The Art of Listening

This book is part of the Peter Lang Media and Communication list.
Every volume is peer reviewed and meets the highest quality
standards for content and production.

PETER LANG
New York • Bern • Berlin
Brussels • Vienna • Oxford • Warsaw

Anthony Arnone

The Art of Listening

Conversations with Cellists

PETER LANG

New York • Bern • Berlin

Brussels • Vienna • Oxford • Warsaw

Library of Congress Cataloging-in-Publication Data

Names: Arnone, Anthony, author.
Title: The art of listening: conversations with cellists/Anthony Arnone.
Description: [1.] | New York: Peter Lang Publishing, 2020.
Includes index.
Identifiers: LCCN 2020011667 (print) | LCCN 2020011668 (ebook)
ISBN 978-1-4331-6293-0 (hardback) | ISBN 978-1-4331-6294-7 (ebook pdf)
ISBN 978-1-4331-6295-4 (epub) | ISBN 978-1-4331-6296-1 (mobi)
Subjects: LCSH: Cellists—Interviews. | Cello teachers—Interviews. |
Cello—Instruction and study. | LCGFT: Interviews.
Classification: LCC ML398 .A76 2020 (print) | LCC ML398 (ebook) |
DDC 787.4092/2—dc23
LC record available at https://lccn.loc.gov/2020011667
LC ebook record available at https://lccn.loc.gov/2020011668
DOI 10.3726/b14801

Bibliographic information published by **Die Deutsche Nationalbibliothek.**
Die Deutsche Nationalbibliothek lists this publication in the "Deutsche
Nationalbibliografie"; detailed bibliographic data are available
on the Internet at http://dnb.d-nb.de/.

© 2020 Peter Lang Publishing, Inc., New York
29 Broadway, 18th floor, New York, NY 10006
www.peterlang.com

Contents

Preface

I have been very fortunate to have studied with some remarkable cellists during my formative years. They were not only great teachers but also wonderful performers and thoughtful musicians, and what I learned from them took me years to fully digest.

I was also very influenced and inspired by other teachers and performers during that time such as Joel Krosnick of the Juilliard Quartet and Paul Katz of the Cleveland Quartet. Listening to their quartet recordings and hearing their sound made me fall in love with some of the great chamber music repertoire and eventually led me to want to become a cellist.

So why did I write this book? Most, if not all, of these great musicians have already been interviewed. My goal was to first document what they learned from their teachers. Their teachers were the "greats" of cello playing. People like Pablo Casals, Gregor Piatigorsky, Leonard Rose, André Navarra, Maurice Gendron, and others shaped the way our current generation of teachers play and teach the cello. I wanted to gather these stories before they were lost.

But I also wanted to preserve this time in history and have a way to collectively compare and understand how cello playing and teaching was viewed in my generation. Maybe I can let Arthur Taylor's words from his book *Notes and Tones* say it better than I can:

My predominant motivation in publishing *Notes and Tones* was that it was inspired by the real voices of musicians as they saw themselves and not as critics or journalists saw them. I wanted an insider's view. These conversations may not always reflect how these artists feel today, but I believe their candid statements represent important insights into a very particular period in history.

I feel incredibly lucky to have spent time with these cellists, and to dig into their lives to learn how they first learned from their teachers, and then later how they learned to listen with ears that hear more than most mortal cellists. I spoke face to face with a group that in total have played thousands of concerts. I sat and had tea with Tim Eddy; went sailing with Steven Doane; watched Gary Hoffman teach and perform at Ravinia; and had breakfast, lunch, and dinner with Paul Katz.

I learned that each of these cellists approached music from a different background, had different goals and expectations, and found their path in very different ways. But one thing they all have in common is a passion for what they do and a desire to improve, no matter how old they are. They all still practice scales! They all are humble and believe there is still so much more to learn. There is respect for the cello and an art of listening.

Acknowledgments

This book had been nothing but a dream for many years. The process was mysterious and exciting for me, and I certainly learned a lot along the way. And I could not have completed this project without the help of many people over the past few years.

I first have to thank the cellists that are in this book. They inspired me not only by their teaching and playing but also with their dedication to art and their sharing of their learning process and their lives. I am thankful to have had the chance to get to know them as people as well as learning about them as musicians.

I am grateful to the University of Iowa library for transcribing dozens of hours of interviews in order to give me a good place to start with editing.

And a huge thank-you to the people along the way that helped me edit. A thank-you to Rachel Gibbons and Brooke Steele for their help early on as well as Jean Littlejohn for taking on some big chapters. Thank you to my mom, Ann Arnone for her beautiful cover art! And a special thank-you to Sarah Hansen for all the editing and proofreading near the end as well as her incredible email to Bonnie Hampton. That will be a great story for years to come. I could not have reached the finish line without her help and support!

1

Richard Aaron

Richard L. Aaron presently serves as professor of cello at the University of Michigan, the Juilliard School, and the Robert McDuffie Center for Strings. Previously, he taught at the Cleveland Institute of Music (CIM) and the New England Conservatory.

Aaron has given master classes in Spain, Germany, France, Korea, Japan, China, and Australia, as well as at many of the leading music schools in North America, including Rice University, Oberlin Conservatory, Eastman School of Music, Mannes, the Hartt School, and the Royal Conservatory of Music in Toronto. Since 2003, Aaron has been on the faculty of the Aspen Music Festival and has taught at many other summer music institutes, including the Indiana University String Academy, Calgary Music Bridge, Peter the Great Music Festival (Groningen, Holland), Aria International Summer Academy (Massachusetts), Innsbruck Summer Music Academy (Missouri), Chautauqua Institution (New York), the Idyllwild Summer Program (California), Heifetz International Music Institute (Virginia), Marrowstone Music Festival (Port Townsend, Washington), and Encore (Ohio).

Many of Aaron's students have won prestigious prizes at competitions around the world, including the Naumburg, Washington International, Johanson in Washington, Isan Yun in Korea, Cassadó in Japan, and Klein in San Francisco. Aaron himself is a frequent competition judge, having recently served the Beijing International

Competition, Isan Yun Competition (Korea), Cassadó (Japan), Amsterdam Cello Biennale Competition, Schadt String Competition, and the Stulberg Competition.

Former Aaron students have occupied principal positions in major orchestras such as Chicago, Saint Louis, Seattle, Portland, and the Metropolitan Opera to name just a few, as well as playing among award-winning ensembles, such as the Biava, Fry Street, American, Penderecki, Linden, Escher, and Aeolus string quartets.

Aaron was a member of the Elysian Piano Trio at Baldwin Wallace College for 14 years; he continues an active chamber music performance schedule.

The Past

Anthony Arnone:	*Where did you grow up and how did you first become exposed to the cello?*
Richard Aaron:	I grew up in West Hartford, Connecticut, and actually I first wanted to play the violin because my brother played the violin. When I was about 7 years old, my parents said, "We can't have two violinists. You have to play something else," so I took up the cello. My first teacher was Sonya Missal (Brittin), who really was very inspiring and made the cello a lot of fun. Then when I was about 11, I started studying with Mary Lou Rylands-Isaacson, who was teaching at the University of Connecticut. She was a wonderful teacher and was the one who really inspired me to want to pursue the cello further.
A.A.	*Were your parents musicians?*
R.A.	No, my mother sings and my father plays the radio, but my uncle is Sam Adler, the composer from Eastman and Juilliard, and my grandfather was a composer. My parents weren't musicians, but music was a very important part of our lives. My brother was a very good violinist and my other brother played French horn so we always had music in the house.
A.A.	*When did you know that the cello was something you seriously wanted to pursue?*
R.A.	I was pretty young. I just knew I enjoyed doing it as it gave me confidence and was really fun. I was also very fortunate to have very good kids my age to play chamber music with. I was in a string quartet with people like Nicki Danielson and Peter Winograd, who were wonderful. And, so we had a very young string quartet that was very inspirational.
A.A.	*When you were a kid did you enjoy practicing?*
R.A.	That was my favorite pastime. It's all I wanted to do, and I was pretty good in sports and things like that, but my love was playing the cello. I didn't practice well and probably wasted 90% of my time but I still loved it and would figure out how to practice much later.

A.A. *It sounds like you were very self-motivated. Did your parents ever have to push you?*

R.A. My parents never had to ask me to practice.

A.A. *You just practiced because you loved the cello so much?*

R.A. I loved it and that's why very often when I see a student that's not totally motivated and working hard, I sometimes question why, because I was very motivated and worked very hard as a kid. So when a kid doesn't work that hard, I have to learn about their motivation. I have to understand what motivates them.

A.A. *Did you study with Mary Lou Rylands-Isaacson until college?*

R.A. No, I studied with Mary Lou until I was around 16, and then I studied with Raya Garbousova and also for a short time with David Wells. They were at Hartt School of Music and so I met them both there. David Wells was very helpful. I went to Yellow Barn with him and he was an inspired teacher. Then I kind of wavered around a little bit and wasn't sure about what to do next.

That was a weird time in my life. I was visiting my brother, who was in a rabbinical program in Israel one December around Christmas time and there was an opening in the orchestra and I won the job. I never really went to university or a music school. My education was playing in the Jerusalem Symphony.

A.A. *How old were you when you went there?*

R.A. I was 18 and it was very lucky. I was at a laundromat doing my laundry just a few days before I was going to leave, when I happened to meet a violist named Richard Wolfe. I said, "What do you do?" And he said, "I'm a violist in the Jerusalem Symphony." I said, "Oh, that's really cool," and he said, "There are Cello auditions next week."

So I took the audition and I won the job, and it was the luckiest break because I feel by having that experience of three and a half, almost four years of just being a professional, my skills of reading improved, as well as my skills of understanding different musical ideas. They would usually have a different conductor every week. That was a really wonderful education even though I was only paid $103 a week.

A.A. *I can relate, I don't have a doctorate, but I worked in the orchestra in Nice for two years and I worked with Paul and Maud Tortelier at the same time, so I consider that worth a degree of some sorts.*

R.A. It's a real education.

A.A. *I agree. It was real live education and a beautiful place to live. So you were there, you said three and a half years.*

R.A. Almost. I left just before I was drafted.

A.A. *You were drafted?*

R.A. Yes, into the Israeli army. I didn't want to do that. I was also very interested in studying the Alexander Technique while I was in Israel. I had three different teachers. And every morning before orchestra I had an Alexander lesson.

A.A. *What drew you to learn about the Alexander Technique?*

R.A. It was just a very enjoyable art form and I thought it helped my cello playing a great deal. After Israel, I decided to move to Switzerland and take an Alexander Technique training course. It was a three-year training course, but I only did it for two and a half years and didn't graduate. I didn't feel the need to be a certified teacher so I just did it for myself. Then I moved to London to continue learning Alexander. I studied with a guy named Patrick McDonald who was a very fine teacher. So there I was in London studying Alexander, working, and playing cello and enjoying life.

A.A.   *At that point, what was your sense of what you thought you wanted to do?*

R.A.   Well, I had no interest in teaching whatsoever. The first time I ever taught was in Israel. There was a lady who had an instrument foundation to give to children who couldn't afford instruments. They had me teach ten students and after one year the kids played worse at the end of the year than they did at the beginning. I only did it for one year and I remember saying to the lady, "I don't think I should be teaching your kids."

     I was very excited to teach them but back then I just didn't understand the process of teaching and when I was in Switzerland and London, being a teacher never even crossed my mind.

A.A.   *Did you think maybe you'd be an orchestral cellist or at least making your living playing the cello?*

R.A.   Yes, I was working a lot in Basil. I was subbing in orchestras and doing a lot of chamber music. In London, I did quite a bit of playing and I always thought I'll just have fun and play. I always thought it was fun, never work.

A.A.   *And, then after London?*

R.A.   I moved to North Carolina. I had an old girlfriend from Switzerland who was in the North Carolina Dance Theater at the School for the Arts. So I decided to move to North Carolina where I lived for six months. I enjoyed living there very much but shortly after I was there, she had an injury and couldn't dance so we traveled all over America. I went to Minneapolis, and I really liked it there, with the MacPhail School and everything, I talked to them and then I said, "Oh, let's just keep on going." I literally traveled for about four months around the whole country in a red Subaru station wagon just deciding where to live. It was great! I remember I really liked Albuquerque and San Diego and I was almost going to settle in San Diego but I thought, "Oh, if I live here I'll never practice, it's way too nice."

     Then I went up the coast and I remember meeting with Irene Sharp in San Francisco. I went to watch her teach and asked, "Do you think I would be able to get students here?" She said no, so I left San Francisco and headed up the coast. I loved Oregon and then I said, "Oh, the last stop is Seattle, let's pick Seattle," and I went to Seattle. I remember it was in the beginning of November and it snowed six inches. It never snows in Seattle! I was supposed to stay with friends on the top of Queen Anne hill and our car couldn't make it even though we had a four-wheel drive Subaru.

A.A.   *What year was this?*

R.A.   It was 1985 because I was there six and a half years, from 1985 to 1992. I should say that when I was in North Carolina someone told me that I should go to a Suzuki Institute to learn Suzuki training. I was not into it at first, but when I learned there was a very good teacher named Gilda Barston, I decided to do it. Gilda and I really hit it off and became the best of friends. I realized that I really didn't understand the pedagogy and the organization of teaching, and in those few weeks Gilder really taught me a great deal.

When I was in Europe I studied with Fournier, and I had lessons with Navarra. I thought I was learning a great deal from them but I didn't learn pedagogy. I think Gilda in that short time really inspired me and after that, when I went up to Seattle I had the audacity to call up the Seattle Suzuki Institute. The lady whom I spoke to said, "I don't believe this but our teacher, Carla Lumsden, is about to retire. We are actually looking for a teacher." I had lunch with them and two days later, I suddenly had four or five students which was very scary because I didn't know what I was doing. It was just real luck that the first student I ever started, the first lesson I ever gave to a beginner, was a boy named Danny Lee, who is now Principal Cellist in the St. Louis Symphony. He was a total child prodigy.

I've never had a student since like this, who literally, when he was nine, soloed with the Seattle Symphony playing Rococo, and at a very high level. Then he went to study with Rostropovich. He was a true child prodigy. That was my first student and I thought all students were like that, so I treated all of the students like him and had very high expectations of other students because my first one was incredible. I built confidence literally from him and actually saw him around four or five times a week for an hour and took a half or two-hour lessons. And, I really learned from him how to teach young students. I knew I was lucky because I know a lot of teachers often teach for years without ever having a real prodigy. I was fortunate to have him and then soon after I had three or four others like that so I had a group of amazing kids in Seattle. I was very lucky too that Carla Lumsden, my predecessor, was an excellent teacher and the students were very well set up and well trained. So, I got into teaching by sheer luck and by the fact that I took over a studio that was brilliantly trained.

A.A. *How long did you stay in Seattle?*

R.A. I was there for seven years.

A.A. *Is that where you felt like you really discovered your teaching voice?*

R.A. For sure. I really learned how to teach and I was teaching almost 50 hours a week. I also was in the Seattle Chamber Orchestra, the Seattle Ballet, and the Opera. I was working like 70 hours a week, working very hard and having a wonderful musical experience in Seattle. I like working hard and that was a fantastic place to do it. And coincidentally Don Weilerstein was visiting the University of Washington for an arts program and heard eight of my students under the age of 11 doing the Villa-Lobos's *Bachianas Brasileiras*. He saw that and said, "I want you to teach my daughter, Ali (Alicia Weilerstein)."

They came out to Seattle a few times so I could work with Ali and then they got me the job at CIM because they wanted me to teach their daughter. That was a really lucky break because if he hadn't gone down the hallway and heard my eight students, I would have never gone to teach at CIM.

David Cerone, the director at CIM, was amazing. He had a real vision and he gave me the opportunity to teach at CIM when he didn't know me at all. But before that, I also had an opportunity from Mimi Zweig at Indiana University. She invited me to teach at her Indiana String Academy. She just called me out of the blue. She had heard about my students and got me the first real summer job that I ever had. Mimi Zweig and David Cerone were the two people who really gave me great opportunities to further my teaching.

The Present

A.A.   *Do you have a teaching philosophy and how has that changed over the years? It's a big question, I know.*

R.A.   Yes, my teaching philosophy would really be the basics. The deeper you go into the basics the better you'll be. Let's say, I find kids really don't know their scales, arpeggios, thirds, and sixths very well. They might know them in a very limited way. But those basics, if you constantly reexamine them where the students constantly make sure that they know those basics, then they improve more. For instance, I teach in the summers at Aspen and I almost always do an extensive scale class and then I'll see them the following year and many often don't remember their arpeggios. I see this constantly. And then those who do remember I find progress much more during the year than those who don't. So I think my job, even though it's not the most fun thing to do, is to teach the basics: Scales, arpeggios, and the geography of the cello.

A.A.   *I still remember your scale class when you came to Iowa.*

R.A.   Yes, I teach scale classes all the time because I really feel a moral obligation to make sure that the kids really know them well.

A.A.   *When you assign sixth and thirds and scales and everything, do you also talk about why they are so important?*

R.A.   Yes because I find that one of the biggest convictions I have in teaching is I really want to give the kids an opportunity to get a job. If I take the responsibility to teach a student, I also take the responsibility that they can find work and that they can make a living. If you go to engineering school, you come out, and you'll do engineering and you make a living as an engineer.

    For some reason a lot of music schools don't take that responsibility to actually help a student get a job. If that is the case, then we didn't do our job. So I take it very personally that if a kid knows the basics, the études very well, their scales, thirds, sixths, octaves, then they have a better opportunity to win a job. So that's the kind of motivation I try to convey to students.

A.A.   *What are some of your philosophies on how to practice? Do you talk to your students a lot about this and is that an important part of your teaching?*

R.A.   How to practice is probably one of the most important concepts to teach a student. And all teachers have limitations. My limitation is always trying to be more consistent, so I find very often I'm not consistent enough and I realize that if I am consistent in asking and constantly trying to get them to practice slower and to practice in a more organized way, then my teaching will be better. I'm always working on myself to be more consistent, and I'm trying to get my students to be more consistent. Consistency is the name of the game.

A.A.   *Do you feel like it's part of your responsibility as a teacher to help them when they're done with school as far as getting a job?*

R.A.   I'm on the phone a great deal. If a student gets a doctorate with me, I feel it's my role to help them find a job. I feel a large majority of my doctoral students have teaching jobs, almost all of them. And, when students have a goal of getting an orchestra job most of them find them. I've been very lucky that a lot of my students have gotten jobs in the past ten years and it's just motivating them to keep up their basics so they can succeed.

A.A.   *And, you teach excerpts as well?*

R.A.   Yes, we have a regular excerpt class. When a kid tells me that they really want an orchestra job, then I really work on excerpts a great deal. If a student wants to go into academia, or go on to get a masters and doctorate, then I work a little differently with them. I'll do more repertoire with them and more contemporary music but if a kid says their goal is to win an orchestra job, then I try to have that as the main focus.

A.A.   *It becomes their bread and butter?*

R.A.   Yes.

A.A.   *How do you keep each student sounding like an individual and how do you balance that with the fact that you often offer bowings and fingerings.*

R.A.   It's very hard for a student to find their own voice, I know that. It took me a long time to really find my own voice on the cello and to express myself the way I wanted. So with students, they have to find their voice but they have to also understand how to find their voice which is the hard part. Very often kids hear from teachers, "You must have an individual voice," but they're not ready to have an individual voice.

For example, my uncle Sam Adler would tell the story very often that when he studied composition with Hindemith, all his own music sounded like Hindemith. It took him many years to not sound like Hindemith but the process of becoming a composer who can imitate is an important process to learn and cello students need to learn how to imitate as well. When they hear a recording, they have to learn how to hear what the voice of that recording is. I am a very good mimic. If I hear a recording, I could mimic that recording. It doesn't mean I totally understand what I'm mimicking but I can mimic it. Mimicking is a good tool to develop because that gives you the skills to find your own voice.

A.A.   *It's a bit like learning an accent with a foreign language.*

R.A.   Exactly, when you're learning a language you have to mimic, you have to understand what that language sounds like, so I like it when students listen to recordings. I want them to hear what other people are saying. So if they're playing a Bach Suite, I want them to hear 10 recordings of that suite but I want them to be able to hear the difference between the recordings and the concepts of tempo and flow, and how people interpret the sound and vibrato.

When a student works with a teacher, they have to find the teacher that they want to mimic or they want to understand the psyche of that teacher. Then you move on to another teacher and learn. I was very inspired by the violinist Gilles Apap. Have you ever heard of Gilles?

A.A.   *No I haven't.*

R.A.   You want to be around Gilles Apap. This guy is such an artist! I'll never forget he gave a masterclass once at Indiana University and he had 10 teachers sitting there with all the students and the first thing out of his mouth was, "Don't do anything your teachers say," and all the teachers just rolled their eyes but what he said was very meaningful.

He said, "You've got to learn from everyone. When you enter a bus, you look at the bus driver and learn about him, learn how he lives his life. When you have a waitress you learn about the hardships of that person, and you have empathy toward people and that's what you're learning from a teacher."

You're learning how to have empathy and how to have an understanding of how to learn and how to learn from all kinds of people. Famous people aren't the only ones we should learn from. We should learn from everyone and that was very meaningful. I hope the students understood what he was saying. I hope they just didn't hear, "Don't learn from your teachers."

A.A. *Right, he could have said, "Don't just learn from your teachers."*

R.A. That's what he was implying and I think the students understood that but I remember that it was a very powerful message. His education is learning from everyone. He goes to India and he goes to Ireland, and he learns from all different types of musicians all over the world. This inspired me to want my students to take one semester off to be in Europe and to learn from different people. I want them to learn different languages and have different experiences. I have a student right now in Helsinki and I was just on Skype with her and she was saying, "Yes, I'm learning so much about how different people think," and I think that's really what I'm after as a teacher.

A.A. *What's the hardest thing to teach a student?*

R.A. The hardest thing is to teach them how to practice slowly. I did not learn how to practice slowly until I was about 25. I find that I tell many of my students a story that after I teach someone for one year I make a list of all their names, I have a little book, I put their names, and I looked at that list. There are hundreds of names and I only had about three or four kids who practiced slowly without me teaching them, so that teaches me it's not a normal way of thinking. How often do you meet someone who meditates, learning how to meditate without learning from someone else? Very few people know how to meditate without being taught.

Learning how to practice slowly is a key to finding your own voice and finding the skill to be a cellist, an artist, and a musician. Just being able to meditate while practicing on what you're doing is so important. The only reason why we don't improve is we don't see what we're doing. If we learn how to meditate on what we're doing and practice slowly then we improve. The breaking of a habit is just going slowly and looking at it.

I work a lot with students doing scales, breathing, inhaling on the down bow, exhaling on the up bow, and just slow everything down so that if they do an arpeggio or scale, it slows them down. Also, it's very important when they're doing the breathing to exhale slower so the up bow is always slower than the down bow, so that you slow yourself down. I'll do any trick to slow them down. I could think of a whole bunch of different ways of doing that but that's a skill that they have to learn.

This year it's funny. I have four freshmen here and I have three freshmen at Juilliard. So having seven freshmen means you have seven students that you have to start new and that they've come from other teachers and have different ideas. So you have to give them the ideas of how you want to teach, and how you want them to move. I move very slowly in the beginning with freshmen. I just do a calendar of events.

The first week we're going to do a major amount of scales, the next week we'll do arpeggios, the next we will do thirds, the next week sixths, and the next week octaves.

For the whole first semester, I will do a different scale with them and it seems very slow to them. It always does. Freshmen, they always look like they're going to fall on me. I just feel that going slow teaches them that they have to practice slowly.

A.A.   *They will thank you later.*

R.A.   Yes, but they won't thank me in the morning.

A.A.   *How important do you feel like the torso is in someone's playing as a way to start the motion of the bow arm. I like to tell students that cello playing is a horizontal art in the sense of how we make sound. I mean, there's releasing energy downward but too often people are playing without any horizontal motion.*

R.A. Well, I try to explain that when you walk, your left knee and your right hand walk in the same flow and your right knee and your left hand walk in the same flow. If the hips are locked, the arms don't flow and the legs don't flow, the sound gets affected. The shoulders and hips are all interconnected so that every bow stroke should feel as though the body is swinging and flowing in a natural way.

I try to get a lot of contrary motion so when you're at the tip you lean left and then you fall to the right exactly like you're walking so that you're constantly in contrary motion. Then, the idea of that shifting always comes from the back muscles and that using the bow always comes from the back. I am someone who really works a great deal on Duport No. 7, but I like a very simple bow arm, so that it moves from the back and that the hand hardly moves. The hand is only balancing the bow and the initiating of movement is always from the back.

A.A.   *How do you get them to do that?*

R.A.   Well, I work a lot on stopping and balancing the bow, so they get to the tip, feel the weight of the frog. And when they get to frog, they feel the weight of the tip. Hopefully when they get to the middle there's no weight in the bow. You just have them stop on every note to feel the balance of the bow and if they feel the balance on the hand then they'll realize they initiate the movement from the body. The hand does not initiate movement.

The biggest problem with students who are shifting is they initiate the movement from the hand instead of from the back. That's why I work a lot on arpeggios and thirds and sixths to feel that the hand never really moves and the back moves the hand. It's kind of like a mantra constantly reminding the students that they start a motion from the back and not from the hands. If you really watch Starker play, he truly moved from his back. Lynn Harrell really moves from his back so beautifully that I often show students videos.

And that's what's fun with YouTube, you can watch them play, even in slow motion, and then you can study how they are moving, which is really amazing to see.

Yes. And, very often I shut the sound off because I don't want them to focus on what they hear, what they see. Also kinesthetically it's very hard to teach someone to learn about kinesthetics and the art of motion. We're really doing things very similar to what dancers do but we very often don't see it that way.

For instance, if we don't like the sound we make, it's the movement we made that wasn't what we like, it's not the sound we didn't like, we just didn't move accordingly. So, we really should only study the kinesthetic and the gesture and movement to make a musical idea. That's very hard to teach a kid because for many years when they're playing, they're preoccupied with just the sound and they don't correlate sound and movement.

A.A. *One of my favorite things to say these days is, "in order to sound different on the cello you have to do something different with your body." It sounds obvious when you say that but then so many people just practice physically doing exactly the same thing and then wonder why it doesn't sound any different.*

R.A. Exactly! Very often I can tell how a student will play by the way they walk in the room. Kinesthetically you can tell.

A.A. *Or even right when they're just about to start you can tell the kind of sound that's going to come out of the cello.*

R.A. You can tell by their posture, and by how elegantly they move. That's why I really think studying Alexander, studying Feldenkrais, studying Tai Chi, and studying yoga are really important. For many years, I had this crazy idea. I said, "Okay, you have four years here, study four art forms. First year do yoga, second year do Feldenkrais, third year do Tai chi, fourth year do whatever you want but you have to do something different every year so that you look at your body differently."

That never worked very well but you can't force the kids to do an art form other than what they want to do, but I have a lot of kids who really get into yoga, and I have a lot of kids who really get into Alexander. I don't personally do Alexander with students even though I spent seven years training with it because it deals a lot with touch and I don't touch my students. I just think that's a kind of a rule of thumb that all teachers, male or female, there might be a misinterpretation of it and it's not worth doing.

A.A. *Do you ever adjust their hands or arms?*

R.A. No, I don't touch. I think in this day and age it's just better not to touch a student because people do misinterpret touch and it's better not to move that direction. With little kids, if I were to teach like a seven- , eight-year-old and the mother was in the room I would facilitate but for college or high school kids, it's better to just use words and to illustrate while playing or to have movements.

Right now, I'm really into core work. Between every lesson, I do a plank.

A.A. *Wow, good idea. I should do that too.*

R.A. I try to have a few minutes between lessons, so I'll do a plank for a minute. I find that all core work is great for the bow arm and great for shifting and fantastic for feeling the balances of the body.

A.A. *Right, my next cello seminar, I'm going to tell all my students, "We're going to do a minute of planks."*

R.A. But you know a minute is too long for most people; most students can't do more than 20 seconds. Have you ever tried it with a student?

A.A. *No, I haven't tried it with a student.*

R.A. Their core is often weak. I started doing this a few years ago and most had a hard time doing 30 seconds. That's why when you're talking about moving from back it's very hard for them to perceive it because they haven't had that much core work. Some though are in great shape.

A.A.   *How do you choose the students you teach? Do you prefer someone physically gifted that maybe doesn't have as much to say or someone very musical that might have more physical hurdles?*

R.A.   Well, that has changed over the years. I'll tell you at Juilliard, students are picked by a committee of seven or eight people, so I'm one vote of eight people and I just really hope that the kids I want get through, and very often they don't. I'm sometimes very surprised, sometimes I want to teach a kid very badly and they don't get in.

A.A.   *So it's not up to you specifically?*

R.A.   No, it's one of eight. When I taught at CIM (for 15 years), I really got to pick. Here at the University of Michigan, I pick my students. It's really interesting because I love my students at Julliard, and I love my students at Michigan, but they are very different kinds of students.

   The kids who go to Juilliard have a very different mentality. Most of the kids at Juilliard don't want to go to a university. The kids at the University of Michigan want to go to a university. There are different types of cellists and sometimes I think kids at Michigan might be better off at Juilliard and sometimes the kids Juilliard might be better off at Michigan, so you never know but they're all so different.

A.A.   *But what do you look for, do you have certain things that you look for in their playing?*

R.A.   That's hard to answer because I try to pick kids who move me. I try not to judge them by how they play. I don't really care how they play because that's not my job.

A.A.   *Is there a certain level of physical playing you look for?*

R.A.   Well, they have to be coordinated. If they're not coordinated it can really be impossible to get to a high level of playing.

A.A.   *Right.*

R.A.   My goal is to get them work and very likely if they're not coordinated it's very hard, but I'm very lucky because between Michigan, Juilliard, and Aspen I see almost 250 kids per year.

A.A.   *And so many of the best students in the country!*

R.A.   Yes, and I know that I'm a very lucky person that way because I know that at many schools, it's hard to get kids to come and I am blessed that way. But, I'm sad every year at audition time because I can't take everyone that I want to teach.

A.A.   *How many hours a day do you tell your students to practice and what do you think is a reasonable amount?*

R.A.   I think that is very different for each student. So, for instance, I have one student now who is a really wonderful, amazing talent and he practices very little but he's always prepared and he's always artistic and he's fabulous, so I would never suggest a certain number of hours with him. It's not the number of hours, but if they're improving monthly, and practicing correctly.

   For instance, if I hear a kid and I just don't see improvement in their playing I take it on myself that it's something I'm doing that's not right. I'm not giving them the right information. If they're not improving, it's my fault because I really feel that it's my responsibility for them to get it.

   If they don't practice enough, it usually means that I'm not inspiring them to practice enough. It's a fact of nature, if you don't have something to play for usually you don't motivate yourself. I'll try to get them to play more in class. I have two classes every week for kids to play in. Or I might try to arrange a concert for them to play in. But if a kid doesn't improve it's the teacher's fault.

A.A.   *What is the best of working on intonation with students?*

R.A.   I use Cleartune (app).

A.A.   *I have that on my phone.*

R.A.   You have that?

A.A.   *Yes, I love it.*

R.A.   I like Cleartune. I use drones with kids. I use a lot of scale work with open strings. I got a kick out of Hans Jensen's book and the concept of harmonics. I use his book a great deal and discuss how you hear the tuning of the harmonics. But I also feel that if you talk too much about intonation you can have a student lose confidence.

And so, if a kid plays out of tune, then I'll work much more on scales and arpeggios with them than intonation. I try not to put too much on the piece, because I feel they will lose confidence. So if a student plays out of tune, I'll work on that with their études and scales and not as much on their pieces. Because it's hard enough playing the cello to lose confidence in that.

A.A.   *Did you have exercises and études that you teach regularly? Has that changed over time?*

R.A.   Yes, I do Duport No. 7 a great deal for the bow as well as Piatti No. 1. I used to do, like 20 for the bow but then I realized if you do Duport No. 7 and Piatti No. 1, and do 50 variations with those, it's enough. And then for the left hand, I try to make sure that my freshman and sophomores know all 40 Popper études.

I usually have a system where I tell them to work on three Poppers every week. I hear one, then we take away that one and then they add one so that they always have at least three to four weeks on an étude before they play it for me. I usually give them the first two or three weeks of school before I will hear one. Then I say, "Okay, it's time to hear some Popper." It has to be very prepared. Expecting a student to play an étude in one week is too much. But if they have three weeks and if they're not prepared, that means they don't know how to prepare.

I'm also into practicing études with double stops so that whenever you play an étude, you always match for pitch and hand position.

A.A. *It's so much easier to tune when you have something to tune a note against. Do you make students play or perform by memory? Do you think that's an important skill of playing the cello?*

R.A.   You know, I find they do without really forcing that. I think they do.

A.A.   *That's not something you really talk about?*

R.A.   I don't really push that. Sonatas, I don't want them to play by memory. I want them to look at the music. I'm especially interested in seeing how they mark their music. For instance, when the kid comes in and the music is blank, they really don't understand how to prepare a piece of music. That, to me, is more important than having it from memory.

For instance, I constantly see the kids thinking that the markings in the music are the things they should do. Like the fingerings, they just go by what's in the music instead of thinking for themselves. I'm just amazed by that. I don't look at any fingerings in music. I finger and bow everything myself. Slurs and articulations, you have to follow the score, the manuscript. But for fingerings, that's an art form and you have to learn how to do it. That takes time to teach. That usually takes about a year or two to get a student to learn these concepts. Very often, I give a student, let's say, "Vocalise." It's an easy piece. I say, "I'd like you to finger and bow it." And they come back and there's nothing in the music. There's a misunderstanding of what it is to learn a piece. So learning how to learn a piece is more important than playing it by memory.

A.A. *What are your methods for teaching vibrato?*

R.A. That's a hard one because I don't like my vibrato (laughs). I usually tell students, "Don't do it like me." But vibrato, I find, is the issue of letting go when playing thirds and sixths. So when you play sixths, you teach yourself how to push a string down and then release the string, and then move to the next note. I find that if you practice a lot of sixths, you improve your vibrato without talking about vibrato. So usually kids who have problems with vibrato don't know thirds or sixths. I usually will say at a first lesson, "Play me a scale in sixths," and it's very rudimentary and has not been thought through. So I find that if a kid has a problem with vibrato, practicing a lot more sixths and thirds and octaves will help a student to understand how to relax the hand, how to have the shape of the hand, and therefore vibrate better. For me, vibrato is about very good shape, balance of the hand and release of the hand. It has very little to do with the movement itself.

I had a student ten years ago who really couldn't vibrate at all. I said, "Okay, let's do an experiment." I had him do ten études, all of them double stop études. He just did them non-stop for a month. Then suddenly he had a beautiful vibrato. And he was shocked. I'm convinced that vibrato is the stability and the strength of the hand. For instance, very often, we have to unteach vibrato rather than teach it. They're not moving from the palm at all. They're trying to move from the finger. So they lock their wrist and palm. Getting the palm to be soft is a hard skill to teach. Most people play with the palm of their hand stiff. So to get a soft palm has nothing to do with vibrato. You have to get that soft and then work on vibrato.

So, vibrato is a really tough thing to talk about because it really doesn't have that much to do with vibrato. I find that it's the relaxation of the hand that makes vibrato happen.

A.A. *Do you still use a tennis ball to help a student find the right motion? I remember you did that when you gave a class at the University of Iowa.*

R.A. I use a tennis ball. But I use that to make them feel from the back, to make feel that the motion moves from the back. But mostly if a kid's vibrato isn't very good, I just really work on sixths.

A.A. *Do you demonstrate a lot in lessons and how important do you think that is in your teaching?*

R.A. I do demonstrate a lot but I'm not always sure that's the best way to get a point across. Sometimes I think making the student hear for themselves is the best way. You know, Rostropovich never played for a student. I know students who studied with him, and they never heard him play the cello, he only played the piano. Because he always said that you have to find your own voice and you don't want to copy what someone else is doing and that you have to figure it out for yourself how to create the sound you want to create.

But I'm not that extreme. I do demonstrate. But I do sometimes think that their playing is the better demonstration. To show them to listen to what they themselves are doing. That's the hard part of making them hear, I think.

A.A. *What about the Bach Suites? What's your perspective of them, the way the historically informed practice has become a way of life.*

R.A. If it was my choice, I'd have all my students play Baroque cello and gamba.

A.A. *That would be a nice thing!*

R.A. I've gone crazy with gamba lately. Every evening around 10 o'clock, I could pull out my cello. But nope, I go right to my gamba and I play gamba almost every evening. I love the gamba. So I'm coming from a background of really wanting to move in that direction. For instance, most students, when I say to them what recordings are they listening to, are they listening to recordings I prefer them not listen to them. I like them to hear Anner Bylsma played, I like them to hear Wispelwey. I like them to hear Baroque cellists play. I like to hear Pandolfo play the Bach Suites. I like them to hear more playing that is representative of the period.

But it's very difficult to get a kid to think that way. For instance, I have a student right now, very proud of him. He's a Japanese boy who won the concerto competition in Aspen playing Haydn in C on cello with no endpin and a Baroque bow. And he played Haydn in C in a very stylized, classical way. I told him before he played I would eat my left sock in the next class if he won. He said, "Why? You don't think I'll win?" I said, "No, you play beautifully, you're good enough to win. But I don't know if you're going to have a jury that will appreciate what you're doing." And he won. So in front of the whole class, I ate my left sock, chewing on it for about 30 seconds. It was a clean sock.

A.A. *Did you actually eat the sock?*

R.A. No, I just chewed on it. I can't eat a sock. But he got a kick out of it. I'm very proud of him because he plays in a very stylized way and not so many kids get that. I love that. I love that when they take up Baroque cello very seriously. I've had quite a few kids who have taken gamba lessons. I have a student here who is the goalie of the Michigan hockey team. And she's now a gambist. I was so proud of her for that. As a freshman, she got into it. There's a wonderful gamba teacher in town in Ann Arbor, Enid Sutherland, and she studied with her intensely and she became a gambist. I love that. I love when kids open up to different ideas.

A.A. *For you and I, when we were young the only recordings we got to know were …*

R.A. Pablo Casals?

A.A. *Well, yes, or maybe a few others. There was more or less one style used to interpret the Bach Suites. But why do you think so many students don't gravitate to playing in a Baroque style more naturally?*

R.A. I don't know why they don't want Baroque cello. It always amazes me.

A.A. *The older style of play still seems to have a hold on many young students.*

R.A. If you listen to, let's say, Daniel Shafran, he was an artist. But his taste is different from other people's taste. So it is a question of taste. I respect Daniel Shafran, a lot of things that he did were amazing. But his taste of, let's say, Bach, is different than, let's say, my taste. Or of Mr. Bylsma's taste. It's a question of taste. And I think our jobs as teachers for four years or two years or however long you have a student is to give a sense of taste to the student. Taste is probably the most difficult and the most important thing that we teach a student. It's a hard thing to teach taste.

A.A. *Along with taste is learning to play in a variety of styles. And that's something that didn't exist as much a few generations ago.*

R.A. I'm very interested in having my students do a contemporary music concert every year. I have a project where I commission sixteen or so composers at the school here and we have a concert playing their music. That is invaluable for the students. Almost every time they get the music, they say, "I don't like the piece." And I say, "Well, tough luck. You're going to learn this piece." And every kid after the concert says, "I love the piece." It happens (snap). And I explain that to them before I give them the music, "You're probably not going to like it. But by the time you perform it, you're going to love it." It's like learning a language. If you just hear the language, you don't understand it. And so, I find it's very important to get contemporary music in their education, to get Baroque music, to do excerpts. You have to have a whole gambit in your education.

A.A. *What is your philosophy on these three pieces that have become so popular even though they're not quite authentic? The Boccherini/Grützmacher B-flat Concerto, the Tchaikovsky/Fitzenhagen Rococo Variations, and the Chopin Polonaise with the Feuermann arrangement?*

R.A. Well, for the Tchaikovsky, I definitely prefer the original. As a matter of fact, I was just converted to that. I was on a jury in Amsterdam and twelve kids did the original which I didn't know that well. After hearing it twelve times, there's no question Tchaikovsky knew what he was doing. And Fitzenhagen was a good musician, but Tchaikovsky had a much better understanding of the balance of the piece.

A.A. *So now do you teach both?*

R.A. I only teach the original.

A.A. *What about the Boccherini/Grützmacher B-flat?*

R.A. I teach that to young kids because there's a lot of value pedagogically to the piece. But my college students generally learn the original.

A.A. *And one more, the Chopin Polonaise.*

R.A. That's a tricky one because I prefer the original. And the kids always come back with the Franchomme, which is very difficult. And also the one that Rose edited, the International Edition. But Chopin knew what he was doing, and the original is very beautiful.

A.A. *Right. And it really features the piano more.*

R.A. Yeah, it's a beautiful piece. If a kid wants a virtuoso piece, I tell them to learn the Franchomme. But I say to him/her, "Treat it as a virtuoso piece by Franchomme." It's a reminiscence of Chopin.

The Future

A.A. *A lot has been made about the shrinking audiences of classical music. Where do you see the future of classical music going in the next generation? And related to that, has technology positively or negatively affected classical music?*

R.A.   Well, the technology has affected music in a positive way because people have the ability to hear more music more easily.

A.A.   *They don't have to go out and hear it.*

R.A.   They don't have to go out and hear it, that's the problem with audiences. The real problem is childhood education in music. That's the problem. It has nothing to do with technology. The budgets have been cut so extremely over the years and childhood education has suffered. The problem is that the kids aren't experiencing playing in bands and orchestras in schools like they did a generation or two ago. And so very often they grow up without having an education in music. That's really what I worry about. There needs to be a lot more support of music for young people. The University of Michigan has a wonderful music education program. We have to support teachers and we have to support building good programs. One of the most valuable lessons I ever had in a lesson was my first lesson at the University of Michigan. I took over some students from the previous teacher, Mr. Bengtsson, and he was a music education teacher. I was a snot-nosed teacher from CIM. I never worked with music education kids and I just thought what's the point. So this student played magnificently for me. I was sitting there in awe, and the first thing out of my mouth was, "How come you're a music education student and not a cello performance major?" He looked me straight in the eye and he said, "I am teaching the future. I am affecting the future far greater than you are." And when he said that, I understood where he was coming from. The next lesson, I said, "I really must apologize to you. Because last week I asked that question in a very ignorant way. I didn't really think about how important music education is. Thank you for putting me straight." He's a big teacher now in the Chicago area and he's also a very fine cellist and he's performing a lot, and he's teaching in the high school. That first lesson at Michigan was a great education for me. It showed me the importance of education.

A.A.   *This is sort of related, but do you think new music is working in the orchestral setting with current audiences here in the US? Do you think there will be a split eventually between hearing new music and the classical standards? Because so many people that go to classical music concerts just want to hear the same eight or ten composers. It seems like orchestras are looking for ways to keep audiences and I'm not always sure that new music is helping or hurting.*

R.A.   Well, I'm a radical with that because I really like new music. I enjoy hearing things I don't know. But not everyone is like that. I feel for orchestras around the country. The conductors are the people who are putting programs together and I know how difficult it is for them to introduce contemporary music. I think it's very important to keep pushing that. But listen, there are a lot of bad classical pieces and there's a lot of bad contemporary music. You have to cipher through all the music to find the good stuff. So I'm very supportive of composers. But I'm unusual that way. But I totally empathize with the audiences who don't really want to hear that music. I think I read recently in Japan, Beethoven's Ninth is played every day of the year somewhere in Japan.

A.A.   *Have you seen the level of cello playing change over the years since you've been teaching, and are there enough jobs for cellists in today's market?*

R.A.   I think there are enough jobs. People always say there aren't. I think anyone can find their own path. So for instance, I believe if you go to a city and you want to teach, you will find 20 students in any city in America. If you're willing to work hard, you can find a community in any city and make a living on cello. You might not make the living the way you dreamed of, being in the New York Philharmonic or the Boston Symphony, but I think that anyone who wants to make a living on the cello can do it.

For instance, how many jobs in this country pay $50 an hour. If a kid comes to a town, and you give a lesson and you charge $50, or $40 an hour and are willing to work 20, 30 hours a week doing that, you make a good living. When people worry about that, I really tell parents never worry about that, because if you have a desire, if you love making music and you love the cello and you love either teaching or playing, you can make it work.

I really find that everyone does make it work in their own way. Some are more successful than others. Some will be able to make a living easier than others, some have a really hard time, but I find that everyone finds their path.

A.A.   *What about the first part that I asked you about, just the level of cello playing over the years? What have you noticed?*

R.A.   I don't think we're old enough to know. I've been teaching for about 30 years. I often think, "I'll never have a student like this again," and then a week later I get a student that's also quite remarkable. I think the level is the same for the past 80 years, but we just don't see it in perspective.

For instance, I hear recordings on YouTube of cellists of 60, 70 years old that are absolutely remarkable. Remarkable. These no-name people. You know *The Recorded Cello: The History of the Cello on Record*, you know that recording?

A.A.   *Yes, but it's been awhile.*

R.A.   There are some amazing recordings out there of people I had never heard of before. I think people are people and the level has always been very, very high. I've been on the jury of many competitions around the world, and the level is very high all over the world, but I can't say whether it's higher now than it was 30 or 40 years ago.

A.A.   *There are maybe just more of those great players?*

R.A.   Bigger numbers. I think the Suzuki Association has really affected that a great deal, because they've brought so many kids into the fold, and I give them a lot of credit for that. I have great respect for Suzuki teachers. I feel that they really do know what they're doing, and I feel that very often they're not given enough credit for what the cello world in this country is by their doing. I've been all over the country, and I find that a lot of the Suzuki training is first rate. I think they have affected the level and the numbers greatly. We have to give the Suzuki teachers a lot of credit for the level. I often ask the kids at Juilliard, or even at Aspen, what kind of training did they have, and almost 50% of the kids are Suzuki-trained.

Close to the Heart

A.A.   *If you hadn't been a musician, what would you have loved to have done with your life?*

R.A.   I think teaching cello is a salesmanship job. We're selling ideas, we're selling ways of practicing, and we're selling how to think on the cello. I don't see any difference between selling something and teaching cello, and I love cars. I'm made fun of very often because every single year I have a different car. If I have a car for six months, I kind of get bored with it and I try to sell it for more than I paid for it. I love negotiating for cars, so I probably would have gone into sales if I didn't do music.

But when people ask me that question, I really can't picture anything else that I would want to do. Why I would want to do anything else. I think this is the most wonderful thing I can do. I literally feel so lucky that I'm doing what I'm doing.

A.A.   *What are some of the more memorable concerts you've ever been involved in? It doesn't even have to be for a musical reason necessarily, just something that sticks out.*

R.A.   I tell you, there are several. Mauricio Kagel is from Argentina and lived in Germany for most of his life. In Israel we did a world premiere of his for chorus and orchestra that was life-changing, because it was so creative. It was so eye-opening to hear a different way of hearing and seeing the world. I will never forget that concert. I don't know why that stuck so deeply, but I was just so deeply moved.

I once did a benefit concert in Seattle for a woman who had cancer, and a group of cellists in the Seattle Symphony put together a concert. That was a very meaningful concert. This was 1986 or 1987 and she needed a bone marrow transplant and didn't have insurance, but we raised a tremendous amount of money. It just felt like a whole community came together and did something supportive for an individual. I tell students about that concert because very often you have to play music for a purpose. You have to play music because it means something, and that was a very meaningful concert to play in.

Playing the Bach Goldberg Variations (the string trio version) was a very meaningful experience as well. My colleagues at Aspen who I played with were wonderful, but just playing that music to me was very magical.

I like listening to singers a great deal. I'm very moved by them, even more so than string playing. There's something very human about what they do. I tell you, the thing that really affects me usually the most is hearing contemporary pieces for the first time. I really enjoy that. Even though, for instance, I have a joke in my studio that whenever you play Elgar for me there's an Elgar tax. You have to put 10 cents on top of the table and I collect it, and at the end of the year I buy a pizza for everybody. The Elgar Concerto is a beautiful work, but I've probably heard it around 3000 times. Enough is enough. I like to hear contemporary works. I like to hear new pieces. Although Popper Études I'll never grow tired of hearing.

A.A.   *Or the Bach Suites. I never grow tired of hearing them either.*

R.A.   The Bach Suites are wonderful, but I don't like hearing kids play Bach Suites until they've studied Vivaldi or Marcello Sonatas or other Baroque music. I don't like starting just with Bach, because Bach is the most profound and the most difficult. I think most students play Bach too quickly and too early in their career. To give little kids Bach Suites is unnecessary when there is so much other Baroque music to learn.

A.A.   *Have you ever dealt with a period of doubt about being a musician or becoming a musician, and how did you get through that period?*

R.A.   I never had that feeling. I've been really lucky in that way.

A.A.   *Many others have.*

R.A.   I have had a few really talented students go through a period of doubt. A few years ago I had a really amazing talent who said to me, "I don't want to play the cello." I said,

"Fine, quit. I don't need to teach you, just quit." He said, "Well, I'm not sure about quitting yet." Then, shortly after that, I had him give a concert, a meaningful benefit concert, and he said, "I could make music to benefit mankind." I said, "Yes, that's why we do this. You have a special gift."

I had another student with that kind of talent who also said that about quitting. I use little psychological games with them, because they often really don't want to quit, they just want to find meaning in what they're doing.

A.A. *What are you most proud of in your life and career?*

R.A. Believe it or not, I'm not so into career. It's like a happenstance that I fell into the situations I'm in. I never applied for a job in my life, and I don't even have a college degree.

A.A. *Have you only taken the Jerusalem Symphony Orchestra audition?*

R.A. No, I've taken many auditions. I was in the Northwest Chamber Orchestra, I was in Basil, I was in London, I've played professionally, but I've never applied for a job in my life. I've been very lucky that I have just fallen into things. I never was really into a career. I'm very proud of my two kids and I sometimes feel I should have spent more time with them and less time with my students. But I think I did a lot with them and I love them very much and I'm very proud of my kids. I'm also proud of my students. A lot of them are very successful and I'm very proud of what they have done.

A.A. *They're like family, in a sense.*

R.A. Yes. I'm very proud of them and I love them and I really feel that they're a very important part of my life. I spend around seven, eight hours teaching everyday so they become a big part of my life. I think that when people think too much of their career, they miss what their career is. Career is not that important. It's being creative and doing things that are creative that really matter. If you think money is important to you, then this is probably not the right career. There's a lot of other ways to make more money, and you shouldn't do it for that reason. You should do it because you enjoy it. Do you agree with that?

A.A. *Yes. I'm all about balance.*

R.A. I'm a little crazy to have two jobs, because I work seven days a week and I do not have a day off, because when I'm not teaching here I'm in New York. Some people might think I'm crazy to do that, but I kind of find it relaxing in some ways. On the flight to New York, I read the news and I read a book, it's a quiet time.

A.A. *Downtime.*

R.A. Yes, downtime. Except for the taxi ride to Juilliard. I don't like that. Also, I used to do a lot of master classes and a lot of teaching around the country and in Europe. I can't do that now, because I can't miss so many lessons, so I don't travel as much as I used to. I do miss that.

A.A. *Is there anything you still want to do before it's all done?*

R.A. Teaching?

A.A. *Anything that comes to mind. Doesn't even have to be music.*

R.A. The word "bucket list" always scares me. I have dreams of riding my bike cross country, but it takes too long.

A.A. *You could even stretch it out and just see more things, if you're with the right group of people.*

R.A. Yes, would you like to join me? That could be a lot of fun!

2

Colin Carr

Colin Carr appears throughout the world as a soloist, chamber musician, recording artist, and teacher. He has played with major orchestras worldwide, including the Royal Concertgebouw Orchestra, the Philharmonia, Royal Philharmonic, BBC Symphony, the orchestras of Chicago, Los Angeles, Washington, Philadelphia, Montréal, and all the major orchestras of Australia and New Zealand. Conductors with whom he has worked include Rattle, Gergiev, Dutoit, Elder, Skrowasczewski, and Marriner. He has been a regular guest at the BBC Proms and has twice toured Australia.

With his duo partner Thomas Sauer, he has played recitals throughout the United States and Europe including New York, Boston, Philadelphia, the Concertgebouw in Amsterdam, and the Wigmore Hall in London. The year 2016 sees them playing a program of Britten and Adès for both the Chamber Music Societies of New York and Philadelphia. Colin has played complete cycles of the Bach Solo Suites at the Wigmore Hall in London, the Chamber Music Society of Lincoln Center, the Gardner Museum in Boston and in Montreal, Toronto, Ottawa, and Vancouver.

As a member of the Golub-Kaplan-Carr Trio, he recorded and toured extensively for 20 years. Chamber music plays an important role in his musical life. He is a frequent visitor to international chamber music festivals worldwide and has appeared often as a guest with the Guarneri and Emerson string quartets and with New York's Chamber Music Society of Lincoln Center.

Recent CD releases include the complete Bach Suites on the Wigmore Live label and the complete Beethoven Sonatas and Variations on the MSR Classics label with Thomas Sauer. Colin is the winner of many prestigious international awards, including First Prize in the Naumburg Competition, the Gregor Piatigorsky Memorial Award, Second Prize in the Rostropovich International Cello Competition and also winner of the Young Concert Artists competition.

He first played the cello at the age of five. Three years later he went to the Yehudi Menuhin School, where he studied with Maurice Gendron and later William Pleeth. He was made a professor at the Royal Academy of Music in 1998, having been on the faculty of the New England Conservatory in Boston for 16 years. In 1998, St. John's College, Oxford, created the post of "Musician in Residence" for him, and in September 2002, he became a professor at Stony Brook University in New York.

Colin's cello was made by Matteo Gofriller in Venice in 1730. He makes his home with his wife Caroline and three children, Clifford, Frankie, and Anya, in an old house outside Oxford.

The Past

Anthony Arnone	*Where did you grow up, and how did you first become exposed to the cello? Were you in a family of musicians?*
Colin Carr	I grew up in Liverpool. My mother played the oboe, and she loved the cello. I was the middle child of three boys, and we all played. My elder brother played piano very briefly and my younger brother played violin very briefly, but I was the only one that stuck with it. Then they shipped me off when I was eight years old to the Menuhin School. That's a boarding school, so that was very traumatic, actually.
A.A.	*Why did they decide to do that at such a young age?*
C.C.	I know. You as a father and I as a father can't imagine wanting to get rid of our eight-year-old child.
A.A.	*Was it because they recognized you were a super talent and you needed to get to that environment?*
C.C.	I think my father was actually a gangster. My father was not a musician. He wanted his children to have respectable careers and professions, and music didn't really count. But, my mother did recognize something. I think she had a frustrated musical career because she married and had children when she was very young. She had two boys by the time she was 23 or 24. The third one came later. So she gave up the oboe to bring up the family and then tried to resurrect her career later on, which was sort of a disaster.

I remember going to a Wigmore Hall concert of hers later, when I was at the Menuhin School. She somehow got a whole group of us from the school to go listen to this recital. It was just so hard to listen to.

A.A.   *You were embarrassed.*

C.C.   Yes, I was.

A.A.   *Did she realize it wasn't maybe what she was hoping it would be?*

C.C.   If she did, she didn't show us. Like any good professional musician, if she was having a hard time, she didn't show it.

A.A.   *Did you know that you were going to be a cellist?*

C.C.   It took awhile. I just did it because that's what my parents told me to do. I'd never heard of Yehudi Menuhin. I didn't know what playing the cello was all about. I guess now that I have a cello-playing son and I see his development. Actually, his development was quite similar to mine, that he played the cello from the same age, five, something like that. But all those first years, I wouldn't say they were wasted, but they were not serious cello-playing years. I think they were probably formative in some way. Just the familiarity with the instrument.

A.A.   *Physically spending time with it.*

C.C.   Yes.

A.A.   *Then, you went to the Menuhin Academy at age eight and you started studying with …?*

C.C.   There was a very fine and wonderful fellow named Christopher Bunting, who was one of the English cellists and something of a pedagogue. He had published some editions of exercises and studies, études, for cello that I think he got some mileage out of those. He was a very jolly English character, but he was only at the school for the first couple of years I was there. Then, Menuhin brought his chamber music colleague, Maurice Gendron, to come teach. Gendron's presence was very infrequent. He was supposed to show up once a month but didn't, and so he had one of his former students from Saarbrücken in Germany come and do the leg work, which was two lessons a week for us.

And I was already, even at that age, 10, 11, 12, somewhat opinionated and also a little bit full of myself. I didn't think I had anything to learn from this person, all the worst things about being young and headstrong, so actually all the way through I didn't really learn very well from my cello teachers. I'm sure now that they had a great deal to offer, but quite frankly I can't remember anything that any of them said.

A.A.   *From all accounts, it sounds like Gendron was maybe not the most supportive and warm teacher.*

C.C.   Gendron was a disaster, from not even being very interested in teaching, to not knowing how to teach kids, to having a problem of even abusing kids in several different ways. Although I was not subject to anything sexual, I was certainly subject to sort of emotional and psychological and even physical abuse. He would whack my bow off the string with his bow as well as other things that were very humiliating, demeaning, and upsetting for me as a child.

Those lessons were not really anything to look forward to. We were all very frightened of him. I don't think any of us felt that there was ever any kind of nurturing happening through a teacher-student relationship. I had this association with Gendron for six years, but I don't remember anything from those lessons that I can bring to my teaching now.

A.A.   *Was he the type that would bring you his bowings and fingerings and say, "You do these"?*

C.C.   Oh, absolutely, that was a hallmark of the way he taught. In fact, everything was color coded. Fingerings, I think, were in blue, bowings were in red, and expressive marks were in green. If he, as he did often, strayed from printed articulations, we had to erase the printed articulations with a razor blade. Some of my music from those early days has been completely destroyed. There are holes where my razor blade technique was not up to par.

A.A.   *Seems a little excessive.*

C.C.   Well, I think that was part of the French system. There was always a system and things that everybody had to do, and that was one of them. It was not a happy time of life at all, and it was surprising to me that Menuhin persisted with it when it was clearly not going well at the school.

A.A.   *So who did you look up to at that time?*

C.C.   I did listen to cellists in those days, much more than I do now. I suppose Rostropovich was something of a hero then. I used to listen to all of those recordings that he made. And Tortelier a little bit. But I didn't have any direct contact with these people. My heroes tended to be non-cello. Menuhin at that time was certainly one of them. We got to play a lot of chamber music with him, and I was very fortunate also to play concertos with him conducting. He loved Elgar, having done the violin concerto from such an early age, so he was also very attached to the cello concerto. I played that with him on a number of occasions.

He had a thing for English music, and he recorded Walton violin and Viola Concertos. The cello concerto was a little more daunting, and I don't think he knew it quite as well, but we did that a couple of times. Nadia Boulanger visited the school several times, and she was somebody that I recognized as a force in music. She made me realize the importance of music just by her very presence. The few times that she played the piano were something I never heard before.

A.A.   *Did you get to know her at all?*

C.C.   Nobody got to know her, really. She'd been mourning for her sister for the last 50 years. She was the most daunting figure. She dressed in gray tweed, and she was blind. I remember playing the prelude of the Fourth Suite to her with Menuhin sitting there as well, and when I finished, she turned to him and said, "I think he understands harmony."

A.A.   *What did Menuhin say?*

C.C.   I think he just nodded in a grim way. Later, I went to Marlboro and I got to play with Serkin, and that was revelatory.

A.A.   *And how old were you at that time?*

C.C.   That was soon after I left. I was probably 20.

A.A.   *Were you more self-motivated as far as practice, and did you enjoy practicing?*

C.C.   Things changed enormously when I became a teenager. I didn't practice much before that. I only practiced when people insisted that I practice. Sometime in my early teens, I think I realized that this is what I was going to do, and if I was going to do it, I'd better be good at it. Then it was nose to the grindstone, and I practiced probably more than was good for me physically. I really put in the hours in those days and have always loved practicing since then. It's just part of my nourishment in the way food and sleep can be seen as something that you need to be alive.

A.A.　*You mentioned that at some point you realized that's what you wanted to do and you wanted to be good at it, but was there any sort of—*

C.C.　Catalyst? There probably was, but I can't put my finger on it now. I'd always been told that I was talented, and I suppose in the very early days I just believed it. But I realized that I wasn't as talented as people would have me believe, and that if this was going to work, whatever talent I had wasn't enough, and that the only way this was going to work would be through hard work. I think probably at that same age I realized that even though I'd sailed through school and academic work quite easily, there wasn't anything else that I was going to be particularly good at, and so I'd better play to my strengths.

A.A.　*It's funny, as you were saying that, I was flashing back to Marlboro again. I remember you told me once how you didn't succeed so much because of your talent but instead from all the hard work.*

C.C.　Well, I've always felt that and still do. I can sit down and sight-read a piece and it'll be tolerably good, but if anything's going to get to the next level, it won't be on instinct alone.

A.A.　*Nothing substitutes for hard work.*

C.C.　Yes, but it's a double-edged sword. I think that probably the greatest musicians, for the most part, do it by instinct and intuition.

A.A.　*But don't you think they went through some period where they had to, at least for a chunk of years, work very hard to build that technique?*

C.C.　I think it varies. If you look at Menuhin, he was playing perfectly when he was 11 or something. In fact, when his playing began to deteriorate and he tried to put in hard work and be analytical, although there was occasionally a wonderful phrase that was perfect and just forever memorable, in many ways the playing deteriorated more by it being more intellectually oriented. I've seen that with other people too. I think that one of the byproducts of hard work in music is knowing how you're going to play something, and that's not always such a great thing. I think that being alive in the moment is such an important part of performing, and if you know how you're going to play something, then you're not truly alive in the moment.

A.A.　*Right. It's almost like you need to develop a technique that can respond to whatever sponta-neous and true impulse that you have.*

C.C.　That's right. That's my aim at the moment, and also something I talk to my students about. There are a lot of coins in what we do that have two sides to them, and one side in music is how much it matters, how important it is, and how crucial it is that we take it seriously enough and put this work in. The other side of that coin is the exact opposite: you have to let go of all that and have the freedom that only comes from a much more carefree approach.

The Present

A.A. *What are some of your secrets to practicing well, and do you consider that an important part of teaching your students? I remember you once said to me, "I'm a fly on the wall. I want to watch you practice."*

C.C. I do that occasionally, but not very often because I think that it's very hard for a student in that situation to just be honest and practice the way they would. It makes them so self-conscious.

A.A. *Do you talk about it without putting them on the spot like that?*

C.C. Yes. Actually, one tool that I used when I was much younger in my own practicing was related to that idea, which is, "Okay, let's pretend that somebody is listening to my practice. Maybe that will make me more attentive to what I'm doing," and it actually does. Part of practicing is to have something in your head, heart, soul or whatever it is that you're aspiring to, which I usually refer to as my inner ear. It's not what I'm doing or playing at that moment, it's just something that exists inside of me, which could be called "perfection." I'm not saying that I'm perfect, but I have some idea of the music that I'm playing.

A.A. *And are you saying musically you're hearing this finished product in your head, with nuance and everything?*

C.C. That's right. The aspiration is to end up sounding like that, and I think that's quite a nice way of looking at it. There's a little phrase that I use with my students, although I don't remember where I got this from, that you don't practice until you get something right but you practice until you don't get anything wrong. That involves a lot of repetition. Something that I've only realized much more recently is repetition is another one of those coins: that it can be deadly.

A.A. *If you're doing it wrong repeatedly.*

C.C. Well, that too, but that's not exactly what I meant. It can be deadly just from the point of view of boredom. But if you're aware of that, you can approach repetition from the other side, which is for it never to be the same. That's always going to be related in some way. That's a very good tool, I think. A good example of that is actually Anna Magdalena Bach. Bach writes sequences in which he repeats phrases in a different key or a new level, new register, whatever, and Anna Magdalena writes them out; every time the articulations and the slowest bowings are different. This is something I learned from Anner Bylsma, who is one of my cello heroes actually. I still like to go visit him in Amsterdam, and we'll chat. I talked my son Frankie, who's playing the cello, into visiting and playing for him. Frankie played him some Bach, and we had a great time. Anyway, it seems to me Anna Magdalena's motto is to repeat, but not the same way. That's very much part of practicing.

A.A. *What about slow practice?*

C.C. Slow practice is wonderful. There's also a question of when you practice, particularly when you do slow practice, are you detached from the music, or are you as involved emotionally as when you're playing for real? I think musicians differ on that. I know some people who would never invest themselves emotionally when they're practicing. They would wait until the performance. I've not been like that. I've always felt that it's necessary for me, whatever I'm playing, to make every note matter during any form of practice. If I'm playing slow scales, that's music. I've developed that idea greatly over the years so that for instance, now, if I get my students to play a slow scale, I'll harmonize it, playing double stops with their slow scale, and make them hear something different about every note of the scale. Each degree of the scale has its character, personality, meaning, and function in the musical phrase. Those are the kinds of things which for me have unlocked the secrets of classical music. But you were asking about practicing. What I do feel, and what I see with my students, is that probably 90-plus percent of practice they're thinking about playing in tune, and even then it doesn't mean they're going to play in tune.

A.A.   *They're just worried about it.*

C.C.   Yes. That's what people are really concerned with. Intonation on its own is a big topic. I've learnt a lot about that over the years, too. My major thirds have now gone down, and my leading tones have gone down. We're hardwired to play them sharp. I see it all the time with my students.

A.A.   *Leading tones and thirds?*

C.C.   Yes. Major thirds. When you check them against open strings they're always too high. Quartet players know this. They've figured it out.

A.A.   *How do you work on that with your students?*

C.C.   I constantly tell them in lessons, "Okay, that F-sharp is sharp. Can you check that with your open A?" If you're playing the F-sharp on the A string, "Check it with your D string." A lot of this is compromise. For the E on the D string in first position, if you check it with your open A, you play it one way, but if you check it with your open G, it's no longer in tune. I think we have to make that compromise.

Another thing I've learnt is that, although we're taught to have a certain left hand shape, the intonation will never be good if the hand is rigid. There's so much flexibility needed particularly for the middle fingers, two and three. I enjoy demonstrating this. When you put your two down for a trill with one, it's going to be a different place from where you put it down when you're trilling with three. The same applies for three. It's that kind of flexibility that I am certainly aware of in my own playing, and I try to make my students aware of it. It's very interesting.

A.A.   *It's a hard thing to teach, I've found. I don't know how you feel, but I've found that if you get used to hearing it out of tune enough, it sounds in tune to you.*

C.C.   Right. Now we have tuners, of course, which we didn't have when I was growing up. When I saw them, I was very cynical about their use, and then I tried it and that was another level of realizing how out of tune I played.

A.A.   *But with the example you used about the E on the D string, how does the tuner know which E you're supposed to be playing?*

C.C.   Well, it can't of course. But if there is any kind of absolute intonation which never wavers for a moment, which is the tuner, then you realize when you're working with one of those just how far from that absolute you are. Some of it may be intentional and some of it not.

A.A.   *Right. It can point out tendencies in your playing that you might just not be hearing.*

C.C.   Well, even the way you tune your instrument doesn't conform to the tuner. We tighten up our fifths.

A.A. *Do you practice performing during your practice?*

C.C. Yes, very much so, and I also encourage the students to do that. It seems to me that you don't want to get out on stage and realize that you've never played the piece before. But there are conductors who will rehearse orchestras without ever playing through a movement. I need performance and practice. Initially, of course, that's not part of the process because you're learning. Initially you may just be figuring out how to get from one note to the next, but part of the process is in constantly enlarging whatever unit you're working with. It may be a phrase, it may be a section of a movement, eventually it's a whole movement, and eventually it's the whole piece.

A.A. *Have nerves ever been an issue for you?*

C.C. Always, and still.

A.A. *How do you deal with it?*

C.C. I think experience is hugely important in dealing with nerves. Nerves, it's another coin isn't it? They can be debilitating, but they can also be hugely positive. There's an excitement about a performance involving nerves that maybe isn't present in a performance that doesn't involve them.

A.A. *Do you think it accentuates any physical bad habits?*

C.C. Yes, for sure. We can think that we're making great progress removing physical tensions from our playing, and then comes the performance, those things do very often raise their ugly heads and come back to haunt us, don't they? I'm so aware of all those things now because of teaching and the realization of how important it is to have a more relaxed approach to the instrument. It was an issue for me when I was younger because I used to model intensity with excitement, and then tension and intensity got muddled.

Tension seemed not to matter because it made things intense, and intense was exciting and good. Now I realize that the music making that I enjoy listening to from the audience rarely involves extreme physical tension in the performer. I used to get through performances with a certain amount of will power because I was tense to the point of experiencing pain. That had to do with overplaying, I think. Now I play a little less, and I'm not as tense and in as much pain.

A.A. *Related to that, how has your teaching evolved, or your teaching philosophy? How do you feel like you've grown as a teacher after all these years?*

C.C. It's been very interesting. Initially I had a sort of one-size-fits-all approach to teaching, which is, "This is how it goes. Do the best you can." Of course, that's the hopeless approach. I also, from being at the Menuhin school and particularly under the influence of the then-director of music, had the idea that if you felt music strongly enough then you could play it. That was very much part of my early teaching efforts. That was, again, an approach that I have learnt to reject, because actually everybody feels music very strongly. It's great music, why wouldn't it affect A as much as B as much as C? The problem is not in experiencing the greatness of the music; the problem is translating it into performance. In those old days, I wasn't well-equipped to give people tools or sharpen their tools, and I've become much more concerned with that. I've also become more perceptive of people's different problems from all these years of teaching. You do see a lot of the same issues cropping up with people, even to the extent that people so often play the same wrong notes. It's so funny.

We are obviously hardwired a certain way in our approach to reading music and playing our individual instruments. I think my approach to teaching has become much more adaptable to the person I'm working with, and I hope more nurturing. I was tough on people always at the beginning, and although I'm demanding now, I'm never nasty to people in the way that I used to be. I ask a lot of them, but I try to be encouraging and positive because I remember how much better I played when people were that way toward me.

I feel more and more that I have to be some kind of standard bearer for things that matter. I feel like old, great composers need people to stand up for them because they get abused. I suppose I felt like that a little bit in the old days, too, but I've gone almost more that way because I feel that they're abused more and more. Part of that problem is IMSLP (a free site on the internet to download music) because it's a cheap way for students to get music, and they never see something that resembles what a composer wrote.

My mantra that keeps coming up is clarity and depth. Of course it can apply just to sound, to have a clear and deep sound, but it also applies to just about everything that happens in your music making, that you have clarity about what you're doing and depth in what you're doing. Sculpting comes up particularly in Beethoven. Virtually anybody can sit down and sight-read a Beethoven Sonata. The notes of the cello parts are not very difficult, but how many people can really sound like they're making an important statement that Beethoven obviously was making himself? Of course, I'd like to think that I am doing that, and that's what I strive for.

Going back to the idea of sculpting, that's something that helps us to make a reality of that idea. You start with the raw material, and you work it and you work it, look at it from all sides, go further away and you look at it, and go around. That's what we're doing. With sculpting, you're taking away, whereas a lot of times we sort of feel like we're adding. A lot of times we make unwanted accents, and they have to be taken away. Very often, we must take some beats away.

I feel that's the way Beethoven wrote, as well. He starts off with something that is often just banal, and then he sculpts and sculpts. He's not happy, and so he reworks, crosses it out, and he starts again.

A.A.   *The last movement of the Eroica Symphony always strikes me that way.*

C.C.   Yes, and eventually it ends with something perfect. In performing and in teaching, that's what I'm trying to do.

A.A.   *What do you think is the hardest thing to teach a student?*

C.C.   That's a good question. I never thought about it. I imagine for me the hardest thing would be to teach a student from the very beginning how to play the cello. I've never done it.

I feel that with experience now, all these things that people say are really difficult to teach—like vibrato, for instance—I can do that now. I can see where problems are. I know exercises to give people. Usually the problem with vibrato is that it's tight. Occasionally it's that it's too slow. I know how to loosen it up, and when it's too slow I know how to practice to make it faster.

A.A.   *Do you have a couple exercises that you might do to slow down or loosen up someone's vibrato?*

C.C.   Well, it's too narrow if it's tight, so you need to widen it but not lose the center of the pitch. Sometimes if you're wide then you're just moving the pitch, which is not a good thing. I have one that goes, I don't know how you're going to write this down but, "Da-dum, da-dum or da-dum, da-dah."

A.A.   *Rhythmic impulses of vibratos.*

C.C.   Yes, control over what you're doing. If people have problems with vibrato, it's because everything is involuntary. Even just slow and wide, and you can be too slow. Being too tight I think is because everything is happening in the finger and not coming through the arm. The arm actually is the motivator for the cello. The violin is not like that. When I see vibratos which are just in the finger, then I feel they never really work.

A.A.   *What about rhythm? For me that's one of the hardest things to teach; it's like you either have the rhythm gene or you don't. All your students probably have the rhythm gene.*

C.C.   No, not at all. In fact, one of the nice things at Stony Brook is we do juries and we listen to not just our own instrument, we listen to all the instruments. I'd see these percussion players, and they have such fantastic rhythm. I think, "Whoa, I've got to think about that." Again, it comes down to the same thing that everything else does, which is feeling like it matters. With rhythm, if you're in any different time signature, what do those beats mean? 2/4 isn't just one, two, one, two.

   Of course, it depends somewhat on the speed of the music and the character of the music. Three is maybe more interesting than two because it's less symmetrical. Subdividing is something very useful in practicing and in performing, as well. In a dotted rhythm, for instance, I'm constantly banging on to my students about feeling the dot. I think that if we're not aware of all the beats in between, very often we just ever so slightly cut these long beats.

A.A.   *Yes, it seems like they're never held too long.*

C.C.   Yes, I think that's right. But rhythm is "up." I teach that a lot. I also encourage learning from other instruments with rhythm, like percussion. For any percussion instrument, there's something that has to go down to make sound happen, but if you don't go up as a rebound, then not only is the rhythm not very good, but the sound is even worse. If you hit a drum and don't come up, then you kill the vibration of the drum or xylophone or any of those instruments.

A.A.   *Even the piano?*

C.C.   Sure. People play the piano like that and just stay in the key. It's the same with strings. I'm always encouraging people to be in the string and then out, rather than out of the string and then in. It can kill the sound.

A.A.   *When you're selecting students, do you have a priority of what's most important?*

C.C.   That's an interesting question. Sound, intonation, and rhythm and the fundamentals. Aside from that, I'm always drawn to people who have character in their playing, people who seem to have a voice of their own that's unique. We all do, and that's what I want to hear. All of my students are graduate students and most of them are doctoral students, so they're older. They have a lot of repertoire required of them at the audition, so actually these auditions are quite long. I think, "Well, if they're this long, I want to talk to them as well." If there's any playing that perks me up, then I'll spend time chatting. On a human, conversational level, it seems like someone that's nice to talk to then is someone who's going to be nice to work with in the lessons. That's all relatively new but important for me.

A.A.   *What are some of the technical exercises or études that you use, and have they changed over the years? Have you maintained a steady diet of Poppers and Piattis?*

C.C.   Yes, there are a couple of Poppers I use. There's the D major one with a lot of thumb position and string crossings. I don't tend to give that to my students, but I play it myself fairly often. I use Number 4, the F-sharp major one, for a flexible left hand. You cannot play that if you just think that everything's going to work in a block.

I also use a couple of Piatti Caprices, such as the infamous B-flat major, Number 3, and the string-crossing one, Number 7. For both of those, the flexibility of left-hand positions is important. As for my exercises, apparently I have something of a reputation for playing scales, but those have evolved and become more refined over the years. It used to be that I would spend an hour or even an hour and a half doing that before anything else, and I've toned that down a little bit. Other exercises have developed from specific problems in pieces that I've had and devised exercises for.

A.A.   *Do you guide students with scales?*

C.C.   I do. I don't impose it on them, but if they ask for guidance, I'm more than ready to give it. I've seen enough people over the years be transformed, if they've taken this seriously, from having a mediocre cello technique to becoming really commanding instrumentalists.

A.A.   *Related to that, do you make students play or perform by memory and is that important? Especially in the sense of being able to think about what you're doing, physically even, or musically?*

C.C.   That's another coin, I think. It can be liberating to play from memory and it can be extremely debilitating for some people to play from memory.

A.A.   *Even for practicing, though? Because I'm not so much asking about getting on stage and going, "Can I remember this piece?" It's more of, like …*

C.C.   Right. Practicing from memory.

A.A.   *Yes.*

C.C.   Well, that's yet another coin, I think. It's related to your question about do you perform as you're practicing. And if you do, you're more likely to be playing from memory. So for me, someone who does like to perform when practicing, I practice without music quite often. But I see my students doing this and then not really knowing or remembering what's in the music. I often come back to the music myself thinking that I'm probably committing the crimes that they are. Indeed, I often am surprised if I've strayed sometimes. I also sometimes find it a little bit inspiring to look at music as I'm playing. It can work both ways. If you've spent a lot of time playing something from memory and then you sit down and you play it with the music, the visual sensation has some contribution to your music-making. What's particularly true about this is if you play from a manuscript, because there's very often some kind of a flow in the writing of the actual notes. Because things are very evenly spaced, in a published, printed page, and in a manuscript, of course depending on whose it is, it is not usually like that. And so you can almost feel where a composer wants motion from looking at the way they've written the notes.

A.A.   *How important is body movement in playing, and have you dealt more with that over the years?*

C.C.   I've always moved. For me, it's important, just as facial expressions are. We're like actors on the stage. They have a script, they become a character, and every movement that they do belongs to that character. We are portraying the character of the music. The obvious two things that people always come up with are happy and sad, right? There's a great deal more than that. There's something incongruous about looking sad when you're playing happy music. It doesn't make sense to the person watching you.

I can see from your demonstration of motion there that when you imitated somebody playing without moving, you thought it was stiff. When you moved a little from side to side, that freed you. Ben Zander, whom you probably remember, used to make people aware of their left and right buttocks.

A.A.   *Yes, it's hard to forget that.*

C.C.   And I think it's good. If we're playing dance music, we should dance. I think if it gets to the point where the motion is a distraction to the listener, then it's too much. We all know cellists for whom that's been a problem, and we all know the cellists for whom the opposite is the problem, the motionless ones. Those people talk about efficiency, and they themselves have made an art of this efficiency. It's been a whole mark of their playing and something quite wonderful, because they've perfected it. When other people try to imitate it, it's very often a disaster.

A.A.   *I agree. One thing I often tell students is that in order to sound different, you have to do something different with your body. People will practice again and again exactly the same way physically, and then wonder, "Why doesn't it sound any different?"*

C.C.   Well, one thing that I've become more aware of recently is, and I noticed you doing this when you were swaying, the idea of motion that's constant. Rather than down bow and stop, then up bow and stop, it's all on one plane.

A.A.   *They're doing circular bowing, is that what you're saying?*

C.C.   Yes. And a lot of that kind of thing really helps people to relax. It's helped me.

A.A.   *How do you teach a clean spiccato, and how do you view the role of the wrist and fingers? Do you have a method?*

C.C.   The first thing for everyone to understand is that it's effortless, that the "chuka-chuka-chuka-chuka-chuka" drum which sounds really busy actually isn't. If you're busy doing that, you'll get tired very quickly. That means that it's the bow that's doing the work, not you. You're guiding it, but you're just helping it to do what it wants to do. If it's faster, like in spiccato, then the arm is not involved. If you're playing something that fast with the arm, you're going to get very tired very quickly. It's just fingers, and wrists possibly if it's slower spiccato. The faster it is, the less it goes left to right. It really just stays in the same place. The down bow and the up bow don't start in different places. If you really watch closely, you'll see that the hair of the bow is not moving as much as the wood of the bow. The wood and the hair are constantly getting closer to each other and then further away from each other. And I think that's helped people quite a lot, as an image. Again, it may not be exactly up and down; it may be just a circle.

But I've also, in these days of not being allowed to touch your students, simply put my hand over the student's hand on the bow to do this. You can make the bow do spiccato, and it's a little bit clunky, but they can actually feel what's going on. Then it's a little bit easier for them to replicate it after that.

A.A. *How much do you tell students to practice? Do you think a specific amount of time, or is it quality more important?*

C.C. It depends just how comfortable they are with their instruments. At a certain point, everyone always has to put in that kind of work. Quite a lot of the time, even with my graduate students, they haven't ever really done it. I do find myself telling them this is what they have to do and to be careful that they're not in pain afterward.

A.A. *Right. Or that you're still being efficient.*

C.C. Right. Then there's always talk about how to divide the practice between what people call technical work and musical work. I don't like the distinction all that much. If you're playing scales and études, I guess you call it technical work. That's fine if you want to label it. I don't think there's an absolute that works for everybody. Certain people enjoy doing the scales more than others. I think the answer is probably to do as much as you're able to while still being fascinated and enriched by it. There's no point in telling them to practice six or seven hours if four of them they find dull.

A.A. *Do you demonstrate a lot in lessons?*

C.C. Much less than I used to. I only play their cello. I don't ever use my cello in lessons. They all say that's helpful. I get real pleasure out of playing lots of different cellos anyway because I always find something to like about any student cello. There's always something, often just the quantity of sound, that they've never understood is possible from their instrument.

A.A. *But why less than you used to do? Was that a conscious decision?*

C.C. Because I'm so weary of "do it as I do" kind of teaching. That's how it used to be. Maybe I exaggerate the dangers of that kind of teaching, but I want my students to be independent thinkers and not imitators.

A.A. *Do you make a point to have your students keep their individuality in their playing?*

C.C. Absolutely. You could always tell a Galamian student. You certainly could never tell a Colin Carr student.

A.A. *But that's not a bad thing.*

C.C. No, I don't think so.

A.A. *How do you feel about these famous transcriptions, like the Boccherini/Grützmacher, or the Rococo (Fitzenhagen), or the Chopin Polonaise (Feuermann). I mean, those are three examples that seem like they're the most popular examples that everyone plays, especially the Boccherini or the Tchaikovsky. Do you teach them with the arrangements? Do you feel like the students should only learn the original first?*

C.C. I actually don't ever ask my students to play the Boccherini B-flat Concerto because I feel like the Grützmacher is such a travesty, and there's so much to the original. I think I've avoided that piece. As for the Rococo, I grew up with the Fitzenhagen version. I've played both, but I've played Fitzenhagen much, much more. The variation that Fitzenhagen had removed is a little bit tedious, actually.

A.A.   *Right, but then on the other side it's what Tchaikovsky wrote, and we don't get to hear that.*

C.C.   If I'm true to my obsession of trying to honor composers' wishes, then I should probably disown the Fitzenhagen version. It's funny, I'm not consistent in that respect. I've played both versions of the Chopin. I've played the version which he wrote where all of the virtuosic things are in the piano, and I've enjoyed it. I feel a little bit like that with Rococo, that it evolved into what people loved.

The Future

A.A.   *I'm wondering about your thoughts on the next generation of cellists and the number of jobs, especially with orchestras. All the technology and the internet, do you think that's a bad thing for classical music?*

C.C.   I think it's a good thing for our instrument that it has branched out. There are lots of different cello ensembles around now doing different things that are nothing short of spectacular. I think that's wonderful. People have been moaning about the demise of classical music since I was a kid. I don't really give much credence to that, because it always seems to survive. It's one of the greatest things man has achieved, so I think that there will always be enough people around who will make sure that it doesn't get killed.

A.A.   *Have you seen the level of cello playing change over the years? And are there enough jobs for young cellists leaving school?*

C.C.   The level of cello playing has certainly gone up. There's no doubt about that. I've been on juries of competitions and just been absolutely shell-shocked. There's always been one or two standouts, but now you can listen to a room full and they can all play superbly. I'm not sure that I could say that they all play with the sort of unique voice that we were talking about earlier, which is something that could be described as art or poetry, but nevertheless, the level of instrumental playing has really gone up.

      As for jobs, I've been teaching at the college/university level now for 34 years and always, always questioning, "What are these people going to do?" It's always answered the same way: they find something, unless of course they decided to have a career change. In that case, they either wanted to make more money than they thought they would make playing the cello, or they felt inadequate or unsuited to having a career in music. If we discount those people, everyone else finds a place for themselves. I'm not that worried.

A.A.   *How much do you help a student find success out of school, and do you think that's part of your job?*

C.C.   Now you're asking the question that makes me feel guilty. It's probably something that I should be more aware of. When students specifically ask for help, then of course I feel it's my duty to provide it. It's surprising how little they do ask for help, though, maybe because they feel they don't need it or maybe because they believe that I'm not going to provide it.

      At Stony Brook recently, I've had a couple of doctoral students who came in sort of like everybody else, thinking they're going to go out the other end and do something relatively normal with the cello. They didn't know what, but they'd find a job of some kind, whether it was teaching or playing in an ensemble. They both developed their singing voices while they were at Stony Brook. They both developed techniques for playing and singing at the same time. I encouraged them violently to do this, because it seemed to me that they were doing something that was challenging, unusual, and potentially very interesting and gratifying. Now they're both out there doing this. That's opened up a whole repertoire of things that they can adapt and transcribe, mostly from popular music, for themselves to play and sing. It's been great.

A.A.   *There's been a big shift to historically informed practice in Baroque music and specifically with the Bach Suites over the last half-century or so. How do you feel about the trend that probably 9 out of 10 recordings now seem to have a direction toward being more authentic to the Baroque period? Has that been a good thing; is that a coin as well?*

C.C.   It's definitely another coin. As I said earlier, Bylsma has been one of my heroes. He was very much the pioneer of this, in cello anyway. His approach was through Anna Magdalena, so that's what got me interested in it at first. I think there's far more to this than just setting up the Anna Magdalena manuscript on the music stand and trying to observe every one of her slurs. If you insist on that as a teacher, you just end up with hundreds of people doing the exact same thing, which ultimately is going to be really dull. For me, what is really fascinating and wonderful about Anna Magdalena is her spirit: it's a spirit of adventure, of spontaneity, of freshness, and of a youthful, anything's-worth-trying kind of approach. There's really no point in just sitting down and doing all these bowings if your spirit is dead. I think I'd rather listen to Casals, actually.

I also enjoy trying to make my cello sound like a Baroque cello. I love non-vibrato; I love the purity and clarity of that sound, but that's another coin, isn't it? Non-vibrato can just simply be ugly.

A.A.   *I remember one thing you often talked about was that on longer notes it's nice to have very little or no vibrato but on the faster notes to keep your hand alive.*

C.C.   Yes, I am very much for that. I still talk about that a lot because it's one of these sorts of counterintuitive things for us, isn't it? We all tend to get going with the vibrato if there's lots of time to do it. Those sixteenth notes can sound really dull if there's no activity there.

Close to the Heart

A.A.   *If you hadn't been a musician, what would you have loved to have done with your life?*

C.C.   Well, that's changed. When I was little I wanted to be a fireman. I wanted to have a pole to slide down. Then, I wanted to be a soccer player. I always loved soccer and I played every day. I was fast. I don't know if I was skillful or not, but that was something I had considered. I think because music has been so central to my whole life I actually can't imagine a life without music. However, I would certainly not play the cello in my next musical life, that's for sure. It's too limiting. I think I would either conduct or play the piano.

I think having control over bigger forces would be exciting. People often don't credit the cello with having as much control in an ensemble as it does actually have. Playing second cello in the Schubert quintet is remarkable for being able to almost direct the entire performance.

A.A. *You did some conducting once upon a time.*

C.C. I did, but I quickly realized how much technique is involved. If I was to do it well, I would want to go to school, and I never really had time to do that. It would also be fun to sing well. I'm always so envious of the ability of a singer to fill a colossal space. I just don't know how it's done. I would love to learn that.

A.A. *Tell me about maybe two or three of your most memorable concert experiences.*

C.C. Playing the Rococo Variations in London comes to mind. I was playing with a Russian conductor, and it was clear from the first rehearsal that things weren't going to go all that well. We got to the variation where the flute plays the theme.

A.A. *The trill variation?*

C.C. The trills, and then there's a little cadenza in that variation. After a short cadenza, the orchestra comes in with the flute playing the melody. So I start my cadenza but the conductor goes to the flute and the flute plays, and half the orchestra played and half didn't. This was in the Albert Hall in London, which is a huge hall, and probably 5,000 people were there. I was young. I was probably 18 or so. I carried on to the end of my cadenza, and the flute carried on. Eventually the whole thing sort of ground to a halt, and I stamped my foot and yelled out, "I want to play my cadenza!" Someone in the audience yelled, "Disgraceful!"

A.A. *And then what happened?*

C.C. I started from the beginning of the variation and got to the end of the piece. That was memorable. I was like a little kid, you know what I mean?

A.A. *Has it become a good memory now, then?*

C.C. Well, it's a good story. Amazing how many people I still meet that say they were there or they were playing orchestra.

A.A. *I wish I could have been there!*

C.C. There's another one. You asked for two or three. I was playing in Turkey for a live radio broadcast with a pianist from Turkey who I'd never played with before. It was an hour concert of the Beethoven A-Major and Brahms E-Minor Sonatas. There was an audience, as well. I came in, bowed, sat down, and I started playing the solo opening of the Beethoven and she started playing the piano part of the Brahms. It was remarkable because it was the same tempo.

A.A. *It would almost work, wouldn't it?*

C.C. It was so shocking that it didn't stop after one measure. We actually played about four measures.

A.A. *Have you ever had to deal with a period of doubt about being a musician in your life, or has it always been a good constant?*

C.C. I think that one of the byproducts of my obsessive approach to cello and practicing endlessly has been that I've never doubted my ability to play. Obviously like anybody else, I have better days and worse days. Occasionally I doubt just the wisdom of spending a whole life doing this. It's limiting, but it can always be justified by the pleasure that it gives me and, I hope, the pleasure that it gives others. It doesn't have to be millions of people. Just a few people whose lives are touched or possibly even changed by it makes it all seem like the right thing to do.

A.A   *What are you most proud of in your life or career?*

C.C.   I'm not a particularly proud person. I don't know. I'm proud of my family.

If someone asked me that, that's probably what I'm thinking.

Yes, I sometimes look at my kids and think, "Did I make that?" and that's wonderful. In terms of career and music and cello playing, I'm really not, which is ridiculous because that's the one thing that I've devoted my whole life to.

A.A.   *Well, you've done so many amazing things. Is there anything you still want to do before it's all done?*

C.C.   No. My colleague Raphael (Wallfisch), who has played probably 20 times the repertoire that I've played, I tip my hat to him because I haven't done it, and I couldn't do it. It takes me time to live with a piece and perform it before it seems like it's the right thing to do. But I am who I am. I think with teaching, although I hate teaching over the internet, using the internet for writing a teaching book does interest me. There wouldn't actually be any students, though. I would take a piece, and that would be a chapter of my book. I would talk about it online and maybe play a little bit. Because I have such knowledge and experience now of hearing hundreds of people play that piece, I know what the pitfalls are and I know the same puddles that people are going to step in. I would make a statement about what's important to me about that piece of music. I think that could be something that might be interesting. I'm not that proud of my recordings that I've done so far; I just don't feel great about them. If I could do something like this, though, where maybe there would be a performance of the whole piece in each chapter as well as some personal statement, that might mean something to people. It's just an idea that's brewing, anyway.

3

Steven Doane

Internationally known as soloist, chamber musician, and master teacher, Steven Doane maintains an active schedule of performances throughout the US and overseas. He travels frequently to the United Kingdom for recitals, clinics, and master classes, and has performed concertos in London, Edinburgh, and Dublin. Concerto appearances in the US have included the orchestras of Baltimore, San Francisco, Buffalo, Milwaukee, and the Rochester Philharmonic. As a member of the New Arts Trio, Doane was awarded the Naumburg Chamber Music prize in 1980.

Doane's New York solo debut was made at Carnegie Hall in Strauss' Don Quixote with David Zinman conducting the Rochester Philharmonic, and was followed by an appearance at the Kennedy Center in Washington.

Numerous recital appearances with duo partner with pianist Barry Snyder have included concerts at New York's Alice Tully Hall, Boston's Sanders Theater, two recitals at London's Wigmore Hall, and numerous other engagements throughout the US and UK. The second in a series of recordings for the Bridge label with Mr. Snyder (works by Benjamin Britten and Frank Bridge) won a 1996 Naird award in the US music press, and the Bridge Sonata was declared "the best performance on record" by BBC music magazine. An earlier disc on the Bridge label of the complete works for cello and piano by Fauré received a "Petit Diapason d'Or" from the French recording press. The duo's most recent release on the Bridge label is the Rachmaninoff Sonata and Études

Tableaux Op. 39 for Piano. In addition to recordings on the Bridge label, Mr. Doane has recorded for Pantheon, Caedmon, Gasparo, and Sony.

Mr. Doane is Professor of Cello at the Eastman School of Music in Rochester N.Y. where he has taught for 38 years. Between 1995 and 1999, Mr. Doane was an associate in cello at the Royal College of Music in London. Following a series of master classes at the Royal Academy in London, he was named a "Fellow" of that institution, and continues his association there as a visiting professor. In November 2014, Mr. Doane received a "lifetime achievement award" from the London Violoncello Society. In addition to recital and solo activities he was also for seven years the cellist of the Los Angeles Piano Quartet.

The Past

Anthony Arnone	*Where did you grow up, and how did you first become exposed to the cello?*
Steven Doane	Well, I grew up in Michigan, in the suburbs of Detroit. Then when I was 13 we moved to Ann Arbor, which was a very lucky break for me and the cello. But my beginnings were as a pianist. I was lucky to have some great piano teachers during my younger years and my parents would take me to the symphony often so I was exposed to music from a young age although it would be awhile before I got my hands on a cello.

I think I actually started playing the cello when I was nine or 10. So I was an extremely late starter. My first teacher was Grace Konopka and then later with Doug Marsh who had been in the Detroit Symphony. At that point it got more serious. When I was 14, I went to the Interlochen Arts Academy, and I realized holy cow! this is really exciting. But the piano's got to go.

That summer I performed in at least one piano recital, I think this was my last "solo" appearance as a pianist!

My teacher at the time Nelita True was very patient with me, but many years later when we were colleagues together at Eastman she told me I was an impossible pupil, as I was never satisfied. I don't think in the end, I could ever find the sound I wanted on the piano. I did realize that summer that I had to stop studying piano, and really concentrate on the cello. After that I started practicing cello very intensely.

And I've often thought that because I was a late starter, I had to think about how to play the cello more, and that might have triggered some interest in teaching.

A.A.	*Do you have siblings, and were they into music as well?*
S.D.	My older brother was a good trombonist, but just played for fun. I used to accompany him on the piano.
A.A.	*What did he do for a living?*
S.D.	He's actually a minister. He's retired, but still working in Chicago.

A.A.   *And were your parents musicians?*

S.D.   My dad was a metallurgical engineer. But he was a very gifted pianist as well. He could play jazz by ear, and he wrote my mom some songs before they were married. His mother was a piano teacher. And so he was very switched on to music, and he would sit me at the piano bench next to him and we'd improvise. He would encourage me to play with him.

A.A.   *That's wonderful!*

S.D.   So it was always fun to play with my dad. He would always encourage me. And then when I was first playing the cello, he'd play with me until I wanted to play too fast. But he was very encouraging. My mom I think was musical, but wasn't trained as a musician.

A.A.   *Was there a point in your teens when you thought this is I think what I want to do, or did that come later?*

S.D.   I think it hit when I was at Interlochen in the summer camp, when I was surrounded by wonderful players in this beautiful setting. It was easy to get excited about what we were doing. I remember feeling a tremendous sense of discovery, and thinking with real excitement that this felt like an expressive "voice" that I was finding.

A.A.   *Did you enjoy practicing?*

S.D.   Yes, very much. My piano practice took place in the living room, so I had to practice "correctly" as I was being overheard. My dad, having taken notes from my lessons, could tell if I was practicing efficiently or not, although I do remember him not minding my improvisation sessions. The cello was a bit more of a private activity, and what I'd learned about practice habits probably carried over, but it was also my own "experiment."

But also when I was about six, I lost the sight of my right eye. I'm profoundly right-handed, so leaps on the piano were a bit problematic, because I couldn't always keep track of both hands. Maybe that influenced things.

A.A.   *How did you hurt yourself?*

S.D.   I had a penetrating injury with a pair of pruning shears.

A.A.   *Oh that's horrible! How did this happen?*

S.D.   I climbed a garage wall. I liked to invent things as a kid, and I had a contraption on my red wagon. And I had it all bound to my tricycle with hemp rope and couldn't get it untied, so I climbed the wall to get the shears and, well, that was that. It certainly changed my life in an instant.

A.A.   *You might have been a pianist if you hadn't had that happen.*

S.D.   Well, I also liked baseball, but I was suddenly unable to really see the ball clearly. I was trying to play Little League and that was a disaster. I think my folks encouraged me with music because it was an outlet. And it didn't hurt that I was very interested in it already.

I think the thing about cello is it's so tactile. On the right side you almost exclusively feel what's going on with the bow, so it's a wonderful kinesthetic feed-back loop on that side.

I also think playing with others was a huge thing. The piano's kind of lonely.

A.A.   *I agree.*

S.D.   I was lucky; one of my early piano teachers, Mark Wessel, was a really good composer and taught us composition if we were interested. So he had me writing pieces. And a lot of them had the melody in the left hand, which was good for my cello instincts.

A.A.   *Were you pushed hard or more self-motivated? I'm guessing it was self-motivated.*

S.D.   On the cello, I was pretty self-motivated.

A.A.   *And what was your primary motivation at that point? Was it for the love of the instrument that made you want to get better, or were you competitive with other people?*

S.D.   Well when I got to Interlochen, Christoph Henkel was the principal cellist. I was amazed by his fluency and confidence! I heard him play the Kodaly Sonata and with a bent endpin no less. And this was 1965 so it seemed somewhat revolutionary.

That summer was a turning point, and the following fall, I started practicing five hours a day and not doing enough homework probably, but it was the next summer I suddenly found that I was in the front of the section instead of the back. The first summer I was lucky to be in the broadcast orchestra and fought to stay there. We had challenges every week. And I think I must have practiced orchestral excerpts 40 hours a week. I didn't mind. We were outdoors, and there was great music going on. And every Friday we had challenges. You would play the chosen excerpt. Your stand partner would play it. Everybody in the section put their head down and voted. And you either went up and down or stayed in place. And the first year when I was toward the back of the section, I'd managed to advance to 7th chair by sheer determination and hours of practice. The next week I slipped back 3 chairs in the section because I'd had to practice the piano quite a lot for a recital—I think that's when I realized the piano had to go.

A.A.   *And then what happened when you were done with high school?*

S.D.   So I was studying with Mr. Marsh right up until the last year of high school, and then I did an early audition at Oberlin and I met Richard Kapuscinski. Norm Fischer introduced us. Because Norm was from Michigan, too. He was from Plymouth, which is about 30 miles outside of Ann Arbor.

And Norm, who's just so full of enthusiasm, said, "Steve, you got to meet Kapuscinski." And I went with him down to Oberlin to hear Kap play in a quartet.

The next day we had a 90 minute lesson, and I think I simply gravitated toward his personal and musical magnetism. He was an unforgettable personality—raised in a poor Catholic family in Milwaukee, and the first of his family to go to university level education. Dick was a wonderfully warm human being—extremely energetic and pretty charismatic, really, and with a simply wonderful cello sound! I'll never forget the initial impression his playing made on meat that moment in my young life! I thought he sounded a bit like Leonard Rose, who he'd met as a teenager and played to quite a bit before going to Curtis to study with Felix Salmond. Many years later, when I heard a recording of Salmond's playing, I got a bit of a shock of recognition: I think Dick had inherited a lot of that immediacy and vocal quality that Salmond's playing exemplified.

A.A.   *What did Kapuscinski give you as a teacher that you hadn't yet received? Did you feel like you already had a pretty solid technical base?*

S.D.   Well, I had some pretty good basics from Mr. Marsh, who had been feeding me all the Schroeder studies. I could see looking back, notations that he made, like loose wrist and fingers, and where to play in the bow. He actually talked about that and was very helpful.

But Dick was different. I think he made you listen on a very high level for detail. He was obsessed with articulation and phrase direction, and I don't think he ever played a boring phrase in his life. He was a musician first. And he'd been in the Boston Symphony, played quartets with Silverstein, and he admired Dumas, the physician/violinist. He'd also talked about Eugene Lehner a lot.

Dick had real reverence for him. And he talked about Rose a bit as well. But Dick had studied with Felix Salmond at Curtis. And I think his sound was a big influence. Because when I heard Salmond on the historic recordings of cellists, there was something about that sound that he made that I thought Dick had picked up.

Dick kept me at certain pieces for a long time until I really had absorbed all the detail he wanted me to. And so that was an education in listening and sound production in terms of control of the bow, especially with the fingers. He was extremely attentive to that.

A.A.   *Did he have you doing a lot of things to build left hand technique?*

S.D.   Not really. I was pretty fluent by that point. But he was really going after how I combined the work of the two hands. I spent a long time on Haydn C and Lalo with him, getting it just right. I had played Schumann on my audition. I hadn't had the sense to realize how hard it was, so I just played it.

Dick was also a role model as a human being. I was kind of a practice nerd, and this was during the Vietnam War, and I would be practicing my Popper studies, and Dick would say, "Steve, there's a peace demonstration on Tappan Square, you're coming." And so he was personally invested in his students. He lived near the dorms and would often come talk to students if they had a crisis. He was extremely engaged in that way.

Dick had famous leaf raking parties in the Fall. He had a big corner lot. And he'd make chili and would get the whole studio out there with rakes, clearing up the leaves, and then he'd feed us. Lucy was Dick's wife and was also thoroughly involved with Oberlin—in fact she was a dorm "mother" or manager, and they lived for a while in an apartment in one of the larger dorms on campus, Dascomb. They were a great example to us of "older" people who completely got what we were about in that very turbulent time in the late 60s and early 70s, and weren't above offering a bit of personal advice when we needed it.

A.A.   *Do you think that influenced you later as a teacher? I mean, just what you saw as kind of the role of a teacher?*

S.D.   I think so, yes. It was hard not to absorb that as well.

A.A.   *It strikes me you're a lot like that as well.*

S.D.   Well, you couldn't help but be influenced when you see somebody like that. He was a Cello Papa.

A.A.   *And so you were there for undergraduate years?*

S.D.   Four years, yes.

A.A.   *Okay, and then what was the next step in your career?*

S.D.   One day I heard the recording of the Beaux Arts Trio playing the Fauré Piano Trio at a party at a friend's, and when they got to the slow movement, I thought, "Who's playing the cello? This is unbelievable." And it was Bernard Greenhouse. It was like, uh oh. How do I get to this person? I'd been trying to get to Casals since I was a freshman in college. I'd read all his biographies. I had written to his wife, to see if I could go and have a lesson or be in a chorus or something, and she always wrote back very politely saying he was too busy. And at the end of my first year at Oberlin, she suggested I try to play to Maurice Eisenberg. And I don't know quite how it happened, but I got admitted to a class in Cascais in Portugal, where Eisenberg was teaching as well as Sandor Vegh on the violin.

It was there that I met the young Steven Isserlis, who was 12 years old. And neither of us knew each other from Adam. He was far from fully grown and was playing on what looked like a ½ sized cello. Milly Stanfield, who at the time was at the International Cello Centre in London was teaching him there. That's as close as I got to Casals up to that point.

And then a couple years later I got into Marlboro, and that was the opportunity of a lifetime because he was conducting the orchestra, and he gave master classes and we all played to him. I played him a good chunk of the Second Suite.

A.A. *Is that when he stopped you after three notes?*

S.D. Well, in the prelude he stopped me after three notes. "This is" and he imitated the vibrato to devastating effect, and said, "This is not music, not music." So I stopped vibrating altogether for a good while, and then he seemed content. And when we were in the Allemande, we were working away and he demonstrated the beginning of the second half of the Allemande, which has some very complex voice leading in it. He finished his demonstration, fixed on me with his beady eyes, and said "do you understand?" "Mm-hmm" said my 20-year-old self. I started playing and there was this very loud shout "No!" And I apparently was so spooked that I hid behind my cello. And I kind of gradually came up and I could see Mischa Schneider in the front row, and Serkin and all of these old guys chuckling. And even Casals, his eyes were twinkly. And I guess the reaction even made him amused and he said, "Next time you will not be so quick to understand." I loved that. I quote that occasionally, because you do have students that want to jump in before they really absorb.

But I still remember the way he demonstrated that phrase. It was totally clear even at 93 or 94, whatever age he was. It was a little scratchy but it was Casals playing, and you knew that sound from hearing his recordings. There is always so much texture and life to everything he did, even in slow motion. So that was tremendously inspiring. Yes, he was definitely my musical god at that point.

A.A. *How many summers were you at Marlboro? Just that one?*

S.D. I only had that one summer sadly.

A.A. *And that was when you were at Oberlin?*

S.D. Yes. I got to play as part of one of the "music from Marlboro" tours, so I missed 3 weeks of classes at Oberlin. The tour was led by the great Italian violinist and founder of I Musici, Pina Camerilli. There were three of us 20-year-olds on the tour: myself, Jerry Grossman (now principal cellist of the Met. Opera orch), and James Dunham (formerly of the Sequoia and Cleveland Quartets now teaching at Rice). The wonderful violist Phil Neagle was another senior member. Pina used to look around during the tour and say of the three of us "Where are the bambini? (children) we must rehearse!" She was an extraordinary musician and person—she played wonderfully, and led with phenomenal authority. She somehow kept her somewhat arthritic hands going by knitting almost continuously during the drives and plane rides.

Peter Wiley was there that summer, and he was 16. Ron Leonard was there. And I went to study with Ron for a semester when he was at Northern Illinois. I went to college a semester early, which I don't recommend to anybody. You should go in with your own class. It was a hard transition.

A.A.   *Why did you graduate a semester early from high school?*

S.D.   Because I thought I was going to have lessons with Italo Babini, the principal cellist in Detroit. He accepted me as a student, but then it didn't work out. My folks just thought well, you've been admitted so maybe it's time to go.

A.A.   *So you finished Oberlin in the middle of the school year?*

S.D.   Yes. So I went to study with Ron (Leonard) at Northern Illinois. He was playing in the Vermeer Quartet for a year. And that was fascinating.

A.A.   *I interviewed him and I remember him telling that part of the story. It's a small cello world!*

S.D.   Well he was amazing. His hands on the cello were like magic. He was such a beautiful player, and I thought this is somebody who I should learn from, you know. It was another no brainer. And then I played for Raya Garbousova once. I wish I'd played for her more—she was very supportive when we did meet, and a wonderfully sweet person and amazing musician.

But then I ended up at Stony Brook with Bernie (Greenhouse). He was touring an awful lot, so I didn't see him all the time. But it was very inspiring when he was there.

A.A.   *Did you also have lessons with anyone else?*

S.D.   I've played to Tim (Eddy) a few times. I wish I had played to him a lot more. We had lived down the hall from each other at Marlboro and had become friends.

A.A.   *Was he a teaching assistant?*

S.D.   I'm not certain of his official status at the time, but he was teaching undergraduates. It was a powerful combination with Bernie. I've known Tim for a long time now as a colleague and he's not only a great musician and cellist, but I believe is also one of the great teachers of the cello in the world today.

A.A.   *What do you remember getting most from Mr. Greenhouse?*

S.D.   What I got most from him was inspiration, pure and simple. Bernie had a very palpable connection to Casals, you could sense it. You could hear it in the playing, you could feel it in the way he articulated and "spoke" the music.

He had that special "magic" that we all should aspire to; the music was spoken when it needed to be, and sung when it needed to be and often in the best way a little of both. It was unforgettable.

At the same time I was frustrated at what I felt were "sticks" for hands, and at not being able to simply "absorb" the malleability he had in his wonderfully soft, yet powerful hands.

And Tim has figured out how to explain it in the most beautiful way. I think Tim has been able to patiently deconstruct what Bernie was actually doing and pass it on. And he's got it in his playing as well. During those two years, I was kind of a lost soul. Dick was so hands-on so fatherly, that I thought okay, I'm ready to go out into the world. And what I didn't realize was that some of the information that he had given me I'd simply "gulped" like a baby bird and never properly digested.

And I think at Stony Brook, I started asking myself how I was doing things, and watching the way Bernie was modeling motion. He was a great musical model. And a very palpable connection to Casals, you could sense that. You could sense it in the playing, you could sense it in the way he articulated and spoke the music.

A.A. *So would you say you learned a lot by just observing and hearing rather than from what he said to you?*

S.D. Yes. At that point in time, I think Bernie was more of an inspirational than analytical teacher. Later on, I think he got much more into detail when he wasn't touring as much. I know he really loved his teaching work, and was a great model for so many of us.

A.A. *Did you feel less confident when you were studying with him than you did at Oberlin?*

S.D. Yes, Dick provided the support I never would have had myself to enter these competitions, which included Hudson Valley, Washington International, and San Francisco Symphony. Each of them led to some wonderful performance opportunities, and as a "side benefit" I was able to quit my pot washing job too! I also had a few other students too, which was fun.

A.A. *I was going to ask about how you got into the teaching part of your career.*

S.D. That was accidental. I "graduated" to teaching a few younger pupils on Saturdays, which turned out to be quite a challenge actually!

A.A. *Do you remember when you first started having any students at all? Was that even at Oberlin, or was it earlier?*

S.D. Probably the last two years of Oberlin, and at Stony Brook.

A.A. *Then what happened after Stony Brook?*

S.D. The opportunity that really was transformative. But first a bit of background. While at Oberlin, I was constantly searching for answers about playing more naturally, and finding the elusive flow in one's playing. I was definitely a "seeker" because I knew these answers weren't completely within my reach as yet. I'd been lucky enough to play piano Trios at Oberlin with pianist Robert Shannon (long time prof. of piano there to this day) and the violinist Kazuko Numanai, a simply wonderful musician who was one of Suzuki's first Japanese teachers in the US in the late 60s when his work began to take hold over here. Kazuko was from Suzuki's home town, and had studied with Dr. Suzuki himself from childhood. She had the most amazing artistry and control and was the first string player I'd met who exemplified a kind of transcendent physical balance at the instrument.

I was also at the time introduced to the philosopher Herrigal's short but brilliant book *Zen in the Art of Archery* and I recognized something in it that I was searching for that reached across all artistic disciplines.

I was also just so curious about the great cellists of the time, including Rostropovich in Russia, Tortelier, Fournier in Geneva, etc. I saw an announcement that the Thomas J. Watson Foundation was interviewing seniors for a fellowship program for overseas study. I wrote a proposal to study cello pedagogy for a year with the idea of meeting some of the great figures of the time, including Rostropovich (I also tried to start learning Russian—that was not a success!), Tortelier, Fournier, and finally Starker, who was doing a summer course in Luzern. (I'd met some of his pupils and knew what a great figure he was in the cello world, but never had played to him.)

William Pleeth, of course, was Jackie du Pré's teacher in London, and I knew there was a wonderful school of cello playing there, so that had to be on my list as well! I wrote Pleeth and had a letter back from his wife, so that was another excellent possibility to explore! This was during my final semester at Oberlin. I was incredibly fortunate to be selected for the Award based on my proposal (and was greatly helped in the interview by organ prof. there Haskell Thompson, who lobbed a couple of "soft" questions to me to help me get over my nerves in the interview!).

I postponed the trip for two years when I got a place in Greenhouse's class at Stony Brook while I got my master's degree.

A.A.   *So you went overseas after your time at Stony Brook?*

S.D.   Yes, by that point I was desperate to get more guidance. When I was at Oberlin the "world was my oyster"—even with all my questions, I was having a great time playing, had experienced some real successes, and was probably pretty overconfident! I suppose at that age a lot of us are ready to conquer the world.

A.A.   *Did you get to get lessons with all these great cellists?*

S.D.   Well I had this incredible list of people I was going to visit although by this time Rostropovich had defected to the US, so change of plan there. But you weren't supposed to stay in one place.

Sensing I'd been delaying the start of my trip, and possibly losing my nerve for the great adventure, Dan (the director of the foundation at the time and the man who'd interviewed me) called and gave me just the push I needed at the time. Looking back, I wish I could thank him for that.

So off I went to Lucerne. I played to Starker for three weeks in the classes, and that was a searing but valuable experience. Then I spent some time in Geneva, where I had a great time staying at the International Student House, speaking as much French as I could with the students there, most of whom were multi-lingual and becoming interpreters for the UN.

And then I went to England, where I knew that Tortelier was chairing the jury of the Imperial Tobacco Cello Competition in Bristol, and that's where I first met him. The opening ceremony was amazing. Tortelier stood up and made a speech about how we shouldn't be afraid to fail in the competition. He used the analogy of Mao, who he said had succeeded because he'd not been afraid to fail so many times. I knew Tortelier was a great cellist, but I didn't know until then that he was a completely dedicated communist. It was quite amazing, and seriously eccentric behavior!

One of the other contestants there was the young Steven Isserlis, who was 16 at the time. We bonded first by both being eliminated in the semi-final round. Tortelier made a speech to each of us, Steven who was declared "zee old man" because he played too slowly for his taste, and myself "you are zee tragedie" because of my awkward bowing style.

One of the other bonding moments with Steven Isserlis was when Tortelier told somebody they should quit, and stalked off in his regal way. And Steven said quite loudly to his back at age 17, "That's one man's opinion." And I thought, this kid has guts. I mean, this is a floppy kid who couldn't keep his shirt tucked in and had this funny cello with all these gut strings. I tried it in the hotel room and I said, "Wow, how do you play this thing?"

But we somehow became great friends. And Steven's friend David Waterman, who was about to become the cellist of the wonderful Endellion Quartet was there with Steven. I remember them driving back to London together in David's car. David had been studying Philosophy at Cambridge in addition to studying cello and chamber music with Martin Lovett of the Amadeus Quartet. At the time I thought I mustn't become friends with them partly because of appearances: David was wearing one of those 70s corduroy leisure suits that were so cool at the time.

But this was the beginning of a new chapter for me. After the rigors of the competition, I wasn't quite sure what to do next, and Steven's mother insisted that I come and stay with them for a while. I ended up living there for weeks on end when I wasn't studying with Steven's teacher up in Scotland. We also started cooking lunches together, and I started "spying" on Steven's practice, which was unlike anything I'd ever heard before. He was so Incredibly patient, and worked so slowly and methodically, but with that inimitable sound of his.

Steven tells of a "famous" incident in which I was trying to figure out visually how he was using bow angle to get a better purchase on the string at the bow change. Steven was playing on his teacher Jane Cowan's Testore cello which she'd loaned him indefinitely, and I was standing on the window sill to get high enough to look down at the bow and see what was going on. And he said he was sure I was going to fall and crush both him and the cello. We really became good friends during that time.

A.A.   *Did you play for each other sometimes?*

S.D.   Yes. I played piano for him in his lessons, too. Because at that point I was still able to play and practice a bit on the piano.

But while I was in their house once getting ready to play to Pleeth, Steven's dad said, "You know, before you play to Bill, you should really play to Jane. She's an inspired genius and she's quite eccentric, but you should play to her first." So I did. And that was an extraordinary moment. It was just like oh, yeah. No choice here. I have to go to study with her.

A.A.   *What was it about her that drew you?*

S.D.   There are some people in your life that can look right through you, and she was one of those. It was spooky. I'd had a lot of early successes, and then things weren't going very well. Jane was entirely sympathetic. We worked for quite a while, and she outlined some principles I needed to consider. At the end of our lessons she simply said "young man, we have some work to do." That was an extraordinary moment.

A.A.   *She saw you and believed in you at the same time.*

S.D.   Yes exactly. She could tell what I needed. And I somehow trusted her right away. And there isn't always a good reason except that you feel something. And also, this kid Steven (Isserlis) was a bit of a genius. And he was devoted to her.

He also seemed to break all the rules of cello playing as I knew them at the time. But somehow I could tell it was working on some level in a very mysterious and wonderful way. The thing that sealed it was hearing Jane's pupils play in a concert in Notting Hill in a church there.

And the sound! They were all playing on gut strings, all the way across the cello. Everyone who studied with her had a raw gut A string, and sometimes an uncovered gut D string as well. I believe Jane was a performance practice "pioneer" before her time, although she was against belonging to any particular movement, and was fiercely independent.

She taught us what she called the 17 varieties of the agogic accent. And we had critical listening sessions, listening to Furtwängler and Klemperer and conductors like that.

It was the first time somebody had made me make the connection between my theory training and my listening to real music, synthesizing phrasing. And she was absolutely a genius at that. She had studied at the Waddell School in Edinburgh as a child. But she met Casals when she was 13 because she was going regularly to Donald Tovey's music college lectures at the university. She was obviously an incredibly precocious kid.

Her mom once got a call from Tovey, and said, "Tell Jane to bring the Beethoven A-Major Sonata to the lecture rooms today, and her cello. I need her to demonstrate the first movement." Well, first of all, she must have been a damn good cellist at age 13 for him to have her do that. And she said she got to the lecture rooms and set up her cello, and there was a funny little bald man sitting at the piano, and they played through the first movement of the Beethoven. She turned to him and said, "My, you are musical." It was Pablo Casals. He was playing the piano for her.

A.A.   *Wow.*

S.D.   And he just gave this great laugh, and I guess they were friends after that. So she met Casals at age 13, and she went to Feuermann later on, three summers in a row for eight weeks. She hilariously said she went to Feuermann to learn how to play the cello, but to also teach him how to make music because she thought he was too dry.

But she loved him. She had imbibed from and watched and had lessons from probably the greatest, two of the greatest cellists of the 20th century. She was an active teacher and performer but then she got married to Christopher Cowan, who was the choirmaster and organist at Winchester School and Cathedral. They had three kids and she basically sidelined her professional activities, but did start teaching pretty actively. So Ben Zander, you probably know Ben, he was a cello student of hers from Winchester School. Many others as well. She had this kind of charismatic personality. She was extraordinarily charismatic, quite beautiful, and very outspoken. And tough as nails when she needed to be, but also she had a heart of gold, and a theatrical personality in some ways.

A.A.   *So you made this trip to Europe thinking you were going to kind of move from place to place, and then you basically decided to stay there?*

S.D.   Yes, yes. I met somebody who became a pivotal figure in my life. It was kind of an accident, and it was through Steven. I mean, it was providential. Because I knew Arto Noras and it wouldn't have been a bad thing to go work with Arto. I mean, he's a great cellist.

But then I met Steven and I was introduced to Jane. And I never did show up at Bill Pleeth's door. It would have been nice to meet him. I think he was very inspirational. But in this case, I think Steven's family just provided a safe haven and also introduced me to an amazing mentor. So yes, I think I would have quit if I hadn't met her. It was an extraordinary time for me.

And it was a unique opportunity, because I was basically in their house. Jane would make the rounds while you were practicing in the morning. We'd all just start by playing Organum. We started in the middle ages by playing in fourths and fifths with each other, and then you'd do your scales. I remember the Spring term her saying, "Where is that boy?" Because I'd be out jogging. And I'd come in and be having breakfast. "Come on, we've got to do our scales." And I would do my scales with her in the music room. And then she said, "Well, I'll be out pruning my roses but the window's open." So it was extraordinary. But then the classes were extraordinary, because she not only did have critical listening classes, but she had French night and German night. So we had to recite Molière and Racine even if you didn't speak French. I spoke some French, so it was fun for me.

And we had German night where you had to try to speak the lines from Goethe's *Faust* and my German was nonexistent. But she said there was no way we should play German music without understanding the syllable stresses and the language. So that was part of our training. It was very interesting. And at the Cello Centre, there were "critical listening" sessions, listening to conductors such as Furtwangler and Klemperer interpreting the classics.

It was the first time that someone had made such a vivid connection for me between my theory training and my way of actually listening to and synthesizing phrasing and form in performance. Jane was absolutely a genius at conveying that.

Jane really helped me put my playing back together. I got a tremendous amount from Dick. But I hadn't quite figured out how to make it my own. I don't know, it's really hard to know what was going on there. Because he had me playing in such an effortless and comfortable way and then it stopped being like that when I was in grad school. And I couldn't figure out what happened.

A.A.   *How long were you in the UK. And what brought you back to the US?*

S.D.   I spent about nine months studying with her. At first I had lessons in London (she was commuting regularly between her activities in London and the branch of the Cello Centre which she and her husband had recently founded in the Scottish borders). I didn't go to Scotland until the following January to become a full-time pupil there.

In the meantime, my parents had been sending me job advertisements from the musician's union paper back in the US, as they knew I would run out of money for my studies eventually. I was learning my orchestral excerpts in the Isserlis' kitchen, keeping warm by the electric fire—Heldenleben on a raw gut A string—that was a challenge!

My parents started sending me the union papers, and saying you know, you're going to run out of money sooner or later. You really should take some auditions.

I went home for Christmas reluctantly, and my folks said look, we'll buy you a ticket to the principal cello audition for the Milwaukee Symphony, because you need the experience. And about a week before, I realized I was making some slightly bad sounds on the raw gut A string so I somewhat reluctantly swapped the top two strings back to steel strings, and realized I was making easily twice as much sound as before I'd been practicing on the gut set up, and with a great deal more ease. That was a surprise, and also made me realize some fundamental changes were taking place. The greatest surprise was actually getting the job! It was kind of weird. I didn't really want it, but I knew I needed to have work.

A.A.   *And that was your first orchestra audition?*

S.D.   Yes, it was a fluke. A real fluke. I think maybe some of the old reflexes from Interlochen kicked in. But I was sure I'd wiped out in the first round. I got in there with a huge adrenalin rush and roared through the Fifth Prelude and the Dvořák exposition, and some excerpts. And I went up to the office of the symphony and looked at the brochure and I thought, damn, it's too bad. It looks like a good organization. And then they said, "Oh, you're in the finals."

A.A. *Was there a screen at that point?*

S.D. Yes, it was behind a screen. I met a lot of quite scary cellists in the warm-up room. A few I knew and most of the others looking awfully serious. I basically went into a corner and played long tones and tried to get my breathing down to a normal level. I tried to remember Jane's advice and thought, there's no use dying of fright. I suspect it was beginner's luck, but I got the job.

A.A. *And then you took the job?*

S.D. I accepted the job, but then I said, "You know, I can't start until September. I'm studying. I'm continuing to study." And so that's when I went back to London, and I stopped for three days at the Isserlis' to get over jet lag and then went up to the Cello Centre. And then I spent two terms there. The winter term which ran January through the Easter break, and then I did the summer term which ran right through to July 4th, I think.

So I finished that year and I think I emerged from that year a different person on a number of levels. When I arrived in Milwaukee and got my first little apartment, I was trying to square the training I'd received in that very remote and rarified Scottish musical setting with what I was now doing in an American orchestra.

A.A. *Was it a fun start in Milwaukee?*

S.D. Oh, a lovely group of people. Kenneth Schermerhorn was the orchestra director, and he was extremely kind to me. And I got to play *Don Quixote* with them.

I just spent one season with the orchestra, and toward the end of the season I met Rebecca Penneys who was the pianist in the New Arts Trio. The trio was breaking up, and I was asked if I'd like to help reform it. Bernie Greenhouse had been in Milwaukee on a tour with the Beaux Arts, and introduced me to Rebecca, and then he referred us to Piotr Janowski, the great young Polish violinist, to play with. Piotr and I had been at Marlboro together a few summers before this. We all felt we'd suddenly "struck gold" in playing together.

So rather rashly I quit my orchestra job after one season and joined this trio. We had a residency at the Wisconsin Conservatory on Prospect Avenue there, and had a seven concert series there as well.

A.A. *Was that a full time job?*

S.D. Yes. It's a small conservatory and they wanted a group to be the nucleus of their collegiate chamber and classical program.

A.A. *And you were also teaching.*

S.D. Yes. That was the beginning of some serious teaching. That's where I found out that the things that Jane Cowan had been doing with me in Scotland weren't just to fix me personally, but rather general principles that I could use well for my teaching. She seemed to understand that there was a chain of command behind all movements. And it didn't hurt that Rebecca, the pianist in my trio, had been Starker's rehearsal accompanist and had toured with him and played for many of his mastery classes.

A.A. *Wow, okay.*

S.D. Rebecca could say to me, "You're having trouble with that bowing because you're not leading with the upper arm." I'd get so mad that I'd go home and I'd say, "Damn, she's right." So I was kind of having second hand Starker lessons, too. Because he'd pointed out all the stuff that wasn't quite right with my playing, it was extremely clarifying although scary.

A.A. *How long did you have the job with the trio at the Wisconsin Conservatory?*

S.D. We were there for four years at the Wisconsin Conservatory. And then Rebecca got a job as a piano professor at Eastman. And the conservator said to us, "Oh, you should re-form with another pianist." And I said, "We can't do that—we've just received the Naumburg Award, and they've given us a really ambitious touring schedule for next season."

And so Pietr and I had to find work. And the principal cello job with the Rochester Philharmonic was open, and I had heard a rumor that there would be some teaching attached. And so I thought well, we've got to go East. I'll take the audition.

And so I went back into orchestral excerpt land for a while. And I was lucky and won the job.

A.A. *I don't think it's luck.*

S.D. Well, I somehow had a knack for that. Piotr got a job teaching at a local college here, and we carried on for a few years. I left the trio after a few years of holding down the orchestra principal position, touring with the Trio, and teaching part-time at Eastman. It all just became too much to manage in the end. Just about at that point a full time teaching position became available at Eastman. Robert Sylvester left the cello faculty to become dean of fine arts in Bellingham, Washington. They put me in as an interim full-time instructor that year, and started furiously interviewing for other jobs, because I thought I might be out of a job at the end of the year. Fortunately I got a nice offer from Bob Freeman, who was the Dean at Eastman at the time. And I seem to have been there ever since.

A.A. *Was there ever any time when you thought about pursuing your playing career and not teaching? Or did you have the right balance?*

S.D. Well, when I was a student, I never planned on teaching or playing in an orchestra. But there is apparently a Chinese proverb: "never name the well from which you will not drink!" Life is full of wonderful surprises—I loved playing in both orchestras—it was exhilarating, and the repertoire is just fantastic! I'm not sure I would have thrived long-term doing that, but it was a great learning environment—in a way another continuation of my musical education.

But the teaching became more and more fascinating as I had to do revisions to my own training. I think when you're going through a period of self-examination, it can become a springboard, because if you find the things you've been discovering are beneficial to others. Then teaching becomes fantastically rewarding. The other thing about teaching is the more you teach, the more you learn, so I'd realized that the quality of my own work was benefiting from the process of analysis with the students. I still joke with them now and tell them if I go home and do exactly what I just showed you, I'll be a better cellist too!

A.A.   *Yes, I feel that way as well.*

S.D.   It's extraordinary. I remember a colleague saying this to me once. If we knew as young-sters what we know now, we'd all go out and win every international competition there is, because the knowledge you get when you're older is exactly what you wish you had at that age.

A.A.   *Are you happy that you've been at Eastman for all this time?*

S.D.   Yes. I made various attempts to leave for other jobs, which were fortunately stymied by the boss. I've come to realize over the years that it's a really, really good environment for the students. It's an intense environment, and sometimes they might feel overwhelmed by all the demands on their time, but it's also extremely stimulating both musically and intellectually.

I'm so lucky. We've got a great cello class, and all of us make a point of encouraging collegiality and peer support. The pupils feel this support from one another, and I've seen it consistently leading to wonderful personal bonds forming as well.

The Present

A.A.   *Do you have a teaching philosophy, and how has that evolved over the years?*

S.D.   Well, when I was first teaching here at Eastman and new on the job, I was obviously a little bit anxious because it's an institution with a long history, and I was only in my early 30s. I told myself, the first thing that was important was to have the students feel that you are supporting them, and that you believe in their potential and you're trying to support them both emotionally and musically. The second thing was to feed them useful information. And motivation too, but a lot of that has to come from within them. But if they have those two things, you can help them. You're not going to fail if they feel supported and they have information.

Then later on I came to believe that if we gave them the tools, especially for under-graduates, and if by the senior year we were functioning as advisors rather than teach-ers, then we've succeeded. If we've given them enough tools for them to problem solve when they're stuck, then we've had success. Ideally, they shouldn't need us by their final year. Or when they graduate. They should have enough information to begin flying under their own power. We sometimes jokingly call this the built-in "teacher obsoles-cence principle."

I try to take pupils who have a strong individual voice. Ideally, they're developing well as cellists and must have a certain level of fluency to get into the school. What really fascinates me is when someone has not only an appropriate level of talent, but also a strong individual voice, and an inquiring mind. Probably the most inspiring moment as a teacher is when you hear that individual voice beginning to emerge, and you see that they're recognizing it and "owning" it. That's a simply fantastic moment, and makes it all worthwhile!

But the process is difficult sometimes. Some of the most talented students can come in with the most physical issues. Tension is so common because your musical intentions understandably get entangled with physical tension. It's very hard, when you're younger especially, to separate tension (or the feeling of "effort") with musical intensity—it's actually a life-long process of dis-entangling this, but it's most dramatic phase is often in one's early 20s, and that's when the students often need the most guidance, and have to learn patience with themselves as well! (speaking here from personal experience!)

A.A. *Well, that was another one of my questions. When you're picking students, would you rather have someone with a strong voice that you feel is there but maybe has technical issues, or do you look for someone who's gifted physically but maybe doesn't have as much to say?*

S.D. I am fascinated by pupils that have a unique voice, because I think the world needs that. I believe one can help a person who's motivated and curious to acquire the necessary fluency. Some individuals encounter more physical challenges at the instrument, and some simply have more natural fluency: that's a gift. It's ideal but not always common to find someone with both the inborn voice and an easy way with the instrument. The two qualities seldom exist in equal measure.

A.A. *Motivation is a word that's come up a lot. How do you deal with motivation with students? Especially if a student lacks motivation. I'm wondering how you've dealt with that.*

S.D. Well, the environment is a huge help. If they're surrounded by gifted colleagues, they will go practice more. And the students inspire each other. The motivation thing is difficult though, because sometimes lack of motivation is fear. You've probably encountered this, right? You have a student who's afraid to really go for it because—

A.A. *Because they might fail?*

S.D. Maybe they won't satisfy their inner ambition, and they might be afraid of either letting themselves down or somebody else down, and I guess that's when the different hats come into play. You said you studied psychology. When you're teaching I suppose sometimes you have that psychologist hat on, don't you?

A.A. *Definitely. I always wonder what is the best way for them to respond or what door can I open to help them.*

S.D. Because every individual that walks in the door has a different learning style, has different issues that they're processing, and sometimes you're a parental stand-in or you're a stand-in for somebody out here, and you don't always know that until you really get to know them.

A.A. *Well, and what someone pointed out to me recently is sometimes you're the only adult that they're able to have a one-on-one conversation with and that they can trust. I hadn't really thought about it until recently, but I think there's a lot of truth to that.*

S.D. I felt that with Mr. Kapuscinski. I was completely stunned that this was somebody I could actually argue with and at the end of the day he was still supporting me. Yes, it's interesting, isn't it? It's a little terrifying to think about it because you suddenly realize you're in a mentor relationship with somebody and that it's pretty pivotal to their development. It's a little daunting to think about. That's when I have to go back to my first point, which is they should feel you're supporting them and believe in them and are gradually giving them some information that's useful. I still remember those first years thinking what gives me the right to do this? Also, as somebody who had had a number of successes and disappointments, I didn't always feel worthy.

A.A. *On a technical level, I'd love for you to talk about your technique book,* Cello Ergonomics. *What motivated you to write that?*

S.D.   It's a book of warm-up exercises that also touches on movement concepts which I can't ignore with my pupils, and that thing evolved from the first 20 years of teaching.

The first title was *Technique for Music's Sake,* and I still like that title, but Steven Isserlis looked through it and put all kinds of hilariously rude comments in the margins, and the first thing he put is "bad title!" So it's like, "Okay, Steve. I'll think of another one." I put between two covers most of the basic exercises I commonly use with the pupils to acquaint them with certain physical principles, and to help them acquire more physical freedom and ease in their warm ups.

The thing that's beginning to fascinate me more and more is this sort of issue of spatial awareness when you're playing, that you own this kinesphere that you're sitting in and that you have to find kinesthetic awareness so that the quality of motion profoundly influences the quality of the sound we make. As seated players, it's especially crucial not to feel constrained by our position, but to find ways of moving sympathetically with the actions of cuing, bowing and shifting. Feldenkrais practitioners, such as my wonderful colleague Uri Vardi who teaches at the University of Wisconsin–Madison, use the principles of that discipline to help achieve freedom in a sitting position, and these principles have helped me enormously in both my own playing and teaching.

The quality of our motion profoundly influences the type of sound we make (basically as string players, we can only create sound through movement …). If we make a jerky motion usually the sound is abrupt or rough, and if you find a motion that's comfortable and harmonious physically, it's kind of like tai chi. If you find a comfortable and harmonious motion that's connected with a sound that really satisfies, that's a golden piece of your cello puzzle. It's that "aha" moment. It's like "Right? You see how we got there." And sometimes we talk about the breadcrumbs, because sometimes they will have a breakthrough moment in their lesson, and at the end of the lesson you try to think about the steps you took to get there. If I'm sensible, I'll go back and say, "Now, how did we get here? This is 45 minutes in, and in this area you've done something very different that we're both pleased with. Can we identify the steps?" Not always possible, but I call it the breadcrumbs like Hansel and Gretel, because they dropped the breadcrumbs and the birds ate them.

A.A.   *Right. So they remember how to get back there.*

S.D.   Between the lessons we talk about that. "The birds ate the breadcrumbs. Okay, we have to go back."

Anyway, the thing that fascinates me, and maybe because I had to rebuild my playing at kind of a difficult moment in my early career, was the thing that Mrs. Cowen helped me find, which was that connection between movement and sound and physical comfort and sound. It's like an infinite loop.

A.A.   *How much do you work on scales and sixths and thirds and things like that with students? Does it depend on what they need?*

S.D.   It's crucial that they have a daily technical routine. (Ergonomics are warm-ups, but they need to "map" the cello with scales, arpeggios, and double stopping.) There's a definite relationship between those who do this regularly and build fluency and confidence and those who don't, unfortunately. My job is to monitor the quality of their movements and sound consistency when they're going through their scales, arpeggios, etc. If they're "laboring" through it, it's not going to produce a great result. Mrs. Cowan used to say "if it's difficult, it's impossible" (i.e., practice is finding a way to make things easy). Using different bowing patterns, mixed slurs, different rhythms etc. helps to combine bowing flexibility with general fluency, and also certainly wards off boredom! I remember Joey Silverstein advising pupils never to play a scale without a specific tempo in mind, a type of bowing pattern, and an idea of the sound quality desired. I also want them to understand as completely as possible the ingredients of good bow mechanics. If they can play their scales with smooth fluency on the left side and beautiful intonation combined with terrific bowing habits, we're really getting somewhere! This is an area where we're also lucky to have teaching assistants to help with a scale class, and a chance for group discussion about challenges which might be coming up.

A.A.   *Oh nice, that's great to have.*

S.D.   I basically have told them that if they don't play scales and arpeggios they can't expect to have the required fluency, and double stops are something they need to practice, because otherwise in a piece they will feel ambushed. Scales, arpeggios, and double stops are essentially our technical foundation.

   What I'm fascinated with is when they do get going with scales, they should also do all kinds of bowing patterns, and I got a lot of those from Jane. A lot of it has to do with using different parts of the bow. She had the Casals's crawl exercise, the two notes down bow and one note up bow, to work your way out and then reversing it to come back. It's really helpful if they can do mixed patterns on either side of the balance point.

   It's really essential for them to understand bowing mechanics. I don't want them to just play scales for the left hand. Yes, you got to be in tune, you got to know where to put your fingers. That's step one, and step two is combining that with a beautiful sense of sound production. If they can play a scale with not only smooth fluency on the left side, but wonderful bowing habits, we're getting somewhere.

A.A.   *What about études or studies? Are there ones that you go to regularly?*

S.D.   The first 15 Poppers are terrifically useful, as are the Piatti Caprices. I'm increasingly convinced for the need of some review studies, such as the earlier Popper preparation to the High School Studies, which are very helpful for the first and second year pupils as well, just to go back over things they may have "vaulted over" trying to get their audition material ready. The Duport studies are also really helpful for string crossing work—I invariably have first years reviewing nos. 2 and 4 to get them acquainted with work above and below the balance point.

   I have a page in the *Cello Ergonomics* book called The Bow Chart, which is an analysis of the détaché stroke and how it changes from the lower third to the middle third to the upper third. It's a great study to see what parts of your bow arm work depending on where you are in the bow.

A.A.   *Do you use your book when you teach your students?*

S.D.   I use it as a syllabus. I want them to use it when they're practicing their scales. There is a unit on mixed bowing patterns, and then there's a unit on shifting, so I have octave shifting, sixth shifting, and then when they get good at it they're supposed to be doing that with double stops. The trouble is, to teach them well I would need two hours a week to do all of this, but the advantage of having (my wife and cello teacher, the mix is that they get about an hour and a half every week between us. So v into more detail.

A.A. *Well, it's hard when you only have one hour a week with a student. There is so much you want to do and it's hard to find the right balance.*

S.D. Well, that's why the scale class is good, because it also turns into a Q&A sometimes with the TA. And also that kids can play to each other and start giving each other feedback.

A.A. *How much do you demonstrate during lessons? Is that important and has that changed over the years?*

S.D. My wife Rosie would say "too much!" We joke about this when we're teaching together in the same room, as we do at the Heifetz festival. But sometimes it's really helpful to demonstrate, and then sometimes it's really important not to demonstrate. When you feel that they're approaching something else on their own, I have to remind myself not to just leap in. But sometimes you want to model something. I find the demonstration really helpful for modeling the motion, or if I'm not satisfied with the sound they're making. I'll say, "If you go into this sounding point, this is what could happen." I also have to remember that I have really good equipment and often they don't. Some of my most fun lessons have been just trying to stop myself from demonstrating and see what they can do.

A.A. *It can be a tricky balance for sure.*

S.D. I think it's a conundrum.

A.A. *I think Gary (Hoffman) told me recently and I've heard the story from a few other people, a Piatigorsky story that you've probably heard where—*

S.D. The guy that was playing worse and worse in his lessons?

A.A. *Yes, and Piatigorsky played badly on purpose and the guy suddenly felt very good about himself. I do think sometimes if I'm demonstrating something and I'm not nailing it, then there's a certain amount of relief in the students of, "Oh good. Well look, he's not playing perfectly either."*

S.D. Yes, you can say "That's precisely how not to do it." I remember somebody in England used to do that.

A.A. *One thing I spend a lot of time with my students on is trying to teach them how to practice, and I'm wondering if that's something that you spend a lot of time talking about with your students?*

S.D. Yes, I talk about it often. It's important in some lessons to say, "You realize we're practicing together now, right? And this is a good thing," and sometimes they've just had an awful week of exams and God knows what else and there's no way to move the lesson. I'll just say, "Bring in something that you're working on and bring questions, and let's plan how you're going to use the time when you have more time. Let's plan what you can do. We can do an A-B-C of how to solve this passage, and we'll do a little of it now."

And failing all else, if they're not sure how to use the lesson, they could start with their questions. That's sometimes just really helpful because it's easy to react to the playing without knowing the backstory. Even with a particular shift. "How do you feel about this shift? It's been beating up on you hasn't it?"

One of the things we're working with them on is not only technical development itself, but that technique should arise from the music making. This is something Jane was just wonderfully eloquent about. One of my favorite things to do when we're working on phrasing is just to get them to play one note with the bowing pattern that they've chosen or that we've chosen. Only play one note, but sing the actual pitches over it as their bowing, until they start to notice that they're doing things differently with their bow than when they're navigating the pitches.

A.A. *Yes, sing and play at the same time.*

S.D. Sing and play. It's a Don Weilerstein trick.

But back to the connection between technique and music though, Jane used to call it the transcendental technique. She got this from working with Feuermann for several summers, for eight weeks at a crack I think. She said that the transcendental technique is one that seems so natural to the audience that it's not noticed. That a technique that disappears into the music making is what we are after.

A.A. *And anyone could do it.*

S.D. Yeah. Exactly! Like, "Oh, cello's easy!"

One of the things that I think is interesting is that to make a coherent connection between what you see on the page, how you would sing it, and how would you translate that into the motions you make. Because playing a string instrument is a process of physical translation, and that's for me the endlessly fascinating thing. Because that's a thing that Jane was able to somehow tell me, whether it was an intuitive process or an analytical process she used.

And watching Starker teach, I could see the process of playing the instrument. There were logical steps that you could take to organize your movements. The thing that was so astounding about him was that the physical timing was so incredibly precise, and he was amazed that nobody else thought it was important enough to take care of that. "Don't you know the secret of clean playing? Anticipation!" Like the whole business of finding the sub-pulse before a shift. Your brain has to be ahead of your hands.

I tried to distill or simplify some of these principles and write about them a bit in the Ergonomics booklet. It leads us to the question of pacing shifts differently for different expressive purposes, and understanding how to do that. The trouble is it starts to look like just a book about fluency, and my research project for the sabbatical is going to be trying to make a more organic connection between movement and fluency and then how that supports your musical goal.

A.A. *We've kind of led into my next question. I've been fascinated by how the movement of the torso affects cello playing and how the torso and arms relate to each other. Because you were just talking a lot about arm movement, and I know that's something you've alluded to in our other conversations too. Have you become more aware of how to use your torso in cello playing?*

S.D. Oh, much more aware of it now, because as you get older, unless you've increased your efficiency and fluency, you're not going to play as well.

A.A. *That's true.*

S.D. When I do it right now I get a better result, but it's because I've had to think through it. I remember Richard (Aaron) talked about "If your hips are frozen, you won't be able to shift as well," and I was thinking, "What's he talking about?" Then I realized of course, that when you do a shift down the fingerboard, your left hip is advancing a little bit.

So sometimes with the pupil's permission you can kneel in front of their cello as they're playing, and push one knee or another to give them the feeling of shifting their weight into a shift. If one pushes the right knee back as they're going up a shift, the result is dramatic, because they often overshoot by at least a whole step. They're often very excited to discover this sense of momentum, and I believe it's a crucial help to us all in large leaps up the string.

A.A.   *What about the bow arm or starting a bow stroke?*

S.D.   Well, yes. The motion is huge. Preparatory motion on a down bow? I'd have to show you with a cello, but if you imagine there's a flashlight on your cello scroll and you're playing in a dark room, you're making circles on the ceiling, either clockwise or counter clockwise, and then if you go a contrary motion with your bow, you're like doing a butterfly pattern, and it's so lovely. Lizzy Simkin showed me some of this. I think she got some of this from Starker, which is a sympathetic motion. I can do it with a cello, but if your circle is with the bow, you get one result, and if it's against the bow you get another.

Of course, moving against the bow helps free the bow. If you want to get rid of the bow or you want a fast bow, move against it, and if you're saving bow, chase the bow a little bit. But I always thought of it in a right-to-left-to-left-to-right, and then I discovered that actually it's circular. You get more depth and more richness from that, and when I do that correctly, my cello sounds so much better.

I kid my students. I said, "Cello's sounding very expensive today." Because they are getting to the bottom of the idea that you're dishing into the instrument, not just in a back-and-forth way.

Then the business of the horizontal plane of the room, I tell them that all the notes are on the practice room wall. Up the string you always go from left to right. And I make a joke about it that an octave is an eighth of a pizza, because an octave shift requires a 45 degree turn of the trunk of the body. Two octaves are at 90 degrees. It's a quarter of a pizza, and you get more to eat!

We start by leading the shifting with the eyes. If you progress up the string, shifting up and down an octave on each successive scale degree, (probably best to start doing this in C major) you're gradually turning to your right as you ascend, and left as you descend, shifting the weight from the hips and noticing that your eyes guide right as you go up. It's very much like "spotting" that a dancer or skater does to keep from becoming dizzy—turning to address the same point in the room, but we're moving much more slowly. I often demonstrate this, and say—"you see, all the notes are on your practice room wall!—you just need to turn toward them a bit, and feel that weight shift."

Also when I do some of these exercises my back doesn't hurt. If I get up in the morning and I'm sore and I practice correctly, that releases tension in the back.

A.A.   *I want to ask you about vibrato too, because I love your vibrato, both in the quality and also how efficient you are with it. You use it in all the places where I get lazy, I think.*

S.D.   The first thing they have to know about vibrato is where the motion comes from. I describe it as "making pizza in space." You hold the imaginary dough with the right hand in a plane that's perpendicular to the fingerboard, and pound it lightly with your left fist to "soften" the dough. Younger kids love this one but everyone finds it useful. It's quickly apparent to them that the tricep (or push-up muscle) is firing the forearm forward and the bicep pulling it back in this motion—like a 2 cycle "motor." Then we can have fun changing the rhythm. Sometimes we call it "slow" or "fast" pizza making. The faster you go, the more the vibrato tends to shrink a bit. You can feel the two muscles opposing each other a bit more. If the vibrato doesn't have enough energy, we have to realize that a bit of effort in this way is OK as long as it's a balanced alternation. Then there's the 3-step process, the upper arm drives the forearm, the forearm drives the fingers, and the playing finger flexing down the string creates what Alan Harris describes as the "throb" in the vibrato. There's an exercise in the Ergonomics booklet called the "pump" exercise (or flexing ex.) which I learned from a pupil who'd studied with Starker. It's basically a slight finger push-up, where the finger ideally flexes from slightly below the pitch to the center of the pitch at the apex of the motion. Of course, when kids first learn to vibrate, they have to concentrate on the motion of the forearm parallel to the fingerboard—and that creates a bit of rotation, which is a necessary ingredient. The Flexing action is something we can do later in our development. We're basically "stealing" this from violin technique. It's a subtle motion ingredient that's essential for centering the vibrato and stabilizing the pitch.

A.A.   *Not having a square hand?*

S.D.   Yes. It also depends on the person's build. So for example, I have a very tapering hand, and a really short pinky. So, I have adapted some of my motions. The little finger, even on a great cello hand, which is more square than mine, is still the youngest sibling. Other fingers have to help hold it up to the water fountain. The little finger has to be in the position where it can drop from the bass joint. It's from Kató Havas's violin playing book. She wrote a lot about the action of the left hand.

   If a person has a more tapered hand, the person is probably more naturally sloping. And the more square hand, they're probably a little more square. Everybody is different. You have to see what their hand naturally forms to.

   Sometimes I describe it as throwing tiny darts with the left hand. That's an easy motion to model—and helps us to become more flexible. Don't the violinists have the arm vibrato, the wrist vibrato and the finger vibrato? We can too! The forearm drives it, but if we don't have some flexibility in the wrist and fingers, the motion doesn't transfer to the string.

A.A.   *Can you talk about teaching a clean spiccato, and how do you view the wrist and fingers with all of this? I loved your video of it.*

S.D.   I hope it made sense.

A.A.   *Yes, it was great!*

S.D.   Well, I'll go back to Jane Cowan who said the Hungarians often described all techniques coming from legato. A good brush stroke I think starts from practicing a smooth détaché near the balance point. Leonard Rose called this action the "paintbrush" stroke—i.e., the arm is the handle of the brush and the fingers are the bristles applying the "paint" to the string. If you use "passive" fingers, your fingers are following the bow. The bow's momentum leads the fingers through the stroke. The last thing that happens is the bow change which I call the breaking wave. The wave comes in and goes kersploosh, as it breaks at your fingers.

A.A.   *I love wave analogies.*

S.D.   But the "undertow" is already pulling you into your downbow, so you've already got this simultaneous pushing-pulling motion. Mr. Kapuscinski called it "belly dancer" motion, because you can feel the up and down motions desynchronizing a bit to create that flexibility—This smooth motion will eventually turn into a good brush stroke or a quicker spiccato if it's developed really well and comfortably. It's useful to make them practice on the string. If somebody's trying to develop a staccato on an Elgar, or even Popper six. I would say, at first, forbid yourself from playing off the string until you can play close to the actual tempo on the string—then the bow will probably take over and help you by starting to bounce a bit on its own.

  To demonstrate this on and off process, I'll have the pupil stand on my left, near enough to see the bow's contact point with the string. I'll start playing fast détaché on the string, make them close their eyes and tell me when they think the bow is bouncing. Invariably when they think it's bouncing and peek they'll see the hair is still on the string; it's actually the stick that's doing the bouncing or flexing and the hair is actually still in contact with the string! I want them to be able to feel that themselves—then they realize you have to have a certain delicacy of touch along with the kick to let the stick do what it's really good at. Of course, they have to find where it will do that. But I think it's important for them to activate the stick without feeling that they are off the string because they think it's from the air. I also make them play on then off, because it's much more interesting. So they're on and then off. They realize that—we call it offish and onish. I want them to feel they can activate the stick without "throwing" it at the string—that's a common misconception especially about spiccato.

A.A.   *If you are giving a student a new piece, are you more "old school" and give them a part with bowings and fingerings that you would like them to do? Or do you start from scratch? What is that process like with students for you or does it depend?*

S.D.   It really depends on the stage of development of the student. I think if it's a first or second year person and it was music that we were encountering together for the first time, I'd probably make quite a few suggestions or I might give them a roughly fingered and bowed part. If I do that though, I always say that I want to work with you on some of these solutions because they are of pedagogical importance. I often will insist that they learn certain solutions for me until I can tell that they have really mastered them. And if I'm happy and they are happy with the way that it's sounding and they find an alternative, then I'm really excited to entertain that and we can discuss it.

  But sometimes there are certain concepts, and it's part of this kinesthetic learning thing, there are certain things I can teach more effectively when I'm using a solution I'm really comfortable with and I've really worked out, like in *Schelomo*, I give them a rough set of fingerings to start with.

A.A.   *Especially for* Schelomo *which doesn't have any fingerings in the edition and has so many unusual scales in it.*

S.D.   Exactly. It's so idiosyncratic.

  With the younger ones, I'm much more proactive about fingering and bowing solutions, but I am interested to see what happens and sometimes something happens naturally that is just perfect and is backwards from what I expect. So I want to be open but more proactive with the younger ones.

I like the analogy that the fingers produce the words or syllables, (speech) and the bow is the voice. Fingerings are musically very important—they aren't just "transportation" they have to be part of the phrasing—if you shift in the middle of a "word" or a musical unit it can sound very illogical. Steven Isserlis calls these convenience mart shifts—they get us there, but don't help the music!

I try to teach them about backwards substitutions and shifting on half steps, especially in classical repertoire, if they can shift almost exclusively on half steps, everything usually comes out better. Then you sound like you have five or six fingers. I want them to play cleanly unless they want me to hear the shift for expressive reasons, and very often they all come in with this somewhat random approach to fingerings. I love it if they can see that there's a logic to fingering choices that is also part of the expression and part of the clarity of the delivery.

A.A. *Do you talk about how many hours they need to practice?*

S.D. I try to see what their expectation is because Eastman is a pretty intense environment. For them to get four solid practice hours in a day is pretty good. And if they can get more than that, that's great. But Jane used to say that Feuermann said if you have to practice more than four hours a day you were not being efficient. And I kind of see the point.

When I was a student, I once had a debut coming up with San Francisco Symphony and I was all of 19 or 20, and I was practicing six hours a day quite regularly. And I thought, "I've got to get it to eight." I actually deteriorated when I added two more hours. I wasn't really focused in the same way. So part of it's quality time. Some of them can do three amazing hours and then they're just done. And some of them can work longer. But I think part of it is that we have to guard against injury because they have orchestra and chamber rehearsals as well.

A.A. *Right.*

S.D. So you have to tack on six hours of playing from the orchestra and maybe five hours of chamber music a week and then factor that in with what they're doing on their own.

I don't know what you think about amounts of hours, but at least I would hope they're putting in regularly three or four hours a day. I don't think they can progress as quickly if they don't do that because they've got to process their scales and arpeggios and their warmups. So there goes an hour, hour and a half, easily. And then they've got to be working through a concerto, a sonata, maybe a show piece, and some Bach.

I try to teach them to rotate. If you can get through all of your pieces in a 48-hour cycle, you're probably doing okay.

On the other hand, at the annual performance exams, there's one jury called the performance certificate where one of the requirements is that you have to prepare a piece without any input from your professors. And some of the most beautiful playing I've ever heard from our pupils has taken place in that segment and that's when you realize that wow, you know, they're functioning independently. I guess you could give yourself a little pat on the back that they're doing it that well, because I've heard people just bring me to tears with some gorgeous playing. And that's been tremendously rewarding.

A.A.   *We talked about learning how to practice. Do you encourage your students to practice performing sometimes? Because that's the flip side. Often a student has never actually played through something without stopping. And then when they're suddenly on stage performing, it's much harder because they are so used to stopping and trying to fix something.*

S.D.   Jane used to say, "Play through. Don't stop to fix things and review passages that don't measure up to your expectations." Because until you go into performing gear, first of all, you don't know what it's going to feel like to deliver a piece that way.

And second of all, things are going to go wrong, even in the performance they're going to go wrong, you've got to get used to keeping going. It's true. Some of them will have a small stumble that brings the whole thing to a crashing halt. You can't have that. And also in the lessons we're supposed to encourage them to sit down and just play. And sometimes they're coming with so many questions that it's a kind of a workshop lesson. But a portion of the lesson should always be a performance of some kind, so they get used to that feeling of not stopping.

A.A.   *What about playing by memory? Is that something you demand for concertos or Bach or anything else?*

S.D.   Playing for memory definitely enhances concentration, removes visual distraction, and encourages a kind of inner vision of the piece that is more compelling. There is a huge range of ability on this front, and it's sometimes a really big job to 'wean" someone off the text. Sometimes they will memorize all the notes but forget the composer's instructions so that is a point of discussion as well. One way that has worked for me is to work my way backwards through a piece; memorizing the end, and then play the phrase before until the end, and so on. I did that for the first time when I was still playing piano for a recital and I was so startled because it worked. I try to talk about that with the students in class, but when I've got somebody who's struggling with memory, we often try that.

And in the Bach Suites, when there are several voices, and they're crossing strings, that's where the most dangerous memory moments are. It's like when the Road Runner looks down, and there's no ground?

A.A.   *I agree.*

S.D.   In Bach, trying to marry harmonic memory with kinesthetic memory is huge, and trying to get them to feel the voices across the string is so important. I'm finding teaching memory though is a huge challenge because it was easy for me, and the things that you do naturally are harder to teach.

A.A.   *I feel the same way.*

S.D.   Do you know the Alexandrian edition to the Bach Suites?

A.A.   *I've heard of it but haven't seen it.*

S.D.   He breaks it over two staves and he puts stems up for voice in the treble and the stem down for the voice in the bass. And he has them stemmed differently so the voices are spread across. It looks like a keyboard work.

A.A.   *Ah, interesting.*

S.D.   So that's where in Bach especially, I sometimes talk to them about trying to find the vertical axis, the harmonic access and not just play melodically. I think a lot of kids nowadays are taught in a linear fashion where they just go with a melodic line, and any information underneath that seems to be just extra.

A.A.   *That is one of the reasons I wrote a continuo part to the Suites. For me, playing Bach by memory is so much about the harmony. That way even if I have a little mistake, I still know what chord I'm going to and I don't get freaked out.*

S.D.   Yes for memory work, if we're not aware of our harmonic context, and if we don't have a sense of the unfolding melodic line and its relation to the bass line, we're going to get into trouble. It's tricky. Some people have a very strong visual memory, some a stronger kinesthetic memory, and this all has to be married to our inner ear and our musical anticipation and imagination. This skill takes a lot of conscious effort to develop!

A.A.   *What about intonation? Another tricky subject. How do you teach that? Do you use drone notes or tuners?*

S.D.   Oh I get into crazy waters here, because I like to explore expressive intonation with them—melodic and harmonic tendencies in intervals. I also discovered in the Fourth Suite of Bach that when I'm playing in flat keys myself I want the open strings to function at times as leading tones, which involves lowering the actual pitch that I'm playing at relative to the open strings.

   We have this luxury in solo music: Obviously when playing with piano we're working with a completely different system, and have to compromise.

   I tend to want to do that to color the sound more because I like the expressive quality of tuning like that but I have to compromise more when I play with the piano.

A.A.   *But have you had students that just might be in more need of some basic intonation improvement?*

S.D.   Yes sometimes it's incredibly helpful to have them play "drone" scales against an open string related to that key to really feel and hear relative intonation and the relation of intervals.

   One of the most key points that you can make to the students about intonation is that they need to tune carefully and really listen to the resonance of the open strings and work with them on sympathetic keys. Also stress that tone quality is inseparable from beautiful intonation. I tell them this has to be a huge priority especially in your warmups because tone quality, and as much as possible, perfect intonation is the way to start your practice. Of course, all of the sensations of freedom and fluency are also essential. I don't want your playing to get tight by trying to play in tune.

   I want them to know that intonation functions on two levels, vertical and horizontal. And that they can organize their listening along those two axes, and the differences are significant. Of course, all the sensations of comfort and fluency at the instrument are essential and should flow from this work.

A.A.   *I always tell my students, if you don't have something to tune a note against, it's much harder to tell if it's in tune.*

   What do you think is the hardest thing to teach a student?

S.D.   You've asked me about memorization, and I think this is very challenging to teach if they're not accustomed to playing for memory. I keep trying to find ways in, including "away from the cello" practice, imagining the performance without the instrument in one's hands, but trying to feel the piece just by sitting quietly.

   I used to go into the library at Oberlin Conservatory and sometimes make an actual map or drawing of a piece, then also I'd use tracing paper on top of my Bach Suites to try to see the interval patterns and shapes—that was sometimes really helpful.

A.A. *Nice.*

S.D. I suppose we have the perennial challenge: "what is our job as teachers" anyway? I think if we can encourage them to listen on the highest level, it will really raise the level of their expectations, that's one of the most powerful tools we can give them to help them grow, and they'll have it for life. All the elements of their playing will benefit from this, especially musical imagination! I remember the great mezzo-soprano Jan DeGaetani, saying to her pupils, "musical imagination is a muscle. Exercise it constantly or it will atrophy."

But if you can raise the awareness, they're listening awareness about all the important elements of playing, like tone, production, intonation and phrase shaping, they're going to lift their whole playing level.

I find that that's more important than fluency, and they'll get the quickness eventually. If they're trying for that before they listen well—I've so many young players that will hack through, blindingly fast through. The second movement of Prokofiev Sinfonia Concertante, and it's really impressive at first. You've probably heard that prodigious flying through and then you realize that about half the notes are slightly out of tune, but they're having a great time and it's very impressive and almost intimidating. Then you realize, well it's pretty messy.

A.A. *Okay.*

S.D. The two things that are really challenging for me are teaching them to be confident about being on the platform. We try to give them a lot of support and try to give them, I guess—oh, I'll have to think about that.

A.A. *What has been your process with the learning and teaching the Bach Suites? I've been asking everyone this because of the historically informed practice movement that has come about.*

S.D. This has brought so much to us, but it's also changed the game. Forever.

A.A. *Everyone I've talked to learned the Suites before that happened. What's your teaching philosophy on the Suites now? Have you gravitated that direction?*

S.D. Definitely. I mean, I'm playing a cello with a modern setup, but I spent two or three full years on gut, which taught me an enormous amount about what the cello likes when it's set up with less tension. That has helped me a lot as a teacher.

Anner Bylsma was a colleague whom I admired greatly. In fact he gave me that fencing master book when he visited us and gave us a class. About two months later, the phone rang in the studio and it was Anner calling from Amsterdam. "So how is it going with the book?" I was embarrassed because I was digging into it a little, but not as much as I should have. And I said, Oh, Anner, it's wonderful! Then it made me realize he really wanted me to give him feedback. He is missed by many.

He came and gave us the whole Bach cycle back about 25 or 30 years ago here. We went out for drinks afterwards and he was enjoying some Calvados brandy. I was just sitting there in complete admiration of how he had managed to control the sounding point with all of these string crossings and with all of this beautiful freedom. I knew how hard it is to make the gut strings just speak. I asked him, "How do you make those strings sound so great?" He said, "Oh Steven, it's like the straw in the stream." I was like, "Oh my God, Anner what is the straw in the stream?" And he said, "You know, the straw always finds the fastest current." Extraordinary Zen-like and beautiful way of putting it!

I realized he wasn't fighting the cello. He was letting the bow find the right place. That was, in one sentence an extraordinary little bit of wisdom from him. When I'm teaching the Suites, I have in front of me the Magdalena manuscript and the Kellner edition. There is also a useful book by Charles Medlam called *A Practical Guide to the Performance of the Bach Suites.* He studied with Mrs. Cowan and he was in the London Baroque, and a wonderful cellist.

Charles' premise in his book is that looking at Bach's own manuscripts of the Violin works, and comparing Kellner and Magdalena. Kellner's is sometimes as clear or more clear than the Magdalena copy. In the cello manuscripts, there are really fascinating differences between the two, and it gives us as performers more options, more choice, which I think is liberating.

I like the old Barenreiter edition which is a good place to start, especially when the pupils need a basic text to work from. You can modify it pretty easily after referring to the manuscripts.

I'll ask the pupils to look at manuscripts which I believe are now available online, and then transcribe things into the Barenreiter. With a new pupil, I'll often recommend a set of bowing solutions that I've come up with, hoping that we'll modify as we go along.

So every student that comes in; rather than giving them a set of bowings, I'll have them start with the Barenreiter and then I'll have them look at the manuscripts and see what they think. Now if it's a freshman I might say, I'm going to give you a set of bowings and then we'll modify. This is what I'm going to do later, but for now do these.

A.A.   *But stylistically, do you have more of a Baroque approach in your sound and interpretation? Things like avoiding slides or not using as much vibrato?*

S.D.   Completely. I mean I was surprised by Rostropovich's recording. Nowadays I love listening to Casals because it's just so original. It's like looking at a Picasso or something. I mean he just discovered the Suites for us.

A.A.   *Right.*

S.D.   And I used to listen to Casals, Fournier, and maybe Tortelier. Those were my three guys when I was in college, and Rostropovich was the new kid on the block and he didn't record them until he was older. I would love to record the Suites, but I'm still revising everything. I used to play the Second Suite really romantically, and it's beautiful that way.

I remember practicing in the music room once in Scotland, just enjoying the acoustics because, it was a room the size of this house with a wooden floor. Jane suddenly stuck her head around the door, two steps up and then said, "Steven you're ranting again" and the door closed. I was embarrassed, and thought a bit, realizing she meant "ranting and raving" like a mad person. That definitely got me thinking about my approach! Now I often have to tell the students to enjoy the sonority of the open strings and lower positions.

Sometimes I just say play that passage, just get rid of the bow, and play it pizzicato. It suddenly sounds so musical. And I said, "Hmm, your pizzicato is blindingly good. Let's see if we can get our bow to do that." So then they have to use the bow to show me all the details that came out so clearly when they played pizzicato! One principle is to always use a different bow stroke for a different voice, to show the voice leading. The bass voice must have a different bow stroke than the upper or middle voices—we have to use different lengths of stroke for adjacent voices for clarity. They're surprised sometimes when I beg them not to connect neighboring voices—"it's not a melody, it's counterpoint!"

A.A.   *There are three accepted transcriptions that I am asking everyone about. The Rococo Variations, the Fitzenhagen one versus the original, the Chopin Polonaise, Feuermann or Rose versus the original and the Boccherini/Grützmacher versus the original Boccherini. I'm just wondering your thoughts on which ones you prefer and which ones you teach.*

S.D.   Boccherini/Grützmacher is a wonderful teaching piece, but it's not Boccherini.

A.A.   *Right.*

S.D.   It's a pastiche of Boccherini and Grützmacher. It's perfect for a high school or junior high kid nowadays. In my day, it was a staple for teens in terms of repertoire. These days kids are playing works that I wouldn't have dreamed of playing when I was a kid. It's sort of terrifying, but Boccherini/Grützmacher is a piece that I cut my teeth on.

    The original is so much more charming and beautiful, but the Boccherini Grützmacher is kind of fun. It's a transcription, if it's done with that spirit, I don't see why not.

    I just played the Chopin original version for the first time and it was very satisfying. It's really lovely and all the cello acrobatics are gone. There are a few bits, but it's mostly music then, it's not about showing off on the cello and the piano gets to shine. Steven (Isserlis) is adamant that we shouldn't be playing the other one.

    The other one is good for kids that want to climb a mountain, but it's a sporting event and it's kind of hard to say whether it works. If it's played by an extremely high-level player, it is played superbly, maybe. I don't know. I'm a little torn. I have played both of them. If students play the transcription, I often make them play the second theme down an octave the first time, the way he wrote it in the original.

    I mean Feuermann went to all his big brother's violin lessons before his big brother tragically passed away, so he kind of thought of the cello as a giant violin. I think he could pull it off, but how many people could play it really cleanly and beautifully? Those transcriptions are what Larry Lesser calls, "of the transcendental technical level."

    I like the original of Tchaikovsky, but I hadn't played it until Steven introduced it to me, and I've played it now in concerts, once on a gut set up and a couple of times on the modern setup.

A.A.   *If you get asked to play it now, which one would you prefer? Do you prefer the original?*

S.D.   I probably prefer to play the original, because I miss the variation that Lizst had Fitzenhagen get rid of, the penultimate variation. It's so whimsical and frivolous. It's a little masterpiece. But it startling to learn it after having done the Fitzenhagen version as a kid.

A.A.   *Well that's been my experience too. It seems like everyone my age and older has learned the Fitzenhagen. When a student comes in, do you steer them one direction or another?*

S.D.   I tend to give them their choice. But I'm pretty pleased when they want to do the original because I think Tchaikovsky knew what he was doing, even if Fitzenhagen, (with Liszt's encouragement) thought he'd improve on it!

    Have you ever played the Fitzenhagen Concert Waltz for four cellos?

A.A.   *No, I didn't even know it existed.*

S.D.   It's got similar things in it and you suddenly recognize his fingerprints.

The first cello part is very close to the modifications he made to the Rococo Variations—the virtuoso tricks he loved to do. He actually enjoyed octaves, and in the original version a lot of that isn't there.

A.A.   *I'm curious to know in a hundred years, what will be the norm and if the Fitzenhagen will just be a thing of the past. It's been an interesting transition to witnesses.*

The Future

A.A.   *Have you seen the level of cello playing change over the years?*

S.D.   Well, as we were saying earlier, I feel that the level has increased exponentially. There has just been a huge increase in the number of people playing at a pretty high level. Also, there are more great cellists than ever out there playing with more variety of styles. A lot of fearless individuals are learning very hard music very young now.

So the world has to readjust one's preconceptions about what's appropriate at what age. Although I am still daunted by some of these works that are being brought in by mid-teen people. But I'm trying to get comfortable with the fact that some of those folks can handle things that we wouldn't have been able to handle in my generation, which is now two generations back.

But generally in terms of the profession, there's so many great players. It's daunting, but it's also pretty amazing.

A.A.   *Related to that, do you feel like there are enough jobs these days? How has that changed?*

S.D.   That's scary. There are so many cellists that play well that you have to feel for young people going into the profession now. Yes, that's difficult, isn't it? I think the standard's gone up. The competition is even more difficult and the one thing I try to say to the students is you probably should think about having more than one income stream. So if you're a great player and you're a soloist, also try to be a wonderful chamber music player. If you're an orchestral player and that's your goal, try to also have two or three other things that you do really well.

The students that play modern cello very well might explore early music, because that's a burgeoning field. It's also a fantastically creative field. The early music people are reimagining the repertoire for us in new and amazing ways and we have to learn from that, and absorb and encourage exploration.

And then there's the new music scene. We are lucky at Eastman to have quite an active new music program with the student-run Ossia Contemporary Ensemble and the Musica Nova Ensemble which is directed by Brad Lubman who is amazing. So it's really nice if they have their standard repertoire knowledge and then they're either exploring new music or early music or maybe both. I think more and more flexibility is being required for sure.

There's also the educational side. I think everybody that studies should also study teaching. It will help them understand the playing themselves better. So there's a lot of different strands. So one hopes anyway, that young people will find their way, whether it's in a more traditional group, or some of the other options out there. We are putting more and more qualified people out there. It's a little bit troubling for those of us in the music profession, because otherwise what are we training these people for?

A.A. *The cello itself hasn't changed much and so many of the pieces that we teach haven't changed, but the internet has been something that has changed the world. I'm wondering just how you feel technology has changed the way young people are approaching music and learning the instrument.*

S.D. I used to say that you should listen to dead string players and try to learn from their recordings. Well, now they can actually see these people playing online, and I suspect that's a really big piece of what's influencing them now. First, it's a fantastic resource because they can see great players and see how people like Piatigorsky play so completely different from Fournier, or Rose. You can see a different physical type interacting with the instrument, which is great.

If you're really tall, see what Piatigorsky is doing with his bow. And if you're more compact, look at Casals who was incredibly compact as a human being and very strong. When I was a teenager, I used to think my arms were way too long because I would see pictures of Casals so I built a chest rest for my cello when I was in college. I got a pair of wooden clamps and stuck them onto the top and bottom of the cello and then built something that would put the cello farther away from my chest, and then my arms felt like they were the right length.

My orchestra director said, what the heck are you doing? And I said "bowing." I basically was trying to turn in my lanky, late teenage self into a shorter person, which was rather silly. But these days, kids can listen to so many performances, and sometimes you have to say to them, "Don't listen to too much." You've got so many options. Try to find your own vision for the piece, your own vision for the sound and the style. But, I have to admit it's such a rich resource to have.

A.A. *Yes, that's in terms of resources too- but I wonder on the flip side of the coin, as far as the shrinking audiences of classical music, whether or not you believe that. Because I think technology has made it too easy now to listen to any piece you want without getting up out of your chair. Just pick up your phone. So I'm wondering how do you think that's affected the music business? Maybe after school when people are out there trying to get audiences. Has that been good or bad?*

S.D. I don't have enough personal experience with social media, but I'm impressed with younger colleagues who are using social media to get their calling card out there and get their performances out. That's a way for them to get in touch with live performance audiences.

The issue of audiences not having to go to concerts because they could do everything through the media is a sad thought. I would think that there's something precious being lost if you're not actually in the room with the player. There's this phenomenon where the audience brings something to the performance that's completely intangible, but it is there.

A.A. *Yes. Oh I agree.*

S.D. And that's why playing a concert is still a memorable experience because you're aware of the audience in a good sense. And also, the audience is playing along with you when you're playing. They're there because they love music, and they want to be there. And if you imagine the audience is there to support, enjoy, and revel in what you're giving them, it can help you go to the next level.

I don't like to look at the audience because it's a little daunting. Occasionally I need to just to remind myself I'm in front of people. But I'm trying to go into my own world, and hope that people come with me. But that's an unspoken contract. You go to a concert, you want to participate with the performer, don't you think?

A.A.   *I agree with you, but what I've seen happen at the University of Iowa is interesting. We have a recital attendance class throughout the University where students have to go to 15 concerts to get an A. So many of them have a hard time not looking at their phone during a concert.*

S.D.   Oh my gosh.

A.A.   *And even music majors! The intermission comes, and the first thing people do is dive into their phones.*

S.D.   It looks to me like another universe.

A.A.   *Well I think our default reaction now is if we have five seconds of empty thought, we need to look at our phone. People are not willing to invest energy to understand something for the first time and try to make sense of it. And that's an important attitude or skill to have at concerts.*

S.D.   Well, they say that great creativity sometimes involves daydreaming. Having time to let your mind idle and then reboot. If you're constantly taking information in, I don't think it's healthy.

A.A.   *I agree. I think in fact I listened to a TED Hour podcast saying exactly that.*

S.D.   Really?

A.A.   *Yes, that's something people are not doing enough of, to just let your mind wander, and think about things. Daydream, like you said.*

S.D.   I was told that Einstein developed his theory of relativity after playing the Bach Ciaccone. He was an amateur violinist, but you can see pictures of him playing, and crossing disciplines may be a good thing. I ask the kids if they've seen African wildlife films where there's a lot of gazelles and a big pasture prairie, and they're feeding, and one of the gazelles, I call it the lead gazelle suddenly puts its head up and smells a lion. And then suddenly you have 1000 gazelles go zoom, and they're off.

So I tell the kids, this is an example of intra-species communication. When you're on the stage performing by yourself, you are by default, the head Gazelle. So anything you do, including your physiological body rhythms, breathing rhythms, motions, everything you do is affecting the people in that space because they're there to participate. It's not just sound, it's motion, it's the interaction of sound and motion. So when you're performing, you're the lead Gazelle.

A.A.   *I love that analogy.*

S.D.   I like the idea that there is this sense of communication with the audience, which is, it's almost tidal. I don't know if you can get that by watching your phone.

A.A.   *Yes, I agree.*

S.D.   But I'm also pretty sure that it's part of human communication that we are in danger of losing if we don't fight for it.

A.A.   *How have you felt about new music and the importance of it, or the acceptance of it with an audience? Maybe I can share what I have seen at the University of Iowa and then get your thoughts. We have quartets that often come to the University of Iowa as part of our*

String Quartet Residency Program. Quite often they play a piece that's been commissioned and play it exceptionally well. In spite of that, it's not a piece that I would necessarily want to go out and hear again, even though it was very well played. I've asked a couple of the groups what they think about the longevity of some of these works and they generally say that it's not really a concern. They just want to get them performed and then move on to the next project. I understand their perspective, that's their job as a quartet and they want to get these composers exposed. Similarly at orchestra concerts, there's usually one piece of new music to help bring something new to the audience. I think by and large most of the audience will find it interesting, but they're really there to hear the Tchaikovsky or Beethoven. I'm wondering if that's good. Or will there be a separation of people that just want to hear new music. I mean there's so many different kinds of music now to listen to in general, how do we keep our audience?

S.D.   Well I would not want to perform a new piece that I didn't have a personal stake in. It really helps to know the composer. I was lucky enough to commission a couple of pieces from my colleague Warren Benson (who's since passed away) at the Eastman School, and also Samuel Adler, and David Liptak, who's currently on the composition faculty.

Any new music piece that I play, I want to feel like I can bring it to life, and if I can't, it becomes much harder to do it. When I was at Tanglewood in the early seventies, I played a lot of new music. Gunther Schuller was overseeing that program then and there were a lot of works by Jacob Druckman, and I think Charles Wuorinen. Some of that music was very jagged and tentative.

We also did *Wozzeck* as a concert performance under Leinsdorf, who was kind enough to do lectures about the piece, with the whole orchestra. That was a huge education because up until that point I'd been a little bit hostile toward atonality, and the effects of that score are so emotionally devastating. I mean it's incredible music. So some of it's a language barrier that you have to work to overcome.

A.A.   *I agree with you from the perspective of a performer, but my concern is with the listener because today audiences have so many options of what to listen to and so many electronic ways to find their music. If some of this music is difficult for the musicians, how much do we worry about the audience?*

S.D.   I remember Fred Sherry's famous comment when he took over the Lincoln Center Chamber Players. When asked what he was going to do first, he said, "I'm going to fire the audience." I think he wanted people to be less comfortable, to push them a little. I probably can't speak to this with as much authority as most, but I still think that as a performer you should do what you really care about, and do it with all your heart and soul. And if it's really creating atonal music, do it, and see if you can bring the audience along. But I think we have to do the things we're most passionate about and hopefully your commitment will then be convincing to the audience.

But I do think going out of one's comfort zone is extremely important right now as a performer and probably as an audience, but the audience nowadays need to have more explanation.

I played the first Britten Suite as part of a recital program at the Pabst Theater in Milwaukee once and I told the audience that before I played the Suite in its entirety, I would give them a quick tour of each of the movements and what's happening here.

I said, "I'm going to do something like a musical whodunit. These are the characters, and you're going to see what happens to them." And many people after that concert said, "We've never heard solo music like Britten before, but it was incredibly helpful to have you give us a little help before you played it." I think that's one of the things we're trying to teach now is that it really helps to give the audience an understanding of how you feel about the music and what the composer might be trying to say.

Who are we? We are the composer's advocate. I make a joke with the students if they're ignoring a mark in the music. I say, "The composer is dead, consider me his lawyer."

A.A.   *Do you help students find jobs after they're done with school? Do you think that's part of your job as a teacher?*

S.D.   I certainly try to help them any way I can. I think your job doesn't end once they graduate. They usually let you know when they need a push or a letter of support for something. One of the good things about computers is that you can store your reference letters and update them by just pulling one out of the file, and it's a pleasure to do that because you start writing about somebody and realize how much fun they were to teach and their wonderful qualities. It brings back a lot of great memories.

A.A.   *Have you ever had to deal with a period of doubt about becoming a musician?*

S.D.   Well, I left high school halfway through my senior year to go to Oberlin College, which was an awkward time to go. I didn't really have a class, I was just this kid that arrived. I had kind of a bumpy first semester, and then Mr. Kapuscinski had me audition for Tanglewood. I ended up at Tanglewood at age 19 with a bunch of grad students. But I had done some good auditions and some good playing for people, and they stuck me in positions of responsibility. There were constant rehearsals, and it was pretty intense; I was beginning to wonder what I was doing. And then I read Rachel Carson's *Silent Spring* which had come out a few years before.

And most of my friends from high school, who I realized I missed dreadfully once I left, were studying biology at the University of Michigan, or places like that. I thought, "What am I doing? This is a pie-in-sky ivory tower profession. The world isn't going to be a better place environmentally because of my cello playing." I don't know; it just seemed like a lot of work that wasn't having an impact on the world that we were living in. I guess that book had a big effect on a lot of people.

My first impulse was to try to transfer back to the university at home and try to do a double major. And then I thought, well, my folks won't let me do that, so I'll take a biology course and see if that's my path. I was never very good at science but I felt passionate about the environment. It was the hardest "C" I ever got! I struggled through that course. I had a wonderful professor who was an amazing lecturer, and he took us on fantastic field trips. We sampled pond water in the arboretum. We had dissections. And he was an avid runner at the beginning of the running boom in the US. He was into the whole aerobic benefits of exercise and was telling us how it affects your body, and what's happening when you're running, and the endorphins. I would see him regularly in the gym, getting ready for his big daily run.

And I loved it. But I'd never had a proper chemistry background in high school, and I was in that course with a bunch of kids, many who were pre-med, so I was hanging on by my finger ends. My cello practice started slipping, and my teacher was a little annoyed. It didn't last that long, but it made me think a lot about what my calling was.

I guess I thought, well my friends that are doing this biological stuff are really good at it, and they all will do a much better job than I would. And I play cello much better than I do in science. I guess it was a wake-up call.

But that was the first moment of doubt, really. And then, I kind of had to just go with it. At first, I got an A- from my teacher. I think we talked a little bit about it all. And then, just seeing friends that had a passion for science and were good at it. I think I realized that everyone has their gift. I loved writing poetry and I read a lot. I loved studio art. I love sketching. I still do sometimes. My dad was a scientist but maybe that particular gene went past me, I don't know. The only scientific thing in my make-up is a sense of analyzing motion, in the sort of engineering of how cello playing works. But that's very intuitive, you don't have to measure and quantify it.

A.A.   *So you're using lots of science in your teaching. Ergonomics and the way the body works?*

S.D.   Yes, it's true. My massage person, Lauren, who's a total dear, was a chemist at Xerox, and she said people would ask her, "Why did you quit chemistry to slather oil on people?" She said, "You guys don't realize, the body is a system. It's just as fascinating as studying anything else. And it works in a very particular way." She also works with cancer patients. She is amazing.

A.A.   *Related to how the body works, have nerves been an issue for you? And do you talk about that with your students?*

S.D.   Sure. I mean, everybody gets nervous. I get really nervous. But, the best way to deal with nerves is to be on the platform quite a bit. It's just a practical thing. Because then you're having to do something repeatedly, and eventually it gets easier. Even playing the solo part in *Don Quixote* with the Rochester Philharmonic got easier after a few nights on the tour, especially after we'd played Carnegie Hall. Even in the Kennedy Center, it had already started to become my nightly routine. I went out there and just played this big piece.

So I keep telling kids when you have only one concert, and you're leading up toward it, and that's the big event, it's really hard. Even a faculty recital is a problem that way, because if it's just a one-off and you haven't played it out of town a couple of times first, it tends to feel like more of a big deal. And so, you get a bit of the first night nerves thing.

My best advice for students is to remind them they are nervous because they care deeply about this; they want it to go well. The flip side of that is because they care so deeply about it they can psyche ourselves out. Or, what is it that I tell them? That, "My saboteur sits on my left shoulder and waggles their finger at me, and says, "You're going to screw this up!"" And I have to say, "Shut up! I'm busy. Go away." Ashkenazy said, "When you go out on stage it feels like there's a tiger on the stage with you," and he said he has to get slightly mad at himself, and say, "That's not a real tiger. It's a fight-or-flight response. Don't be stupid!"

So thinking rationally helps a little bit. Physically the first two things you lose most easily under nervous stress are the sense of gravity (body and arm weight) and flow of breath. If you can keep consciously keep in touch with these two forces, that's very important. Often it means sitting in the Green Room and just being with the instrument as calmly as you can—I do a lot of exhaling!

And then, the other huge ally is positive projection. "I'm sharing something that I love. These are amazing pieces. I'm probably the best prepared person within two square miles to play this program tonight." I keep telling kids that, "You're the one that's practiced this particular material the most, so you've earned the right to do it. And if you've practiced well, you've especially earned the right."

I also try to tell the kids to imagine that they have a wave of support from the audience and that people are there because they love music. If they're not there because they love music, they deserve to be ignored by the performer and the fellow audience members. If they're there to be music critics, they should go jump in the lake! So that helped me a little bit, too. Because I went through an awful stage in my graduate school training when I wasn't getting very regular lessons and things were getting more and more difficult, rather than easier. And I was angry. I wanted to go out on stage and show them I really knew what I could do, and that's possibly the worst attitude to have to go on stage that I can think of. It makes you play for all the wrong reasons. I was, like, "Damn it! I'll show them." And that's awful. It's not about music, it's about your wounded ego.

Close to the Heart

A.A.   *If you hadn't been a musician, what would you have loved to have done with your life?*

S.D.   You mean, if I could go back and do it all over again?

A.A.   *Sure. Or if you couldn't be a cellist.*

S.D.   I don't know. That is interesting because what do they say, "Music isn't a profession, it's an addiction."? It's something that kind of takes over and you just end up going with it. So I guess from age 15, I probably was feeling a very strong pull in that direction. But I was very interested in writing, and I was very interested in visual arts. I loved drawing and sculpture. And I was fascinated by the design of string instruments. So part of me at one point thought, if I couldn't play, I would want to make them.

I am really fascinated by people that create things with their hands, whether it's making instruments, or even building boats. The trick with being a musician is the results are so intangible: you practice and practice and you may create one beautiful thing, but if you don't keep practicing, then you can't recreate it.

I'm also concerned about what's going on with our planet and climate change. I'm trying to figure out how I can connect my concern about that, with what I'm doing as an artist.

But it would have been amazing to be a photographer or some kind of artist I think, to observe. I just find that sometimes I'm riveted by a visual image, or just being in the natural world. The extraordinary beauty and variety that it has. That's a nourishing and replenishing thing, I think. So maybe it would have been, either some kind of writing or some kind of artistic endeavor.

A.A.   *What are a couple of the most memorable concerts you've been involved with? There are so many to choose from I'm sure.*

S.D.   One of the most memorable rehearsals I ever witnessed was Jacqueline du Pré rehearsing the Elgar Concerto with the Boston Symphony at Tanglewood, and laughing with the cello section as she was swooping through these enormous shifts. She was obviously having the time of her life. But the first time I heard her I was 15. I'd just gotten off work. I was working in the University Law School kitchen to make money for my summer studies at Interlochen. I was either washing dishes, cleaning the grill, or even polishing floors. I went straight over from work, and got there in time to get a standing room ticket at the back of Rackham auditorium. This completely radiant person came out on stage with her Strad and Steven Bishop-Kovasovich, her pianist. They played Debussy, Beethoven A Major and Brahms F. It was just classic cello repertoire. As I stood there, I felt almost giddy—I'd never had alcohol or champagne before, but I was having a sensation like I was almost drunk! Maybe another great memory was playing in the orchestra at Marlboro when Casals was conducting.

A.A.   *That must have been amazing!*

S.D.   I was sitting right in front of Julius Levine, the great bassist, and I felt like I was being wafted forward by the power of his sound. I was 19 or 20 and at the back of the cello section. Ronnie Leonard was leading. Ray Still, the principal oboe of Chicago Symphony at the time was also there. There were these incredible players in the orchestra. I mean, it was crazy. The Vermeer Quartet was in the front circle and Julius's sound, and his rhythmic and musical energy were just unbelievable.

Casals would go to the podium, and you'd think he wasn't going to make it onto the podium; he'll die before he gets there! And he'd pick up the baton and drop about 50 years, and he would suddenly become a 40-year-old maniac, just completely in the moment. It was amazing

Maybe another one was hearing Rostropovich play the Dvořák in Cleveland, with the Cleveland Orchestra and Szell conducting. And seeing grown men, very dignified people, bursting into tears all around me. I mean, there was so much communicative power in what he was doing. The force of his personality was extraordinary.

A.A.   *What are you most proud of?*

S.D.   Good grief! Well, when you asked me that before, the first thing that popped into my head was how proud I am that our former students, mine and Rosie's, are our friends. We have a community of wonderful friends. And you don't know you're building it at the time, do you? It's funny because you morph from being a guide, to being an advisor, to being a peer, and I think that's kind of a magical progression. I hope that is what happens in parenting children, too.

It's incredibly touching when they reach out to you as adults. It's lovely because then, when they get married or they have a special person in their life, they want to include us. Then you realize you have made an impact on their lives, even if it's been a while since they've connected, and that's just delightful. I love it when they come back and want to play something, or just have a coffee.

You know, it's something you don't think about, necessarily, when you're teaching, you think you're trying to help people play the instrument, and then you realize that you're also, inadvertently a part of their development as a person. One of the great rewards of having the arrogance to be a mentor is learning how humbling it is in the end.

A.A.   *Is there anything you still want to do, that's on your bucket list?*

S.D.   Oh, the bucket list!

A.A.   *Yes, the bucket list.*

S.D.   Oh my gosh! Are you talking about life, or music, or both?

A.A.   *Either? Both?*

S.D.   I want to spend more time looking at the moon! You know, we're sitting looking at the moon over a beautiful lake. I could think of a lot of worse ways to spend some time. I want to continue to be physically active and interacting with the physical world, and trying to celebrate it. I would like to try to help raise public awareness of some of the issues that we're facing as a species. We're all such tiny parts of this thing. But I don't know whether it involves political action, public awareness, or doing something through music.

     I'd like to keep playing because I keep learning more, and I love performing; it's becoming more meaningful. I was playing with my colleague Elinor Freer recently while working on Beethoven's C-Major Sonata, and I said, "When you're starting to see life a little more in the rear-view mirror, some of this stuff really pops out. Some of this stuff becomes even more meaningful, more apparent, and it makes you want to live in that moment, more, when you're playing."

     I think one of the biggest things to find now, is balance. You've only got so much energy. I'm always going to want to teach, but I want to balance teaching and perform-ing. And, maybe, do a little better job with both of those. And maybe spend more time sailing on my boat as well.

A.A.   *Okay. Do you have desert island pieces? If you had one CD that you could only listen to, and you could put whatever you want on it?*

S.D.   Oh my gosh!

A.A.   *I know it's a hard question.*

S.D.   If somebody asks me that, I always think that when we're rehearsing a lot, we carry the pieces around in our head—so in that way we've got our own Desert Island Disc.

     But wait, what about Glenn Gould's early recording of the Goldberg Variations, or the late Beethoven Quartets, or Britten's music for *Midsummer Night's Dream*, or the late pieces of Fauré—his music has an absolutely magical quality about it—(he was quite deaf by then like Beethoven) sometimes it's really hard to parse what he's doing, but there's this incredible energy there.

4

Timothy Eddy

Cellist Timothy Eddy has earned distinction as a recitalist, soloist with orchestra, chamber musician, recording artist, and teacher of cello and chamber music. He has performed as soloist with the Dallas, Colorado, Jacksonville, North Carolina, and Stamford symphonies, and has appeared at the Mostly Mozart, Ravinia, Aspen, Heifetz, Sarasota, Chamber Music Northwest, Santa Fe, Marlboro, Lockenhaus, and Spoleto music festivals. He has also won prizes in numerous national and international competitions, including the 1975 Gaspar Cassadó International Violoncello Competition in Italy. He is a member of the Orion String Quartet, whose critically acclaimed recordings of the Beethoven string quartets are on the Koch label. A former member of the Galimir Quartet, the New York Philomusica, and the Bach Aria Group, Mr. Eddy collaborates regularly in recital with pianist Gilbert Kalish. A frequent performer of the works of Bach, he has presented the complete cello Suites of Bach at Colorado's Boulder Bach Festival and Vermont's Brattleboro Music Center. He has recorded a wide range of repertoire from Baroque to avant-garde for the Angel, Arabesque, Columbia, CRI, Delos, Musical Heritage, New World, Nonesuch, Vanguard, Vox, and SONY Classical labels. He is currently professor of cello at The Juilliard School, is Professor Emeritus at SUNY Stony Brook and the Mannes College of Music, and he was a faculty member at the Isaac Stern Chamber Music Workshops at Carnegie Hall.

The Past

Anthony Arnone	*Where did you grow up and how did you first get exposed to the cello?*
Timothy Eddy	My earliest memories are from Chester, Pennsylvania. Our family was living in a row house while my dad was working on his PhD dissertation at the University of Pennsylvania while teaching full-time.

We moved around quite a bit. In my preschool years as my dad was working on advancing his career as a French teacher. He actually had a mentor for his PhD degree that he was following around, first moving out to the University of Oklahoma in Norman, and then after one year, back to the East Coast, just like musicians find and follow their mentors. We latch onto somebody as long as we can because we're getting so much from them, which is what I did with Mr. Greenhouse and Mr. Silva before that.

A.A.   *Was your dad French?*

T.E.   No, he wasn't French, but he was near-native in his abilities to speak and write French. As his career developed, he became one of the pioneers of redirecting the American foreign language teaching system toward an initially audio-lingual approach and away from using reading as the initial and primary way of learning a foreign language. Part of the reason that some Americans traveling abroad had developed the reputation of being "Ugly Americans" (referring to Americans who were insensitive to the idioms and styles of different languages and cultures) was that the US was so much more culturally isolated at that time. European countries are geographically so close, and their cultures have been mutually accessible and mutually influential for so long. Even when communication and travel were not as easy and fluid as they are now, familiarity with different cultures has always been a more natural part of life in Europe. Americans would come to Europe and often would speak French, Spanish, German, and Italian with the "sound vocabulary" of American English, because we didn't hear native speakers of these languages as a normal part of our daily lives. So many Americans visiting France, for instance, since they hadn't had the opportunity to live in a French speaking community, spoke in a way that native French speakers couldn't recognize or understand. My dad was tremendously dedicated to improving the quality and ease of communication between people and cultures through the respectful study and reflexive learning of the idiomatic characteristics of foreign languages: for instance, their characteristic sounds (phonemes), diction, rhythm, melodic inflection, vocabulary usage, and syntax.

The next place we lived was Frederick, Maryland, just north of Washington D.C., where my dad was on the faculty of Hood College. When he eventually took a position at Georgetown University, we moved to Bethesda, Maryland.

Then, when I was in ninth grade, my dad was hired by the publisher Holt, Rinehart, and Winston, to be an Editor for a language-teaching-materials project, and the company wanted him to be living in New York. When our family moved there for a year I went to the High School of Performing Arts, and for the first time, I was in a school where all the students were musicians, dancers, or actors. I finally felt surrounded by like-minded peers. That one year had a big impact on me, being immersed in the vivid cultural life and society of New York City. But right after that year, we had to move back to Bethesda. Fortunately, the Montgomery County public schools were great, so I got a good high school education there.

That leads me to the second part of your question, asking how I first learned about the cello and got interested in it.

My story isn't the kind of romantic story that's told sometimes, where someone hears an instrument at an early age, something clicks, and their destiny is sealed from then on! At the beginning of my life with music, I was a somewhat reluctant piano student of my mother. I wasn't comfortable having my teacher living under the same roof; I didn't like practicing where my teacher was always within earshot. I certainly wasn't particularly committed or serious about music then, and I didn't feel that challenged or stimulated musically outside my home.

My mother taught piano to young children in our home as I was growing up. My parents were both very gifted musically, though my dad was never trained as a musician. My mother began playing piano as a child, but one of her greatest regrets, ultimately, about her musical life was that she didn't get good training early enough to enable her to have a shot at a professional life in music. But, as my mother, she put her frustration to good use, vowing to herself that I would have good enough musical training at an early age to enable me to pursue a life in music, if I chose to. By the time I was 13, I was getting first-class, inspiring teaching.

A.A.   *Were you playing cello or piano at this point, at 13 years old?*

T.E.   At that point, it was only the cello. The most important factor that led to my starting the cello was the public school music program that was available to me at my elementary school. As a fourth grader, I took home the mimeographed sheet that described the school's music program. My mom felt it would be a good idea to see if there was something for me in that program. She knew I was talented and enjoyed music.

At school, I got tested for the musical sensitivity of my ear -- I remember it to this day. I went to the auditorium in my small suburban school, and the music teacher tested my ear by doing things like playing two notes and asking which was higher. I remember it being very simple and primitive.

A.A.   *Probably very easy for you.*

T.E.   It was, but since that ear test apparently showed that I had a good enough ear, I was sent home with a note saying that I could study a string instrument at school. It turned out that my maternal grandfather owned a cello, and when my mother inquired about it she found out it wasn't being used and was stored in her father's attic.

A.A.   *Did I read that you were interested in trumpet too but you had hurt your mouth?*

T.E.   Yes. That's right. When asked what instrument I wanted to play, that's what I was interested in doing, but in third grade I'd had a jungle gym accident. I don't know if jungle gyms exist anymore or if they're any safer than they were then, but they were just steel pipes that were bolted together into a bunch of cubes so that you could climb around them. I had my hands on the top rung of a pipe, my feet on the next rung below that, and when my feet slipped, I fell down and my mouth went right into a steel pipe. It broke the root of one of my front teeth. I began seeing a dentist regularly then, to make sure that everything was done to keep that tooth alive. The dentist said that playing the trumpet wouldn't be good for me because of the constant pressure of the mouthpiece on my front teeth.

A.A.   *If that hadn't happened, who knows what your life would have been like.*

T.E.   It could've been very different. But I adapted and moved on, signing up to study the cello instead. I was in fourth grade, and since I was too small for a full-size cello, I started out on a rented three-quarter-size one. After a while, I graduated briefly to my grandfather's cello, but that instrument was not proportioned well. The fingerboard was set extremely low on it, and my teacher realized that it wasn't healthy for me to continue playing it.

My teacher, Luigi Silva, found me a modern French cello made in the 1920s. But even with this good instrument, as with the piano earlier, I wasn't really serious about the cello. But I did enjoy it, and I enjoyed the fact that my mother didn't play the cello. I was glad to have an activity that was really my own. It wasn't the French language, and it wasn't the piano.

A.A.   *Did your brother play an instrument as well?*

T.E.   Yes, he did. He started in the public schools, too. His band leader hooked him up with the bass clarinet (he needed a bass clarinetist in his band). My brother, as he played Mozart's clarinet concerto on the bass clarinet, heard other people playing it on the B-flat clarinet (the instrument it was actually written for), became curious what that would be like, and eventually he switched to that instrument. But when he went off to college the clarinet never resurfaced. My brother's musical outlet, later on, turned out to be singing: he has a beautiful voice, and he has taken great pleasure in singing in amateur choruses throughout his life.

Singing turned out to be important in my life as well. We belonged to an Episcopal church in Bethesda, MD, and our denomination has a very strong liturgical music and classical music tradition, including a hymnal with a lot of very beautiful and uplifting music, including many chorales by Bach, hymns by other established classical composers, and earlier music, too, including Gregorian chant. (My choirmaster's graceful pacing of Gregorian chant, I'm convinced, helped inspire my own sense of rubato later on.) My dad also sang in his church choir as a young man. He was brought up in the Episcopal church in Saratoga Springs, NY. I've always felt it was a beautiful coincidence that the name of his childhood parish was Bethesda Church.

I've come to realize that being a member of the Boys Choir in our church was one of the most important formative experiences in my development as a musician. We had an absolutely wonderful choirmaster, John Spaulding, who cared for us like a surrogate father and held us to high standards of skill and beauty.

I vividly remember my first performance as a fledgling cellist. I played "The Swan" by Saint-Saëns at an assembly in my elementary school, and my mom played the piano part (in the same auditorium where I'd had my musical ear test!). But later on, what really woke up my deeper love and passion for music and for playing the cello was going to Kneisel Hall in Blue Hill, ME. Being there was my mother's doing entirely. I had been studying in my suburban public school music program, but since she was determined that I would have the chance to get started in music on a stronger footing than she did, she found a more challenging and stimulating environment for me: Kneisel Hall.

A.A. *Do you think she wanted you to get that training in case you decided you wanted to be a musician?*

T.E. Precisely, and my dad was very much with her on that, even though he didn't have the same personal connection with music or the need for music that my mother had. At home, our family would listen as our classical music radio station broadcast the Library of Congress's Budapest Quartet concerts from the time when we were back in Frederick, Maryland. I wasn't particularly drawn to the string quartet when I heard it at that point, but that obviously changed.

I first went to Kneisel Hall when I was 13. There were 17- and 18-year-olds there who played as well as the professional recordings I'd heard. I saw how accomplished young students could be. It was inspiring, intimidating, and exciting, all at once. I went to Kneisel Hall for three consecutive summers and I heard so much great chamber music repertoire there. It was amazing. And I wanted so badly to play it, and play it well.

The first summer I was there was when I started working with Luigi Silva. That was, again, my mom's doing, finding the place that had Luigi Silva on the faculty. He was one of the most significant cello teachers of the 20th century. I don't know what her initial perspective was on him, but she knew that Kneisel Hall was an excellent summer festival. She had driven me up to New York to audition for the school. I played for Marianne Kneisel (daughter of founder Franz Kneisel), who, upon hearing me play, picked up the phone and called Mr. Silva, asking him if he had time to hear me. While we were still in New York, I played for him. It turned out, this was an audition, and they accepted me. I wasn't an advanced player, but I must've shown enough talent that they saw some possibilities. That summer, as I saw what was possible, some seeds were planted by hearing friends, and fellow students do amazing things.

After Kneisel Hall was over and the school year began back in Bethesda, and since Mr. Silva was teaching at the Peabody Conservatory in near-by Baltimore, my mom took me there so that I could continue my studies with him. I auditioned for the pre-college program and got in and became a member of Mr. Silva's class. Once a week, I'd go have a lesson in Baltimore.

I had previously been studying with John Martin, the long-time principal cellist of the National Symphony. Before that first summer at Blue Hill, my mom drove me up to New York to have a couple lessons with my new-found teacher, Mr. Silva. During this time, I stopped studying with Mr. Martin because the things that Mr. Silva had on his agenda for me were so different.

After my first summer at Blue Hill came a full year of studying in the Peabody pre-paratory department. But within a couple weeks of the end of that year, Mr. Silva told me that he wouldn't be able to teach me anymore because I wasn't practicing enough. He said, "I have people waiting to study with me that are willing to work." I was absolutely crushed. I wasn't that invested in it, but being told I wasn't good enough to continue working with him was a very painful and important wake-up call for me. I cried many tears. I was so upset at the thought of not continuing with him. It made me realize how important the cello and Mr. Silva were to me, so I went home and really practiced. I finally practiced in a focused and determined way—I was desperate to turn things around.

A.A. *He saw that and kept teaching you.*

T.E. Yes, and then my second summer at Blue Hill was really a revolution in my life, it was the time when I literally got hooked on music. I practiced five or six hours a day, and it was intoxicating for me. It was so exciting to be making progress rapidly and to use my new-found commitment, determination, focus, and hard work to produce results. I had my hands on the steering wheel of my life in a way that I never had before.

After that summer, I was living in New York and going to The High School of the Performing Arts. Murray Perahia and I were classmates, and we wound up performing a lot together. We did the Schumann Fantasy Pieces in the school assembly, at the Mannes College at a preparatory department concert, on WPIX-TV, and on WNYC radio. (Years later, Murray and I were at the Marlboro Festival together and then played a particularly satisfying Music from Marlboro concert tour.)

Around that time, I had a Nathan Milstein LP recording of Prokofiev and Handel Sonatas for violin and piano. That's the first time I saw Artur Balsam's name and heard him play. I eventually came to understand that he was a giant of a pianist and musician. I wound up studying chamber music with him at Kneisel Hall before I went to college at Manhattan School. I had a piano quartet there, studying with Balsam, and our violist left in the middle of the year. Earlier that year, a lovely lady and superb violist had just transferred to the Manhattan School from Eastman. On behalf of my group, I invited her to join our piano quartet. Linda Moss accepted our invitation, and some years later, she became my wife.

A.A. *That worked out pretty well, I guess.*

T.E. It certainly did. We have a wonderful life together, with two grown children, a daughter and a son, and are now raising an adorable and feisty Cavalier King Charles puppy.

A.A. *What were some of the most valuable things you got from Mr. Silva and Mr. Greenhouse? Did they complement each other?*

T.E. Absolutely, they complemented each other wonderfully. I was very lucky. Luigi Silva was such a thorough, thoughtful, and effective pedagogue. He had ways to practice everything. For any issue of cello playing, any type of playing with the bow or left hand, he had an understanding and a strategy for mastering it.

He gave me the experience that cello playing could be seen and understood through one giant outline, encompassing all of the divisions and subdivisions of topics. Within the "left hand" topic, for instance, there are patterns and configurations within a position that need to be learned reflexively. There's shifting. There's vibrato. There are also fingering styles and principles. He had all of his students show up with a blank manuscript book in which he wrote his strategies and exercises for all kinds of left hand patterns. Scales and arpeggios have always been universally understood to be building blocks of technique because they're building blocks of Western classical music. But he also addressed how you can best practice scales in double stops: in sixths, for example, by first learning how a scale in sixths is constructed, and then learning what the left hand physical patterns are in major and minor keys.

He shared many strategies for mastering thirds in neck- and thumb-positions, too. There is only one practical fingering for playing thirds in neck position. But in thumb position, you can play "fingered thirds," with two thirds within each position, with octaves serving as the framework for your hand. And he pointed out that to play diatonic music in thumb position in a major key, moving through all of the positions in the key, requires only four configurations of the left hand, that's all. He had me playing scales in sixths, thirds, octaves, and tenths. (I later added scales in sevenths and seconds as preparation for contemporary music that is based on those intervals.) And he also had exercises for diminished seventh patterns, octave skips, string-crossings, and up-bow or down-bow staccato practice methods, etc. In short, he handed us the tools to effectively pursue mastery of technique.

He had, then, an encyclopedic understanding of how things work and of how to train oneself to master them. My perspective, built on this experience, became that every problem and challenge is solvable. You just need to step back and observe the nature of the particular issue you're dealing with. As soon as that's understood clearly, then common-sense strategies come to mind as a direct result. Experimenting with those strategies and modifying them as needed usually leads us to effective solutions.

Suddenly, though, after two and a half years of extremely productive and inspiring work with him, Mr. Silva died.

A.A.   *That's what I read.*

T.E.   I was desperate and felt cut adrift, very much like the time he'd said earlier that he couldn't teach me anymore.

A.A.   *How old were you when he died?*

T.E.   I was 15, still in high school. Every Friday afternoon, I'd get on a Trailway bus in Washington DC and go to New York, stay at a friend's house, and go to the Juilliard preparatory department on Saturday. Mr. Silva had stopped teaching at Peabody, so I had to come to New York on the weekends. In the Juilliard prep department orchestra, Itzhak Perlman was sitting third stand in the first violin section. Pinchas Zukerman was playing viola. Once again, as at Kneisel Hall, my eyes and ears and heart were opened up to new horizons.

A.A.   *Was Mr. Silva intimidating or nurturing in lessons?*

T.E.   He was very demanding. He expected a lot. He gave us tools, and he expected us to use them. You didn't want to come to your lesson unprepared, or not having learned what you'd just been taught last week. I remember an incident when I was first working with him up in Blue Hill when I wasn't very serious yet: once, when I wasn't catching on to some change with my bow hand, he took a pencil and rapped it sharply on my right hand. It didn't hurt, but he did it without warning, so it startled me. I realized I needed to follow through more thoroughly to make changes happen.

When Mr. Silva died in November of '61, Juilliard prep arranged for Mr. Greenhouse to finish teaching Silva's students for the remainder of the first semester. At that time, having just lost my beloved teacher, I didn't want to study with anyone else; I had idea how meeting him would affect me, that day, and for the rest of my life.

When I arrived for my first lesson with Mr. Greenhouse, at 101st and Riverside in NYC, he was teaching in his living room, which extended off to the left of the entrance foyer. I had to be very quiet. As I listened to Mr. Greenhouse demonstrate, I was very moved by the sounds I was hearing. They were so beautiful and deeply expressive.

Mr. Silva hadn't emphasized sound production that much with me. I think he was quite individual in the way he taught each student. Later on, I came to learn that some of my experiences with Silva weren't parallel with other students' experiences. While he was moving quickly through repertoire with many other students, he was very systematically working with me on building a solid technical foundation. For instance, he was taking me through all of the Popper études—every one of them—along with Piatti Études, Kreutzer-Silva Études, Guerrini-Silva Études, and a couple of Paganini-Silva Caprices.

When I began studying with Mr. Greenhouse, I had the fingerboard well mapped out and could play accurately as long as it wasn't too fast, but I couldn't move fluidly or easily. My playing was tight. Mr. Greenhouse showed me very quickly how I could work less strenuously, but more effectively, and produce a much more generous sound. The first piece he assigned to me was Bloch's *Schelomo*. He wanted to loosen me up, emotionally, and in my sound production and fluidity of shifting.

A.A.   *Do you think he helped you find your voice on the cello?*

T.E.   Absolutely. There's no question about that.

He was extremely busy with the Beaux Arts Trio. They were having great success, and were establishing themselves as one of the world's finest Piano Trios. He was also the solo cellist of the Bach Aria Group, a position I eventually held, later on. The passionate texts of the cantatas we did in the Bach Aria Group gave me a new understanding of Bach as a human being and as a composer. I would go to Beaux Arts Trio concerts and Bach Aria concerts to hear Mr. Greenhouse and to see what could be expressed with music through the cello. It was very inspiring to see and hear my teacher playing. He was such a poet.

A.A.   *Did you always have a pretty clear path on what you wanted to do with the cello? Did you ever make a living playing in an orchestra?*

T.E.   I have never been part of a professional orchestra. It would have been good for me in many ways to have that experience, but I was also fortunate to be active enough as a chamber music player, in formed groups and free-lance, playing traditional and contemporary music, teaching, and playing some recitals and competitions, that I didn't have the time or need the income at that point.

I worked with Mr. Greenhouse for my Bachelor's and Master's Degrees as well as a couple of years before that. His way of teaching me changed a lot during those years. He was much more didactic at the beginning. There were things I needed to experience and try out with his guidance so that I could have a wider range of musical vocabulary and technical skills. He didn't try to produce "clones," but he asked us to be able to play the way he was playing so that we would have the experience of making music and playing the cello using his technical and expressive vocabulary.

I'll never forget when I was asked to substitute for him in a Bach Aria Group concert. Have you ever heard a recording or seen a video of that group?

A.A.   *No, I haven't.*

T.E.   It was comprised of nine people—four vocal soloists, four instrumental soloists, and keyboard. Our home repertoire was the arias within the cantatas. We didn't perform that many complete cantatas. The particular mission of that group was to bring the exquisite vocal/instrumental chamber music of Bach's arias to the classical concert music stage.

I had seen Mr. Greenhouse play continuo and obligato parts with the Bach Aria Group for years in NY when I was studying with him in school. When I was asked to substitute for him and play continuo in the Group, it was such a challenge! There were so many different continuo-player roles to fill, in order to establish the foundation of each piece's particular character. There were 25 different pieces on the program, and I needed to know the text, character, construction, and counterpoint for all of them. When I had one of my first rehearsals for that concert, Mr. Greenhouse was sitting in the front row, and I was onstage sweating bullets as he gave me hand signals, indicating that I needed to play here louder, there shorter, now more delicately, then with more verve, etc.

I mentioned above that he was didactic at the beginning of our time working together, but more and more, as time passed, I would bring in pieces and he would just listen to me play. Eventually he said, "I'm here waiting for you to reach me, and if you don't, if there's some interference in communication or lack of clarity in what it is you're saying, I'll speak up about it. Fundamentally, I'm waiting for you to reach me. I'm here listening."

Taking it one step further, one of my most unforgettable lessons was up in Wellfleet, MA, his summer home. He had come to the rental house in Orleans MA where a number of his students, including myself, were living and having lessons once a week. (Often, at his home, he'd have a barbecue or take us out on his sailboat. There was a very lovely feeling of apprenticeship, beyond the usual dimensions we got from school lessons.) I played for him, and I had worked really hard. When I finished playing, he said it was skillfully done and very conscientiously learned. It was musical—but, he said, "I'm no better off now than I was before you started playing." Clearly, he was challenging me to do something and say something with my music that would be much more deeply valuable to him as a person, as a human being. With this remark, he effectively set my sights as a performer for life, making clear the ultimate potential role of a performing artist.

That reminds me of my thoughts about another one of your questions, "Have you ever wondered whether or not you could be or should be in another field?"

I have. These feelings and questions tended to come up in the spring when I was an undergrad because of my "burnout" from a hard year's work. It wasn't just the lure of Spring that I was grappling with, I wondered what good I could accomplish as a musician compared to being a physician, for instance, where I would be assured of having the opportunity to make critical differences in people's lives, their families, and their physical health and overall well-being.

I'm glad I had the sense to take my own doubts very seriously and think them through. I thought about what music had meant to me in my life. I was at the Manhattan School toward the end of my undergraduate years. I loved doing what I was doing. I found it exciting and fulfilling. It gave me a strong sense of purpose. What I was questioning was whether this sense of significance and value extended beyond my own life or whether it was just what you might call a "vanity project." As I thought about how I had been affected by concerts that I had witnessed or played in, I could only think of a handful of times when I was completely overwhelmed by the experience of the music, when it just meant so much to me that I could hardly bear the beauty of it, the meaning of it.

One of those times was at a recital by pianist Artur Balsam at Kneisel Hall. He was an aristocrat and a poet and a powerhouse as a musician. I had never been so powerfully drawn to the piano before, but this recital made me feel so emotionally full to over-flowing. Afterwards I didn't want to talk to anybody because I thought no one would understand me. I had to move, to do something. So I finally just burst out of the Hall and started running, downhill, and I ran until I was exhausted, spent, emptied out.

Another one of these extraordinary times happened when I was in Kingston, Jamaica, having been brought in to bolster the cello section of a municipal orchestra for a combined choral/orchestral concert. I'm really vulnerable to choruses. Wonderful choral singing can be overwhelming to me. It wasn't a large group, but the sound these singers made, the rhythm of it, the jubilation of it, it just knocked me out—I was so moved and elated!

So as I thought about what music has done for me in a few extraordinary experiences, how I've felt, what it has meant to me, and the way it has nourished me, ener-gized me, and enlightened me, I thought, if I could just make music like that, then I might have a chance of making a significant difference in someone else's life. Once again, my sights were set. Following through was not going to be simple or easy, but it would be meaningful and gratifying.

On another subject, when I was having one of my annual recitals with Gilbert Kalish at Stony Brook, I was, once again, feeling incredibly nervous and afraid to play, and I'm glad I worked hard to try to figure out what I was so afraid of. The introspec-tion spurred by my stage fright led to many important realizations that have helped me ever since.

Sometimes a student will talk to me about something they're afraid of, or that they're worried about in their future, or they will reveal that they've had deep concerns or reservations about pursuing a career as a cellist, or that they have a strong, enduring interest in some other line of work, like being in music management and production, instead of performance. One such former student is still very active as a cellist, but she became one of the key administrators of a major chamber music presenter. Another cellist who was studying with me had grown up since a young age always being serious about the cello, and he said, "I'm just having trouble concentrating on practicing. My mind keeps wandering." I encouraged him to listen to his doubts and questions, par-ticularly since they were recurring frequently over a long period of time, and see where that leads. Sometimes it makes sense to dedicate a month in the summer, for instance, to try out another primary focus, temporarily, and see what you learn from it.

Do I consider people's success and happiness in general life and professional life my business? I certainly care very much that people are doing well, altogether, but I don't bring up subjects outside of music, myself.

In terms of people that have helped me live a better life, in general, and in the largest sense, Gil Kalish is one of the people that inspires me the most. I'm very close to Gil. Do you know him personally at all?

A.A.   *I've met him.*

T.E.   He's such an admirable human being who is really true to himself. His life, vividness, passion, care, suffering, and joys are present whether you're talking to him or you're making music with him. Clearly, for Gil, playing music is a natural and magnificent way to experience and savor and share one's life. I've been inspired by Gil and by other people who have a deep passion for life and music, together. Life feels most real and gratifying to me when I'm dedicated to living it that way.

A.A.   *When did you think you would want to be a teacher? Was it a natural progression for you in your life?*

T.E.   It was quite a natural one. When I was an undergraduate student, one of my fellow students was always picking my brain, and I was always interested in trying to answer his questions. And Mr. Greenhouse said from time to time over many years, "Tim, I'd love to see you do some teaching for me." I think he was expressing his faith in me by saying that, and I felt encouraged by it.

If I hadn't gone into music, as I mentioned before, being a physician was a possibility. I've always been interested in science and math, too: seeing the logic in cause and effect, the beauty of the way things work out in a math equation, and taking up the challenge of solving a puzzle. I also love to help people. Teaching provides a rare, extraordinary opportunity to make a difference in someone else's life.

The Present

A.A.   *You almost answered this earlier, but what is your teaching philosophy?*

First of all, I believe that everyone who is in front of me for a lesson, no matter where they are on the ladder of their development, has potential that hasn't been fulfilled yet.

Secondly, I find that listening and observing without any agenda enables the clearest perception and evaluation of a student's qualities and abilities at the moment, which can then naturally lead to the most specific, clear, prioritized agenda for that student.

Thirdly, since mastery is achieved through the development of a network of well-trained reflexes and habits, students need a disciplined, purposeful progression of study: both a comprehensive agenda whose goal is overall mastery, and a specific individual agenda that balances and integrates all aspects of their playing in the service of beautiful music-making, right now.

But what is it that makes music-making sound beautiful to us?

The more we can understand why and how music can be so meaningful, the more effectively we can work on cultivating those qualities, ourselves, and with our students.

Looking back at my life as a performer and teacher, some principles, values, and interrelationships have come into focus, shedding light on the nature of music and how to best bring it to life and send it out:

Heart, mind, soul, and body need to work together to discover how to speak the expressive language of music, and then to channel our instinctively expressive language of physical behavior that enables us to express ourselves clearly through the sounds of an instrument.

It's good to make your instrument sound like you're singing. First, actually sing your phrase with your voice and listen to your singing. Then sing it again in a way that you find even more beautiful. Then, get ready to sing again, but this time, make those singing sounds through your hands with the instrument. This is a wonderful way to work, leading to awakenings of a more personal relationship to the music through our voice, which is, after all, our original and very personal musical instrument.

For me, though, our *speaking* voice is an even more fundamental and more nuanced source of musical guidance and inspiration than singing, since it is actually the music (the singing) of our speech that unfailingly, eloquently, and most naturally communicates emotion. All aspects of speech carry the symptoms and evidence of the speaker's feelings: the sounds of our speech always have pitch, rhythm, tone-of-voice (timbre), articulation, and melody, and these elements are all constantly changing and evolving as the speaker's emotional state flows and evolves. Everything that makes speech expressive and emotional, then, is actually music. It's clear to me now that even when people say that they don't have a musical bone in their body, they actually do, because we're all constantly revealing who we are and the way we feel through the music of our speech. We can't help it. We're put together that way.

Building and refining our instrumental technique is like learning verbal vocabulary and improving verbal diction, which is, in itself, important and admirable. But verbal language provides a medium and a conduit primarily for facts and ideas, not feelings. It's the musical language of sounds in the particular way that we speak that springs instinctively, inevitably from the passions of our hearts and souls that makes another human being find our sounds emotionally beautiful and meaningful, whether we're speaking with words or with music.

Artists, then, are ideally spokespeople for the true inner lives of human beings. As a player and as a teacher, I find it's good to keep that ultimate role in mind.

A.A.   *Do you spend a lot of time helping students learn how to practice well?*

T.E.   Yes, I do. As I'm trying to help guide a student, sometimes I need more perspective, and it will take going to their recital or hearing a student's jury to help me realize that I haven't been working as effectively as I could've been on some subject.

I do work with students on how to practice, including sharing with them the tremendously helpful basic technique exercises, strategies, and perspectives I learned from Luigi Silva.

How to practice involves so many things. Mr. Silva had a sequence that I've come to consider normal and healthy: practice basic technique first; then work on études as a transition that integrates technical and expressive elements; then finish with repertoire study, where technique is clearly put at the service of the music. Becoming a master of the instrument is like becoming a native speaker of a language. The things you want to say and the way you say them just come to you by reflex when you have trained yourself well.

Our bodies are the experts in "natural movement," they move naturally in everyday life—unless there are inhibitions, tensions, injuries, "cultivated" or "contrived" habits, or maladaptions. Alexander Technique and Feldenkreis study can each help to achieve a more truly natural, optimally released and naturally responsive physical state. In everyday life, we usually use our bodies without thinking about how we're going to do things. When we want to open a door, we step toward it first and then we extend our arm out.

A.A.   *We don't miss the door handle.*

T.E.   No, not usually! Because we unconsciously aim with our eyes. Aiming is one of the most important and helpful things to do when playing music: to lead by aiming with our ears. Music begins and ends with the ear, first hearing the ideal "image" of the sound in our mind's ear, then hearing the actual sound in the room.

One of the reasons why the advice "Relax, take it easy, don't try too hard" used to confuse me was that I was being sincere and energetically pursuing a good and ambitious goal. My teacher probably meant that I needed to relax physically, but I think I must've assumed it was meant as advice about mental effort. (W. Timothy Gallwey's *Inner Game of Tennis* is very valuable in its examination of our internal dialogue as we try to achieve a goal. He advises using clarity and intensity of perception over intensity of mental management or dominance of will, to achieve a desired result.)

It's true that it doesn't tend to work out well when we struggle. When we're not struggling to do things, our bodies can more easily work in a balanced, adaptive and fluid way. Instead of trying to make things happen by stopping everything and grabbing control, much of what's best will happen most easily and reliably if we "release" into our playing, which is my favorite word to use instead of "relax" (which has a connotation of passivity). I work a lot on form with my students.

A.A.   *I've been really curious to ask you your feelings on torso movement and body movement when playing. I've heard a lot of different opinions on this, and one thing that helped me a lot in my own playing was a feeling of having motions start with the torso, like a backhand tennis swing. It's a result of a bigger motion. Is that something you taught or believe?*

T.E.   Yes, I do. I'm very familiar with it, and for tennis players, baseball players, bowlers, ballet dancers, etc., it's just the norm. The torso is the biggest, most intrinsically powerful part of ourselves. As it effortlessly begins with some small motion, that motion and energy can then easily flow out through our arms and hands into the instrument.

Here's a specific example of that: For me, the fundamental nature of the bow stroke is that it's a pendulum. The way I usually introduce the experience of having a pendulum-produced bow stroke is to have a student walk around the room, just walk. Then after a moment, I'll ask them to observe what their hands and arms are doing: do they swing? Why do they swing? Are they using muscles to make them swing? (No, not normally, or ideally) It turns out that the bottom of your torso just twists and shifts forward as we're taking a step, and since our torso is flexible, that twisting makes its way up to our shoulders, which makes our dangling arms swing. If we're walking quickly and taking big steps, our arms wind up swinging naturally quite a lot, and that's all with no muscle effort. That's an example of a "natural resource" that can be harnessed and directed into our playing.

A.A. *How do you keep a student sounding like an individual? You mentioned you want to maintain a student's individuality. I'm wondering if that's a conscious decision in your teaching to try to make their way as convincing as you can.*

T.E. I'm not afraid of modeling and imitation; I think it has a very valuable place by building perceptiveness and a more specific sound and movement vocabulary, and by requiring adaptability. As a phase of experimentation and learning, I don't find that it stifles individuality. If a student is playing from their own passion and sense of imperative, they will sound individual, just by being themselves.

A.A. *Like Mr. Greenhouse did for you quite often, by demonstrating.*

T.E. Yes, for sure. Students will need to make some very specific adjustments to really "clone" your motion. But then, it's theirs, as soon as they've done it, and they can use it if and when they want to and in whatever way they need. Mr. Greenhouse: "What I'm teaching you when I'm asking you to do this, is vocabulary."

A.A. *Do you give them your bowings and fingerings initially?*

T.E. I do, and it's for the same purpose of sharing a means to an end. We know as players that some fingerings just work better than others. Some fingerings tend to fall out of the hand more easily, more reliably, and more accurately. When I'm starting to teach somebody, I'll say, "Learn this piece so that you can do it this way, and present it to me this way." Later on, if they're getting closer to a performance, for instance, and they're not playing something as well as I know they can, I'll often suggest, "If there's something that might work better for you, try it and then do whatever works best."

As I worked with Mr. Greenhouse and with his fingerings, I got a feel for the ways he used his hands, ways that often wouldn't have occurred to me at first, on my own. As I ask a new student to learn a new piece starting with my fingerings, I explain that this is an efficient way for me to share some very important things with them. It's efficient because we're not taking lesson time for me to explain every fingering to them. It's also effective in ways that can't be explained in words, because one only truly experiences what fingerings are like by actually using them. I also tell them, "I'm not giving you my fingerings because I think they are the only fingerings or even necessarily the best ones that could possibly be found. But they're the best that I've found so far, and I know there is a lot of value in learning them."

Choosing fingerings always involves considering both practical and aesthetic issues. Using a teacher's fingerings gives the student the chance to experience some ways their teacher has chosen to address and balance those challenges and opportunities.

A.A. *What is the hardest thing to teach a student?*

T.E. To really trust their instincts. To really give over control of their playing to what they instinctively and emotionally need to do. That's what often separates a compelling artist from a partially successful one. To be present, passionate, and in character, you need to develop a sense of what feeling is behind the music. Who is speaking? What part of yourself is really finding expression in this phrase? Then, follow your own lead. Experiment, and listen for what's most convincing to you.

A.A.   *When you pick students, you must hear lots of wonderful students auditioning for you. Do you pick someone who, maybe, has a lot to say but doesn't feel physically comfortable saying it yet, or do you pick someone who seems to be physically gifted on the cello but isn't trusting what they want to say yet?*

T.E.   Both kinds of applicants can be wonderful to work with. We hear valuable, worthy people in all sorts of conditions of incompleteness, where the greatest opportunities lie in identifying and addressing relative weaknesses, and then working to pull it all together into an integrated whole.

Since the most valuable thing in music is not how well you're saying something, it's what you're saying, I'm drawn first to the person to whom sounds are just inescapably meaningful, one who doesn't have to try really hard to try to make it meaningful. It just is. When the music means a great deal to you, it tends to come out basically reflecting your sincerity and conviction. But it usually takes experimentation, guided by imagination and "listening for the truth" of what's coming out, to fully discover just what we mean to convey and just what actions and sounds truly say what we mean. I've seen some striking changes in students as they become better connected with themselves in that way.

On the other hand, I recall hearing a young boy play an audition as a freshman who was trained in a wonderfully disciplined way, technically, but who was pretty mechanical-sounding. Nonetheless, I felt that there was a real heart there that was trying to come out, and I heard that it couldn't help but come out at certain points. I had my consultation lesson with him right after he had played his audition. After that lesson was finished, he said, "You were talking about the bow all the time. In my country, we didn't talk about the bow as much." This young man was so gratifying to work with and his playing evolved and opened up beautifully. His disciplined early technical training continued to be a priceless virtue and to provide a secure foundation, even as his technical/physical approach to playing became far more varied and specific in its expressivity.

I have a kind of mantra for myself, to help get my instincts in control of my playing, which is: like a method actor, "get in character" and then physically "behave the way you feel," since the instrument's specific sounds will be a direct result of the way we physically treat the string. Just like we are inevitably expressive with our voice, we inevitably have an instinct to move in character with our emotions.

A.A.   *How many hours should a student be practicing each day? Is it just as much as they need, or would you tell a student they should be doing a certain amount of time? Does it depend on where they're at in their development?*

T.E.   This is something that I could be doing better in my teaching. I help them know how to practice, and I do that in very detailed and explicit ways at times. I could be more alert to whether I should be advising them to spend certain amounts of time.

In terms of organizing their practice, I counsel my students generally to work on the sequence that I learned from Mr. Silva: Practicing basic technique gives you an opportunity to refresh your skills and build those skills, including establishing your ideal intonation, in your ear and in your hands. When you're playing thirds, play them better than you did yesterday. People often shy away from playing thirds because they're so difficult. People often shy away from doing daily practice of octaves and arpeggios, also, because they're difficult. If we bring our fullest idealism, in terms of the standards of our playing, to our basic technique practice, then we will build a foundation that we can trust, that in turn enables us to release more into the instrument. The more disciplined and idealistic training we give ourselves in our octaves, thirds, sixths, arpeggios, scales, and other fundamentals, the more those skills become solid and trustworthy. As we are able to release more into the instrument, we can capitalize more on some natural qualities that become more available: vibrato becomes easier and more natural, and the left hand balances itself because it's released.

Basic technique work is isolated and abstract, but études are an incredibly valuable tool for integrating the different aspects of our technique into fluid, coordinated teamwork; as with pieces of music, études are written in phrases that go through harmonies, and there are different personalities to them. (The Piatti caprices, for instance, are wonderfully characterful!) Our sensitivity to harmony and to sound should not be turned off while we're working on technique, and études give us a chance to develop more beautiful, seamless integration of left and right hands, and of the rhythm of music and of technique, while always shaping our sound into phrases.

A.A. *What about intonation? How do you help the student play better in tune?*

T.E. Lead with your ear—hear the note very clearly first in your mind's ear, then ask your fingertip to "hear" where it is on the fingerboard before you play, and without testing first. Learn to know where you are on the fingerboard by "feel" alone (without testing or checking).

A.A. *Do you have them do drones? Do you use electronic devices or double stops?*

T.E. Yes, because intonation is a relative thing, a drone really gives you a solid reference point. Tuning to open strings or drones is really helpful. I do use a tuner in limited ways, myself, and I encourage my students to use a tuner in particular ways, and I use a metronome in a similar way: I use them both as consultants. There are certain degrees and types of ear development that come from following the lead of the tuner, but we ultimately need to cultivate our self-sufficiency: we need for our own ear to imagine a note accurately first. As a phase of practice, a tuner serving as a check can help us to sharpen the acuity of our ear. (And metronome practice can function the same way as a check for the way we feel rhythm in our ear and in our body.)

When I've gotten in shape, daily, I can tell whether I'm in tune before I play, so I can trust my hands to follow the lead of my ear. When that happens to us, it means you can release into your playing confidently. You feel secure enough to go for the sound that you really want. I started realizing that by experimenting in my practice, I could keep track of whether I was in that "attuned" state or not, and I could cultivate it. Instead of just trying to pound good intonation into my left hand ten times in order to make sure I remembered where it was, I could use leading with my ear as the primary means to find the notes. What I've learned to do is not to micromanage physically, not to think, "I've got to physically place my finger a little higher than I thought since I was flat on that note." The ideal training mode for practice is for playing always to be simple, direct, led by our ear and accomplished by a released and therefore flexible left hand, and not to depend on micro-corrections. (Some micro-corrections, though, are a part of real life as a performer, and in performance, they actually can help us "home-in" on our best intonation.)

There's often not just one way to pursue things. I may experiment a little bit by playing first to find where a note is, and then I'll try to just get the sense where it is, hovering just above the string. It doesn't necessarily mean I'm going to play in tune yet just because I'm concentrating really well on where it is. But for each pitch that I want to land on, I'm going to try again to hear the note first, then sense the sound of that note with the tip of my finger, and then I'm going to drop the finger there and see if it's just right. If it's not "just right," I'll start over again by clearly hearing the note, then sensing what feels like that note with my fingertip, and then dropping my finger there again, until my systems catch on, and I find my accuracy. (This association of hearing with physical sensation of place is not new; my strong hunch is that it kicks in for most of us when we feel "in really good shape," or "really well warmed-up and ready to play," or when we're playing a piece that we know very, very well.)

Working in this way has been a tremendous help to me. It's like an archer's having his eye on the target—my ear is on the target. It's also like meditating on it: Can you hear and then feel that note? And then physically going for it. I've been repeatedly shocked at how well that works when I give it a chance and when I dare to trust my hand to adapt to the leadership of my ear. We are so much more subtly physically sensitive when we're released.

A.A.   *Do you make students play by memory? Is that an important part of what they learn?*

T.E.   I should do more of that, because it really is constructive.

I do coach my students about how to memorize. There are different types of playing from memory. One is physical memory (muscle memory of the series of actions that cause our playing to happen).

Another is structural memory of the music. (Observations and analysis of the music's structure: What key am I in? What chord am I in? Where am I modulating? What notes are principal and what notes are embellishing? etc.) This is the way I finally succeeded in memorizing the Bach Fourth Suite Prelude and was able to get really secure with it. At first glance, that movement is a complex blizzard of eighth notes, but as soon as I discovered the organization of it, I knew the place and function of each of those eighth-notes, and knew what was happening harmonically for the entire piece. When the structure's organization and aesthetic logic become clear, a piece is often more beautiful and "memorable" to us because it's so much more meaningful. Structural memory can help us experience exactly where we are in the unfolding of a piece, and give us an explicit understanding of the emotional steps that the composer's structural choices create for us. I regard structural awareness as an aid and stimulus to my instinct which helps me more fully receive the experiences that composers build into their pieces—experiences which it is our role to have and to share with our audiences through our sounds.

So, structural analysis, then, goes to the very heart of a performer's role: it reveals the nature of the experiences that the composer is reaching out to share with us, and it's our job to then share that experience, generously and eloquently, with our audiences. Musical structure, far from being "dry" and "intellectual," is profoundly evocative, and filled with symptoms and clues about the state of a composer's heart, soul and mind. I got so much more than I expected from analyzing the Prelude to Bach's Fourth Suite; I didn't just learn what the notes were, I learned why they were there and came to love and need them, in exactly their design, to have the great experience of this piece.

Playing from memory by playing by ear, I had a challenging experience at the Cassadó Competition when I entered it for the second time. (I had won third place the first time, but I decided to see if I could do any better.)

To make a long story short, there was some confusion about whether or not Sonatas had to be played from memory, and I finally learned, for sure, that I was required to play them from memory only two days before performing them in the Competition. Fortunately, they were standard repertoire pieces which I had performed a number of times before, but never from memory.

After wondering whether I should continue in the Competition, I decided to see if there was a way that I could still play the next round. If I could just stay cool enough, then maybe I could do this: play by ear instead of off of a page of music. Essentially, that's what I did; training my playing reflexes to be led by my ear, I advanced through the next rounds of the competition and ultimately won the top prize.

"Playing by ear" to me is the most natural way to play from memory, but physical and structural memories provide additional layers of knowledge and security.

A.A. *What is your philosophy on teaching the Bach Suites, and what do you think of the performance practice that's evolved over my generation to have more historically informed performances?*

T.E. There are many valuable things that have come out of historical performance study and practice, particularly convincingly as many historically informed performances have become so much more characterful, imaginative, and vividly expressive. I suspect that people at Bach's time were still individuals with as different personalities, idiosyncrasies, conventions and styles as human beings usually have. While what most makes music meaningful to me is the evolution of its emotional, aesthetic experience (some kind of emotional story), a sensitivity to performance practices of the time definitely helps to take us to a distinctive and exquisite aesthetic world within which we then have our own personal and emotional experiences with the Suites.

I take some cues about temperament, timing, and motivic character from the music's structure and from certain idiomatic aspects of slurring, not all of which are necessarily explicitly in the Anna Magdalena Bach manuscript. In the Anna Magdalena Bach version of the Courante of the Second Suite, for example, there are a lot of broken thirds written without slurs, most of which I choose to play as couplets, which gives the experience of two voices traveling in the same direction, with the upper ones being primary. The string crossings of many of these couplets serve to still articulate the second notes of the couplets.

I choose not to use much vibrato in these pieces, not mainly because I'm trying to be correct, but because I prefer it. I find that vibrato can often distract from fully experiencing the harmonies and the specific timbre and shaping of sounds created by the bow.

A.A.   *I agree.*

T.E.   I find the personality and expressivity of vibrato to be far more generic than the speci-
ficity of the effects of clarity of pitch and nuance of tone quality. I know from quartet
playing that tones don't combine into harmonies nearly as well if one uses more vibrato.
Also, responding to the basic harmonic rhythm is very helpful to me since, as harmonies change, we take steps into different emotional worlds, which helps our phrases feel
like specific emotional journeys.

If other notes (outside the apparent basic harmony) in a bar look and sound like
they're wandering around within that chord, then they are doing just that—exploring
and savoring the feeling of that chord. When you get to another chord, you see how
that one makes you feel, and make sure that it sounds the way you feel. Those simple
distinctions wind up dealing with one of the most important issues in playing Bach,
finding the simple structure that is behind the written-out embellishments, and then
experiencing the piece fundamentally from those basic features.

This music was written at a time when embellishments were being written out far
more than in the early Baroque. I've been inspired and influenced by some of the
eloquent, literate Baroque music interpreters, harpsichordists in particular, that I've
worked with over the years who are free spirits and who don't shy away from doing
something personal, in terms of affect and embellishment. If historical idioms start
dominating too much what's personal and individual about the playing of a piece, then
one's at risk of diluting the humanity of the experience.

A.A.   *I'm wondering what your thoughts are on this next topic. There are three popular transcriptions that people perform, and I wondered if you enjoy teaching them. Those include
the Grützmacher Boccherini B-flat, the Fitzenhagen Tchaikovsky Rococo, and the Chopin-
Feuermann Polonaise, a piece in which you rarely hear the original. They're all pieces that
we've learned. Do you have feelings on those?*

T.E.   The Boccherini B-flat Concerto is an excellent teaching piece and a lovely piece of
re-composed and arranged music. This is Boccherini processed through another lens,
though, and I personally prefer hearing it in its original form. (On the other hand,
Mendelssohn, in his D-Major Sonata for cello and piano, op. 58, wrote a slow movement that is clearly inspired by baroque-style chorale and recitative, and brought the
particular type of fullness of the romantic spirit of his time to that music. I find that
movement to be absolutely beautiful, eloquent, and valuable music.

I enjoy Tchaikovsky's Rococo Variations equally in both the original and Fitzenhagen
versions. It's an excellent piece of music, and a very valuable piece to study.

I think the Feuermann transcription of the Chopin Polonaise is also a beautiful
piece, and it's a great piece to have in our repertoire. Composers used to arrange, re-or-
chestrate and recompose things frequently. Bach and many others did it with their
own music. (The first Bach Viola da Gamba and Harpsichord Sonata also exists in a
two-flute version, for example, and there are countless others.) I think we shouldn't be
too uptight about that. Different arrangements and instrumentation often shed a new
light on a piece, which may or may not be to our taste, and may not sound as well as
the original to us, but I personally like to remain open to new versions of old pieces.

As a footnote, I happened to hear Bach's famous Chaconne in D Minor for solo
violin on the radio recently, played on the mandolin! At first I was shocked, but the

piece (which was not changed at all) drew me in and left me once again marveling at how eloquent and magnificent it is. And the new "flavor" added another dimension to my love of this piece.

A.A.   *Similar to what we talked about earlier, do you demonstrate often in lessons, and how important do you think that is?*

T.E.   It can be very valuable.

A.A.   *Is it something you do fairly regularly?*

T.E.   Yes, but I don't do it all the time. Sometimes I don't do it because a piece is not in my repertoire. Other times, I don't do it because I'm interested in trying to help my students be self-starters. If I feel like somebody is merely playing the notes on the stand in front of them, before starting to demonstrate, I'll often identify some feature of the writing to react to more specifically or colorfully. By throwing out verbal advice or challenges, I mean to give them encouragement to use their imagination and search their instincts for a more personal and compelling purpose for playing.

At other times, I'll realize that words aren't best, get out my cello and make some sounds of the sort I'm encouraging them to try, which demonstrates not only the sound but the means of achieving it, and the feeling behind the sound.

Most often, my students already want to play in a character that's similar to what I'd like, too. People can often articulate how the music should sound better than they can actually play it, sometimes because they're not yet actually feeling that way while they're playing, sometimes because they're not deeply enough into their experience and genuinely needing to reach out with it, and sometimes they're simply distracted. Students are normally very dedicated and idealistic and are doing their utmost, but sometimes they haven't realized yet that you can't share a feeling that you're not first having, yourself, and that what's going to be projected (whether you intend it or not) is whatever you're actually caring about the most while you're playing.

As performers, we have a very specific role to fulfill at a specific time and place. To have the best chance succeeding, it helps to first define our ambition and purpose for playing a concert, our goal.

My own goal when playing a concert is to send out a vivid celebration of our lives by candidly sharing our own inner life through our sounds, as we experience the emotional stories of our composers and literally share communally the experiences of living at the deepest, most personal level.

To have the best chances of reaching our goal, we need to be living in "performance mode," welcoming our passions, trusting our talents and skills to be our medium, without hesitation or looking back in judgment. I find it very helpful to consciously leave "practice mode" behind as I shift into "performance mode." Practice mode is for advancing our skills; performance mode is for using them. It gives our skills a job to do, and we need to trust them so that they can be free to serve their purpose.

"Method actors" are very inspiring role models for me as a performer. They set out to live a part, to be that person that they're playing, to get inside their skin, to empathize to that extent. I find that's the ideal approach for me to emulate since one of my greatest aspirations as a performer is to be emotionally authentic, that is, to be honest and candid in the moment. I most want to speak about and share the experience that

I believe the piece is about. It's very helpful when I've worked on and found that kind of identification in my practice room and rehearsals, well before the performance. And then I especially want to be full of those feelings when performing, but it's easier by then because I've formed a stronger emotional relationship with the music, and the audience helps draw me out since they're listening hard, wanting to share that feeling.

A.A.   *Do you tell your students to practice performing sometimes? I think so many students are so used to being in the practice room that when they get out it's so scary and different.*

T.E.   It's extremely valuable to practice performing. It's something I particularly encourage my students to do as they're approaching a recital, by playing in my weekly cello class, for example, but also to "practice for performing." There's a lot of repertoire, and there are many issues that they need to be working on, and it can be quite overwhelming. I advise them to do slightly slower slow-motion practice in "performance mode"; that is, to go through a movement without stopping but as if in a slow-motion video with every bit of the character, inflection, etc., so that they can still be guided by the essence of the music. At this slightly slower tempo you have a little more time to put features into your playing, and you have a little more time to hear what's actually coming out. In the meantime, you've made a rule for yourself that you're not stopping, which is a normal part of performance, and which helps us experience and trust the flow of the piece.

It's so important and helpful to stay fully engaged in the spirit, the feeling, the way you are moved by a piece that makes everything happen in your performance, and that gives it its reason for being. (In addition to getting ourselves "on message," this kind of focus leaves less room for worries and distractions.) The best reason for performing music, as far as I'm concerned, is to celebrate our lives, together with our audience, through the lens of our innermost and deepest feelings.

The Future

A.A.   *Where do you see the future of classical music going in the next generation?*

T.E.   Well, every single time any of us gets up on stage and gives any kind of performance, we owe it to each other as human beings, and to our music, to give it a chance to reach people and be valuable to them. Don't play notes on a page. Don't play something until you've found out how you feel about it. You've got to put distractions aside, and sometimes that's really difficult. It can take a lot of effort, for instance, to put aside that you're suffering or that someone in your family is suffering. We need to stand up and fulfill our role, we need to get engaged, and share the way our lives and the experiences in the music move us.

When musical communication happens on the deepest level, we are literally less alone. If the music's really beautiful, meaningful, and really pulls at your heart inside, then you can really make a difference. A central aspect of this "calling" is to find out who you are, be who you are, and share it. That's a good thing in the moment and a good thing for the survival of our art—to give our listeners an experience that's nourishing and valuable.

A.A.   *Let me ask, where have you seen the level of cello playing go in the last 30 years?*

T.E.   Oh, it's amazing, particularly in the level of craftsmanship, and often in artistry and creativity, too. It is still rare, though, to hear playing that is poetic, that in the larger sense fully reveals the true richness and depth of our inner lives.

A.A.   *Related to that, are there enough jobs for cellists in today's market? Have you seen a change in that with all these great cellists coming out of school?*

T.E.   It partly depends on how broadly our students define what they would accept as jobs, what jobs they see as creative, important, and fulfilling. But we need to also make the case for our music to keep living and doing its good work in our lives and communities, by supporting and participating in the life of local arts organizations, all the while feeling the responsibility and opportunity we have anytime and everytime we make musical sounds: people are listening, and we've got to speak to their hearts and souls in a way that makes a difference. I'm looking forward to delving into Joseph Polisi's book, *The Artist as Citizen*, to hear his thoughts about what we're facing and what actions we can take, for ourselves and for our society.

　　　Another response to this challenge is to encourage my students to think "outside the box" of the paradigm of the "typical serious classical cellist" and to take stock of their own particular musical interests and skills and consider how they could all contribute to a good and sustainable life for them. Many of my students, it turns out, are fascinated and engaged by other genres of music (pop, jazz, bluegrass, world music, etc.) and by various outreach, educational, or therapeutic musical activities. There are some that could certainly be hired by a university to oversee two or three aspects of the needs of a department.

A.A.   *You said a key thing to me about music, that people need to be there listening to it. What worries me is that you and I can hear pretty much any performance from our couch so easily. I hope that the idea of having to go and sit and experience music together never goes away. I find today classical music has to cater more and more to technology.*

T.E.   Right. Everything is recorded now.

A.A.   *Yes. Everything's on video.*

T.E.   There's all of this incredibly comprehensive circulation and availability today. Every single time we play, we have the possibility of feeding people's personal and musical needs. Every time our playing is captured, we have the possibility of touching God knows who, God knows where. This new location, which is everywhere, is a goldmine at the same time that it's a hazard to live concerts and to experiencing the "community of hearts and souls" of a live concert.

A.A.   *Do you think the concert hall will become obsolete in 50 years?*

T.E.   Do you think rock concerts are going to become obsolete?

A.A.   *They might, although I definitely think younger people like to go to rock concerts more than classical concerts.*

T.E.   Yes. My son goes to rock concerts.

A.A.   *It's a much different experience in a way. There's so much visual.*

T.E.   True, there's a lot of the experience that's visual, which reminds me that I get very turned off sometimes seeing some classical musicians trying to be visually appealing in a way that dilutes or distracts from the experience of our sounds. As musicians, we believe in the ability of sounds to connect us with each other. We need to make a case for that power of music, of musical sounds, every single time we play—that's one of the most important things we can do—even as we also acknowledge that there's great value and obvious normal appeal to the full "live" experience of having audio and video together, capturing what appears to be the "whole experience." But the whole experience is really being there, so that one experiences the give and take between performer and audience, and the communing all around, with your fellow audience members, too.

I'm all for things that can be done to give people more connection with the performers in a classical music concert. I think it's great when people talk briefly from the stage, for instance, as long as it's used to draw people in, and welcome them into the distinctive and universally valuable experiences we have to offer.

Close to the Heart

A.A.   *If you hadn't been a musician, what would you have loved to have done with your life?*

T.E.   I'm very interested in lots of things. By the time I was finishing high school, my interest in the humanities had been heightened tremendously, and I was very stimulated by literature, poetry, and creative writing. I was fortunate to find a humanities teacher at Manhattan school who was a Dante scholar. He was a deep thinker and reckoner of the human condition, and a sort of "Pied Piper" to his students, welcoming us into very personal experiences with great poetry and prose. I studied Shakespeare, modern poetry, and philosophy in very probing ways with him.

I've always been attracted to science and math. I find biology astounding, for instance, in the unbelievably sophisticated and responsive systems that are within living organisms. I could have pursued something related to medicine, biology, or physics. Actually, as an instrumentalist, I frequently look at physical issues through the "lens" of mechanics in my teaching. Sometimes, if a student asks me about their bow hold and I see it isn't working well, I'll say, "Okay, let's take a look at how the angles and vectors work best." There's a useful place for the clarity of physics as we set out to achieve our practical, artistic, and personal goals.

A.A.   *What are some of the more memorable concert experiences you've had?*

T.E.   I'm really fortunate that I've had many really wonderful experiences playing concerts, in all kinds of roles, playing string quartets, sonata duos, concertos, unaccompanied works, in all kinds of places, playing all manner of repertoire—it's all been a great experience and privilege.

I've also found it deeply satisfying to play for my son's wedding and for my neighbor's funeral.

A.A.   *What did you play at your son's wedding? I'm just curious.*

T.E.   The Bach G-Major Suite Prelude.

A.A.   *What are you most proud of in your life and career?*

T.E.   My marriage, my children, and my students, first of all. As a musician, I'm proud and happy to have sent out some sounds that really do sound like I feel.

A.A.   *Is there anything you still want to do that's on your bucket list before it's all done?*

T.E.   Oh, I've got an appetite to do all kinds of things, but I'm doing one of the most important ones right now. I'm recording the Suites.

A.A.   *Oh okay, that's great. That's a big one.*

T.E.   Yes, it is. This is something I've wanted to do for a long time, so I'm very glad to finally be doing it now. It's a wonderful experience and a great challenge.

A.A.   *I'm just curious if you had any desert island pieces? If you could only listen to a couple pieces, which ones would they be? Does it depend on the day?*

T.E.   Something that's always been transporting for me is the Air from Bach's D major orchestral suite. When I was an undergraduate at Manhattan School, I'd put on my LP (vinyl) recording of this piece, plug in my headphones so that I had fantastic sound quality, and just go to another place.

Another piece that I'll mention, because I was recently reminded how much I'm affected by it, is Schubert's Fantasy in F Minor D940 for piano four hands. It's not a comfortable piece to listen to, but it's very beautiful. It's just heartbreakingly beautiful.

5

Stephen Geber

Stephen Geber, the longest-serving principal cellist in the history of the Cleveland Orchestra, served for 30 seasons in that post from 1973 until 2003. Born in Los Angeles into a family of professional cellists, he studied cello with his mother, Gretchen Geber, as well as with Gábor Rejtő, Stephen Deʼak, Ronald Leonard, and Zara Nelsova. He graduated from the Eastman School of Music in 1965 with a bachelor of music degree and a performerʼs certificate. While at Eastman, he was a member of the Rochester Philharmonic, and prior to joining the Cleveland Orchestra as a principal cellist in 1973, he was a member of the Boston Symphony Orchestra and a faculty member of the New England Conservatory of Music.

With the Cleveland Orchestra, Mr. Geber has been featured as a soloist in two world premieres and three Cleveland premieres. In 1998, he gave the world-premiere performance of Samuel Adlerʼs Cello Concerto with the Eastman Philharmonia under Christoph von Dohnányiʼs direction. The concerto was commissioned by the Eastman School of Music in honor of Mr. Geber, who received Eastmanʼs Alumni Achievement Award during the concert.

In addition to his frequent performances as featured soloist with the Cleveland Orchestra, Mr. Geber has been a guest soloist with orchestras throughout the United States, including the Boston Pops, Dallas Symphony, Eastman-Rochester Symphony, and the Florida Orchestra. He has collaborated in chamber music with a number of leading artists, including Vladimir Ashkenazy, Julius Baker, Rudolf Firkusny, Grant Johannesen, Yo-Yo Ma, and Lorin Maazel, and has performed with the Emerson, American, and Cavani string quartets.

Regarded as one of the leading cello teachers in this country, Mr. Geber heads the Cello Departments of the CIM and Kent/Blossom Music, and is a faculty member of New World Symphony in Miami, Florida. Former students of Mr. Geber hold positions in nearly all of the major American orchestras, and in several leading chamber ensembles. He has taught masterclasses throughout North America, Europe, and Eastern Asia. In 1994, he taught and performed in the Georg Solti Orchestral Project at Carnegie Hall, which brought together talented young musicians and principal players from major American orchestras. The following year, Mr. Geber was one of four Cleveland Orchestra principal players chosen to lead their respective sections in an orchestra assembled under Solti's direction for a special concert in Geneva, Switzerland, to honor the 50th anniversary of the United Nations.

In August 2003, Shar Music Company released his CD recording of 18 prominent orchestral cello solos. In 2007, Stephen Geber was appointed to the advisory council of Chamber Music Two at Lincoln Center. In 2008, he received the prestigious Eva Janzer Award from Indiana University. This is given in recognition for lifetime contributions to cello performance and teaching.

Mr. Geber is married to Lisa Wellbaum, principal harp for the Cleveland Orchestra, and he is the father of four daughters.

The Past

Anthony Arnone	*Where did you grow up, and how did you first become exposed to the cello?*
Stephen Geber	I grew up in Los Angeles, California. My first exposure was when I was born. Both my parents were cellists. My father was a member of the Los Angeles Philharmonic cello section for nearly 40 years. My mother was a very well-known teacher in Los Angeles and also did a lot of studio work as principal cellist at the Fox and MGM studios. However she was primarily a teacher and developed some wonderful students.
A.A.	*Do you have brothers and sisters?*
S.G.	I have a brother David who is also a highly respected cellist, chamber musician, and teacher. He has taught at the Manhattan School of Music for many years. He was also a founding member of the American String Quartet, which he performed in for 29 years.
A.A.	*Walk me through your early path in music. When did you know that you wanted to do this for your life?*

S.G.   I started piano when I was five and a half. I played piano for about a year, but I didn't particularly enjoy playing it. Sometimes I wish I had the skills to accompany students even on simple things, but I let it go. I begged to play the cello. At six and a half years old, I started the cello with my mother, and it didn't work out very well. We were together for about a year and a half and we were not getting along well.

A.A.   *It's hard to teach your kid.*

S.G.   Yes. I found that out with my own daughter. They put me with another teacher for a while, and I yo-yo'd back and forth between Stephen De'ak, who is my godfather as a matter of fact, and Gábor Rejtő. Stephen De'ak had formerly taught at Curtis, and then he moved to Los Angeles to teach at USC. After working with him for six years, Gábor Rejtő then taught me. I wasn't really taken with the cello to the point where I wanted to have a career yet. I was a late bloomer, you might say. I wanted to be a kid, date girls, and play baseball. I got through high school on sheer talent and then went to Eastman. I really enjoyed myself there and made up my mind that this was what I wanted to do. Before I went to Eastman, I had even toyed with the possibility of taking a year off and studying medicine. I thought about that, but I did miserably in biology. I just couldn't cut it. So, music it was. I was very fortunate to land a position with the Boston Symphony when I finished up at Eastman.

A.A.   *Who did you study with at Eastman?*

S.G.   I studied with Ron Leonard. I did a lot of chamber music there too and got into the Rochester Philharmonic right away. Back in those days, they allowed students to play in the orchestra there.

A.A.   *Ron Leonard must have been close to your age.*

S.G.   He's nine years older than I am.

A.A.   *Was it difficult to have a teacher so close to you in age?*

S.G.   No not at all. We got along famously and still do.

A.A.   *When you decided to go to Eastman, did you know you wanted to major in cello?*

S.G.   Yes, absolutely I was 18. I had taken a year away from serious study of cello and that was good for me. It centered my thinking. I was at Eastman for four years, and in my senior year I auditioned for the Boston Symphony and got in. It was then that, after a year or so in the orchestra, I realized that there was a lot more I wanted to learn about the cello. I decided that it was important for me to continue taking some coachings, so that's when I started working with Zara Nelsova during the summertimes at Tanglewood, where she and her husband would go and stay for two months. There was no concertizing, only learning repertoire and relaxing. She was a wonderful influence as well.

A.A.   *What do you think you learned the most from her?*

S.G.   I would say there was something in her sound that I really wanted to emulate. I always had a nice sound, but the tonal color that she was able to produce on the cello while always projecting was something that I was trying to break through.

A.A.   *Do you feel like you already had a strong overall technique at that point?*

S.G.   Yes.

A.A.   *Do you credit Rejtő?*

S.G.   He was a wonderful and patient teacher. He was one of Casals' students. He was very methodical, very detailed, and no nonsense. He was also Larry Lesser's teacher. In fact,

Larry used to come in after me for his lessons, and I used to say to him, "Gee, I hope Mr. Rejtő is going to be in a better mood for you than he was for me. I may have put him in a bad mood."

A.A.   *Was he pretty influential? I'm curious to know who really helped build your foundation.*

S.G.   He did. He helped. I had a great start with my mother and wonderful lessons with Stephen De'ak. Once in a while, I would even have lessons with my father, although he wasn't that serious about teaching back then. Of course, Ron and then Nelsova were also very influential.

A.A.   *You spent your summers at Tanglewood and were still in the BSO. What was next for you?*

S.G.   Well, I had eight years in the Boston Symphony, from 1965 to 1973. In Boston I gradually worked my way up to assistant, but something was still missing in me. I wanted to play more. I wanted to do more solo playing and teaching, although I did teach at New England Conservatory while I was with the Boston Symphony. For eight years, I taught there in the college division. In 1973, I auditioned for the Cleveland Orchestra and began my career there as principal. Lorin Maazel was the music director at the time.

A.A.   *Had you been wanting to have a principal cello job?*

S.G.   That was something I had in the back of my mind.

A.A.   *Other than your teachers, did you have any other major influences in your musical life?*

S.G.   I used to attend many concerts of the LA Philharmonic. Back in those days, they would have Saturday matinees in the old Philharmonic Hall downtown Los Angeles. I used to go to concerts pretty regularly and sit in the fourth row, looking right up at my father on the stage there. I remember when I was a boy I heard this fabulous cellist come through and play the Shostakovich Concerto. I remember it was a premiere in the United States, other than when it was played with the Philadelphia Orchestra. Do you know who I'm speaking of?

A.A.   *Rostropovich?*

S.G.   Absolutely. He had just recorded it with Eugene Ormandy and the Philadelphia Orchestra. Here I was in the fourth row looking at this guy up there. All I knew was that the piece was totally unfamiliar to me. After he played, the audience booed the piece. They didn't like it, but now it's a mainstay. That had quite an impact on me. It was at that point when I started to get more interested in going to the Hollywood Bowl concerts and the Pilgrimage Theater concerts out in California. I heard Piatigorsky, Primrose, and Heifetz concerts.

A.A.   *Did you get to watch Piatigorsky teach at all?*

S.G.   No, I didn't. I don't recall him being a prominent teacher back then. He was still concertizing. He and my mother got to know each other quite well. In fact, I have a picture of him at home that he signed for her.

A.A.   *Did you enjoy practicing?*

S.G.   No, not at all.

A.A.   *So what motivated you? Did your parents push you to practice?*

S.G.   Oh yes, we fought over it. We had many, many arguments about it. I would say, "I want to go play baseball" or "I want to take Susie so and so out." We fought over it a lot, but I really am grateful my parents didn't push me too hard. There were no threats. There was a lot of love in our family. They allowed me to be a kid. Some kids are kids longer than others, and I was one of those. It wasn't really until I went to Eastman that I really started to get serious.

A.A.   *Were they happy as two cellists to see their kids become cellists as well?*

S.G.   I think so, but we rarely talked much about it. We would talk more about the orchestras. I was in Cleveland and my dad was in LA. We would talk about the weather. They had no interest in sports, nor did my brother. I was a loner in that regard. We would have very simple discussions. It's a family. I am grateful that they let me be a kid.

A.A.   *When you got the Cleveland Orchestra job, how long after did you start teaching at CIM?*

S.G.   One year later in 1974. I didn't want to do any teaching my first year. They offered me a job at CIM as soon as I got into Cleveland Orchestra. Bill Kirshbaum was president back then. He called me and he said, "Would you please join our faculty?" I told him, "No, I want to take a year off and just concentrate on the orchestra." After a year, I started teaching with maybe four students.

A.A.   *Did you do any teaching when you were in the BSO?*

S.G.   I did some private teaching. In fact, one of my most prominent students out of that class is now the assistant principal of Boston Symphony, Sato Knudsen. He's been there a long time, of course.

A.A.   *How many years did you teach at CIM?*

S.G.   42 years.

A.A.   *How many years were you in the Cleveland Orchestra?*

S.G.   30 years. I was full-time at CIM for the last 12 years. I was teaching 20–22 students. I had the big classes.

A.A.   *How did it feel when you left the orchestra but were still teaching? Did you miss it?*

S.G.   There were certain things I missed. I missed the music, of course, and I missed the people. I didn't miss the tours and the time away from family. My wife, Lisa Wellbaum, was the principal harpist of the Cleveland Orchestra. She retired three years ago. She and I would cry every time we'd have to leave the kids. We did a lot of traveling. We saw the world. We were on the road about ten weeks a year. It was very glamorous in the beginning, but you get tired living out of a suitcase. You travel and play a concert one night and then get up the next morning early to travel again.

The Present

A.A.   *What are some of your secrets for practicing well? Did you consider that an important part of your job as a teacher at CIM?*

S.G.   Absolutely. The first thing I try to help young people with, unless they are really on a great track, is how to practice. It's like trying to learn how to run. You want to be able to walk before you can run. I've seen so often that kids come and they play material that's way over their heads. They have no concept of how to play it technically or musically. It affects the intonation; it affects everything. I teach them how to be methodical by practicing slowly, carefully, and focused. After that, we go to work and polish the music.

A.A.   *Along with that, do you teach scales, thirds, and arpeggios?*

S.G.   Absolutely. I know Richard Aaron and Ron Leonard do too. I know that there are teachers that don't, but I believe it's a process that we all have to go through.

A.A.   *As a performer, do you practice performing? I feel students are often in the practice room stopping and fixing something, but when they have an audience they're not used to actually having to keep going. I'm wondering if that's something that you remind students. Do you make yourself play through nonstop?*

S.G.   Eventually yes. It's important to practice slowly and then gradually work it up. There needs to be a good mix of digesting a piece and then letting yourself feel what it feels like to perform it. Don't gulp in the whole piece in each sitting. In fact, I would generally assign about two pages a week as well as scales, arpeggios, thirds, octaves, and an étude.

A.A.   *For all your years of playing solos with the Cleveland Orchestra, were nerves ever an issue for you? How did you deal with that if they were?*

S.G.   I believe that a person who doesn't get at least a little bit nervous in a performance is going to have the dullest performance you've ever heard. I've heard some magnificent technical players, but someone who comes in and tries to play perfectly all the time doesn't say much. I've been worked up at times, but I can't say it's affected the performance. That's not to say that every performance I had was perfect. There were some imperfections.

A.A.   *Have you had students that have had nerves really get in the way of their playing?*

S.G.   They talk about it a lot. They ask, "How do you feel, Mr. Geber, if I were to take beta blockers?" I say, "I'm not a doctor. I would never recommend anything without consulting a physician. That's not my place." We hear that sometimes members in the orchestra take beta blockers. Maybe they're ordered to do it for blood pressure or heart regulation reasons. That's not my business or your business. How do you feel about it?

A.A.   I've often told students that that nerves can accentuate a bad habit that you might have physically, but if you are prepared, you're able to handle it better.

S.G.   That's the key. Preparation is the greatest relaxer. If you're not prepared or if you have any sense of doubt when you walk out, that's going to add to your nervous anxiety. It gets back to that knowing how to practice. We don't all have the luxury of being able to practice four and five hours a day.

A.A.   *Do you suggest a certain amount of practice for your students?*

S.G.   It depends on their schedule. Some kids have a more rigid schedule than others. I like to suggest you always practice when you're fresh. Don't wait until the very end of the day. Get two hours in the morning. Take a short break between the two hours. Go have a drink or do whatever you want to do. Come back and keep the door closed.

A.A.   *And your phone put away.*

S.G.   And your phone put away, exactly.

A.A.   *If you had to summarize your teaching philosophy, what would it be? And how has your teaching evolved as your philosophy changed over the years?*

S.G.   My teaching has changed through the years because of where I've been more focused musically. When I was younger, the focus was more on the technique, and it got to that point again when I was out of the orchestra. I had more time to really focus in on that.

A.A.   *What do you look for most when you're picking your students?*

S.G.   I frankly look for someone with heart. I look for someone with intelligence and who is wise enough to know they're out of tune. In fact, one of the questions I ask when

I interview a student is "What are the issues you feel you have in your playing that you really would like to go to work on?" I choose the students that can say, "I need to have a more systematic and concise way of playing." I don't want to hear, "I want to learn how to play from my heart." That's a God given thing. We all don't have that. Those of us that do are fortunate. That's what people are listening to. Music has to reach out and touch people.

A.A.   *How do you keep each student sounding like an individual? And not necessarily related, do you give them bowings and fingerings? Are you pretty consistent or do you let them discover their own?*

S.G.   I used to be so regimented in that regard. You take these bowings, you take these fingerings, and that's it. I got away from that. I would demonstrate for them. This is what works for me. You try it. If it doesn't work, then you find a way and show me. It gets them thinking.

A.A.   *Do you try to have them find and keep their own voice?*

S.G.   Absolutely. In fact, I encourage them to sing the phrases. I've been advocating for years for a program that includes one semester of voice lessons so that students could, for example, take a phrase out of the Schumann concerto to a qualified singer. We have a wonderful vocal department here at CIM, and they are behind it 100 percent. It's a matter of trying to work it into the curriculum.

Sometimes my students will come in and play inhibited, and I tell them, "Go to that window. What's it doing out there?" They'll look and say, "Oh, the sun is shining." I say, "What do you mean the sun is shining? Is that the way you want to sound at the cello? Tell me how you really feel about that sunshine. You haven't seen it for three months." You want to get excited and passionate about what you're doing.

A.A.   *What is more important in a potential student: their musicality or their physical approach?*

S.G.   I think that technique is more important. How can you be really musical if you're not set up well and can't play in tune?

A.A.   *What's the hardest thing to teach a student?*

S.G.   How to be consistent. I think it's such an individual thing. Every kid is different. I've had kids that can play anything on cello but have very little projection of personality or sound. I've also had kids that could play with so much passion, but they play out of tune.

A.A.   *How do you work on intonation with students? Do you use drones or tuners?*

S.G.   First of all, I think one of the biggest things that affect intonation is vibrato. Excessive vibrato at the wrong time is uncalled for, especially when it's so wide that you can't tell what pitch they're on. I try to develop different kinds of vibrato. Thinking about the vibrato and what you're creating with it is what really helps the intonation. I tell them to practice scales without vibrato, unless they have a major vibrato problem where they can't vibrate or keep it even. You sometimes have that issue too. If you're playing a piece of repertoire, slow it down and play non-vibrato for a few days to really work on the pitches and then gradually work the vibrato back in.

A.A.   *What do you think about tuners? Do you think they're beneficial?*

S.G.   I personally didn't use them, but I see no harm in it.

A.A. *What are some of the technical exercises and études that you use frequently? Have they changed a lot over the years?*

S.G. I give pretty much what I studied between Rejtő and Leonard.

A.A. *Popper études?*

S.G. Absolutely. If it's a less advanced student I'll go back as far as Merk or Cossmann, although Cossmann is awfully boring. The Popper and Franchomme are lovely. Working up I have students who play Piatti and Paganini caprices. If you're going to play things that advanced, like some of the Popper, Piatti, and Paganini, you're going to have to think about music too.

A.A. *Do you make students play or perform by memory?*

S.G. I think memory is important because if you can memorize it, you really know it. I've done several world premiers with the orchestra. For those I used music, because it was unfamiliar territory.

A.A. *Do you make students perform something by memory in a master class, seminar, or a recital?*

S.G. Yes, but I tell them to use the music when collaborating on a sonata.

A.A. *How important is body movement to you in playing, such as the use of the torso and the back? Is that something you talk about a lot in your teaching?*

S.G. I think it's important that you look for tension right away in somebody when they play. Life is too short for tension. If you're going to be a stick, you're not going to get out what you want. You're not going to be able to communicate what you want. Without being ostentatious, I think body language is important.

A.A. *How do you help a student find the right kind of body movement?*

S.G. Sometimes I will film them and let them see for themselves.

A.A. *They are probably surprised by what they see?*

S.G. Yes. I recommend a mirror to them, but not to get married to it. Don't sit for three hours and practice in front of that mirror, only 20 minutes or so. See how you're doing and then turn the chair and continue your work. Do you like that concept?

A.A. *Very much. I'm a firm believer in trying to let motion start from the torso as in backhand in tennis. I also emphasize that the cello is on an endpin and not firmly planted. It allows us to have this movement. To find that, you need to have freedom in the hips and shoulders.*

S.G. I think that's what helped me, because I used to have tension in my playing. When I went to Eastman, I was pretty tense because I was always trying to be perfect. I remember Joseph Knitzer, a famous violin teacher at Eastman, came to me after a jury said to me, "My boy, relax. Play for me something." He told me to keep breathing when I play.

Ron Leonard is a very relaxed, natural player. He studied with Rose. He was one of Rose's greatest students. I wanted to go to Julliard to study with Rose, but my parents wouldn't let me because they believed I wasn't ready for a big city like New York City. They said, "Don't go there. You'll just get swallowed up. Go to Rochester. You'll still be getting the Rose training." Years later I spoke with Rose. He came through and played *Schelomo* with the Cleveland Orchestra. I spoke with him and he said, "I'm sorry you didn't come to Julliard, but you're still part of my family." That was very nice of him. Leonard Rose is my favorite cellist and always has been. I used to hear him play all the time when he would come out to LA. We would always go and he developed a wonderful friendship with my parents.

I'll tell you another story about Rose. Years later, when I was in the Cleveland Orchestra, about half of our section had some training in the Rose school with either Ron Leonard or Richard Weiss. We decided we would have a party. I had frequent parties at our house, maybe three times a year. Everyone would come, bring their cellos, play through music, and listen to recordings. One of the cellists said, "Rose is very, very sick." The rest of us didn't know about it. I asked him, "How long has he been sick?" He said, "He's been sick now for several months. It's cancer. Let's call him." So we called him. Sure enough, we found him right away on the first or second ring, and he talked one by one to each one of us, all 12 of us. It took probably an hour of conversation to get through everybody.

I was the last one that got on. I picked up the phone and said, "Mr. Rose, this is Stephen Geber." He said, "Stephen, you don't know what it means to hear that a principal takes the time to get his section together. You'll always be grateful that you did that. When I was with the NBC Orchestra, nobody talked to each other." That included his cousin, Fred Miller. They sat together on the first stand but didn't speak. He said, "It's so important that you keep comradery going in your section." I'll never forget those words. Two weeks later, he passed away.

Another person that I got to know and I liked very much, although I was never really enamored with the playing, was Starker. He could play anything. About ten years ago, he wined and dined my wife and I. We even spent some time at his house with him and had a really glorious time. He told me this funny joke that he made up. There were three cellists that died all at the same time. One by one they went up into heaven and went to the gates of St. Peter. St. Peter was there to greet them. He opened the gate for the first cellist and said, "What did you do back on Earth?" The cellist replied, "Well, I was a cellist." St. Peter asks, "With whom did you study?" The cellist responded, "I studied with Leonard Rose." Immediately, St. Peter slammed the gate. The next cellist comes up and St. Peter asks, "Well, what did you do?" The second cellist answers, "Well, I was a cellist, a well-known cellist." Again, St. Peter asks, "Who was your teacher there?" The cellist tells him, "Rostropovich." Immediately the gate slams. St. Peter opens the gate again, and the third cellist steps up. St. Peter says, "Now, what did you do?" He answers, "I was a very well-known cellist." "With whom did you study?" St. Peter asks. He answers, "I studied with János Starker." The gates open, the lights shine, and the trumpets are blaring. He says to the cellist, "Come on in. You've already been through Hell."

A.A. *I haven't heard that. It would have been great to have been able to speak with him as well.*

S.G. He had a great sense of humor. He could be a caustic guy. He could also be very hard on the students, even nasty to them. I remember him in a class when he was chewing out a young lady saying, "You know, dear, they are looking for burger flippers at McDonalds. Maybe you could find a career there." Underneath that, he could be a pussycat. He could be so nice and embracing if he liked you.

A.A. *What is your philosophy on teaching the Bach Suites? Do you teach in relation to the historically informed practice, the movement that's happened over the last generation?*

S.G. I'm very well aware of it. To a degree I support it, but I remember having a long talk with Yo-Yo about this. We live in a modern age. You won't find any two editions alike of the Bach Suites. I always go to Barenreiter. They're unedited, and I think they're the most accurate. That's not to say that you should play them barren of all expression. You're never going to hear two people play them the same either. Even students that are in the same class are not going to play any movement exactly the same way when they're performing. I think we all have to study scores. We have to get familiar with the language as best as we can.

A.A.　*Do you demonstrate often when you teach, and how important do you think that is?*

S.G.　I do, and I think it's very important, although this last year I wasn't doing too much playing because I have a tear in my rotator. I wanted to avoid surgery.

A.A.　*There are three specific pieces I want to ask about that are all arrangements or transcriptions. I am wondering how you feel about them. The first one is the Boccherini B-flat Concerto arranged by Grützmacher, the second one is the Fitzenhagen's version of the Tchaikovsky Rococo Variations, and the third is the Feuermann edition of the Chopin Polonaise. Some teachers really feel strongly about playing the original and others have a lot of flexibility.*

S.G.　It's not only teachers. Do you see, especially in the big competitions, these kids want to know which edition of the Haydn Concerto, which edition of Dvořák, or which edition of Bach to play? I've heard of instances where kids go off and they do very well, but they don't advance because the jury didn't like the edition they were playing from.

A.A.　*Do you teach the Grützmacher-Boccherini B-flat?*

S.G.　To be honest with you, yes. I do. That is the way I learned the piece.

A.A.　*I think it's a good piece. It's not Boccherini, but it's still a really good piece for students to learn.*

S.G.　That was the only thing that was available when I was growing up.

A.A.　*What about the Rococo? Have you taught the original?*

S.G.　No. I use the old International Rose edition. I don't know how far it will get you if you are going to play a competition.

A.A.　*How do you approach the Chopin Polonaise?*

S.G.　I used, again, the International edition. When I was studying with De'ak, because he worked with Feuermann as well as Casals, I took a copy of that and pasted in the Feuermann markings.

The Future

A.A.　*Where do you see the future of classical music going in the next generation, and has technology positively or negatively affected classical music?*

S.G.　I think that both in chamber music and orchestral playing that programming is changing. It's becoming more geared to the younger generation without forgetting the older generation. You have to change with the times.

A.A.　*How is it changing?*

S.G.　There's a balanced program, usually including a piece that's brand new and a standard piece. I think that there's not enough emphasis on contemporary music still.

A.A.　*You've experienced this for so many years. Orchestras seem like they try to put in the one unfamiliar piece, but the audience, from what I read, generally comes to hear those 12 composers that are familiar. In your experience in both Cleveland and Boston, do you think the new music pieces were working for audiences?*

S.G. I think they are. I think it depends on the style of the piece. There have been some flops. Audiences that have come in and booed. I think overall it depends on who's up there. Pierre Boulez was someone who really knew how to convince an audience. He could take a piece that no one would know and he knew how to rehearse it. And he knew how to bring the orchestra together to enjoy the work. He was the consonant modern-day conductor when it came to contemporary music. He knew exactly what he wanted, how he wanted it, and what the composer wanted.

A.A. *Do you think that the internet and technology have been good for audiences? How much do we need as musicians to accommodate for that?*

S.G. Well, you and I grew up with records, and that's what we relied on. Today people go to the internet for everything from paying their bills to listening to music. People are getting everything off the internet.

A.A. *Do you think that's been good for classical music or orchestras?*

S.G. Business-wise, no. I don't. You can buy really cheap sheet music off the internet. You can even get it free. If you want to look up Beethoven's fifth symphony, you don't need to go to Ovation Press and pay for one part. You can go print parts that are unedited. That's the disadvantage, but you get nice, clean parts that you can get off the internet for nothing.

A.A. *I worry that people are less inclined to go out and hear concerts live because they can hear almost anything from the comfort of their home or phone.*

S.G. I agree with that, but there's nothing that replaces the live performance. The thing that scares me more about attendance at live performances is the cost. It's expensive. Now the government wants to cut back the NEA.

A.A. *And music education for kids.*

S.G. That's another thing. The arts, to me, are not a privilege. They're a necessity of life.

A.A. *Have you seen the level of cello playing change over the years?*

S.G. My goodness, yes. Haven't you? The thing that I'm concerned about is that many of the kids are not getting the proper training in the very thing that's going to be their bread and butter. Let's face it. Where are the jobs going to be when you graduate from a conservatory or from a university? Are you going to be a soloist? Are you going to be a first class chamber player? Maybe. That's a tough life. I know from my brother. Are you going to be an orchestra player? That's where the jobs are. But how many schools have an orchestra repertoire class? How many schools have teachers in them who have had some experience they can offer that to a student? I get called all over the country to teach master classes, even now that I retired. I say, "Let me come and do an orchestra repertoire class. You don't need me for a solo class. A repertoire class is what they really need."

A.A. *Do you think there are enough jobs for cellists?*

S.G. I don't. It worries me. I see kids sit around for four or five years after school. It's not just my students. It's throughout this whole system, in all instruments. They're waiting for an opportunity. Then, I tell them this story. Do you know Elaine Douvas? She's the principal oboist at the Met. She auditioned many times before she got her first job, which was the Met. In other words, if you keep pursuing, if you keep trying, if you get the right kind of instruction, then it's going to happen.

A.A.   *Do you feel like guiding the student after they're done studying with you is an important part of your job?*

S.G.   Yes. I do. I feel that mentoring is a very important part of it. I get very attached to the kids. I really do. They come into our house. They meet my family and we keep our relationship alive. That is very important to me.

Close to the Heart

A.A.   *If you hadn't been a musician, what would you have loved to have done with your life?*

S.G.   I had a little bit of interest in medicine. I did miserably at it. I thought about even being a pilot at one point too. I thought about taking flying lessons while I was in the Boston Symphony. I used to fly pretty regularly with a fellow, William Stokking, who was in the orchestra and had a pilot's license. We shared a stand together for about two years in the Boston Symphony.

A.A.   *What are some of the most memorable concerts you've ever been involved with as a musician?*

S.G.   I'll never forget when Danny Kaye, who used to go around and do special pension fund concerts for orchestras, came to Cleveland. He came and he conducted and he was doing a stint with the concertmaster, Daniel Majeske, and me. We were to hold him up, me on the cello side and the concertmaster on the other side. He wanted to be the elderly gentleman conductor who had to excuse himself for personal reasons. We had to lift him off the stage, and I'm holding my cello and his arm. I lost it. I was crying. It was so funny the way he was doing it. The whole audience wasn't laughing at him. They were laughing at me. We got through it. The following week he went out to Los Angeles to conduct at the Hollywood Bowl and my father was in the orchestra. Danny Kaye said, "Excuse me. Is there an Ed Geber here?" My father says, "Yeah! Yeah, that's me." He responded, "I wanted to tell you I just came from Cleveland, and I want you to know I met your son and he's disgraced the Geber name." It was very funny.

Another memorable concert experience was when Rostropovich came and played Haydn with us. I was thrilled. He rehearsed with Pooks. Do you know who Pooks was? His dog. This little dog would come out with him and be right at the edge of the podium while he was rehearsing for the performance.

I think one of the biggest thrills I had personally was when I played *Don Quixote*, Brahms' Double, the world premier of the Tippett Triple, and a piece by Moravitz that was written for me. And Sam Adler wrote a concerto for me. I did all this at Carnegie Hall with the Cleveland Orchestra.

A.A.   *Did you ever have to deal with a period of doubt about being a musician?*

S.G.   I like the idea of diversity. I mixed my career with the orchestra, teaching, solo opportunities, and chamber music. I was with a quartet in the Boston Symphony for eight years, and I moved into Cleveland then for 26 years. We had a quartet amongst the principals before Preucil came. It was really wonderful to have that diversity. That's what kept me going. I didn't ever think about changing careers.

A.A.   *What are you most proud of in your life?*

S.G.   My family. Without a doubt.

A.A.   *Is there anything still on your musical bucket list, such as a piece you want to play?*

S.G.   I think I would like to continue working with kids to help them with the orchestra repertoire. I want to get more involved with that, because I see a need for that all over the country.

A.A.   *If you had to pick three desert island pieces of music, what would they be?*

S.G.   You know who asked me this question once was Dohnányi.

A.A.   *Oh, really?*

S.G.   Yeah, and I was very guarded. I think I would probably go back and revisit the Prokofiev Concertante. I never really got in depth into that piece. I only got to the point of working it technically. I think that's a powerful work. I'd only be doing it for myself. My favorite piece is the *Schelomo*. I recorded that with Cleveland. If I could only play one piece on cello, it would be that one.

A.A.   What about non-cello pieces?

S.G.   How about Billy Joel's "Piano Man"? I like all genres of music. I really do.

6

Bonnie Hampton

Cellist Bonnie Hampton leads an active music life as a chamber musician, soloist, and teacher. A founding member of the Naumburg Award-winning Francesco Trio, she has also performed as the Hampton-Schwartz Duo with her late husband, pianist Nathan Schwartz. Her solo debut with the San Francisco Symphony Orchestra was followed by appearances with orchestras nationally performing the entire standard repertoire and many of the 20th century cello concertos.

Ms. Hampton's chamber music guest appearances have included performances with the Juilliard, Guarneri, Cleveland, Mendelssohn, Alexander, Budapest, and Griller String Quartets, and concert tours have taken her to Europe and Asia. She has performed in halls throughout the United States, including Davies and the Opera House in San Francisco, Alice Tully, the Library of Congress, the Kennedy Center, Jordan Hall, and many chamber music venues throughout the world.

A student of Pablo Casals, she participated for many years in the Casals and Marlboro festivals. She has performed at many festivals including Tanglewood, Ravinia, Santa Fe, Kneisel Hall, and Yellow Barn. Her early studies were with Margaret Rowell, the Griller String Quartet, and Zara Nelsova.

Her Francesco Trio Residencies have included Stanford University and the San Francisco Conservatory of Music, where she taught for 30 years. Ms. Hampton was awarded an "Excellence in Teaching Award" from SFCM and Indiana University and was a member of the Juilliard School's Cello and Chamber Music faculty from 2003 to 2012. In 2018, she was awarded an Honorary Doctorate Degree from the San Francisco Conservatory of Music.

The Past

A.A.   Let's start from the beginning. Where were you born and raised, and how did you first become exposed to the cello? Was it a family of musicians?

B.H.   I was born and raised here in Berkeley, California.

A.A.   How did you get started on the cello?

B.H.   Well, the cello wasn't the first thing. When I was four I happened to notice there was a piano in the house. I started fooling around with it, and the next thing I knew I was having lessons. The first four years or so, I studied the piano.

My mother was an amateur violinist and so I remember, even before I went to school, listening to informal quartet sessions in the house. When I was about eight, I wanted to play with some other people. I did feel that the piano was lonely, but I loved it. I loved playing, and somehow the cello evolved and I started with Margaret Rowell. She was such a compelling personality, but also such a great teacher, that I became very attached to the cello and continued both instruments until I was about 10; and then the cello just took over.

I think we were pretty lucky here in Berkeley at that time because there was a lot of music in the schools, and so right away I was playing in ensembles in elementary school. There was an elementary school orchestra and the same thing in junior high school, and they had music classes with chorus in those days. All those things have been cut out so much now.

A.A.   Was it hard to start with Margaret Rowell right away? I mean, was she in the habit of taking beginners?

B.H.   She had every age. Absolutely. She was wonderful for a beginner because it meant you got really good habits right from the beginning.

She had so much imagination that she made it fun. You found out about the bear hug right away, so you were embracing the cello and getting connected with the instrument. She was willing to do some crazy things, but you were just involved. It was hands-on, she was very physical in her teaching. Probably she wouldn't be able to get away with quite as much without permission now, because she just would grab your arm and shake it if it was getting tight and have you do all kinds of things that really kept you very free. I feel very lucky.

Also, the environment was terrific because there were other kids my own age, especially as a teenager. Of course, at first I was younger than a lot of them, but she had a lot of students. There were monthly workshops, and there were always quite a few cellists there. As a young kid I remember being very impressed with these college-age students.

A.A.   Did you have siblings too?

B.H.   Yes, I had an older brother and sister, quite a bit older than I, and my sister played the violin pretty much up through high school. With my brother, the trumpet only lasted into junior high school.

There was also the Young People's Symphony, and it was actually at that point the only youth orchestra here in the Bay Area. Now there are probably six or seven or eight. The whole area was just a beehive of musical activity. This was a very good youth orchestra which I was involved in, and I played my first concerto when I was about 13.

A.A.   *Was it around this time that you knew you wanted to be a cellist for the rest of your life, or did that happen later?*

B.H.   Well, I think that happened really early. I loved it and I had fun with it. I think probably some of the early experiences that I had drew me to the cello, but I hadn't really thought consciously about doing it with the rest of my life. It somehow always had to be a part of my life—I knew that. But I remember, I was in junior high school, I think, and I was chosen to go up to Sacramento with a youth orchestra, assembled from all over California or all over the west, with a very dynamic conductor—Stanley Chapman, I think. He was English, very dynamic, and we played the Brahms First Symphony.

Having that musical experience was just overwhelming, and about the same time, when I was about 12 or 13, I went to the national music camp at Interlochen in Michigan. That also was a great experience because I got to play all those symphonies in the high school orchestra even when I was in junior high school intermediate camp. I knew after that, that that's just what I was going to do. I was definitely bitten by the bug, let's say.

Then soon after that, when I was still a teenager, the Griller Quartet came here. They were an English quartet in residence at the University of California and also active at the San Francisco Conservatory, and so I got involved in chamber music with them. Before that, I can remember hearing my first string quartet. It was the London String Quartet, and I still remember the visit. I can visualize it. William Primrose was the violist, and I thought he was absolutely the greatest. Warwick Evans was the cellist, and John Pennington was the first violinist. This little guy was the second violinist and Pennington was very big and had a big personality, and I always felt sorry for the second violinist.

After that, so many quartets came. In those days the university concert series couldn't afford the big organizations or touring orchestras, but they could afford chamber music; so there were a lot of quartets that came every year. Then the Griller Quartet had their series of about six concerts a year. It was a very, very rich time. I also started getting invited to chamber music evenings, reading. You know the amateur scene, with older people and adults and that sort of thing. I don't know how good my sight-reading was, but it improved pretty quickly. I got to play a lot, and this led to quite a few concerts and concerto opportunities in those early days.

A.A.   *Do you remember back then if you enjoyed practicing, or was it something you had to make yourself do?*

B.H.   Oh well, it was just part of what I did. It's very funny because somebody else told me once that if you're going to be serious about the cello and really want a professional life, you have to work very, very hard. The instrument is a very hard task master, and you really have to put in your time, no matter what your natural ability is. You have to really work; and then I thought about it afterward and I said, "You know, that's not true. I've never worked hard in my life." What I mean by that—I always wanted to do it.

A.A.   *It didn't feel like work.*

B.H.   I guess I was a normal kid and I loved to run around with my dog and ride on my bicycle. I loved to ride my horse and all kinds of things like that; but once I was about

12, the cello really took over. It was always what I wanted to do. I don't know how disciplined I was, however. The way Margaret was, she'd assign me things—études—like Klengel, and she said, "You have to eat your vegetables." But in the lessons we'd be working on other repertoire, so she wasn't a great one with études.

I remember the teacher at Interlochen, Louis Potter. He was very good. He liked Merk études. We had to produce one every week. I remember one summer, though, as a teenager, I decided I should learn the Popper études. So I just worked on all of them. I worked on all of them that summer.

After those first two years at Interlochen, I didn't go to various camps. We did have chamber music courses here with the Alma Trio when I was about 14 or 15. I participated in a couple of those where I got to play, and they also had their series of concerts, which were great, and the Griller Quartet also had some chamber music courses in the summer.

A.A.   *Do you feel like Margaret gave you just the foundation that you needed?*

B.H.   Yes, I had to do a lot of other work, and I studied with Zara (Nelsova) when I was about 16 or 17, and she demanded études every week and Grützmacher Book Two, nice difficult études, which I like very much.

A.A.   *Did you study with Zara here in the Bay Area?*

B.H.   Yes, she had come from Toronto to teach at San Francisco State College. She had a sister here, and so she was hired one semester per year for several years. She was an incredible cellist. I would go to her sister's house, which is just a couple of blocks from home actually, and she would play at me. That was what those lessons were about. I would play some things, but there was a great deal of her playing for me—but just being around that kind of playing had an enormous impact. There's no way that it wasn't going to have an impact. Every lesson consisted of a Bach Suite, an étude, and a concerto. I remember one time, I had to repeat Grützmacher number 17 to the following week, and that was just a terrible thing.

A.A.   *Were you still studying with Margaret then or had you moved onto another teacher?*

B.H.   I don't know that I moved on, because Margaret had me playing for all kinds of people. I remember having a couple of lessons with Gábor Rejtő—when he first came in the early 40s, she opened a lot of doors for him, and so I played for quite a few people. I would say I studied with her until I was about 15 or so.

After that, all her life, I would go up and play for her, but not in a directed way. Very often she would just make a comment that was absolutely to the point. She had that sense of what was the important issue that made a lot of other things come into focus around it. She was a remarkable teacher and a remarkable human being.

I was very lucky, because she had me start teaching when I was about 16. She arranged for me to teach a couple of young boys who were 10 or 11. The parents had wanted her to teach them, but they weren't that serious and she was busy with students who were very committed. That was my very first experience with teaching.

When I was about 10, there was another interesting situation. She had me practice with an 80-year-old man who had wanted lessons—a very sweet Englishman who sort of played the cello not very, well, I don't know exactly what to say. I would practice with him every week for an hour, and I got a dollar and a chocolate bar, which was pretty good for a 10-year-old. It suited me just fine. Yes, that was very rewarding.

I started teaching at the San Francisco Conservatory in the pre-college when I was about 18, and I had beginners and various age groups, and the adults actually were the hardest. I even had a Nobel Prize winner physicist who was really tough to teach, because he was tone deaf and very tense. His family had said he needed to relax, as he was very tight, and that was tough. He also had no time to practice.

A.A.   *Did you start school at 18? What happened?*

B.H.   I was homeschooled the rest of my high school years and then started at the University of California, but not as a regular student. I had no wish for a regular degree. It was a very different era. I took courses, especially music courses as well at the San Francisco Conservatory, but I didn't want to do the full curriculum because I was spending so much time with music. Really my life was very, very full of music. What's interesting now is to see so many kids around the pre-college at Juilliard and other schools who are totally homeschooled. It was more unusual back then.

A.A.   *When did you first play for Pablo Casals?*

B.H.   I first played for him when I was 16. I went to the Casals Festival, and I was urged to play for him. I hadn't necessarily planned to play for him, but one of his friends urged me to do it and set it up. I went to a lot of rehearsals before the festival and the festival itself, and then I stayed on for a lot of recording sessions afterward. Then at the end I played for him, and he said he would take me as a student but felt I was too young to come to Prades at that time.

A.A.   *You were 16 at that time?*

B.H.   Yes, I was 15 that year and just turned 16 at the end of that summer, and Casals thought that I should come back in a couple of years. It was actually four years before I got back. After that he moved to Puerto Rico, and I went down there for more lessons; but then he came to give classes here in California. A lot of those tapes still exist from those classes.

The recordings of those classes are very good because when some of the players didn't play as well—and unfortunately, there were some that shouldn't have been there—he would play a lot more. He was in his 80s already and, all through the lessons that I had with him, he was still playing marvelously—really marvelously. Everything! He had a remarkable level of playing. You just had an insight into what it must have been like when he was in his prime. It was a whole other world.

A.A.   *Did you go and live there and study with him for a time?*

B.H.   Yes, for about eight months. The first time I was in Prades and then in Puerto Rico. I went for about four months the first time, and then after that I was playing in the Festival every year in San Juan. So I often would stay for some lessons after the Festival. It was a magical time for sure.

A.A.   *Did you realize at the time how magical this time in your life was?*

B.H.   Of course. There was no question. You just knew that this is how music had to be. It was an incredible orchestra, because there were a lot of first-chair wind players from the New York Philharmonic or Philadelphia; and in terms of the string players, you had a lot of concert masters, principal players, and quartet players. It was an amazing orchestra. They were there because they wanted to be there, so they really gave and would go with Casals wherever he went with the music. Over the festival years, we played with all of the big conductors. It was an incredible experience that way, but also in the positive attitude.

There were always, in his playing and in lessons, these ah-ha moments. You weren't expecting them necessarily, but all of a sudden you have that moment when something happens. All of a sudden you realize, that's the way it has to be.

I remember one time playing with many of these guys who had played with Toscanini, so they'd been under the gun. Frank Miller was the first cellist with the festival for quite a few years there, and he had been Toscanini's first cellist. After that Leslie Parnas, who had just won the Tchaikovsky competition, and I were also up there in the first stand playing. It was very exciting!

One time we were playing Schumann's Fourth Symphony, and Casals's rehearsing was very, very detailed. He would sing, gesture, and put it together like chamber music. His music-making was always very flowing and full of motion. There was nothing static about it. It was always very alive, with nothing staying still or being flat. It was all ebbs and flows and motion. He worked for the first hour in a very, very detailed way over nuances and sound, and then he started letting us play on through the movement. By that time, everybody was so sensitized that it was remarkable. It was just so beautiful and so good because these are terrific players; and at the end, the whole orchestra just stood up, because it had been such an experience for all of us. These were musicians who had been around playing a great deal, and yet it was that feeling that you played it for the first time. It was a special, special experience for all of us.

A.A.   *Did you feel at that time you already had a sound technical base?*

B.H.   Oh yes. If you study with Casals, everything is by memory because he taught so directly. You didn't have time to have any music or look at it or put any marks in. You went home and put your marks in to remember things, but at the lesson it was just very, very direct and a very intense interaction.

It was curious. I think it was because people had asked for his fingerings and bowings, so he was very detailed in that way although he would not always play things the same way. For instance, I asked him if he had ever thought about making an edition for the Bach Suites, especially because they were so special to him. He said no—that if he did that, it would be carved in cement and the music would go dead. He would say, "Play with character. Say something, even if tomorrow you say it differently."

I remember with the D-Minor Suite, he played the Prelude for me, and I had to get everything he had done from the beginning by watching. I had to just take it all in and then play it back to show him that I understood. Then I went home and wrote it down. We students shared with each other. But then we'd go to a lesson all prepared, and he would sometimes change the details. His feeling, as I understood it—he didn't talk about these things typically—he wanted one to understand the harmonic and contrapuntal phrasing. Whether you take this up or down bow, that was not as important. He had changed some details since the time of the recordings; where you can tell how he's bowing things and which were based on some of the older nineteenth-century editions, which had many more slurs. Now with more Urtext editions, there are many more separate bows, and he was taking many more separate bows at the time I was studying with him. The articulation was enormously important to him.

Absolutely you had to have the basic repertoire you studied with him memorized. I practiced seven or eight hours and day. In Prades, it was so cold that it took half an hour to get warmed up. If you dared to stop, you'd have to do it all over again, so you just kept playing. There was a lot of work that went into preparing things, because you needed to know everything you took to a lesson very well.

A.A.   *I remember you telling me a story when you were in Iowa that you once played the Bach Fifth Suite Prelude for him, and he had had maybe a bad morning or something, but he said something like, "Thank you for that." Am I remembering that correctly?*

B.H.   The lessons had a lot of interaction and were very intense in a great way. We were playing at each other, so to speak, and it was wonderful. It was very inspirational and you very much got his feeling for the character of things. At the end, he had this really beautiful smile on his face and said, "Thank you. I feel better." Yes, that was real Casals, absolutely wonderful.

A.A.   *Let's talk about making the transition from a student to a professional. You don't have a degree from any university, right?*

B.H.   No, I'm uneducated, if you want.

A.A.   *You are hardly uneducated!*

B.H.   Well, the Griller Quartet said if you want to be a musician, go be a musician. They didn't urge getting a degree, and that suited me just fine. It would have been different if I had gone to a school; but I'm not sorry that I didn't, because in my life I was constantly learning. Sidney Griller told me, "If you can read, you can find out an awful lot." I always read an enormous amount, and I still do. I'm curious about things.

I've always poked around in libraries, music libraries, book stores, and music stores where you could rummage through music. In that way, I've acquired a certain amount of knowledge. It's a funny thing—I notice that some people, once they've gone through school, don't go on searching out so much.

I'm kind of surprised and a little bit upset that some of my students or some other people aren't more curious about things. I've always been enormously curious. If I track onto something, I want to find out everything about it. I remember the early days going to libraries and music libraries in the universities and colleges and just listening and finding out about everything I could, because I get on a track and trace it down like a detective, one thing to another.

I've had the fun of taking in a lot, and I want to continue to do that because it's so interesting. It's endless.

So turning professional just evolved. I had to join the union when I was 17 so that I could pay Leon Kirchner's trio with him. It was the first performance in San Francisco. He had just written the trio, and it was quite a wild experience because we were playing from manuscript and he didn't play at all what was in the manuscript—so we chased him around the performance. I'd been playing a lot of contemporary music around here already in those years, as well as playing recitals and concertos.

Around that time and also into my 20s, I was enormously busy. I think that was around the first time I soloed with the San Francisco Symphony. I was probably in my early 20s, but I'd played already with some smaller orchestras before.

A.A.   *You were never hired full time to play in one orchestra?*

B.H.   No, just the Casals Festival Orchestra. I was given some offers in that way, but I even turned down a recital in Sacramento when I was 17. It was at the museum, where they had a very nice series. I wrote back as only a 17-year-old can. I said, "Oh, I only play chamber music." I wish they'd offer it to me now, but oh well. I had an opportunity to play with a violinist named David Abel. We are about the same age, and he had his early debut when he was about 13. He played with the San Francisco Symphony on one of the youth concerts, and then he did the Columbia Artists thing: traveling around, playing community concerts, and sometimes touring with an orchestra.

Then at one point he was back here looking around to see who was the most active cellist, and I guess he decided I was. He wanted to play the Brahms Double Concerto, and we had several dates to do it. I worked very hard on that because it is one of the great works for cello. I'd started practicing the Dvořák concerto when I was about 15, and I fell in love with that piece as well. I can't imagine how it sounded, but still—the biggies, you want to get a crack at them. Well, Brahms was a whole other thing, one of the big mountains, and you get your playing up to such a level for it. Besides, it's such a wonderful work that it's worth the effort.

I feel that I got my playing up to a different stage during that time. I don't know if I want to say that that was the first time, but as far as playing in a way that could hold up anywhere, I think that was one of the first times. Otherwise, often I was a talented young person who was doing their thing—but this was something that would hold up.

I played with the San Francisco Symphony around that same time, as well as the Oakland Symphony. Both of those were supposed to be debuts, let's call it. And playing the Brahms Double with David led to the forming of our piano trio, because we read the Brahms through with (pianist) Nathan Schwartz, whom I had played with at the University of California, Berkeley.

The Griller Quartet urged me to learn by playing. They maintained that if you played a performance ten times, then you might know it. I was playing for University noon concerts—my own repertoire—sonatas, but also a lot of chamber music.

I also played a lot at these dives in San Francisco. It probably wasn't legal because I was under 18, but we played so many times there. A lot of sonatas, trios, or piano quartets. I was playing a lot, and I find that I'm glad of that experience of playing in all kinds of situations.

I'm very lucky, because at that point there were a lot of opportunities here that I would not have had in some other metropolitan areas. I probably wouldn't have had as much opportunity if I'd been in a regular school or conservatory.

A.A. *I was just going to say, these days so many performance majors don't get to perform nearly enough.*

B.H. Right, and what really disturbs me is that they often don't really take advantage of situations that come their way, because they don't understand that concerts aren't easy to get once you're out of school. They don't understand that you learn to play by doing it, and you jolly well better get yourself ready. This area became known as a very cello-friendly place, and so many young cellists moved out here. They thought this would be a good place to start, and it still is.

It's very different today than when I was growing up; but just the same, if you put in the effort, you can create a lot and have the opportunity to do a lot. Some of these young professionals who come play for me are pretty busy doing a lot of things.

A.A. *What was your first real professional full-time job?*

B.H.   During my early 20s, I was teaching at Mills College, which was part-time. Everything was part-time. I was playing in a contemporary group—well, we played Brahms and Beethoven—but we played a lot of contemporary music. I also had a private studio. I was teaching over at Dominican College, then Stanford found out I was doing okay at Mills College, and so they asked me to come down to Stanford to teach as well.

Joseph Schuster had been teaching there and had a lot of very good students, but he left and the director asked me to come and teach. So here are all these students that had come to study with him but got me instead, and I was maybe a couple of years older than the students. It was an interesting time at both schools, because you would get students at such different musical stages. The serious ones were never a problem. We just got down to work. It was only the ones that weren't so serious—only a couple, maybe more at Mills, who tested me a little bit. Fortunately, I'd been teaching long enough that I felt I was able to hold my own.

I was playing a lot of contemporary music in all kinds of groups at that time. The Mills Chamber Players was basically a piano trio plus clarinet, so we played the first performances on the West Coast of Messiaen's *Quartet for the End of Time* and a great deal of other contemporary music. Other players would join us to expand the group, which developed into one of the Rockefeller groups with about 12 players and did many things with that.

There weren't really and full-time performance jobs in chamber music except the Griller Quartet. But that was how it was—they didn't have to make full-time jobs, because there were enough musicians in the area that they could hire everybody by the hour, which was much cheaper. During this time period, the Francesco Trio also developed. After several years of playing concerts mostly on the West Coast, the Francesco Trio—my trio with David Abel and Nathan Schwartz—was invited to come to Grinnell, Iowa, to be the trio in residence. We'd been together for about four years at that point, and they offered us a real job. They had to, otherwise we would not have gone! We had already been in residence at Stanford, but part-time. They were horrified that we could leave the great Stanford University to go to Grinnell, Iowa.

It was a real job with health benefits and retirement; and now, at this point in my life, let me tell you, I'm very happy. In about three years, Stanford got us back by making us a more full-time job.

A.A.   *So you were at Grinnell for three years?*

B.H.   Yes, and it was very good. I'm really grateful that we did it. We had gone on a tour earlier, to Alaska and British Columbia; later on, we never could've gotten away for five weeks, but that was the second year of the trio. We had about 20 evening concerts and about 40 or 50 school concerts.

The tour helped to consolidate our playing as a young group, and then at Grinnell, two-thirds of our contract was playing concerts, which was extraordinary. It's wonderful for a young group because it means you're learning repertoire by putting on that many concerts. It was a really great time. I don't know if we've been treated so well any place as we were at Grinnell, but we still came back to Stanford where only one-third of our job was playing concerts.

It was right after Grinnell that I also started teaching at the San Francisco Conservatory. I was teaching about 30 hours a week, combined cello and chamber music. Plus, we were playing about 70 concerts a year. We were pretty busy!

It's just what you did. It was good. I taught some chamber music at Cal, because I had that early association and I was grateful for what I had gotten there. A lot of the best players were in computer science or in biology, but I felt that I could help them open the door on chamber music.

Cello teaching had always been interesting and important to me. I've always been very curious about so many of the editions of the Bach Suites, because I'm curious about what other people have done. I've been very curious about any books that have been written about cello teaching and playing. I have found that violinists are much more organized about their pedagogy.

The Present

A.A.   *If you had to summarize your teaching philosophy, what would it be? And how has that changed over the years?*

B.H.   Well, I was much more sure of myself earlier, in the sense that I was willing to be very strong. Maybe it was because I was younger and I felt I had to prove myself, I don't know. For a lot of years, when I was teaching cello or coaching chamber music, I knew I was rehearsing because it's something you learn on the job. About 20 years later, I was wondering, "Am I still rehearsing?"

But seriously, teaching is communicating. Teaching is somehow finding out how that other person is going to learn in the best way. Everybody's somewhat different. In other words, I definitely do not have a method that I just put on a person. That can be quite successful at times because some people that do have a method can turn out very good "products."

I do have a lot of what you might call method ideas. I have a lot of things that I believe in, but the skill, the craft has to be bound up with the musical intentions. The two have to be an organic whole, and they all have to balance each other. In other words, even from a first lesson, one is trying to find out how you do this, how you do that, how you hold the bow, what the strings are, and so forth. All those things are important; but right away, one wants to be developing those basic musical qualities, the fact of an ear, of a true ear, because if you aren't hearing the pitches, if you aren't somehow becoming very attuned to the idea of listening, that's a problem because that's so basic.

A sense of rhythm is basic. That's just musical. As far as cello is concerned, sound is basic. To get a beautiful sound, your body has to be free. I don't think you can get a beautiful sound if you're stiff or tight. You see that with kids. When they go out, they're playing ball, they're playing around, they run around, they use their bodies totally naturally. Then they get with an instrument and they're being shown, "You do this, and you do that," and these poor little kids are all stiff and tight trying to think of all the right things.

With a kid, especially, you have to help them experience things and find out how they're going to learn and use a lot of analogies. It always amazes me that anyone learns how to play the cello. I mean, it's kind of a miracle. It's a human connection. I think it's helping a person learn, and I hope I can guide them. I can give them information.

As students move on through their experiences, the connection, the purpose of the skill is very important. You have the notes, and there's no mystery about all the basic skills of playing, but it's taking that into the musical realm, and hopefully the musical realm is happening right from the beginning of study. That's what I feel is the most important thing about playing an instrument: having that sense of what one's doing and why one's doing it.

A.A. *Over the years, as you were hearing all these auditions at the San Francisco Conservatory or Juilliard, did you tend to look for students that were more gifted physically on the instrument or students that had more to say musically?*

B.H. It's a hard question, especially in a place like Juilliard, which is so over-applied. There'd be 180 applicants and 100 that we would actually hear, for perhaps 20 slots. So it's very rough. We have enough good conservatories, music schools, and music departments with good teachers. And some of the kids, even at Juilliard, I felt would have been better off and happier at a college or university where there's a good music department, with a good teacher that they wanted to study with. But the thing is, the audition process is like a concert tour, and they try everywhere, which they should. They have to, and they'll get in if they have the ability. A basic musical talent needs to have appeared by that time.

The person's habits are important: whether one's going to have to do a lot of repair work, or whether one can just move on into the music. And that varies from school to school. It is hard, but it's whether you feel there's a strong musical impulse. The skill has to be there, but if the skill is there without a musical impulse, then something is missing.

I remember finding my musical impulse when I was about 14 or 15, just about the time you start waking up emotionally as a person. It's really important that one's musical instincts are nurtured at that time, that they're encouraged from one's cello teacher and connected with the instrument. Not just how you play the instrument—because I've heard some students that have had that, but their teacher would teach musical expression through the vibrato or various other things, rather than asking, what is the character of this work? What are you trying to express? In other words, it was always approached through the instrumental technique, per se. It's okay for it to be both, but if the musical impulse isn't nurtured, it will be more difficult later. I've heard and coached some kids who couldn't talk in more general terms of exploring character, exploring musical things.

In other words, their imaginations had not been developed, where they had an idea and then wanted to try to find out how to do it technically; but if you asked them to use a little more vibrato there or do something specific, then they could do that. They hadn't connected it with the purpose. And if we don't have the purpose for why we're doing something—Why we are playing these notes?—then it's only part of the picture. It's so much fun with the kids because they're doing many things for the first time. It's a sort of discovery and they're so excited about it. Somehow when they get into college, they're not so excited anymore, or it's just not cool to show it.

A.A.   *Do you make an effort to have your students sound like individuals when you're teaching?*

B.H.   Yes, it's really important to find your own voice. And listening is one of the biggest elements; and it's not so obvious because we're so "eye" oriented in our education. We're very left-brained in our basic education. And so the listening process and really hearing how one is sounding is not always right up in front.

I was very lucky with Margaret in that her students all had a beautiful sound because she got our bodies working very freely—we were aware of the beauty of that. She would say, "All right, now play a blue note. Now play a red note." That got your imagination going about the different qualities and different sounds and, of course, playing different music, which really demands so many different qualities and tonal colors.

You want a young player to really listen and allow their imagination to develop. I talk about, "what kind of sound can you imagine that could be?" Even if they can't do it yet. If one can start their imagination going on how you really want it to sound and then we talk about the skills involved, it gets the student to think about all the variety of bow use. We think through our left hands so much because we have to play the notes through the left hand. But it's really the bow that's making the sound, and it's really how we use our bow and think through the bow that makes the music. Thinking of music through the bow is such a crucial thing for sound. But it's also getting that personal sound. What's interesting is that every great player really has their own sound. They really do.

These days I find it harder to recognize an individual player. With the old guys, you hear them and you know who they are. But these days, there's so much playing that gets developed for the big halls only. Players are taught to play down in the bridge and really power out the sound, so the instruments don't have the chance to find all those different resonances and all those different colors with the bow.

A student's sound can evolve well, and people are really happy when they start finding that because it's theirs. Nobody can take that away from them. It's theirs, and it's so important.

A.A.   *Do you teach scales and all that goes with them?*

B.H.   Oh, yes. I believe in scales. Absolutely no matter what. Other technical things too, but scales are so important. But musical scales, in other words, with all the nuance and color. Over the years, I've put together an awful lot of material that I've completely plagiarized from other wonderful cellists. There are so many gems. There's Klengel, the old formal scale patterns of two octaves and then 12-12-123, or even before that the Grützmacher, just 12-12-12 all the way. Then there's the Magg system, the Matz system, and of course Feuillard. There's Galamian and what Jensen did with his cello method.

You have to get a basic, solid pattern, which you do for everything. But then later, when you come across a scale-like passage in music, it is hardly ever played the same way that you practice scales. I mean look at Variation 4 of Tchaikovsky's Rococo Variations. It's so much better going up, across, up, across on the four-octave scales. But usually when we practice scales, we go across to the A string and then all the way up. Of course, Magg does it going up the D string a bit and then across and up. But for my materials, I went through concertos, sonatas, chamber music works, some symphonies, and some of the standard repertoire and took examples: What kind of scale would you have to practice to be prepared to play this with the best fingering?

And the other thing is that very often a scale-like passage in music will be just one octave or so. So while I was teaching at Stanford, I created a worksheet of one-octave scales that went through the circle of 5ths. Every major and minor key!

And I would tell my students, "This takes me 4 minutes. Go through it carefully and well, at different speeds. And if you don't have four minutes a day to practice, then I'm sorry, I don't want to listen to you." Actually, I remember one final I was really mean; I really made everybody show me that they could do it. And one pre-med student had figured out a pattern fingering so she could do those scales without really knowing the notes. She had a good enough ear that she could do it without really knowing what she was doing. She played it pretty well because she figured out there were eight notes and so you need three groups: one group of two and two groups of three. And that was very funny—I thought, "Well you're right, that's okay."

But it's also useful to practice it in different parts of the cello, just do that circle of fifths up the A string or up the D string or across the strings. In other words, not just to practice it one way. So that was the start of some of this exploration of all the different ways to practice scales. One thing I still like is the Klengel Book Two section with the twelve different variations on a scale, where you're constantly coming back and forth over the same notes. So your intonation needs to be very good, since you're coming back to the same notes and, you hope, not fishing too much.

And it was very funny once—Felix Galimir was out here for one of our chamber music festivals, and in his quartet, the Galimir Quartet, in New York at that time, Tim Eddy was the cellist. And he was saying what a serious and wonderful cellist he was. But he was so serious, he said, that when he goes on tour he has a book of Klengel. It's the only book he takes for cello technique, the Klengel Book Two. And I said, "That's what I take too." Because it just keeps you clean. I think when you're playing a lot, it's really important to do a little bit of basic, solid technical work just to keep yourself really honest in that way. So yes, I think scales and arpeggios are a very basic thing to keep yourself in good shape.

There's another thing, though. Now this is a little bit of sacrilege, so I don't know if I want to be quoted on this. A couple years ago now, I had a really bad bout of sciatica, and I was a basket case because it was very, very painful. I could only sit and play about 40 minutes a day. But what I did, which was a pleasure and sort of kept me from feeling so much pain while I was doing it, was to play a Bach Suite every day, all the way through the sixth. I just kept going around. It was wonderful that it kept me in pretty good shape, and it meant that I really enjoyed that 40 minutes that I was playing, but also because Bach is just scales and arpeggios. I remember thinking, "You know, Bach is a lot more fun than scales." But I don't dare tell my students that.

No, I really feel it's important just to keep a basic routine going, and I usually do. I encourage a student, apart from checking in on them, to play a scale just to warm up at the beginning of a lesson, rather than to jump straight into the music they're working on.

A.A   *What have you found that has been the hardest thing to teach a student?*

B.H.   Oh, that's difficult (long pause). Probably vibrato. One always hopes that a student will just start using vibrato, because it's a very personal thing. Unless a kid is really free, it's hard to get a good vibrato. I believe in a live hand—that one's hand has this sense of aliveness about it, spring and bounce and so on. But to get them feeling that motion, not only the vertical motion up and down the string, but the rotation motion, can be difficult. I often don't direct things at first when I'm teaching it. I think it's been a pretty long time since I've actually had to do the beginnings of vibrato.

One thing that often doesn't get talked about as much is developing vibrato in terms of hearing a vibration on the A string and then adjusting on each of the lower strings because the vibrato needs to be a little bit different to tune in to the physics of it—to tune in with the slower vibrations of each string. Sometimes people use the same vibrato on the C string that they use on the A string, and so you don't really hear that much vibration.

In the Brahms E Minor, for instance, it's not going to do much good at all. So you're not going to have that deep throb. It's harder. That was something I got from Casals right away—finding the variation of the vibrato. I had been playing often for Zara (Nelsova), and she was a very hyper, electric cellist and had a very virtuosic fast vibrato, very exciting, very stimulating. I played for Casals that first time after I came back to start the lessons, and I was trying to play the best I could. And Casals said, "It was very exciting, but pretty soon it gets really boring because it's all the same." Okay, I get it.

I often have students turn their heads away so they can't see their hand. You see, if you're aware of the movement of the vibrato, you expect that you're hearing what you see. And yet if you turn your head away so you can't really see it and really listen to the vibration actually coming out, then you have to start dealing with it. It's not easy; it's the physical control, but then ultimately it's also part of one's sound and one's own voice. So it's really challenging for a person to see what they really intend, and often it changes when they really start listening to it.

I have a thing about fingerings too—how sometimes people finger Bach or Beethoven, for instance, according to the kind of music it is. Or the fact that when playing with the piano, you need to finger more harmonically. In all these slides, it's beautiful on some of these lyrical pieces like Fauré to go up the D string. It's wonderful.

However, the piano can't do all those things. In Beethoven, I think one needs to pay more attention to what kind of music it is. A lot of it is harmonic. With Bach also, I feel that these beautiful fingerings that go up on one string just don't work. That sound is just wonderful for Dvořák, and for Brahms, but not necessarily for Bach or others from that era.

A.A.   *One thing I still haven't quite figured out what I like is the first two notes of the Beethoven A major.*

B.H.   Oh. Try everything.

A.A.   *Do you cross over or do you go up the G string?*

B.H.   I do everything. I have done everything.

Earlier I'd always played going up the G string. And it's so beautiful. And then the piano comes in; nice, open. That whole movement is made up of these open intervals. That's the whole essence of Beethoven. So often, like in the G-Minor Sonata, Beethoven takes a dotted rhythm and he makes practically a whole piece out of that kind of musical idea. I've experimented and I actually have even tried all these things in performance.

I'm getting simpler in my old age, and I still would just go up the G string because it's so beautiful. That's why I love the Bärenreiter edition of the Beethoven Sonatas, because there are no fingerings; you just have Beethoven's phrasings. Which are not always bowings, even—I mean, some of them are impossible.

A.A.   *I have spent a lot of time with my students trying to just teach them how to practice. I'm wondering if that's something you talk about with your students?*

Absolutely. It's tricky, you know? But I think it's very important. I don't mean it's tricky, exactly; I was just thinking about time distribution, which you were talking about, too. An awful lot of effective practice comes through problem solving.

I started playing contemporary music as a teenager, and when you come across contemporary music that has never been played before and has techniques that Popper doesn't help at all, you have to invent your own technique to help you be able to do some of those things. It makes you want to become very aware of how you do things.

For instance, if you have a problem and even after practicing it quite a lot, it's still not working, then there's something wrong about the way you're practicing it. So you have to take it apart and really dissect it. What are the problems here? Shifting, for instance, is one of the bigger things, because we have to go all these distances. That's why the cello's so much harder than the violin, where everything's right under their hands. Of course I can say that to you; I can't say it in front of a violinist.

So, really analyzing how we shift and which finger we're shifting on, really measuring, finding the marksmanship so you know the absolute distance. You know exactly where to go, without hearing anything, you know this note and that note. In an absolute way, I call it marksmanship.

A.A.   *Target practice.*

B.H.   Target practice, yes. And then to coordinate it with whether it's a change of bow, whether it's on the earlier bow, all those things—to really be conscious. Especially at the college level, it's a very important time for the students to start being conscious about how they do things. Because often, it's so long ago that they started the cello. And often the teacher would show them how to do something, and maybe give them a couple of verbal things to help guide them when they get home. But because they've done it, they already have experience, and the experience is so important. Later it's very important that they really understand how they're doing things, as it comes up within what they're working on. We've all had this experience, when you're in the middle of a performance and with something you've always been able to just do, all of a sudden you're not sure if you can do it.

You sometimes have to think your way through it for the moment. It's very public, you know? That's why public performance is a real learning experience. Yet it's sometimes very painful because it's a very public place to be learning things. So that's why, as things come up, I ask a lot of questions of students.

How I've decided to do something might help somebody else. But really, they have to discover how they're going to do it. They have to figure it out for themselves, with some guidance. You can help them, and you can question, but the real learning, I think, comes from their own discovery.

Kids are sometimes shy at first; they try to tell you what they think you want to hear, you know? But then when they start thinking for themselves, then that's a real asset. And they get interested in trying to figure it out. If they're going to teach ever, it's really crucial to be able to analyze that.

I was very lucky. I was about 15, and Margaret had had some lessons with a man named D.C. Dounis, who at that time (1950s) was an amateur violinist, a doctor, and a respected string teacher. Actually, some well-known violinists, violists, and cellists would go to him, some of them up the back stairs, if they were having trouble with some technical thing. It was a kind of cult at that time.

He lived in Los Angeles, but he would come up to San Francisco or he would go to the East Coast to teach all of these string players, some of them quite famous. Well, Margaret had had a couple of lessons with him. He would give these four-hour lessons, with two check-ups. He would go through all the aspects of bowing, all the aspects of shifting, all the aspects of articulation and finger action. She then would come back and teach some of these things. And then she wanted me to go and have a series of four-hour lessons.

I guess I had two four-hour lessons with two check-ups. Or maybe I just had one set- anyway, I saw him a few times. But he wasn't here that long. And it was very funny. I was playing the Saint-Saëns Concerto around that time, and I went in and there was this incredible cellist playing Saint-Saëns. I was thinking, "Oh gosh, I have to go in there and play?" It turned out it was George Neikrug.

Even George Neikrug based his whole teaching career on the Dounis ideas. The bowhold, all the fingers, all the different things with the left hand, and shifting, everything. Dounis analyzed every aspect. He had this scientific mind, and he had dissected everything about string playing.

A.A.   *What about torso movement, or just movement in general in cello playing?*

B.H.   One of the things I've heard for a long time is "You have to play from the back." Well, where is my back? How do I experience my back? This is hard to talk about but important in playing. I remember at Juilliard when I was first there, there were these big freshmen who might have been mistaken for football players because they were big guys. And they were just playing from muscle.

And us poor little females, we have to use a lot of thrown energy. This is an exaggeration, but the point is I was lucky that Margaret had made me so aware of playing with freedom. But you know, in teaching it, in trying to help a person find that, you could say, "Play from the back." And even Margaret could do a kind of osmosis on you and get you in good shape, and yet it didn't necessarily hold up when you got nervous on stage. You'd tighten up just to protect yourself, in a way.

So, the magic: you have to really know what you're doing so that you can get it no matter how uncomfortable you may be feeling at that moment on the stage, so you can access it right away. I've certainly learned how to do that. But the first thing is getting back into the shoulder blades, feeling that motion. And then also being aware that there's a huge sheath of muscles all the way down either side; so if we start tapping into it, there's no way you could get to the end of that energy.

I know when I have played the Dvořák Concerto sometimes with orchestra, I've really tapped into that because you need a lot of sound. You have to make a lot of noise in that piece. And, for instance, with bow changes it's important that you don't sit and play with your arms. You have that give and take, that motion. And I say sometimes, even though it's very subtle—change your bow with your body.

If you have that feeling where everything is moving and is proportioned, then you're really feeling. I can show this very easily to a student. I put one hand on the shoulder and one hand back on the shoulder blade and find out whether they're using it at all. Often they're not. Often they're just playing, and then I try to help them move that muscle, just to be aware of how to get it moving.

I get them to come over and put their hands on my shoulder and back, just to feel the difference. I play with just my arm, so they can feel that, and then do it with the shoulder blade actively there. The difference in sound—and it can be a perfectly good sound, just playing from the shoulder, you can get absolutely good sound—but then you put it into the back and it's so much deeper, and there's much more natural resonance. It's very funny: sometimes when I've helped a person tap into that, they say, "But it's so much easier this way," as if that's a bad thing.

A.A.   *Right.*

B.H.   Those physical things took me awhile because I had been told for a long time, "Play from your back." Okay, great. I'll be glad to. How do I do that?

A.A.   *I often hear the analogy that bowing is like throwing a frisbee or hitting a backhand in tennis. Do you agree?*

B.H.   Yes. I remember when Primrose was here playing with the Griller quartet. One time I was down in Los Angeles, and for some reason he invited me over to his house. And he loved to play golf. So he gave me a lesson in how to swing a golf club. He said, "That's just like a bow."

A.A.   *What about training the ear? How do you work on intonation?*

B.H.   Many different ways. Anything that works is fine. I believe in the premise that if you're tight, it's much harder to hear. You turn off the listening device if you're tense. There's a whole hand-ear relationship. If you're really hearing well, the hand will often go to the note without knowing why. It just wants to be there.

This goes with the idea that it's not in your fingertips, it's in your ear—let the ear be in the driver's seat.

I work a lot with the overtones of the instrument, when you're in the center of the note, especially the notes that have natural overtones: the G's, the D's, the C's. Then you really hear the difference. As for tools and tuners, doing things up a string with a drone can help. And it can help get the intervals that much more in your ear.

You can become just as clear with the seconds and sevenths as you are with thirds or sixths. The fifths are tricky just because our cellos are never in tune.

The octaves are obvious. Another one is the first finger up from the open string—that note is often out of tune. We tend to go sharp.

A.A.   *Yes, I still do that often.*

B.H.   I find the fourth to the string above, a very good one because it is an open interval where you really can hear whether it's in tune or not. So, that's a guide that I have kids check a lot. Especially if it's this thing of the first finger being too high.

One other thing that I discovered, while I was at Grinnell, I had this kid—she seemed hopeless, and she was trying, but she was playing so out of tune. She just could not seem to hear the difference between when it was in tune and when it wasn't. It was very interesting: I asked her to sing it, and she was beautifully in tune.

I said, Okay, your ear is fine. It's not that you have a bummed out ear and it's been mishandled. So, it's a finely honed thing, developing your ear to have an elemental intonation and to still be within the expressive range you want.

There's one other rather subtle thing that I don't think about too often. Sometimes I think about it consciously, though. I learned that there was a school in England where they were teaching deaf kids to play the cello and, I gather, the bass, too, and these kids were learning how to play pretty well, just by feeling the vibrations.

Once you start thinking about that and start playing, then if you have a sensitive, live finger, you play a note, and if you really start thinking about the vibrations, you can have the sensation of whether it's in tune or not. But we don't even think about it; we're not even aware of it, most of the time.

At first, you have to think about it a little bit consciously, but then you start feeling. You know what was very interesting—I got to play Casals's cello for a couple of weeks, when the Manhattan School was putting on a special concert honoring him. I was asked to play some Bach on his cello and also one of his own pieces (this was maybe four or five years ago).

Casals's cello was amazing. I had a little trouble the first couple of days. Casals's widow, Marta, had said that it was a difficult instrument to play, and she was right. The first couple of days, it just growled at me. I just didn't know what I was going to do. I tried all the bows that I had there, and nothing was really working.

Then I got a bow out of the case that looked kind of tattered, you know, it was all worn off here and the hair looked terrible. I started playing it- it was a Frank Torres bow- and it was obviously going to be the best bow to use.

The bow hair was really worn out, and I just kept putting more rosin on it and played with it. When I told Marta what had happened, she said, "Well, of course, it hasn't been rehaired for 30 years."

What helped me to get it sounding well after a couple of days was that I started trying to imagine his bow arm, to imagine the balance of it. It was an incredibly perfect bow arm. Then the spring, the liveliness, the bounce and the spring and the resilience of his left hand, which was so alive.

I started playing that way. Then the cello said, "yes, yes, yes, I want to be played that way." It was kind of amazing that it spoke so quickly, that I felt this immediacy of the life of the cello, of the vibration. Then, on that instrument, I really felt this sense of vibrating.

That was very interesting, and it made me think, all right, is this because that's the way Casals played it all those years, and that's the way the instrument wanted to be played? Or was it just that that was the way that cello needed to be played?

A.A.   *Do you make students memorize things and/or perform things by memory?*

B.H.   I encourage it, you know, because when their brains are younger, they can retain those pieces for years. But some things I learned a couple of years ago, I'm not so sure about. I do absolutely encourage it. I think too often people learn a piece and then they memorize it. It should be happening at the same time.

On the other hand, it's good to check back in, because very often one forgets certain subtleties. I do like the visual, as well. I really encourage students to practice in front of a mirror for certain things, especially with the bow. There's a certain kind of reality about it. When we're playing, we're imagining what's coming out, which isn't necessarily what we're actually doing. If you see that other person over there in the mirror, you're able to be more objective.

Whenever I would play a concerto, I would always do the difficult technical passages with the metronome quite a lot. Even things I'd played before, just to build it up so that you're in shape and very solid and good with it.

I have two ways of practicing with a metronome. Sometimes, notch it up. But also, you can practice something exactly half tempo, carefully and well, and often it transfers into the faster tempo. In other words, the inner pulse can stay constant.

It's amazing, like with the seventh variation of the Tchaikovsky or the second movement of the Elgar—it has to be there. Just build it up. You could say, "Oh, but that takes so long," but if you just take it up, not even single notches, but three or four at a time, it's amazing how quickly you can get from here to there. On the other hand, if you just practice it slowly and then try to go to tempo and see how it is, it's not necessarily there. It's the process of building.

Yes, there needs to be slow practice, and I always tell a person, "Start from where you can play it really well, really the way you want to play it, and then build it from there."

When you're playing in front of an orchestra, you've got to be certain; otherwise you not only mess yourself up, but you mess up a hundred people behind you. That's just the reality.

A.A.   *I was going to ask you about slow practice too, but you answered that.*

B.H.   Unfortunately, we probably don't spend enough time on things, in the sense of really accepting them, incorporating them, and digesting them. What I've noticed, with somebody like Casals, is that if they have repertoire coming up, they start working on it way ahead. Way ahead! Way ahead, even though they have all kinds of other concerts all the way along in between. Working on something a whole year before they play it. That's what bothers me when kids at college are getting ready for recitals. By that time, they're on to the last three suites, and they say, "Well, I want to learn the E-Flat Suite and play it on my concert in X number of months." I say, "No, you work on the E-Flat Suite, get it where it's ready—and that can take a year—and really play it well, and then you schedule it."

A.A. Yes.

B.H. There are certain works that you just need time for. With the Brahms Double, we started about a year and a half ahead.

I was in New York recently. I went to a concert of kids from age eight to about 20, I guess. People from all over the country who would audition and get chosen to play on this concert so they could play in Weill Hall, but they would be able to say, "My debut in New York was at Carnegie, at the age of eight."

Of the 25 kids that played, I would say, if I'm generous, about a fourth of them deserved to play, as far as really being ready. I believe in performance, I feel that absolutely teachers need to have their students practice performing in the studios, but I don't think one has a right to invite somebody to come and listen to them unless they're really ready.

A.A. *That brings me to asking about nerves. Do you deal with that a lot with your students, and how do you help them with stage fright?*

B.H. Yes, you have to talk about it, especially at college age. You need to discuss the difference between playing your own concert or recital and preparing psychologically for an audition. At that age, they have to do a lot of auditions to try to get scholarships, to try to get into summer camp, to try to get into another school, and all these things are great preparation for trying to get a job. In orchestra auditions, you have very little time. You have to hit the ground running because you have to get the best from yourself across in a short amount of time. They're going to be judging you, that's just the truth.

So there are no illusions, it's important to be psychologically prepared for that. Whereas if you have your own concert, you hope the people have come to enjoy the music. You have the chance to bring them in to listen to the larger things.

You know, I've had students who were fearless. If they're fearless and play very well, I don't want to mess them up by putting problems in front of them. Usually then at some point they wake up and start getting nervous.

A.A. *Do you demonstrate a lot when you teach, and do you think that's an important aspect to teaching the cello?*

B.H. Yes, I do. In the past, I have taught a lot from the cello. Depending on the age of the person, I don't just play at them a lot, but I demonstrate specific things or how to do something or how to analyze a particular technical thing.

The only reason I'd play a section or a phrase is to try to get something of the spirit across. I don't want students to copy me at all. Sometimes, it's just to show them what it takes to bring something to life, just the energy that has to go into playing, to get past the third row.

I also question a lot. I like to have them physically experience different things on the cello. I will often start by asking permission—"Do you mind if I manhandle you?"—to try to help them feel something or experience something physically, especially the back thing. It's tricky. Especially in master classes, it can be very valuable to demonstrate something.

On the other hand, sometimes you see somebody who is using a master class to get themselves across, rather than to help the student. My goal is always to find one or two points that I'm wanting to get across. Hopefully, you can really help that person sound better on that right now.

When that works—and it often does, because I don't make them big complicated things—if you can unlock something or help them understand something and can say, "Look, you did that, you just did that, and you didn't go home and practice for four hours, you did it right now," that's what's most satisfying. That's not by just demonstrating to them.

A.A.   *What is your philosophy on the Bach Suites and teaching them, and how has the historically informed practice movement affected your teaching?*

B.H.   I love working on the Bach Suites with students, especially at this point in my life. The Suites bring me so much pleasure these days. I think what's so important with Bach is getting the character, getting the life. Each suite has its own character, which the preludes show us. Then, each dance within the suite has its own version of that basic character, which has to do of course with Bach, the key and what it represents, and all those kinds of things.

Also, it's different every day. You don't say the same things the same way even if you're saying the same things. It's a little different every day. It's the same with Bach—it lives. I try to get that across. There are some basic elements. Since it's so tonal and you're on your own, it's important to hear the tonality within phrases and play within a key area. You must have the sense of notes within the key areas and really listen in that way.

I feel the left hand is speaking and the bow is singing but also articulating. It's a double-edged thing because you want to have a really singing détaché, and that's where I started getting baroque bows in the 1960s. I learned so much from the baroque bow because you play in a different part of the bow, so you can get a really singing détaché; our modern bows are made to have much more beginning bite, like consonants. No matter how legato you try to play, especially down in the lower part, it has that articulation just from the bow itself.

Whereas with a baroque bow, you can really get the vibrations, especially if you're playing with gut strings. But you can get it so the vibrations are holding over. It's not as intense or as deep a sound, but they're holding over so you can catch them, so that you can play actually quite legato. And it's legato sounding, but also with the clarity of the baroque bow and the overtone resonance. It's a different way of producing sound, with the baroque bow. I learned a lot, and it meant that I could translate a lot of that sound and technique to a modern bow, too.

So I found the tools of baroque playing to be very useful. And especially with my cello, which was an old cello. Once I played the Fifth Suite tuned down. I learned it first with the normal tuning, and then later I was asked to play it at a Bach festival, so I thought, I'm going to learn it tuned down and play it with all gut strings. I put on a raw A and an aluminum-covered D and then silver-wound guts on the G and C. When I was traveling a lot that became difficult because they don't stay in tune very long. My cello said, "I can breathe more." It liked it.

And the sound was very dark; it was wonderful and the whole instrument was just ringing. It wasn't as intense a sound coming out, but it was so resonant. I got so much overtone resonance. In the cello suites a lot of the phrases are very linear, and that's why the nineteenth-century cellists made their editions with big slurs all over the place. Whereas we get the urtext and see that there are these different bowings, of course we don't have them from Bach, but we have the Anna Magdalena, and then we have Kellner and Westphal and all of the others. I've got the new edition with all the different markings, including the lute version with all the other notes in the Fifth Suite. Of course, I've had that for a long time, but it's really nice to have them all on top of each other, because then you can just really compare directly. I like that we can play with the urtext, but I don't feel that the pieces need to be played literally. Anner Bylsma talks about that in *The Fencing Master*. He's such a wonderful cellist, and he was one of the first really good instrumentalists to start getting into historical performance practice. I knew him before he got into early music.

A.A.   *Really?*

B.H.   Yes. We had a four-hour bus ride together, and he had me laughing the whole time. He had just won the principal cellist job with the Concertgebouw. At that point, he loved the Duport Études. And after several years he started getting into early music.

I love what I've learned from baroque bows, and I still use a baroque bow if I'm playing Bach in a not too large space. I once played on a series at Casals Hall in Tokyo, and every cellist played a Bach Suite to start the concert. I played it with a baroque bow—there are probably about 800 seats, and a lot of wood. It was a great hall to play in because it was so resonant, and some of the college-age kids had never heard a baroque bow sound like that. It's a very full sound, not in the intense way we make with our modern pressure projecting the sound, but with the sound just flowing out. It's a sound that goes out and amplifies naturally.

I think the sound that we've learned from the baroque bow is very, very important. It's a much clearer sound. It's always working with that overtone resonance, and I love that. It has so much more vibration because of the overtones, such that if you add vibrato, it can contradict. I'm not saying don't use vibrato—I play with vibrato, absolutely, but much less and much more carefully. Not something we just put on like frosting on everything.

And that's how vibrato is used a lot of the time. It's just there, you just do it. No, vibrato should be part of the expressive thing. And certainly Leopold Mozart and some of the earlier people talked about vibrato, but as an expressive thing, so those are the things we consider—so I find it's not even a question so much of deciding on this performance practice or that performance practice. When you approach the music with that ear, with that sense, you don't want to use a whole lot of vibrato. You want it to come out of the center of the music.

A.A.   *I have in my mind something I thought you said once that I've often repeated to students, something to the effect of, "You don't play Bach, you speak Bach."*

B.H.   Yes, the articulation is spoken. Then whether it's separate bows or legato bows, it's singing. With a baroque bow, there aren't as many consonants; there are some consonants, but there's an awful lot more where the ring is going on, like singing. And you're working with resonance and the vibration of resonance. Actually, when you think about it, an open string has an incredible amount of vibrato. You say, "The piano can't do vibrato." But when you listen to a piano chord, there's an enormous amount of vibration coming out of that chord.

I think it's a question of getting it in sync with whatever you're doing. And when you start listening that way, you tend to naturally do what's needed. The really important thing is to have a very live left hand and not just dead fingers. It's not vibrato, but it's not dead either. I don't say do not use vibrato at all because very often what can happen is that when you tell a person to stop using vibrato, their bow goes dead. Therefore, their sound goes dead, and that's a double whammy. There's something wonderful about a non-vibrato note that's ringing, but it's not going to ring unless the bow is alive. It's subtle. When you're changing habits and changing ideas, it needs to come out of a total understanding of what you're trying to do.

A.A.   *Okay, on the opposite end of the spectrum, there are three pieces that are often played but they're not exactly original: the Boccherini B-flat Concerto (Grützmacher), the Tchaikovsky Rococo Variations (Fitzenhagen), and the Chopin Polonaise Brillante (Feuermann). How do you feel about those being part of the standard repertoire but not being original? Do you support them being played even in their non-original form?*

B.H.   Yes. I love urtext, and particularly manuscripts, because I like seeing what the composer wrote in their own hand. You get such a feeling for a piece. I remember Kreisler owned the original Brahms Violin Concerto manuscript. He's the one who gave it to the Library of Congress. I listened with a friend to a recording of the Brahms with Kreisler playing and following it on a facsimile. The places where Brahms was writing faster and sort of tumbling down the hill, Kreisler went tumbling down the hill with him. Other places where it expanded and there was more space between notes, Kreisler expanded. It was really fascinating to see how he did that.

Now I don't know if he was just playing the way he thought the music was, or whether since he had owned the original manuscript and, undoubtedly, studied it, he was affected by that.

But anyway, one of the first ones I heard was a Chopin, an old recording on 78s of Chopin with Feuermann, and I'll never forget it. I'd never heard a sound that affected me the way that did. Of course, often the first performance you hear of a piece, if you're really impressed with it or you're young, is the one you remember, even though there are plenty of wonderful ones. But I've never heard another performance with the kind of core intensity and focus that I felt from that sound. He played it marvelously.

In my own life, however, I have only played the original version of the Chopin. Maybe I was just too lazy to play the other stuff. I objected to playing the piano runs, because frankly they sound better on the piano. It was very funny—when I was driving Navarra around, he was playing it on that tour, but he was playing his own version. He was incorporating different piano-part licks. Of course, it's a good technique-builder. So I really don't have an objection to it.

I was so happy when the Rostropovich recording of the Chopin was the original. I thought, "Okay, then it's all right."

For the Tchaikovsky, it's interesting because we all grew up with the Fitzenhagen, and now we have the original, which actually has some pretty good stuff. Evidently Fitzenhagen's version was okay with Tchaikovsky, at least that's what I've read. It made it a very effective concert piece. It used to be played on recitals a lot more than it is now. Both Zara and Leonard Rose used to play it on recitals all the time.

I didn't play it until quite a bit later. I never studied it with anyone, and then I was engaged to play it a year and a half ahead of time, so naturally you say, "Okay." I was in New York and Zara was at Juilliard at that time, and so I asked her if she'd listen to it, because she played it like the dickens. She played it marvelously. I told her I'd never played it, and she said, "What, you haven't played it? Well, I hope something can be done." It was a real Zara thing, it was very funny.

Actually, I've never heard the original performed with orchestra. I have the score, but I've never actually worked on it. I heard Paul Tobias play it, but not with orchestra. He told me once that he was giving a master class and had told this story about me. He was about 11 or 12 and was fooling with radios, taking them apart and putting them together. He came to his lesson and said, "I took this radio apart and put it back together, and so I just have had no time to practice at all." I said, "Well, great, thank you, Paul, but I don't want to hear you if you haven't practiced." I was evidently the only teacher who ever kicked him out of a lesson. I had completely forgotten about that.

But back to Tchaikovsky. Certainly if somebody wants to play the original, I'm happy to hear it. If somebody wants to play the Tchaikovsky, I might give them a choice and try to interest them in it, but I wouldn't insist that they play the original.

The Boccherini is a fun one because I was able to get from the University of Edinburgh some manuscripts of the three versions of the Boccherini B-flat. The first one is for two violins. It's much shorter and is basically the themes with a different slow movement. Then I'm not sure whether the sonata or the concerto was next in the original.

I've played the original concerto, which I like very much. It's got a lot of music that Grützmacher didn't use, which is nice to have. It's got a different slow movement, and the sonata version has a few tempo changes that Boccherini doesn't make in the concerto version.

I don't feel it's a crime not to play from the urtext, necessarily. I think urtext is important, and there's a lot of stuff that absolutely you want to play with that. And then there are other things that might not get played otherwise but are still good music, like the Grützmacher/Boccherini Concerto. I don't feel so purist about that. That was just performance practice in the nineteenth century, and cellists were used to making their own versions. Grützmacher simply used material from Boccherini's other concertos.

The Future

A.A.   A lot has been made of the shrinking audience in classical music. Where do you see the future of classical music going in the next generation, and especially how has technology positively or negatively influenced classical music?

B.H.   Well, I wonder whether the audience really is shrinking. There has always been that core audience, and while concerts as we've known them are going to change, there will also probably be some aspects and some venues that are going to stay the same, in the way that art galleries and museums have stayed the same. There are also going to be changes in the way careers are built.

In the olden days, we would book our concerts, we'd get our brochures, we'd put up our posters, we'd do all those things to put on a concert. Now so many more people are using YouTube to introduce themselves. They want to get concerts, yes, but in different ways. You don't just book Town Hall anymore. I don't think recitals are being given as often as they used to be, as a way to get your career started or get yourself known. That's already a way that technology has changed how people are building their careers.

A lot more young players are doing crossover projects, and I don't think it's because it pays more—although probably it is more lucrative than classical music. But for the most part, people that do that need to be classically trained. That's how they're going to really learn the instrument. I also think that younger players are being more proactive and finding different ways to get out and play their music and have a musical life, rather than just waiting by the phone for somebody to engage them or waiting for some manager to come and make their career. They're being more proactive about getting out there and playing in all kinds of situations, and I am definitely for that.

I think my own career has evolved in the same way, and that's great. Music should just be a part of life. There have never been that many who have earned their living just from playing concerts. Mostly, you have some other job that sustains you, and then you play the concerts because you want to share, you want to express. It's part of what we want to do. It's one of the things that perhaps attracted us to being performers. We're wanting to get it out there. I've felt for a while now that the way music happens will continue to change in the future.

A.A.   *Do you think classical music is becoming more visual?*

B.H.   Well, that's part of it—we're so stimulated with so many different media. It's why a group like the Kronos Quartet does so well. They earn their living by playing concerts, and their production has the visual, has the sound, has everything. It's more like what rock musicians do; it's a whole other kind of entertainment.

A.A.   *Yes, everything's video now.*

B.H.   That's one of the reasons why opera is terrific on DVD. Just sitting and watching a video of a string quartet doesn't work as well unless one's really a music lover. Even then, the actual experience of being with all those other people sharing it has an attraction to people, rather than just being in your Brave New World cave.

I have a DVD of the Juilliard Quartet in the 1970s. It was very soon after Joel (Krosnick) joined them, and I remember it as a sort of Romantic revival period, where everybody dressed up in their fancy cuffs and fancy shirts, and maybe velvet jackets and things like that. In this video the Juilliard Quartet was playing Beethoven in a beautiful library in Germany, a really gorgeous baroque building, and they played Op. 18, No. 4, Op. 59, No. 1, and Op. 131. They were absolutely at the top of their game—Bobby Mann was still young—and they were all playing marvelously. It was really wonderful, except the camera crew obviously hadn't done their homework. A couple of times the camera wasn't necessarily on the person who should have had the attention, but mostly it was. But the camera shots were moving around so much that it was really distracting. They were trying to make something that was very exciting to watch from a visual perspective, but I felt it needed to be calmed down a little.

A.A.   *How does new music fit into the continuation of classical music, especially orchestrally—how can orchestras find the balance of getting people to appreciate new music while still giving them the standard repertoire, which is really what most of them seem to want to hear?*

B.H.   Well, I think that Michael Tilson Thomas has done a really good job of that here in San Francisco because he has programmed a lot of contemporary music, and he presents it in a way the audience can understand. He has put on a whole series of contemporary concerts, and he absolutely packs them in. I think his mentor, or certainly his model, was Bernstein, and like Bernstein, he communicates very well.

I started playing contemporary music in the 1950s, which was one of the roughest periods as far as some of the brutal music being written, because it was not that long after the war. Some of the European composers, especially the Polish composers like Penderecki and Lutosławski, were writing music that was so hard. It was like machines. It was so hard, and bitter, and tough. Some of their later works were not as cruel, but they had lived through a pretty cruel time, especially in Poland and nearby countries.

Also, it was so experimental. It was the time when the Buchla Box and tape music were in use. Hollywood did all those sound effects much better. Back then, the composers were rather primitive with the tape sounds (except for Davidovsky) and then the computer music started. Schoenberg was still down in Los Angeles making tone rows.

At one point we played for a seminar with a whole bunch of composers there. It was a composium, I guess you'd call it. I was getting so frustrated with playing some of the music, because as the cello part in a quartet with a terrible manuscript and a terrible cello part, I was growling around sitting on the lower two strings, just growling. I said, "Ugh, I'm going to write a piece that only composers have to play." They didn't laugh. They didn't think it was at all funny. I thought it was very good.

I was glad to get asked to play these pieces, though, because you find out that you have to put in the work and learn a piece before you can even tell whether it's at all a good piece and worth playing or not. I played some good ones- I played the premiere of the Elliott Carter Cello Sonata out here and got an incredible review for him. I sent it to him, and then I played it on my debut in New York.

Now that piece is our classical twentieth-century sonata. It's marvelous, and we played it a lot through the years. I have always loved playing the slow movement, which is so dramatic, and so beautiful and emotional, but the second movement with all the jazzy stuff, we got so that we could just toss it off, have fun with it. Often I would find some of the younger listeners especially would really respond to it and would come back and talk about how much they liked it. We had a great time playing that.

A.A.   *Have you seen the level of cello playing change over the years? And are there enough jobs for the cellists in today's market?*

B.H.   Well, there have always been great cellists, certainly. We were so lucky to have had Boccherini, Feuermann, Duport, and others. And then, of course, we had Casals. Casals was a departure. He never did so much the performance right of his time, performance practice, let's call it. Neither did Kreisler. Neither did some of the others that have transcended a playing style of their time, the ones that we want to keep listening to, that didn't have so many of the characteristics of a certain period—the ones that took it beyond what was just the fashion of the day.

The other thing about Casals was that he had an amazing facility and clarity of playing, but he also brought out the music's purpose, the musical intention of the work and the artistry of the little pieces. He always had something that would really move you. With some of the other playing, it could be very good cello playing but not necessarily very great music playing; but for Casals, the musical intention was always primary.

Yes, the young cellists are playing better technically, and they are getting better faster and younger. And they are learning modern music so much faster than my generation.

For a year, I was a substitute in the Sequoia Quartet down in Los Angeles. They were a part of a consortium that commissioned the Carter Fourth Quartet. That was the first thing I played with them. A Carter Quartet instead of a Haydn, which would be more usual to start with. We had to work hard, as it was very difficult and had not been performed.

The following summer, I was at Tanglewood, and there was a student group playing it and being coached by the Juilliard Quartet. The group learned it very quickly. Of course, by then there were recordings to listen to. I said to my colleague, Jorja Fleezanis, assistant concertmaster of the San Francisco Symphony, and very involved in contemporary music, "That's not fair. We had to work so hard, and then the kids come along and are just playing it." She said, "Well, somebody has to come along and blaze the trail for the next generation."

But there's something about music that will only be learned in its own time. Ultimately it's the players that get more deeply into the music who are going to move people and have a more important impact. Look at the Casals recordings that are still on the market; and they wouldn't be on the market if they weren't being sold. He obviously had something that was special.

A.A.   *And what about the job market for young cellists these days? Are there enough jobs?*

B.H.   Well, in the 1950s, the Griller Quartet and the Budapest Quartet were the two quartets touring in this country. In Europe, it was the Busch Quartet and the Griller Quartet. Look how many string quartets there are now, trying to get those same concerts. There are not as many concerts. At UC-Berkeley, they used to have all these quartets coming through from Europe because they could afford them. Now they might have a quartet playing a series, or maybe two quartets a year, a trio maybe once every five years. Otherwise, you have big dance companies, you have the touring orchestras, you have all these big, spectacular things. In that sense, it's tougher. But on the other hand, organizations like Chamber Music America have helped—the only thing is that there are so many more groups.

A.A: *Right, but a lot of them are finding residencies at colleges and universities around the country.*

B.H: Both Juilliard and Guarneri performed a lot but also found residencies. I don't know if they could have totally made a living back then by just playing, but they wanted the residencies too. The big orchestras still give a very good living. That's what our society really does support.

I get sad about the orchestras the next couple of tiers down, with a smaller series, where most of the players have to have other jobs. It gets difficult when the musicians try for more money, and then the board either can't or won't pay it, and then an orchestra folds. And when an orchestra folds, it's very hard to get it back. Those things are difficult, and there are more and more players being trained because the whole education thing has become so much of a market.

Naturally, everybody wants to stay in metropolitan areas, especially if they can get a good job. It's a little sad when a person gets a job right away because then they get used to a paycheck and maybe lose motivation to see what else they can do. It's important to try to find out what's out there because you might find some things that you like to do that you didn't know about, and maybe you'll find out you're good at some things you didn't know and develop more of your abilities, not just playing that instrument. There are many things a musician gets to do, and naturally, at some point, they want to come in out of the cold, with a more substantial and assured income. But I think there's nothing wrong with getting a broader experience.

I've played in about 40 of the states, and some of them quite a few times. You can always tell a town that has some musicians creating a larger musical environment, because of the people that not only come, but the kids that come back to talk to you after a concert- and then sometimes come to study with you. Margaret Rowell made a huge difference here, as well as some of the other teachers here in Berkeley. There was an atmosphere for it here, so I was very lucky. You can always tell whether the civic-minded people or politically minded people are putting on the "requisite cultural concert" to do their civic duty, compared to the places where there's a real grounds— and we're a very big country. The woman who started the San Francisco Conservatory played the San Francisco premiere of Beethoven's Emperor Concerto.

A.A. *That's amazing!*

B.H. You see, we're pioneer stuff. Europe has had many more years to develop music as part of their life and culture, and the question might be whether this country wants European music to be part of the culture.

It's doubtful in many places. If kids are not exposed to it in their own families, and if their school doesn't have it, many of them are not going to find it. At Grinnell College, for instance, I did a teaching program with some of the cello students and told them, "You don't teach in a vacuum. You work with people, and you learn how to do things by trial and error. You learn on the job. We have cellos here where the students can go practice and then put them back, so they don't take them home. They're there for the next person, and you need to find somebody who doesn't play a string instrument who wants to do this."

Then I went into the schools there and found a trumpet player who was trying to teach all the different instruments, so I offered my Grinnell students to work with the three or four of these kids. There were two or three junior high kids that were struggling along, and my students would give them lessons and help them. The teacher was delighted to have that help.

One day the chairman arrived in my studio with the hero of the football team. He had his bass, and he didn't know how to read music but would improvise along with records. He'd learn off the records, and he did pretty well. He was quite talented, and he wanted to learn how to read and learn more about playing.

I wrote to the Berklee Jazz School in Boston and got the bass book about all the chords and how to learn to jazz bass. Then I also got a Simandl (*New Method for the Double Bass*)—that's the bass book for learning how to read, learning the scales, learning some of the basic harmonies, and just bass playing in general. I pulled out my cello endpin and stood next to him. Actually, it was kind of fun. He didn't say anything, but he was a good guy. And he had some talent. I got him to bring along one of his records to hear him improvise with it, and he really did very well. That was how he taught himself.

That's the thing, in a small liberal arts college like that; the more different things you can do or are willing to try to do, the more valuable you are to the community.

Close to the Heart

A.A.   *If you hadn't been a musician, what would you have loved to have done with your life?*

B.H.   I don't think I could have not been a musician. That's a good question to ask any kid that's thinking about it, "Can you imagine anything else you would rather do?" If they have some other things they'd rather do than have music all their lives, go on. I've said this to students who would have a really hard time earning their living with music and with the cello. I've told them, "You may have to earn your living in some other way for a while or always, but it doesn't mean you can't go on growing as a musician all your life." Because I know some of the older guys used to say to students, "Ah, forget it. Don't try to be a musician. You just haven't got it." I don't think that's fair. I think that a person, if they love music and want it, they should be able to do it. They just have to be clear about the economic side of it.

I don't know. I like books a lot. I read all the time, and I always have, but I don't think I would have been happy just having a bookstore or being in a library. I don't think so. I think music just was too much there.

A.A.   *Did you ever have to deal with a period of doubt about becoming a musician in your life?*

B.H.   Yes, a little bit, as a late teenager, in making that transition from being a student to becoming a professional. I had already been earning quite a lot of money with teaching, even though I think my fee was 3 dollars at that point.

A.A.   *Wow.*

B.H.   That's where I started, and I remember when I hit 10 dollars, that was a big event. It's really funny. I think it was that identity crisis time, the late teens into 20, when you start doubting everything. It's sort of the last hurrah of adolescence, and I had a stormy adolescence. I had passionate feelings about stuff, and one does mellow out, I have to say. Life mellows one, and unfortunately, I didn't show feelings very much, so they built up more. I was alone a lot, and that's another way that it could build up. In other words, it was probably not just about music and the cello; but since I identified myself so much with music and the cello, it meant that I was questioning everything and then there was that desperation: "Well, what am I going to do? This is what I want to do." I don't know that I had doubts about my own ability.

A.A.   *Or desire?*

B.H.   Desire, no, I don't think so. I think it was just a question of how I was going to make the transition into having it become something. I remember specifically saying, "Well, maybe I can find a job in a hotel that has a palm tree, and play behind the palm tree." All those ridiculous adolescent things. I think that's just part of life.

A.A.   *What are maybe just two or three of your most memorable concert experiences?*

B.H.   That's hard. It's very funny, but when I am given recordings digitized from old reel to reel or cassette performances, and I listen to them, I think, "Oh, that's pretty good. Oh, I had forgotten that we could play like that. Could I play that well? I didn't know that."

Playing the Schubert Quintet in the Library of Congress with the Juilliard Quartet was very special. Not only was it such a great work and a great group of musicians, but it was such a great hall. It's a place where the acoustics are so good; the hall is like an instrument, so you want to play very, very well, because you can hear everything. You really get the sense of how a hall can enhance one's playing. After the concert, a gentleman said to me, "I felt Schubert had arrived from the heavens. You made my wife cry." That is Schubert!

I remember another event that was pretty moving. It was the Casals Festival performance, and we were playing the Ninth Symphony of Beethoven. We had been sent by the state department to the Dominican Republic, and we were told to stay in the hotel compound because there was fighting going on. We could hear gunfire all over the place. It was not only the orchestra and Casals—it was Maureen Forrester and all these really great singers. Warfield, I think, was the bass, an incredible bass, so it was really all-star stuff. Well, we came out on stage before the concert and started to tune up. The audience had been there for hours to be able to get a seat, and they were absolutely silent, like they were frozen. I remember that when we were tuning up, I was thinking, "Oh boy, am I glad I live in a free country," because you could feel the tension and the nervous energy. It was just radiating. I think the performance must have started with the Fauré Requiem or something that Shaw was conducting, because for the Ninth Symphony, they had the Cleveland Chorus there also—it was a lot of people for this event that the state department set up.

With the Ninth Symphony, there was something with Casals's energy, what he brought to it. It was over the top, a live, profound statement of something, the Ode to Joy and all that expresses; and afterward, the audience absolutely exploded. You know, it was their one chance to let out how they felt. I've never heard a response like that or seen a response like that. It was frenetic, and it went on, and on, and on, and on, and on, and on until they finally had to turn the lights out and tell them to go home.

A.A.   *Wow.*

B.H.   The energy that went into that concert was an unbelievable experience. I don't know that I've ever played Beethoven's Ninth with such electricity as I experienced on that night.

One more concert that was very important was our debut in Tully Hall with the trio. We had won the Naumburg, and the performance was one of the things we were offered. There was something about the Tully Hall concert. It's such an incredibly wonderful hall, and it was the first time the trio played in New York. That was very special partly because of how I felt after the concert. If one understood the different alpha, beta—the different mind levels, I must have been on a really high one, because it was quite a while before I was really back to being in the here and now. In other words, whatever energy it was that had gone into that concert put me in a whole different time space, which was a new experience for me. I don't know how that affected my playing, but I think it was pretty good. I think we played our best.

A.A. *Do you remember what you played?*

B.H. We played a good program. We played Ives's trio to start and played Brahms's C major next. And we played a premiere by Seymour Shifrin, who had been a student of Sessions—it was very involved, difficult—and then ended with the Beethoven Op. 70, No. 2, in E-flat.

A.A. *That's a big program.*

B.H. It was, but we did our best. What else can you do?

A.A. *What are you most proud of in your life or career?*

B.H. Well, I don't know that I would use that word exactly, but something that has been one of the biggest perks has been teaching so many students. I wish I had started a list of all the different students I had taught, because it would be quite a bookful. But by the time I thought of it, it was way too late to start. But over the last ten or fifteen years, I've been invited to quite a few places around the country to do a masterclass, play a mini recital, give a presentation with chamber music. Sometimes I've conducted a cello ensemble.

What's been such a joy is seeing students I have worked with and how they are active in their communities, how they're developing and how they've grown as musicians themselves, with their playing and in what they're contributing to their communities.

The people that are working in a community make such a huge difference. Those are the things that make it all make sense. One has a job because one needs a job. But I've always thought of teaching as kind of a calling, not a job. Otherwise I would have left the Bay Area. I was offered positions at other nice schools,, but I felt I could make more of a contribution here. New York has plenty of cellists.

On the other hand, there have been times when students, even at Stanford, would go out and start earning twice as much as I had ever made right away. Even musically, getting a job in an orchestra where they would have earned a comfortable living. That was nice to see.

I do believe if I had stayed on the East Coast, I would have had a more visible career, because the marketplace is on the East Coast. Several years ago, after my husband Nathan passed away, my longtime friend Joel Krosnick asked me to come teach at Juilliard. I decided to keep my house here in Berkeley, but I had to get rid of a lot of old programs and such. I'd keep one or two just as a memento, but I went through them; and the thing is, we played an unbelievable amount of music. We played so much music over the years, and we had the option to create our own series, and we created audiences—and that's what it's about, playing the music. It's not what fame you might have, because fame goes by pretty quickly. The one thing that I'm sorry we didn't do more of in those days was to record more, but I've got a lot of things and probably there are some performances that could be put out on disc. I have one that's really good, but then somehow the tape machine stopped just in the last two or three movements.

A.A. *Oh, no!*

B.H. But anyway, we played so much. That's what it's about- the experience. I feel so lucky that I've had the life I've had.

I wish I could play some of the things now as well as I used to play, because it's gotten harder. I can play some, and some of it's not too bad. I'm just so glad I've got music in my life, because I can't imagine what my life would be without it. Life is transitory; and so if you get to do it while you can, what's better than that?

It's been so interesting to see how careers are made in music and how that's changed over the years. I can't speak with complete certainty, because I'm not in the scene so much anymore, but I think there's still not that same career intention here in the Bay Area. When you get to New York and you're around musicians, right away, you're very aware of it, because everybody's on the make. Everybody's talking about what they're doing and want to do. Even guys that have been there forever and have already had great careers, they're still promoting what they're doing, so that you'll know they're still being very active. I always think, "We know how great you are. You don't need to tell us. It's all right. Yes, you did that when you were 20, but you don't need to do it now." I don't mean to criticize at all. It's just part of life. Mainly I just wanted a "Life in Music."

A.A. *Is there anything you still want to do, though, before it's all done? Anything on your bucket list, or to play a certain piece or something? Because you've done so much!*

B.H. Well, sure. I wouldn't mind playing some more- some of those pieces I particularly loved playing. The only problem is, I want to be sure I can sound well enough. The Schubert B-flat Trio. Actually, I was rehearsing it with a wonderful violinist, quite a well-known violinist; and we were going to be playing it, not so long ago, but that was when I got the sciatica. There was just no way I could play. I couldn't even stand up straight. But you see, I'm not necessarily needing or wanting to play new things. It's just there are some things that I loved playing so much.

I've been at a lot of the summer festivals, and I've also moved around a lot by choice. I turned down Banff last year partly because of my knee, and also because I found, the previous time when I had gone to Banff, that the altitude was hard on me. I found getting around up there hard for me, so I decided I'd better just do the things that I can do.

And for instance, I've had this situation more recently where some colleagues said, "Oh, Bonnie, you shouldn't do that, because that's not at your caliber." Well, I don't know if it is or not, but it's going to involve some of my younger students, and it's a new place; but the students I'll be teaching are just fine. There are some younger students going with me and I'll be coaching a lot of chamber music, which I love to do, so it'll be up to me how it is; and again, I might contribute something to it as well. But the point is, I would rather be doing things that I like to do and can do than not. I could sit at home on my high horse and not be too happy. But instead I have something that is meaningful and active, you know what I mean?

A.A.   *Do you have any desert island pieces?*

B.H.   Oh, the Bach Suites. I would want to take the whole bunch. I always loved them, but now they mean so much more to me. They're so satisfying to me.

A.A.   *I find that as well, as I get older.*

B.H.   The same thing with the Beethoven Sonatas.

A.A.   *Except you'd need a pianist on the desert island with you.*

B.H.   Yes. You know the thing that I've never heard a bass player play, but, because of history, they'd have a perfectly legitimate claim to? The second Beethoven Sonata in G minor. When Beethoven wrote that, he didn't have a cellist to play it, but I guess he had a contract with Dragonetti and asked him to come over and play it with him. So he played it with this bass player Dragonetti, who was famous for his concerto. He was a virtuoso, and when he got in the last (rondo) movement, he really played it. Evidently, Beethoven jumped up and gave him a bear hug. So a bass player could play it, and they could have a legitimate story to go with it.

A.A.   *Do you have anything more to add?*

B.H.   Yes, how very important it is for us to remember as performers, that it is our role to delve into the character and spirit of the music we study and perform. We are so lucky to have so many incredible masterworks and it is for us to bring them to life. Likewise, it is so important to be a part of our current times and play and interact with the composers and works of our own times. We are all on that continuum which is a musician's journey, one person to the next.

7

Gary Hoffman

Mr. Hoffman made his debut at the Wigmore Hall in London at the age of fifteen, quickly followed by New York. At the age of twenty-two, he became the youngest faculty appointee in the history of the Indiana University School of Music. After winning the Premier Grand Prix of the Rostropovich International Competition in Paris in 1986, he embarked on an international career, appearing with the world's most noted orchestras, in major recital and chamber music series and at prestigious festivals.

Although he has great affection for the classical cello repertoire, Gary Hoffman does not neglect contemporary music, of which he is a committed champion. Numerous composers, among them Graciane Finzi, Renaud Gagneux, Joel Hoffman, Laurent Petitgirard and Dominique Lemaître, to name only a few, have dedicated their concertos to him. He is a regular guest with the Chamber Music Society of Lincoln Center in New York, and is a remarkable and much sought-after chamber partner. He has made recordings for BMG (RCA), Sony, EMI and Le Chant du Monde, and now records on the La Dolce Volta label. Gary Hoffman has lived in Paris since 1990. He performs on a 1662 Nicolo Amati, the 'ex-Leonard Rose'. In 2011, Mr. Hoffman was appointed Maître en Résidence for cello at the prestigious Chapelle Musicale Reine Elisabeth in Brussels.

The Past

Anthony Arnone:	*Where did you grow up, and how did you first become exposed to the cello?*
Gary Hoffman:	It comes completely from the fact that I was born into a family of musicians; I'm the second of three brothers, and both parents were musicians.

My father was a conductor, and my mother was a violinist. My older brother is a pianist/composer, and my younger brother is a conductor; he was a violist and still occasionally plays. My sister, who unfortunately passed away, was a harpist. So from a very early age, I was living on a daily basis with the experience of listening to music, and eventually started an instrument myself. I have fond memories of going to see my parents, especially my father, who was the Music Director of the Vancouver Symphony (which is where I was born). So music was always there and always a big part of my life.

A.A.	*How did you pick the cello? Or did it pick you?*
G.H.	I started on the violin when I was seven and was studying with my mother, but it just wasn't very natural for me. My aunt was also a cellist; she was a member of the Chicago Symphony for many years. One day when I was nine, I was at her place and saw her cello, and I started plucking some notes. When I came home, I said to my parents, "I want to play the cello." And I think they had the wherewithal and the foresight to understand that perhaps that was a sign of destiny, that I was choosing something that was coming from within me.

So I switched, and from then on it was a totally different story. The cello was clearly the right instrument for me. From the beginning, I knew that the cello was the instrument I should play. I was lucky to have parents who could understand that.

A.A.	*Did you start lessons shortly after that?*
G.H.	Yes. I actually started with my aunt, but that wasn't really the right situation. I needed more regular attention and that kind of thing, so I started with a great teacher from the Midwest—at the time living in Chicago—Karl Fruh, whose name is known to some people. He always called himself the Midwestern Leonard Rose.
A.A.	*How old were you when you moved to Chicago?*
G.H.	We left Vancouver when I was almost eight.
A.A.	*So it was shortly after you moved to Chicago that you started to play the cello.*
G.H.	Absolutely. It was really in Chicago where it all began. Obviously the two years of playing the violin gave me something, but mostly it was trying to get out of habits that related to violin positions that were not suited to the cello. That took some time, but it was clear that with the cello I found my voice, both physically and also in terms of just finding a means of expression. I remember feeling that the violin was not right. Strange how those things happen.

A.A.   Was there any certain cellist that you heard, or that really you thought, "Wow, this is great. I want to sound like this." Maybe other than Karl Fruh?

G.H.   Definitely Karl Fruh for sure, but I would say at that time it was really listening to recordings of Feuermann and Piatigorsky.

A.A.   Was there a point that you remember when you thought, "This is what I want to do with my life."

G.H.   Yes. I was 11, and I understood that I was either going to be a baseball player or a cellist. Later on, I thought of something else, but it really wasn't in my thinking at that time. But I've wondered in retrospect if I had grown up in a different environment, whether I might have been something else. This is a peculiar thing to say, because it can cause a lot of interesting reactions—if not negative reactions. I happen to be somebody who lives in Europe—as you know—and in Europe, especially in Spain, somebody who feels about it the way I do is referred to as an aficionado. I'm talking about bullfighting.

   I sometimes wonder if I had grown up in a different environment, if I might have actually wanted to become a bullfighter—which seems for some people just barbaric. I get these comments all the time like, "How is it possible that a classical musician like you could like that?" I don't know the answer to that question, and maybe that's something we'll get into later. But at the time (I was 11) I knew deep down that what I wanted to be was a musician. And I was not forced to do it, none of us were forced. In fact, my father actually didn't want any of us to become musicians; he thought that it was too difficult a life. Since we showed aptitude in other areas, he thought we could make a living doing other things and have an easier life than the one that we would end up having if we chose the path of music. As luck would have it, we all chose music … in spite of his efforts.

A.A.   Is it fair to say you were self-motivated? Did you enjoy practicing?

G.H.   I loved the cello, and I loved music. Yes, I was motivated to practice. I was motivated to improve so I could express myself. When I was upset, or feeling troubled, my first reaction was always to go and play the cello. Always. That became my voice, and it became my way of working out difficulties—a sort of therapy in a way. I could also say it became like a religion. I was never forced to play the cello, and I was never forced to become a musician.

   It was made clear to all of us as children; if we chose that path, we had to be the best we could be, and we had to be serious about it. It was not in any way a hobby. And if we're going to do it, we're going to have to work.

A.A.   Do you think, looking back on that, it was a good lesson?

G.H.   It was a good thing, because I learned discipline early on. That might have happened anyway—I'll never know—but that was something that was made very clear. Yes, I think it was a good thing. These are things that last throughout your life. There's no question that the kind of discipline that I learned, and that I understood was important at that point, has helped me through lots and lots of difficult times on many different levels. We can call it what we want … discipline or a certain attitude about maintaining a standard that you set. Or as my teacher, Mr. Starker, would have said, what it means to be a professional. Not falling below a certain standard. Ever.

A.A.   *You learned that very young.*

G.H.   Yes, that was in my family already. I didn't have to learn that from Mr. Starker—I knew that already long before. That was part of everyday life, and it also included school-work. It had to be the best grades—not sometimes—but all the time. It was a lot of pressure. I did do things other kids did, but I had to have time to practice and do my homework. I had to. If I did do other things, it couldn't be at the expense of that.

A.A.   *What was the next step in your cello journey?*

G.H.   When I was 15, our family moved to Florida. My father had founded an orchestra now called the Florida Orchestra, but it used to be called the Florida Gulf Coast Symphony. When we were in Chicago, he was the Associate Music Director of the Chicago Symphony for one year before Solti came. Then Solti took over, we went down to Florida, and I was faced with what to do about a teacher. In fact, for a couple years, I didn't have a teacher. I was completely on my own.

A.A.   *Did you have an orchestra program in your school?*

G.H.   No.

A.A.   *That must have been a lonely existence at times.*

G.H.   I was the only classical musician in my high school, so I was on my own. I had my fam-ily, but that was it. We played chamber music in the family, and we did some concerts. For those two years, I was really learning on my own. In retrospect, that was probably a helpful thing to learn independence. It's an unusual thing at that age to do that, but circumstances brought that on.

A.A.   *It's amazing your drive for cello didn't diminish, without having a teacher or an orchestra or something to give you a sense of belonging.*

G.H.   No, not at all. That remained, because that was something that I had this intensity for. That wouldn't have stopped it at that point.

A.A.   *How advanced were you when you got to Florida, as far as the kinds of things were you practicing and performing? Did you feel like you had a fairly strong technique already established?*

G.H.   I had already been playing in public; I played this recital in Wigmore Hall when I was 15. It was the kind of recital that one wouldn't play anymore. It wasn't so strange in those days; but if I tell you the program now, it seems odd. I played Saint-Saëns Concerto, Tchaikovsky Rococo Variations, and a Brahms Sonata on that concert. I was learning concertos and sonatas and Bach, so I don't know what you would call that.

A.A.   *I would almost say you were a prodigy then, if you were playing Wigmore Hall recital when you're 15. I don't know if you ever felt like that, or if that term was used for you.*

G.H.   I had heard it, but I wasn't thinking in those terms. I just had an aim to want to be a musician, and also this drive, which probably came from my parents too.

A.A.   *Did you win a competition to get that recital opportunity?*

G.H.   No, that was something that was organized through my parents with the help of some other people. Some things flowed from that, but that wasn't something that was pushed that hard. Which I think in retrospect was a good thing; because at that point I had already seen people who had been pushed very hard only to have their interest waned, and then you never hear from them anymore. Some people met very sad ends.

        I'm actually thankful that I didn't have that experience, but I did have the experience of having a certain amount of pressure and similar objectives which gave a focus to what I was doing. And I was learning repertoire, so I wasn't getting stuck on the same pieces. I was learning chamber music, and shortly after that, I started studying with Starker. I took some lessons with him in Bloomington my senior year of high school. Then I went to Bloomington, where I was just eating up music and learning a lot from Mr. Starker.

A.A.   *How did you happen to first get to play for him? That doesn't happen every day.*

G.H.   My father had conducted for him a number of times, and they contacted him and asked if there would be a chance that I could play for him. He was in Fort Lauderdale; so I went there with my mother, and he agreed to teach me and give me a couple of private lessons. Then I went to Indiana. I didn't apply for any other school—I didn't really consider any other teachers.

A.A.   *How did your experience with Mr. Fruh compare with your experience with Mr. Starker?*

G.H.   I think what I got from Karl Fruh was an incredibly solid basis in making sound, making expression, and singing on the cello.

A.A.   *Would you say that you already had that sound in your head and Mr. Fruh helped your body be able to find it?*

G.H.   I think it was probably there in a very vague way somewhere, but he had a very natural and healthy way of playing. He was also very concerned with singing and a vocal approach to the instrument, in terms of how to use the left hand and the bow, that was invaluable. So I think in that respect, it obviously had suited what was inside me. I'm not sure that I could tell you that I actually heard something inside before.

A.A.   *Do you feel like you were physically pretty natural on the instrument?*

G.H.   Yes, I did feel that right away. I needed to adjust some of the things I learned from playing the violin; but after that, it seemed natural right away. The violin never seemed natural to me. I think Karl Fruh instilled a strong basis in the cello as an expressive instrument, and I'm sure that has made a big difference in my life. When I went to Janos Starker, I sensed that I needed to have more awareness, more information, and more development in the physical aspect of the cello.

A.A.   *Of how you were doing what you were doing?*

G.H.   Yes, and understanding it. I don't think I was a mindless player—it came fairly naturally to me—but I sensed somewhere that I needed to get to another level and have more to bring to it. I'm not so sure that was Karl Fruh's strength. We moved down to Florida, so a change was going to be made at some point. Then when I started studying with Mr. Starker, I started to lose a lot of what was natural to me, because I became very conscious of everything.

     I remember my parents being a bit worried, because I started to lose things that were just me. I remember in my second year as a student, I won the concerto competition playing the Elgar Concerto. When I listened to a recording of the performance, I was shocked. I didn't realize how I had actually come to sound like him. That wasn't my or his intention, but happened because of the strength of his personality and all the things that I was being conscious about at the time.

A.A.   *Were you happy about this?*

G.H.   No, not at all. That was a moment of awakening. From that point, I was into trying to find my own voice. Obviously I had gone through this process, and that was continuing. But this process actually involved, at least momentarily, losing the natural instinctive aspect of who I was as a cellist and a musician. That was not an intentional thing. The intentional aspect was that I needed to learn more about the cello and how to play it. This happened too, but I just didn't realize what else was happening.

I was never at odds with Mr. Starker, but I realized that I needed to start figuring out what's really deep inside and how I was going to put these things together. That was a very long process. I realized I had to stop listening to many of my idols, because that would be a dead end. I started to understand that best that I could be would be the best version of Gary Hoffman and not a lesser version of anybody else. That meant it had to be about what I am, and that was going to be a difficult process to figure out. That's what started it all, hearing that recording, and hearing that I had become something that I had never intended to be.

That started that process, and that took a very long time. But I owe Mr. Starker the largest debt of gratitude that one can have for somebody, because I've always felt that there is and maybe never will be anybody who brought teaching of the cello to that level. The greatest thing that he taught me, and I think any teacher can give to any student, is the ability to teach oneself. Because like with a parent and a child, you haven't quite done your job if they leave home and they're not equipped to deal with the world without you.

A.A. *It must have been interesting for you in a sense to not "leave home" since you started teaching at Indiana University right when you finished studying there as a student. Was it hard to teach there and find your own identity, but still be under Starker's wing?*

G.H. There was a position open in Bloomington, and he wanted me to take it. I finally did, but I was only 22 when I started teaching. It might not have been the best thing for me in terms of making my career mark as a young cellist, but that's how life went. It did teach me a sense of responsibility toward others; as well as the necessity to be your own person, to be able to see what you do and to understand it. And finally to be able to impart that—to communicate and articulate it in various ways—through playing, speaking, standing up for certain values, whether they be moral or musical.

Mr. Starker was obviously an incredibly intelligent person and intuitive, and somewhere he thought that I had the capacity for that. I don't think he would have put me in that position if he didn't think I would succeed. I didn't think about that then; I just thought about doing my job, but I didn't really think about what that meant for him to put his neck on the line for me.

A.A. *How many years did you teach at IU?*

G.H. I guess seven-and-a-half years.

A.A. *Did you feel like during that time, you had the space to be your own teacher? That must have been hard to have someone like Starker right there, in a way, watching over your shoulder.*

G.H. It was tricky. Before I made my own reputation as a teacher, he ended up accepting students that he knew that he couldn't have time for right away. He sent them to Gary Hoffman, and eventually maybe they would go to him. That's normal—but in that way, I was still a little bit like his assistant … but I wasn't his assistant. There were people who came and studied with me, but they didn't really know me. I was 22 years old, and I hadn't really made my mark as a performer or teacher so that people would want to study with me. So he would take more students than he could handle, and some of these people were not always happy. Then it was my job to convince them that they weren't going to be wasting their time. Another responsibility. In a way, his presence nonetheless was always acutely felt. Eventually, I had to leave Bloomington partially for that reason. Not because of anything he did wrong, but because I was still part of a situation where I couldn't be totally my own person. I maybe could leave and come back and be my own person, but at some point I'm going to have to leave.

A.A.   *So you knew when it was time.*

G.H.   Absolutely. There was a day when I knew I needed to leave. I went into the studio, and I said, "Mr. Starker, I have to talk to you." He said, "You're leaving." I said, "Just please let me tell you my own way." Which I did, and he understood. I think he always knew that one day that was going to happen. Others had studied there and then stayed for many years, but that was just not who I was.

A.A.   *How did you feel, especially compared to when you were 22 and started there, about your direction in life with the cello? Did you want to pursue a solo career? Or had teaching become a focus in your life?*

G.H.   Teaching wasn't something that I was thinking about, but Starker saw that it might be something that I would have a certain aptitude or ability for—he saw that in me. When I left Bloomington in 1986, I actually didn't teach anymore for 25 years.

A.A.   *Wow.*

G.H.   I gave master classes and taught at summer things, like here—at the Steans Institute. Until I started with a class again at La Chapelle Musicale Reine Elisabeth, or the Queen Elizabeth Music Chapel in Belgium eight years ago, I didn't have my own class. That was 25 years.

A.A.   *What did you do when you left Indiana? Was there a lot of work for you? I know you won the Rostropovich Competition in Paris in 1986, right about when you left IU.*

G.H.   Yes, I was pretty busy. I was playing chamber music all the time. A lot of those things don't exist in the same way in Europe; these series where they're just people that know each other and they're playing. That's starting to happen in Europe, but those things don't exist in the same way. That's hard for a lot of young musicians, but they have to make those things happen more.

When I lived in New York for example, there were times I was playing four or five different programs in one week. Playing in Bargemusic, playing in the series in New Jersey, playing this pickup thing and that. Suddenly, I'm playing four or five different programs in the same week and rehearsing nine hours a day. That got old at a certain point. But you make some money—not enormous fees, but some—and it keeps going. And some solo concerts here and there, but I wasn't teaching then. I had married a French woman. We were living in New York when my son was born, and she was unhappy there. She wanted to move back to Paris, and I thought this could be a good life change for me. As fate would have it, a year later, she wanted out of the marriage. My son was three, and I was faced with a decision; I had left the rest of my family in the States. I had been doing a lot of things in the States, and now I had to figure out what's going to happen. I thought, I'm staying close to my son.

So, I supported myself totally on playing for all those years. The reason why I started at the Chapelle was that I understood that at some point in my life, I'd want to go back to teaching. That seemed like a good fit, because it didn't require me to leave Paris—and I wanted to stay in Paris. It gave me a kind of freedom; it was a reasonable and easy commute, I didn't have to change my lifestyle, and I could have a class again. That's the reason why I did it. All those years before returning to teaching, I was doing it on my own; and it wasn't always the easiest thing, but I was okay with that.

A.A.   *Were you happy with the opportunities that were coming your way and feeling a good balance in your life?*

G.H.   Yeah, absolutely. I had freedom. When it comes to performing, I've managed with good fortune over the years. I also had a certain effort and focus, a sense of purpose, and the ability to do more and more of what I just really feel good about doing and what's important to me. Less of doing what I feel like I have to for whatever reasons, including financial. There's nothing wrong with that, but it's nice to be in a situation where you don't have to say "yes" to everything.

It's interesting—my father came through the Depression times, and I was taught that opportunities are hard to find; there are not very many guarantees in life, and it's good to have security and all that stuff. I never thought in those terms. So, for all those years, I was living without any assurance that from one year to the next I was going to be able to manage. But I have to admit, it never really bothered me.

A.A.   *Like a bohemian lifestyle.*

G.H.   Yeah, I think I'm like that. I guess you could look at it in different ways, but you know as well as I do that to get up on stage and to do these kinds of things, you can have lots of self-doubts and a lot of insecurities. Somewhere you have to have a sense of self confidence; there isn't any other way to do it. If you don't have that, you can't do it. You just can't. I think I knew that I had that. I didn't know if other people would recognize what I had to offer—or if I had anything to offer—and if I would have any possibility of really making it without some steady income.

But year after year, I kept going that way, and I started to see that I could manage this. I stuck with that. I'm one of those people, I guess, where independence of spirit and independence of thought is crucial to my being. Even through the difficult times, I've always had that. I remember having a very serious conversation with a friend of mine who was teaching somewhere (so he had a salary) and had just won a top prize on violin in the Tchaikovsky Competition. He said he was offered a position as a concertmaster, which was a very high paying, prestigious position. We were talking about it, and he said, "What do you think? What should I do?"

I said, "You just did this competition, you got a top prize, and you've got this teaching job, so you've got an income. It sounds to me like you were planning to pursue this and see where it leads you, so why don't you just keep doing that?" He looked at me and said, "I'm not like you. I need to have the car and the condominium and to know that I've got the money coming in and all that. I need that." I said, "Okay, then you've got your answer." I knew that I'm not like that. Some people might say that's arrogance or whatever, but I just think I knew what I wanted and the way I wanted it. That's it.

I just had this belief that it was going to be okay. I didn't know exactly if it would be what I wanted life is not like that. But I was still aiming for it, and I still thought that

I should give myself a chance for that. I could readjust later on if I had to, but now's the time—not in 20 or 30 years. I don't know—I guess nobody can tell the future; but if you make those choices for the right reasons, then you're doing something positive for yourself. You're putting yourself into a situation where at least those things can happen. If you don't do that, then they never will happen. I didn't want to live with that.

A.A. *For me, I always told myself that if I was going to actually try to go into music—because I started a little late—that I want to make sure I'm really happy, and not just take the job that comes. Might as well do something else.*

G.H. You're right. You know, it's interesting, because I got an email this morning from a friend of mine. She's French, and she had been trying for a few years to get an orchestra job. She finally got a good position in an orchestra in the North of France, so it pays a good salary. We're not talking about American standards like Chicago Symphony New York, but by French standards it's a pretty good salary. It's a pretty good orchestra and a nice city ... a lot of things. She's obviously having lots of second thoughts, and wondering what to do. She said, "The thing is, you have this life where you simply don't have to answer to anybody."

Then she was talking about these people in the media—not just in music. She just can't accept their values, or lack thereof, and the kinds of things that they do to try to achieve their own purposes. What they're willing to do and how they treat people. She said, "But you, you just do what you want. I respect and admire that." I thought it was nice for her to say that, but actually that was always important to me. Having said that, I have to make lots of concessions like everybody does. We're not alone in the world, but in the end it's true. I really don't have to do anything that I don't want to do.

A.A. *When you started teaching at the Chapelle, did you feel like you had rediscovered something you had missed from not teaching for all those years?*

G.H. No, because I was always in contact with students. I always did this kind of thing in the summer. I would see many of these people on repeated occasions in other places, so I was developing relationships with students and other teachers. I would start to go to Curtis and give classes there and that kind of thing. It's not like I was out of the teaching world. When the Chapelle offer came, I realized that it was the right fit for me. It fit my lifestyle, and it gave me the opportunity to teach in a situation that I thought would be productive. The level is incredibly high, which is nice. It's not a salaried position; I get paid for the lessons I teach. There's no particular risk I'm taking, but I don't have a signed contract or tenure or anything like that. For that reason, some people wonder how I could accept a situation like that?

The answer is because I trust them, they like me, and they're happy with what's going on. I've been offered nice salaries in other places, but it just didn't fit my life. I know that some people have told me that when you have a situation like that, you don't think about it. You take it. I always thought that was strange. You mean you don't have a choice? No, you don't. You're offered something like that, so you do it. But somebody else is deciding your life for you, and I don't want that. "But this is the opportunity you have, and look at the benefits." I get all that, but you're telling me that I need to give up something that's essential to me. I can't do that.

The Present

A.A. *How has your teaching evolved from your start at Bloomington into the way you teach now? Do you have a philosophy? It sounded like, from the way you were talking earlier, that there might be some similarities to being a parent.*

G.H. I don't know if I have an exact philosophy, beyond the fact that I think that I see my role as giving these young cellists—as best as I can—the tools to go forward in their life and not to be dependent on me or any other teacher. To be dependent on themselves, whatever that entails.

A.A. *You made me think of this earlier when you talked about your time as a student with Starker, and it resonated with me. I think a lot of people when they're young and they start off studying with a very big personality, they might lose their own voice. At least initially, they want to imitate, they don't quite know who they are. Is that something you're aware of as a teacher?*

G.H. I'm very aware of that. I don't play much in lessons. That's not really a conscious choice, but more by instinct. My instinct only on occasion brings me to play, and usually just a couple of notes, demonstrating one thing that I just feel that is best heard rather than said with words. Earlier, when I was showing Natania that bowing in the Beethoven, I just wanted to try to get her to achieve the most natural motion possible. I thought the most natural way of doing that was just doing it, instead of talking about it.

A.A. *Don't you find some students may learn better by just hearing and imitating sound, as opposed to words being spoken to them?*

G.H. No doubt, but the danger is they will be influenced by what they hear. So in a lot of ways I prefer to find other ways to communicate other than playing. As it is, I notice that sometimes students are playing like me, and I really don't like it at all. I guess you could take it as flattery, but I don't take it that way. But inevitably, unfortunately, all that stuff is out there ... CDs, YouTube—and you can't stop it. I'm not happy about it at all.

A.A. *But if a student is going to learn—let's just say a Beethoven Sonata, or Brahms E Minor or something, do you think recordings or YouTube should fit into their learning of a piece like that?*

G.H. Only after they develop at least the beginnings of a relationship with the music. On the other hand, it's almost impossible that somebody who's 14 or 15 years old would start the A-Major Beethoven and have never heard it before. Even if it's not a CD or YouTube, they've heard it played live. You can hardly avoid that. But when students have to play a new piece, the first thing they do is listen to somebody play it. I insist that they don't do this, but I know they do it anyway.

I've had students ask me, "How do you learn a piece you've never heard?" What do you do if you're doing the world premiere of something? "Exactly, what do you do?" That's where you need all the things you can bring to the table—and by the way, I consider that very liberating. "What?" It's you and the music, and there's no comparison with anybody, at least in your mind or anybody else's. They never heard anybody else play it. In other words, the piece is in some respect partially created by you. It's about what you think about it and what you feel about it, and what it is you gleam from what you see. Or maybe it's about the relationship you have with the composer or what that music suggests to you based on other music you've played. There are any number of different reference points.

"But how do you know you're on the right track?" I said, "That's the point, you don't know." Ok, so you don't know. But what makes you think you know just because you heard other people do it? Are they all right? Especially young people are constantly asking, "What do most people do?" And my first response is, "As if that matters what most people do. Why is that a criterion?"

A.A.   *I think that's the danger of smartphones these days too, it's just way too easy.*

G.H.   All that stuff, it allows you not to have to think. It allows you not to have an opinion and not to have to go through the process. Somebody went through the process somewhere along the line, and everybody else benefited from it. It's great when I hear people imitate Janos Starker—how he plays the Kodaly Sonata—but when they do that rubato, it sounds different than when he does it. And why? Because he went through the process, and they didn't. They don't understand that. "But, Kodaly ..." I know, but he went through a process, and you need to go through that process.

How do you go through the process? Now we have a discussion. Now we have something we can talk about. How do you go through that process? That's a reasonable question. There is a way, but it's difficult. Especially when you've been inundated with all that stuff that has come to you, because other people have done the work and you haven't. So it's tough, but it can be done. Maybe it can't be done in the same way that you'll do it when you have to play a piece that nobody else has played, but you can try to get to the source and try to have your own relationship.

To get back to your question—I always make this analogy: let's say you're going to read a book. Do you want to hear 25 opinions before you read the book? No. What do you want to do? You want to read the book. After that, discuss it with people if you want. Then you work on a piece, get some ideas, get a reaction, and see how you are with that music. Don't go to YouTube, don't listen to somebody play it. You start to get a feeling about something first, then watch it. That's like having a conversation about the book you just read. What do you think about this piece?

A.A.   *That's a great analogy.*

I believe if people do that, they're going to come a little bit closer to what the music is for them. But a lot of them don't have either the trust or the conviction or the certainty that they're going to be on the right track. That's where I try to underline to them that nobody knows that for sure. The point is not whether it's the right track, but to find what makes sense to you inside. You're not going to find it if you just mindlessly do what somebody else did.

It doesn't relate to you; so while you might do it very well, it's still not you, and it's still not going to be the original. The original will always be better, because it is the original. Period. Sometimes people ask me, "Who do you think the greatest cellist is?" And as far as I'm concerned, there's only one answer to that, and that's Pablo Casals. The reason for that is because there wouldn't be anybody else, if it wasn't for Pablo Casals. For me, that's the end of the discussion. You can prefer this one or that one—but he was the greatest, simply because we wouldn't exist if it weren't for him.

There were other cellists before that, but from all reports Casals brought the instrument into a totally different universe. I have to believe that, because it couldn't have been that he just played a little bit more in tune or his tone was a little bit more pleasing. It must have been a giant leap. From what we can gather and from what I've heard of recordings of some of the cellists of the past—close enough to that time—we're talking about light years away. Starker talks about it when he met Casals as a kid, and heard the cello played in a different way.

A.A.   *Related to interpreting and learning a piece, do you tell your students to listen to other works by the composer they're playing?*

G.H.   Very much so. It's very shocking to me if I'm working with a student on say the Brahms F-Major, and I make the parallels with the Third Symphony but realize they don't know the Third Symphony. To me, that's impossible. It's not a problem—it's impossible. You had better know these pieces. That will help you get to some certainty about what this music is about. Recognizing gestures, understanding the language. We're talking about language; we're talking about understanding a language. I understand the meaning of that word, but how does he use that word? In other words, having a deeper understanding of what at least the composer is attempting to communicate. After that, three people hear that composition or those expressions and will hear different things. I'm not talking about that. Three people look at a painting and see different things, that's normal.

But the painter had some desire to say something, so it's important to have some kind of deeper understanding of what those things are. It's a language—there are symbols, and there are references.

A.A.   *You almost have to develop a certain accent in your musical voice depending on what composer you are playing.*

G.H.   This is essential as well, but also to have a greater knowledge of the general repertoire. The Chopin Sonata is a piece I love. Sometimes people have thought that I have some innate sense of this music, but as a kid I was listening to Chopin all the time. I checked out recordings from the library when I was living in Chicago, I listened to Lipatti playing Waltzes and the B-Minor Sonata, and Rubinstein playing the Nocturnes and the Polonaise. I listened to this stuff. So you get a sense of what these kinds of rhythms mean to Chopin.

What's behind all that? And how do you know unless you have some sense of what this language is? So yes, that strikes me as essential. Of course, I had the advantage of growing up listening and hearing this music at home. Hearing my mother playing violin music. Going to concerts and seeing my father conduct all his big symphonic works and things like that. That was a built-in education—I don't deny that.

A.A.   *But still, I find so many students aren't curious to know what the Brahms Symphonies sound like. It's not like going to the dentist.*

G.H.   It's astonishing. When I talk to young college students and say "You know the Brahms G-Major Sextet?" And you look at them, not only have they not played it—which is a little surprising—but at least they've heard it. No! They haven't heard it. Really? The Brahms Second Sextet, you never heard it? First of all, I want to say to them, I'm jealous. Because it's the most unbelievable feeling when you sit down and play this music for the first time. In a way, it will never be quite like that, because the first time is something unbelievable.

A.A.   *It just blows you away.*

G.H.   You just can't believe what you're part of. They look at you and think, "Okay, good." Yeah, I had better listen to it. And I'm thinking, why did you wait this long? What are you waiting for? You don't have colleagues that ever want to sit down and read? Sit down and read—it doesn't matter how good it is, but get experience. What do you want to play music for, if it's not to experience that stuff? Sometimes it's shocking to me. When I was in Bloomington, I would check out music, there was a pianist or two that I would play with, and we would just read through stuff all the time. Would spend evenings—three or four hours just playing through stuff.

"How did you know about this piece?" That's how I knew about it. I remember years later, when I was in Kronberg, there was a festival that was dedicated to the memory of Piatigorsky. I was asked to do a recital. I remember when I was in Bloomington, that I had seen this music of an original piece that Piatigorsky wrote called "Scherzo" and I had never seen it again. I was going back to Bloomington for something, and sure enough it was there. I copied it, and I played it in that program. I never even would have known about this piece if I hadn't checked out stuff when I was a student. And there I saw, Piatigorsky Scherzo. It doesn't change your life, but it's a charming piece that I was able to program then. In this concert I played a piece by Piatigorsky, not a transcription, but an original piece by Piatigorsky. People thought, "How did you find it?" I didn't tell the whole story—but that's how I found it, because I was curious to see what that was. I don't think that's any great thing, I don't understand why they're not more curious about stuff like that. "How is that you play this sonata?" Because I read about it, I got the music, and I thought it was a great piece. "You never heard anybody play it?" No. "Then what made you want to do it?" Back to that again.

You need somebody to show you the way first, before you're willing to take a step? Is that the way it is? I guess so. That's where I feel differently about these things.

A.A.   *How do you help students find their own voice? To not rely on imitation as much as exploring the process to discover what they really want to say in music?*

G.H.   Well I'm aware that some teachers in the past, as well as some teachers today are basically about "This is how I do it. Do it like I do." That can be interesting if you're interested to know how somebody does something and what you should do to sound like them.

But of course to me that's clearly not the goal. Imitation is always an important aspect of learning because it allows one to identify certain things and figure out how one does it, but that's of course not the objective, to imitate somebody and play like somebody. To me the important thing is for each student to develop his or her own vision and to get them to think for themselves. I'm not sure if I'm successful at this, but what I would like to think I am and I'd like to hope that I get students to actually think about aspects of what they're doing instrumentally and musically, that I feel are important.

So in the end it is going to be partially about my values and my vision of what it's all about. But that strikes me as normal and in fact crucial because otherwise why are they coming to study with me?

So I can't completely ignore my participation in that. But in the end, my objective is to try to get them to individually approach learning in their own way and ask themselves these questions that to me are crucial and important in their development. How they see the instrument and how it's going to be used to produce and communicate the musical thoughts and ideas that they have. That for me is the goal. And as I said, that's not a simple thing. But I've noticed that over the years, without making it a conscious decision, that I don't play very much in lessons. And it's funny because it's not something that I really thought about that much, but over the years it's evolved in that direction. And then there are times that I noticed that I just have the cello and I start to play bits and pieces. Sometimes even a few phrases but rarely more than that.

It's not because I'm afraid of what playing for them might do. But I have noticed that at times when I've done it, I thought it was a shortcut—it was too much of a shortcut. It became too simple. That very often these young talents can absorb things quickly. But I've noticed that with certain students, that they just wanted to hear me play and hear my solutions and start writing things down. And I'm like, "Wait, wait, wait, don't write things down." And over time I realized that through verbal communication and perhaps other aspects of communication can be used other than playing for them, and can often induce a positive response.

There was an interesting story about Gregor Piatigorsky who talks about a student who came to him who wasn't an enormous talent. The student could play but Piatigorsky noticed that every time he demonstrated, the kid played worse and worse. And so then he started to play badly in lessons and then the kid played better and better. And at the end there was a class recital and he played and other people played and there was a party and he said the kid was going around to his colleagues saying, "Oh boy, Mr. Piatigorsky, what a great teacher. As a cellist, not so good, but a great teacher." So Piatigorsky was very happy because he felt he accomplished his goal.

A.A.   *It seems like just from watching you teach that you're not the old school, "Here's my bowings and fingerings, play it that way," but rather you let the students find their own way and guide them when needed.*

G.H.   Absolutely! I remember I once had a student who was studying during the year with another teacher and came to me for a summer session in Bloomington. She came to me and said, "What do you think I should work on?" And I don't know why, but I had this idea that a good piece for her to learn would be the Dohnányi Konzertstück. I said, "I think the Dohnányi Konzertstück" and she said, "I don't know that piece." I said, "Good." And she said, "Okay, well I'll go buy the music. And what should I do about fingerings and bowings? Could I have your part?" I said, I haven't played the piece. And suddenly I saw panic on her face and she said, "Oh, what should I do?" I don't understand your question. "What should I do about fingerings and bowings?" I said, "Decide fingerings and bowings." This is a master's student. She said, "I've never done that." I said, "Well now you will." That's what we spent the summer doing.

And she was actually very grateful at the end of the summer. She said, "You know, I had no idea how to do this." I said, "Well, I'm glad because that was really important for you to learn." What are you going to do when you don't have a teacher anymore? You can't just play the repertoire that you learned with the teacher and do just that. But you're absolutely right—I do it for that reason, to develop independence of thought. The most important thing is to have some kind of reasoning process and to have some way of arriving at something that would be useful and musical. And there are obviously principles and logic behind this. Without that, it's just like walking in the dark, you have no idea where you're going.

A.A. *If you are looking for potential students, what do you look for most? Is it if they have a strong voice, something to say, but maybe they have some physical limitations? Or the other way around, if they're very gifted physically but maybe don't have as much to say?*

G.H. I wouldn't say that it's one or the other. I would say that we all have our weaknesses, but there has to be something ultimately somewhere that suggests that this person has something to say with music. And that for me still is more important in the end because I feel like certain things can be learned but certain other things can be awakened, developed, improved, clarified, magnified, or expanded. You can lead a horse to water, but you can't make them drink. And if somebody doesn't have anything to say about music and doesn't have that essential ingredient, I don't know that you can teach that.

A.A. *Do you think scales and études are a necessary part of students' development?*

G.H. Absolutely. And it doesn't end just because they already play really well. I think that's something that should be kept going. Maintenance and pushing to the next level and that sort of thing.

A.A. *Do you still do scales?*

G.H. Yes. Every day!

A.A. *Everyone I've asked has said that.*

G.H. It's therapeutic. And also gives me a chance to get physically on the right track.

A.A. *When I asked Larry Lesser what he still wants to accomplish in this life, he said, "I still want to learn to play in tune." And I laughed a little and he said, "No, I'm serious. I want to learn to play in tune."*

G.H. We all want to learn to play in tune, that's for sure! But intonation is not absolute. For example, Heifetz played in tune. But Heifetz was constantly adjusting intonation depending on what he was playing. So if you listened to him play Porgy and Bess Suite, he's playing flat sometimes intentionally. So this idea of mechanized intonation doesn't exist. Heifetz was capable of doing that, but he didn't see intonation that way, as this absolute objective and once you achieve it then you just do that. For him it was part of expression. Intonation was part of expression and should change based on the matter at hand.

A.A. *Was there something that helped the way you practiced for your intonation to become wonderful? Was there a process you went through? A lot of double stops or playing with drone notes?*

G.H. Those are very helpful but for me, the best way I could address that subject is to use an example of somebody who came to me at the Chapelle who I thought was very talented but had a basic problem with intonation. It first had to do with the fact that he clearly wasn't hearing what he was playing and that he wasn't disturbed enough by it and he wasn't bothered enough to make it an objective. That was the first thing. Once I got him to start really hearing it, he got really disturbed, so I of course became happier because now it wasn't my problem. It was his problem and that's important. After that we started getting into issues which are esoteric but essential; he was doing all kinds of fingerings that were basically designed to decrease his chances of playing in tune. Sometimes because he had a musical idea. Good. But what I was telling him is if it's not feasible, if you can't execute it, it doesn't matter what musical value it has. If you can't do it, it's a bad fingering.

But there are passages where I have many possible fingerings, and somewhere among them should be at least one that will be the best solution for you, based on your hands and how you want to hear that passage. Then you have to understand the kinds of things that could create intonation problems. So we talked about all kinds of matters. He would play passages that had a fairly consistent pattern and would be constantly changing the pattern. Let's look at that. You're constantly changing the pattern. That creates an extra burden mentally on what's going through your mind and what you have to accomplish as you're playing under stress.

There are chances that maybe nine times out of ten it will work instead of, on a good day if I feel good and I've had enough sleep that maybe three out of ten. That's not good enough. Why is it not good enough? Because you play one phrase that's in tune. The next phase is three notes that are out of tune. After a while, the listener is disturbed by this because it gives the impression of slovenliness. It gives the impression of not understanding its importance in terms of the sound you make, the harmonies you're playing within and all of these kinds of things.

So we started examining things. I said, "Okay look. Look at the fingering you're doing there. Why are you doing it?" "Because I want to." "I get it. Well, what about this way of doing it?" Okay. And "Why would I do it that way?" Because chances are if you do the other thing, you follow an extension by an extension and then there's a shift in everything, then there's not a point where you're stable in this whole passage. So chances are, unless you get it all completely right and understand every nook and cranny, it's just going to be out of tune.

So he started to get all that and you know something? He started to play in tune and he appreciated that. But that was something he had never dealt with. And so of course it's a complex issue, but I think it comes from a desire, an objective to play in tune. Not because that way nobody can criticize you, but because you hear it as an integral component in the process of making music. And then to figure out from a physical and instrumental standpoint, what kinds of things you can do to increase your chances of playing in tune, assuming you hear it. And also working on how you should be hearing, melodically and harmonically and this kind of thing.

A.A.   *I spend a lot of time helping my students to learn how to practice. Is that something you work on a lot with students? And related to that, do you have practice, tips that you find are really helpful to you that you could share, even if you don't spend a lot of time on that with your students.*

G.H.   Actually I often practice with my students, but they don't realize it. We will go back to a certain spot and I'll ask them to try something. So not playing the passage exactly as it's written, but just a certain aspect of it. And then I'll ask them to incorporate something else in the passage. So in my mind I've broken it down into various elements on that specific piece and then try to put it back together again and then they get to play in tempo.

I say, "What we just did was practicing. That's what that was. So that's why I went through that process. To give you an idea of how at least in my mind, it's the most efficient way and useful way of practicing, to sort of identify a problem, see what that relates and to try to isolate the various issues. And once you've understood what that's about, try to put it back together." It's a kind of general way. But in essence the idea of how one practices, because I think obviously there's the kind of mindless repetition, which over time will probably guarantee that you'll play it better unless you're practicing the same problem over and over again. In which case it's just going to instill the problem.

A.A.   *It's obvious in a way but I remind my students if you want to sound different, you have to do something different with your body. Because I think a lot of people do the same thing with their body and keep expecting it to sound different. It's not going to happen.*

G.H.   Exactly! We saw, for example, with Jason in the Strauss what he's capable of doing. He's so not aware of this tension that he creates in his neck and his jaw. But when he keys in on that, suddenly the sound gets so much better. Like you say, if you're not going to do anything differently, you can't expect it to sound any different. And if you continue to practice the same problem over and over and over again, all you're doing is instilling the problem deeper and deeper into your system.

A.A.   *Sort of the other side of the coin of breaking things down in practice, do you ever practice performing as it gets close to the concert? Especially If maybe it's a piece you haven't performed a lot?*

G.H.   Yes, all the time.

A.A.   *Because I find a lot of students are so used to stopping and trying to fix something at the moment, and then they're on stage and they're not used to the fact that they can't stop anymore.*

G.H.   That's a very good point. That is something that comes up a lot because I remind students that we're in the business of trying to improve our playing and improve instrumental issues and try to hear more in music and understand better what the music is about and how we can accomplish that. But in the end, the point is that we're going to perform. And that's something that we don't really practice enough. And they ask, "Well, how do you practice that?" And I say, "Well, you're working on certain problems. You're trying to achieve certain things. You're trying to learn certain things. You should spend every day some time, 20 minutes, 15 minutes just performing. Whatever you're trying to accomplish, whatever you're doing, you need to get back to your instinctive being, and if you spend all your time analyzing and practicing, and you get on stage, and you're not really playing, you're practicing. In other words, you can't expect to perform on stage if that's the only time you ever do it.

Performing is not sitting there going, "That wasn't good, that was not good, that that was not good, I didn't like that." Don't sit and judge yourself. Just listen, and go on and remember, and then you'll have a better idea of what you need to practice. Most of the time they will agree. I always say that you learn far more in one concert than 100 hours of practicing. Now you know what to practice.

A.A.   *How do you feel about playing by memory in lessons, or at concerts? Is that something you have your students do?*

G.H.   I do think it's very important to develop one's memory. And not just to be able to play by memory but to develop it, because I think memory is an incredibly important aspect of everything that we do. To remember things, to remember what we heard, to remember music that we've heard, and how it relates to music we're playing, and all the different aspects of memory. I think if we don't have a sense of memory in our playing, and I don't mean specifically related to playing, performing by memory, but the registering and the retaining of information, in a deep and permanent way, then I think we're missing something that is incredibly important to the whole process of instrumental playing, and music making. In the end, it makes no difference to me whether people play from memory, or they don't play from memory. But I would definitely urge them to develop that. In the end if I understood that somebody really had made a solid effort, and in the end they feel uncomfortable, that's ok. I don't have a problem with that. But they have to have gone through that process, and they have to try to get over that mental block. I do think it is possible for some people to actually feel freer with the music.

A.A.   *Do you deal with stage fright with your students? I'm wondering if that's something you've ever had to deal with?*

G.H.   I think we all do have to deal with nerves, and I think there's certain physiological things that are important. Obviously, you know that limit of the heart beating faster, tension in the body that increases with nerves. But I always go on the supposition that these things may happen with nerves, but they're still there somewhere. Even when we're playing in what we consider to be a relaxed state, and so the element of being nervous when we play gives us an opportunity to perhaps see what becomes heightened, but may in fact be present, that we better pay attention to, and there are various philosophies I have about that. That this idea when people say, "That never happened to me when I practice." I understand that, but I think that's probably not true. It just wasn't that noticeable, or even that important because you were thinking about other things, and you thought that was okay, but suddenly the thing that you never really paid any attention to was not okay, because you got nervous.

   You never really practiced it. People say, "There's no point in practicing something you know how to do." Maybe not, but maybe you need some kind of awareness, because if you don't deal with that, it can come out like a hidden monster that bites you because you never bothered with it.

A.A.   *What do you think is the hardest thing to teach a student?*

G.H.   Why taste and scholarship are so important? Because I guess I can't teach anybody the importance of these things. I once had an experience with the third movement of the Brahms F-Major Sonata. When the student got to the mordant, he played a trill. And I wasn't sure I was going to let him play the Da Capo, because we were running out of time, but I thought, "I want to hear it again, because I want to see what he does."

   And then we did it again, and he did the same thing. And at the end I tried to play dumb, and asked, "What edition you have?" And this and that. "But you know those are mordants, not trills." He said, "Yeah I know, I know. So what, what's the difference?"

He was an arrogant student who later did become less defensive. But it was a moment where I couldn't teach *What Does it Matter?* It's something inside you. It's a question of conscience, and you know what it is all about. So I don't know, I guess in a way that's the hardest thing to teach.

You know Starker used to say, "You can define everything in music." Everything, and he's right. You can explain every single thing in instrumental playing. There isn't one thing that can't be explained. And in music making too. You can identify, you can analyze it, you can break it down, he said. But the one thing that can't be explained is why some people can, and others can't.

Was that something we referred to as talent? But it goes beyond talent. Of course, it's also just what's important to you, and what it all means, and I guess that's the thing you can't teach. That maybe some people would say you can't teach talent. Maybe that's a simple way of explaining what it is I just said. But you can't. You can't teach talent. But there's no question, and I agree with Starker with that. You can explain everything, every single thing, you know? And I consider it important for me to be able to do that, and I don't mean this as criticism to teachers, or colleagues, but I'm surprised very often that some people seem not to be aware, or able to pinpoint a problem. You know, with Starker, he could explain everything to me. That's why I considered him supreme, because he knew everything, and understood everything, and could articulate it. It's just absolute complete knowledge, and that was unique really, I have never seen anybody else like that.

A.A.   *I have loved watching and hearing your vibrato over the past few days. It's obviously something you have thought a lot about and use it as an important tool in your expression. Did you deal a lot physically with how to achieve that, or was it more from your imagination and conception of sound?*

G.H.   What I do over the years, and what I still do listen for, is constantly the relationship between vibrato, and what the bow is doing, in terms of the various parameters. Obviously, the ones that we know. Where the bow is being placed, the pressure, or speed, and how that all is combined. For me, it's all predicated on the central notion that the essential aspect of the character of the sound that we produce comes from the right side of the body, meaning from the bow, and that the left hand adds that element that the bow cannot provide. That has to come, and flow from what the bow is doing. So the vibrato should enhance, and add that element that will complete the picture. But if we gave a percentage, I would say it's 95% from the bow, and 5% for the left hand. Maybe there are times shifts a little bit, you know, but I would always say that the essential aspect of the character of the sound is coming from the right side of the body.

For example, if you want to give that kind of shimmery sound, which is quite light with the bow. Contact, but very little pressure, lots of speed. So the impression is that one is not working very hard with the bow, just moving along, gliding along the top of the string. But you want the sound to shimmer. At that point, the string is not vibrating that much. So, the vibrato actually starts to work to create the sound. The vibration that's missing from what the bow can do, and the combination creates that shimmering sound that we sometimes like to have, and that's where the vibrato of course will create that missing ingredient. But that has totally of course to do with how the two function together. With students, this is often very difficult because they haven't yet learned to separate the hands. They haven't practiced like that yet.

And equally interesting is something that often doesn't come up. Playing with different parts of the finger. I see many young people playing always with the same part of their finger. "Can you get a thicker sound there?" They start vibrating wider. No, no, no. I'm not talking about the wider vibrato. I'm talking about a thicker sound. Then there's a puzzled look on their face.

"Contact the string with more flesh? I don't know what that means."

"Well, you're always playing the tips of your fingers. Do you ever play toward the inside, toward the first joint? "

"No, I never did."

"Well, you could use that part of the finger. Get a thicker sound." They put it down. Yeah, oh. That's the new idea, okay? Now you're covering more surface of the string. Now your vibrato becomes more efficient. In other words, the smallest oscillation. You're covering more string, so you're getting more of it to vibrate. Ah. okay. Do you actually do that all the time? All the time. I mean you're actually changing contact points on the finger all the time? Really? That's like, that's a new idea. I learned this from Karl Fruh.

But this is not a way out. There's a logic behind that, right? Of course, one can be using it at the wrong time. Obviously if you're looking for precision and speed, probably better not to be playing flat fingers. If you want to look for quick articulation, probably play more on the tip. You want to look for thicker sound inside. But you know, we're not talking about the very tip next to the nail, or next to the first joint. We're talking about a fairly small area, but it makes a big difference, you know?

A.A.   *I agree!*

G.H.   And then of course the angle. You know, I remember understanding fairly early, because I was always fascinated by vibrato, that actually a perfectly perpendicular hold creates a vibrato that to the ear is fairly monochromatic, and one dimensional because it has only one component to it. Up and down in the direction of the fingerboard. It's an okay sound, it just sounds a bit flat and uninteresting, and when you add to it a slightly diagonal component, it starts creating different kinds of sounds because you're hitting different parts of the finger as you rotate in a motion, and that creates a more interesting sound.

So I would talk to students, and show them that, and they say, "Yeah." So that's why the slightly pronated approach will help to create a more colorful, interesting ringing sound because you're doing that. In addition, when we want to produce singing lines, we're more in the business of creating horizontal connections between notes, rather than vertical connections, and the pronated approach will help to increase that aspect because you're not attacking from above, and in the vertical way. Having said that, there are many times when you want a speaking singing sound that you want to attack more from above. Possibly a little bit more at a right angle, and possibly not. For me, the master of that, and that's virtually a vanished technique, was Casals. There's almost nobody who plays like this anymore. To actually speak with the left hand, and sing with the bow. These days it's sing with the bow, sing with the left hand. Speak with the bow, speak with the left hand. What about the sing with the bow, and speak with the left hand? What does that mean? Well listen, so lift fingers, do this kind of thing, and give different attacks, different timing. Sort of different rhythm to how fingers come down, and how notes begin. I mean, there's so much one can do with that, and you rarely hear anybody playing like this anymore. Greenhouse used to play like that.

A.A.   *I was going to say that I heard Joel Krosnick talk about that too, and yes, it doesn't seem as common in today's playing.*

G.H.   Oh it's an art that's been lost very much. And it's surprising to me that when I talk about playing with different parts of the fingertip, how many people never have been taught that, or told that, or even thought about it.

A.A.   *It's true.*

G.H.   They were taught probably at an early age to play at a certain point, and never thought about it again.

A.A.   *What about on a bigger scale? How do you feel about torso movement, specifically involved in playing the cello?*

G.H.   It's very important. That's something that comes up a lot, and I often show because one of the things that comes up that torso movement can really help to improve, are those very difficult moments. For example, playing with the first finger in the upper positions, or in half position, you know? And that getting that nasty thin sound that nobody wants.

When many people get into the upper positions, they will break the last joint of their first finger, and try to vibrate that way because they feel they're getting more surface area. I recommend that they maintain the position that they have, and just think of not pulling their arm back, not pulling their shoulders back, but rotating their torso slightly toward the right, so that they maintain the same relationship of their arm/shoulder to the torso, but that they then contact with the first finger on a slightly fleshier part at a better angle, and vibrate, and it always works. Not just sometimes it works, it always works. Because it's fundamentally sound, you know? And it makes sense, and the adjustment is very small.

Now some people think, "Really? Rotate your torso?" I asked them to play a C major scale from the low C to two octaves up the A string, like four notes. The simple thing, observe what you do. Didn't you rotate your torso when you went from the C, to the G, to the D to the A? Yeah, a little bit. That's all I'm talking about. This is a motion that we always are using, because if you negate it, and don't use it, you can't play. You're like a robot. You're like a statue, you know? So just going from the C up to the A involves a slight rotation of the torso. So this is not a motion that's foreign to what we all normally do.

A.A.   *What about for the bow arm? Not so much for a string crossings, but if you're starting, let's say a fairly fast bow motion. I've often heard the analogy that it's similar to a backhand in tennis or throwing a frisbee. I've used that analogy sometimes, too, that the motion maybe would start from the torso. Do you believe that?*

G.H.   I actually hadn't thought of it that way, but yes, I would believe that, because of course, I think the origin of all of these motions are not in the hand, they're not in the forearm, they're not even in the upper arm. They're somewhere in the lower body, pelvis, lower back, torso, all of these things. So yes, I totally agree.

One of the analogies that I make, which isn't exactly what we're talking about, is the whole issue of pulling and pushing the bow. The French way is actually very good because of course, as you know, down-bow and up-bow in French is "tirer/pousser", or "pull/push." We know what it means, but unfortunately, it doesn't describe at all what's really happening. We accept it now, we know what down-bow is. So it's not like, "Really, why is that down-bow?", but we think about it. "Actually, why is it down-bow?" There's nothing more down about this or more up about that. It's completely arbitrary.

But pulling and pushing is exactly what's happening, and that I often say, think about how the French identified these strokes. We talk about pulling and pushing, but how do you feel pulling? For example, you pull the bow. Imagine you put your arm out like you're holding the bow. Okay, now you've got a very taut rope in your hand, and somebody is pulling on it, and you're pulling against it in the direction of the way the bow should be going. That's the feeling you want to have. That's what pulling means, and now when you don't have that taut rope, but you just have the bow, you're not clutching it. So you release the tension just to the point where you're able to hold the bow, and it's not going to fall and you're fine.

But the feeling that you want to establish in the arm is pulling. There's some kind of resistant force pushing, like you're pushing against something that's resisting you as you're playing on bow, and sometimes I actually put my fist against their upper arm, or I hold them so that they feel this force against which they should play, whether it's down or up, and that they need to establish that feeling, without my being the one to impose that force to induce that muscular feeling, and I would say that, of course, that's focused basically on what they're feeling in the arm, but in fact, as you say, it's coming from farther back than that.

So yes, I think that kind of analogy, whether it's backhand, or you suggested Frisbee, these are all good analogies. I mentioned the rope idea, because we all know in school, tug of war, but that is the feeling. Anything like that, I think, is extremely helpful, because that way they can relate it to something that is so familiar and that they've always done that actually is a useful motion and how it translates to the cello.

I think one of the greatest difficulties in cello playing is just the idea of trying to produce natural motions, and realizing that we need to find a way to produce motions on the cello that are motions we know and use, and that we don't suddenly get panicked when we are sitting behind the cello, and suddenly don't know what to do.

A.A. *How do you feel about a bent thumb on the bow? From watching you, it looks like you play with a bent thumb.*

G.H. I believe that the thumb being bent back the other way and blocked is bad because it creates excess tension and restricts motion. But I did have a student at the Chapelle who was so double jointed that her thumb had to lock. A lot of people do this. Sometimes I make mention of it and sometimes I don't in master class situations like this past week as I do think it's an important thing, I'm sure I learned directly from Starker that the thumb should be held on the bow simply the way it naturally falls, and that since, for most people, it doesn't fall by being bent back that way, there's no reason to do that when one holds the bow. My impression is that if they can do it, there's some more flow and richness in the sound, but I've been told by some young people that they intentionally collapse the thumb because they feel they get a bigger sound that way, because they have less flexibility. They put the pressure in, and the bow does not buckle underneath, but what I hear is not a bigger sound. It's just a hard sound.

A.A.   *Related to that, I've asked a lot of people about pronation as you get to the tip of the bow. We all learn that word and teach it to a certain extent, but when you get out to the tip, how much can you maintain your weight rather than having a high elbow and getting most of your sound by pronating.*

G.H.   Yes. You can exaggerate the pronation, I agree, because that can cause another tension in the other way.

A.A.   *Well, just in observing you, it looks like you're very relaxed as you get to the tip.*

G.H.   In my early days studying with Starker, I over pronated, and I actually got incredibly tight in my forearm as I got to the tip. So I realized I was exaggerating that idea. But what I do think is very important, and I feel strongly about, is that I don't think you should lift your fourth finger when you get to the upper half of the bow. It's true that you may not need it as you get to the tip but as you come back, you will need it again. Why add an extra action by lifting it when you're going to need it again? It's not because you leave it there and don't press it that it's disturbing. Leave it there. So the intensity has shifted more to the inside of the hand because it has to the inside of the arm, but leave the fourth finger. Don't lift it. It'll come back. You'll need it again. Why add another motion you don't need? Keep it simple, keep it organic.

Also, there are times that may need unique solutions, and people have different ways of dealing with those. Rostropovich, when he got to the end of the Shostakovich first concerto, would often have a cramp in his thumb, so he would grab the bow like a baseball bat and play the last section with the thumb underneath the frog. I understand it, because basically what you're talking about at that moment is survival, because if you have a cramp, obviously it was a point you're going to drop the bow.

Tortelier's way of dealing with it was to take the fourth finger and put it on the other side of the frog, but I noticed that there's some connection between what we should feel in the outside of the hand, especially as it relates to the fourth finger in those times of trouble, and what happens to the tension resulting between the thumb and the first finger, that muscle, and I noticed that if I pressed very hard between the thumb and the first finger in the bow, and then intentionally placed the fourth finger against the frog and press, that that relieved some of that tension.

Then I noticed that if I put the fourth finger on the bow, and pressed it against the frog, that some of that tension in that muscle between the thumb and the first finger was distributed more across the hand. So I theorized that in fact even at the tip, in times of trouble, when you're feeling that extra tension, that actually the presence of the fourth finger is helpful, and even at times when I'm playing a big moment or sustain a long loud sound, I'm actually very conscious of the fourth finger in that moment where normally you wouldn't be, because actually, that helps to distribute tension.

There's still tension in the hand but it is distributed across the hand more instead of being located in one place, which eventually will cause a muscle cramp, and then you're stuck and then you have to grab it like a baseball bat again.

A.A. *What about teaching a sautillé stroke? I've come across a number of different teaching procedures or philosophies of making circles or just finding a bounce up and down, a vertical bounce. What is your process for teaching that?*

G.H. Well, I think it still all comes from the same motion, it comes from basic legato motion, meaning you pass the middle of the bow and your forearm starts to open up. Then when it gets to a certain speed, that becomes cumbersome and awkward and stiff. So you have to get to the point where the motion is fluidified by the forearm opening up. So that's definitely somewhere passing through the middle or above the middle. The faster the tempo, the higher it goes, probably because there's less and less weight in the stroke and it's probably lighter and lighter. But for me, the whole issue of the sautillé or spiccato stroke, any stroke of that nature, comes from the legato stroke at a much higher speed, and then the question is, how does the bow leave the string?

And that, I think, is a question of finding a way to shake your arm so your hand starts moving in a direction which will allow the bow to then leave the string. So that's going to be somewhere between completely horizontal and completely vertical. So I often give this exercise where I ask them to take the bow away, and to shake the arm so that the hand moves in a completely horizontal way. So the motion is not coming from the hand, right? It comes from the arm still, but the hand is moving back and forth in a horizontal way.

A.A. *And the wrist is very loose.*

G.H. Yes, the wrist allows that motion to occur, and then depending on what you're looking for, it could be more toward the vertical or more toward the horizontal, but the hand will be moving in some type of diagonal fashion. So then when you place the bow in the hand and you do this on the string, it's actually causing the bow to bounce. Then it's a question of being able to practice, and I do recommend without the bow in the air, so that you can produce an absolutely consistent motion so that whatever diagonal stroke you're describing with your hand in the air is as consistent as possible in terms of where it's going and how far it's going, because that consistency will ensure that the sound will actually be useful and usable.

And then of course it's adjusted to a certain extent by what part of the bow to use, given the speed and volume.

A.A. *What is your philosophy on teaching the Bach Suites and how has the historically informed practice ideas of the past generation affected your teaching and playing of the suites?*

G.H. When I was younger, there was certainly none of this Baroque research that has now taken place. My ideal when I was growing up was always Casals, and to a certain extent still is. Not because I want to play it that way, but I just find that his way of playing this music is utterly convincing because it comes from the deepest place, and every cell of his body is involved in it.

Having said that, I knew Anner Bylsma, and I learned a great deal from him, and I think that in this day and age, it's impossible to be completely separated from what's going on. I think a great deal can be learned from that, and should be learned from that, because I think it illuminates many issues, and I don't see why the knowledge of this is in any way counterproductive or disturbing. The real problem for me is, how does one incorporate that into today's playing. I don't think today's goal is to play the suites exactly how they were played back then.

There were probably certain things that were common to what most people did that are maybe very different than what we do or what we've done, and that's interesting to know. For a whole year I played Bach holding up on the bow to figure out what that did, and then I eventually changed it back because of the basically modern setup that I play the cello with. But I learned a lot from the balance of the bow and how to produce certain strokes that maybe wouldn't have come so easily unless I had held up on the bow. But in the end, my experience with Bach, from listening all these years to different people in many of the older generation is I've come to realize that Bach that I find convincing has zero to do with style. Zero. Nothing to do with style.

I can accept all different kinds of styles. The only kind of Bach that, for me, is convincing is when it comes naturally from a person who has gone through the process of what is important, like in any other music, and if it's unnatural to try to sound like a Baroque player when you're not a Baroque player, then it's not the right approach. How to find the right approach is the most difficult thing, but I think it has to do with, with some understanding of who you are, how you hear music, whether it's Bach or Beethoven, or music of our time, and that one has to consider things that clearly have illuminated important aspects of Baroque playing or early classical playing, and I've certainly been influenced by it. I've listened to Anner Bylsma a lot and read his books.

I remember having a conversation. We were in Amsterdam listening to something, and I'd been complaining for years about why everybody starts all trills now from the upper note. It doesn't even matter whether they're playing Baroque, classical or romantic or 20th-century music, and where did that come from? All trills from the upper note, all the time. I ask people, "Why do you do that?" Not all trills start from the upper note. When did that start? I was taught that Baroque trills start from the upper note, except when the note appears in the line right before and then it's redundant to repeat the note. Early classical music is different. But I don't think that trills were systematically started from the upper note. Some people say, "Oh no, no, in Beethoven It's done all the time." I don't believe it. I just simply don't believe it. My intuition tells me that that's not right, and yet I notice that people are doing it all the time.

So I asked Anner Bylsma about that. "Anner, what do you think about starting trills?" His answer was, "What do you think?", and I said, "This is what I think," and he said, "That's what you should do." I had it from the expert. That's what I would've thought. It was nice to hear it from Anner Bylsma.

A.A. *Yes I'm sure. That's awesome.*

G.H. So in other words, here's the great Baroque player that everybody admires and bows down to and he says, "Trust your instincts." Of course, he told me that because he assumed that I'm reasonably intelligent, that I think about these things, and that I care about it and I don't want to do it any old way. So his point was to inform yourself, try and figure it out, but in the end, the best guide is your instinct, and that's what my feeling is about playing Bach.

A.A.   *There are 3 famous pieces that are not originals that have become standard repertoire. I'm wondering if you have some thoughts on the Boccherini/Grützmacher B-flat Concerto, the Tchaikovsky/Fitzenhagen Rococo Variations and the Feuermann version of the Chopin Polonaise Brillante.*

G.H.   Well, let's go piece by piece. Let's start with Rococo because actually I have to play it soon, and people are always asking, "Well, what version do you play?" It didn't used to be that way, of course.

A.A.   *Yes, it seems like Steven Isserlis pioneered the original version several years ago.*

G.H.   First of all, I happen to think the Fitzenhagen version is a beautiful piece. Second of all, I've heard and looked at the original version and I think it's absolutely performable and viable. I'm not prepared to say that I think it's better or worse. I think it is what it is, and I think both are possible. So if anybody wants to play the original version or the Fitzenhagen version, I simply have no problem with either one.

I've had students who learned the original version of Rococo. Great. No problem. I would never ever tell them you should do the other one. They know the other one exists. They chose that. It's all good. I'm fine with that. I am like you. All my life, I've played the Fitzenhagen version. There are other things to do in life than to relearn the whole piece unless I felt like it would turn it into one of the greatest masterpieces of all time. It's not. I don't think it ever was in the Fitzenhagen version, and I don't think it is in the original version.

It's a very beautiful piece, and it has a great deal of charm. It has a tremendous amount of style and all that, but it's not a piece that for me is going to change my life. If you told me there was another version of the Brahms F major, which was 10,000 times greater than the one we know, I would jump on it. And if I felt that, I would relearn it, but that is a different kind of piece. That piece gives you more and more and more. It's like a bottomless well. No disrespect to Rococo variations. It is what it is, but it doesn't have that quality to me.

Having said that, if I started out today with today's consciousness and everything, I probably would play the original version, not because I think it's better, because it's the original and now you can get the material and you can actually go and play it somewhere, and you won't be caught with a version that simply now you can't play because the orchestra's don't have the material.

What I'm more surprised about, honestly, is when people don't play the original version of Pezzo Capriccioso. The version that people play is different than the original version.

A.A.   *Oh, I didn't know that.*

G.H.   Yes, and you can't even find the original version. It's very hard to. I have it. It's from the collected works of Tchaikovsky, this old Russian volume. And I'm surprised that people don't play that. It's not a different piece, but many of the passages are different. But you know, we've gotten on the Rococo thing, and eventually somebody's going to get on the Pezzo thing, and then people will ask why didn't you do that? And then that's going to be a thing.

As for the Boccherini Grützmacher, I'm like you. For me, it's a non-discussion the original version is the Boccherini B-flat Concerto. The Grützmacher edition is another piece. I've tried to get it programmed for the last 15 years. Nobody will have it.

A.A.   *I'm surprised. Why is that?*

G.H.   Because they don't want to be accused of being musical idiots. And I tried to explain to them that this is not an uninformed version of Boccherini. This is a different piece. People did that then. Grützmacher took themes by Boccherini and turned it into another piece. The second movement is from the G major concerto with some small changes. But instead of looking at it like a bad version of Boccherini, we could look at it as a piece that's based on the Boccherini B-flat Concerto.

As far as the Chopin, my first experience with it was playing the Feuermann version. In those days it was published by International and it was listed as the Leonard Rose arrangement. It was not. Rose makes a cut of the Feuermann version and then called it his own.

In the original version, that music exists, of course it doesn't sound like the Feuermann version, but that music is actually there. In the Rose edition, he cuts a sequence out, but the rest of it is all of the Feuermann arrangement. And then International printed the correction and said, "In fact, this is the Feuermann arrangement of the Rose edition." And that's how I learned the piece. And that became a piece that I played a lot. My father loved that piece, so I had to play it a lot in the family concerts and things like that. And there was a point when I just got sick of it.

And then I played the original many times. And I think it's actually fine. But these days I only play it when I'm playing a program that's either all Chopin, or maybe Chopin/Schumann or something like that because it makes a nice program.

The Future

A.A.   *Our technological world is changing so quickly, and what seems to be happening with many orchestras and audiences, at least in my mind, is the audiences are having a shorter attention span, and not being able to sit and absorb things that they don't know or understand. I mean that's a subject that I want to get more thoughts on when we talk about new music. But I'm wondering if you can speak a little bit about where classical music is going, where you think it's going, and if technology is influencing that, or if things are becoming more visual. It's a big question.*

G.H.   Yes, I'm not sure which way concerts are going. What I do know is what I feel comfortable with and what I think is me. I know that these things are happening. Things like more visual elements and talking to the audience. I'm not against it. It's just that I know that a lot of these kinds of things are not really what I'm about. In this day and age, very often you go to play somewhere and they'll ask you, "Are you going to talk?" 20 years ago that nobody ever asked the question. I always talked, but not the way people are talking these days. If I play a recital, I don't keep my mouth shut from the beginning to the end. There's a point where I'm going to say something, and it could be completely off the cuff. But it's not going to be what I see often today with young people.

And that's why presenters like this because they feel that helps to bridge the gap with the audience. I'm not going to agree or disagree with that, but that's not what I'm going to do because, for me, talking was always an option. But I come from the basic premise that music speaks for itself, so I don't need to present this music verbally to people. They need to sharpen their ability to receive this music through oral means and not have to be explained what the experience is meant to be.

Having said that, I'm always open for questions or to aluminate certain things. I very much believe in people coming to open rehearsals. They see a process, they understand, all those kinds of things. What I don't like so much is feeling this obligation now because many of the younger generation are doing that, and they all feel that it's the right thing to do. Or they're doing it because everybody else is doing it, so I should feel some obligation to follow the herd and do it. I don't believe in it, and I won't do it.

I will talk to the audience in my way, and it's going to be spontaneous. It's not going to be because they're expecting it. I'm very adamant about that. And maybe that's a hard line approach, but it's like thematic programming. I always did thematic program, not the way that people are thinking about it today. Excuse me, but sometimes it's complete bullshit what people are doing. They put Schubert, Mendelssohn and Brahms together, and they call it the "North Wind." Come on man, who are you kidding here?

Recently, I was asked to submit a recital program and I did. And then without asking me, they wanted me to do a contemporary piece. And they took out a piece I had programmed and put their piece in, and then sent me the program. And I was not happy with it. I said, "You should have asked me to do it." And I finally agreed to do it, but then I said, "This is going to change the program. I can't just remove one piece and put another in there because it happens to be the same length." As if it's all interchangeable. No, there's a reason why I put those pieces together on the program.

A.A. It's like preparing a really nice meal.

G.H. Yes exactly. It doesn't have to be Spanish night, but it might have a Spanish piece on it with other pieces that make a connection in some way to that.

A.A. *Kind of related to this, it seems like orchestras, especially these days, are always wanting to have one new music piece on the program. And I wonder, if there will ever be a divide in what orchestras and chamber music presenters decide to present to audiences instead of putting new and old music together on a program. For example, we have a lot of quartets that come through the University of Iowa as part of our Quartet Residency Program. And there are a lot of commissions these days for these new works which are performed at a very high level. And I've asked some of the members of the quartets, "Do you feel like this is a piece that's going to get played a lot more in the next ten years?" And quite often they get played 15 times that year, and then they disappear. And the quartets don't seem really concerned about the longevity of the piece. I'm wondering how you think new music fits in with what a huge percentage of the public wants. They want to hear the same 12 composers over and over again. How do you feel about that?*

G.H. Well, I think it's important and it's our role to continue to help to sort of lead the way. And I don't believe in this attitude that some people have that we need to give the people what they want. No disrespect to the public, but the people don't know what they want. We're the ones that know this repertoire, not them. So I believe in establishing a certain trust, and embrace our role to reveal these pieces and to give them their due because we're in the business of discovering these things and understanding the importance of people hearing this music.

I'm constantly playing romantic period pieces that people don't know and that even cellists don't know. And when people hear them they think, oh, how's it possible you never hear this? So I'm very gratified when that happens. But very often, presenters refuse to accept that on the program because they think it'll scare the public away.

Piatigorsky used to say, "People don't want to see the same movie twice, they don't want to read the same book twice, but they always want to hear the same piece of music." So there's unfortunately something sort of basic to how people are when it comes to music and there's some comfort or reassurance to hear something that they're familiar with rather than something they don't know. But countless times people are interested in hearing something they don't know and are happy to hear a piece that they end up really enjoying that they didn't know before. So I think presenters very often have this wrong. I really do.

But the presenters have to have the trust of their public because they have to get the people in the hall. And that's part of their job to establish an element of trust so that people can say, "I don't know this performer. I don't know this piece, but I have a reasonable expectation that it might be something I would like because usually it is." That's the presenter's job.

A.A.   *Do you think it's okay for an audience to hear a piece, a new piece, a contemporary piece that they enjoyed hearing that once, and they probably don't want to hear it again, but they enjoyed it that night? Do you think that's okay?*

G.H.   That they only hear it once?

A.A.   *That they don't want to hear it again, but it was like a nice balance to a meal. Again, I'm using that analogy.*

G.H.   I think it's okay. But for that, I come from a little bit more of the composer standpoint because my older brother is a composer. And we know that it's not so difficult getting a first performance. The great difficulty is getting the next performance.

A.A.   *Right. I mean University of Iowa, Iowa City's a pretty liberal town. The people that go, they support classical music. These are people that are literate with music, and they know composers. And I think a lot of times, they have a hard time taking in a very new piece that's maybe not as tonal, for example. They appreciate the artistry of the group—*

G.H.   It's a somewhat unfamiliar language.

A.A.   *Exactly. And I've talked with a lot of them after the concert and they would say, "Wow, that was interesting but I'm not going to want to hear that one again." But they appreciate the experience of how it felt to be there live. I guess that's what I'm getting at, maybe live versus listening to a recording.*

G.H.   That's all you can really ask is that people are at least open to the experience. I remember a performance many years ago in France of the Lutosławski Concerto. The orchestra asked for it, so I was very happy to do it because it's a great piece. And for once, I didn't have to shove it down somebody's throat. So because the cadenza at the opening is so important to the piece, I played the cadenza at the first rehearsal. Normally you don't play a cadenza in the first reading, you wait until the dress rehearsal. But in this piece, it's different. It's not just the cadenza like in a heightened concerto. It's five minutes of the whole opening.

I mean, the piece doesn't make sense if you don't play that cadenza, so I played it. And I hear a woman in the second violin section, it was in France, and she said in French, "What is this shit?" I'm thinking, okay, and now we have to convince a whole audience if you've got people behind you playing in the orchestra who feel like that. Well fortunately, some of those attitudes are dying away and you can get a piece like that performed, but you have to fight for it. One of the things that we will always be incredibly indebted to with Rostropovich is not only all the pieces that were written for him and pieces that he coerced people, and cajoled them, and intimidated them into writing, but also certain pieces that he played over and over again and insisted, "If you want me to play, I'm going to play this." And those pieces have become part of the repertoire like the Dutilleux and Lutosławski Concerti, not to mention the two Shostakovich Concerti and the Prokofiev Sinfonia Concertante. And that was thanks to him playing them on repeated occasions to the point where they went from being Rostropovich's pieces to now being standard repertoire pieces, and we have to thank him for that. But that could only be done by doing it that way. Other people who have had many new pieces written for them, played them once and that's it. And I've tried to have those pieces programmed. Nobody wants to hear them.

So, they're gone. You don't hear these pieces. Dozens of good cello concerti were written by contemporary composers that you cannot get performed. The original person who premiered them could probably get a second performance, but doesn't do it. And their reasoning is, I'm not here for that. I'm a midwife. Rostropovich put these pieces on the map. That's why they're part of the repertoire. The other pieces will never be part of the repertoire.

A.A.   *Have you seen the level of cello playing change over the years? And related to that, are there enough jobs for cellists in today's market?*

G.H.   Clearly there are not enough jobs for cellists in today's market. And I sense a basic panic amongst young musicians about what they are going to do. Because essentially, there are no more jobs, there's just a lot more musicians. But that's also motivated people to create their own niches.

A.A.   *That's what I was going to ask you about next, if you see that with the younger generation.*

G.H.   Absolutely. And I think they all have different ways of doing it, but they see the necessity of it, and that makes a lot of sense. As far as the level of playing, I would say the level of a certain basic technical solidity and excellence has gone higher. Whether the level of music making is now greater than it was before, I'm not so sure. I think in the end, if we're discussing a basic technical level, consistency, intonation, solidity, being able to perform under stress with a certain degree of technical proficiency, all that. Those kinds of things, yes, it's higher today than it was 30 years ago.

A.A.   *I agree! Why do you think that is?*

G.H.   I think it's true for probably a lot of different reasons, and one of them is probably because of the internet. Things like YouTube, and the accessibility of being able to just repeatedly hear, hear, hear, hear, without even thinking about it. It seeps in. I think it's because there's been such an accent placed, probably from a teaching perspective and also learning perspective, to somehow keep up with the expectation of the comparison to recordings. And the fact that you can get it on a recording as close to perfect as you possibly can. And that there is some, let's say motivation to achieve that, let's say consistency in performance, where maybe to that degree, that was never a criterion. And to that extent, almost obsessively so. And probably a lot of other reasons. I think that the accessibility of recorded material has made a very big difference in what happens in the development of playing today, and not necessarily always for the good. Very often not for the good.

A.A. *How has it not been good?*

G.H. It's something that you alluded to yesterday and I was thinking about it more. If you compare what one hears today and you compare it to, let's say the time of Heifetz and Kreisler and Casals and people like that, you would hear one or two notes of those guys and you knew who was playing. Today you can hear 10 violinists and you can't tell the difference, things have changed.

I think there's a lot of different reasons for that. I think one of the reasons is what I just mentioned. That people have the same source. Instead of being motivated to think for themselves, they're also motivated by trying to be successful, and assume that what's out there and what is currently successful, will be successful for them. And without giving it a lot of thought or examining it, they just go in that direction.

But I even think that in the days when Heifetz, Kreisler, Ysaÿe, or some of these people were growing up, they didn't have recordings to listen to. But they did hear people, because people came through town and they played. So if they went to a concert, they had to assimilate everything from that. Or from their teacher or colleagues, friends. Let's say they heard a great violinist play in their town. Let's say whoever that might be, it doesn't matter. Ysaÿe is coming, go here and play. You better retain what you heard. You better have honed your ability to hear and understand and retain and observe. Because that's your one opportunity to do so. And when you go home and you want to figure out how they did that, you better have absorbed it.

Now, we had recordings before, but YouTube is even easier than that. Now you don't have to think of anything. You just put it on and mindlessly let it seep into your consciousness. So you hear 20 cellists around the world who've studied with different people, they're all different people and they come from different nationalities. And they'll play the Debussy Sonata in exactly the same way with the same mannerisms, the same stuff. You think, how is this possible? And you go on YouTube and no doubt, the first thing that comes up is the one they listen to.

One of my closest friends who teaches in New York said he asked a student of his, "How did you learn this piece?" "I listened to something on YouTube." "How did you decide what to listen to?" "The one that had the most likes." This girl was absolutely dead serious and saw nothing wrong in what she said. So let's not make any mistake about it. It's happening. And I know, because I know people are hearing me too. I see what they're picking up. It's flattering, but when I divorced myself from the ego part, I'm thinking, let's be honest. It's not any better than if they're hearing anybody else. It's still not what they ought to be doing.

But in those days, they needed to be able to absorb that. They needed to be able to recall it and understand. And that way, when they went home and they figured out how they did that, it became them. It became part of them. What they're doing now and the way it's entering their consciousness and into their playing, it's not becoming them. But we're in an era where people are so gadget technology conscious that they're able to do it any old which way. But to actually have you have a conviction about something, that is the difficult part.

Close to the Heart

A.A.   *If you hadn't been a musician, what would you have loved to have done with your life?*

G.H.   Well, I love bullfighting, and wish I could have been a torero, but I never had the chance because it wasn't in my family and it wasn't around me, so it would have been difficult. I would've had to grow up and either southern France, Spain, or Mexico. But I did seriously consider becoming a baseball player. But I realized that the pull to music and the cello was stronger.

A.A.   *You've probably played thousands of concerts in your life. Are there any particular concerts, not even necessarily that you've played, but concert experiences that stick out? Any stories or thoughts?*

G.H.   Yes. A recital of Rubinstein. Arthur Rubinstein.

A.A.   *That you attended?*

G.H.   Yes. It was probably the greatest musical moment I've ever experienced. And it wasn't even his playing. It was the way he walked from the stage door to the piano. That was the greatest musical experience I ever had.

A.A.   *Where was that and how old were you?*

G.H.   It was in St. Petersburg, Florida, and I think I was around 17. The stage door opened up, Rubinstein walked out, and the moment he walked out, it was like he embraced the whole audience. And you felt this warm glow coming around everybody in this horrible auditorium that had a terrible sound. 3,000 people, dry as a bone. And he walked, which probably took, what, four or five seconds, from the stage door to the piano. I'll never forget that moment as long as I live. That was the greatest moment in music I've ever experienced. And then he played, and then that was just an extension of what I had already experienced. And I wondered what that was about. It obviously had to do with him and how he saw life and what he was doing there. The feeling was like, we're here in this privileged moment, to experience this time together. It was just an extension of him. You can call it what you want, charisma or whatever.

But that's something that I often talk about, that moment, because I think students can get very much wrapped up in practical things. This was out of tune, I missed that shift. Is that what music is about? Well, what are you talking about? And then I tell this story. So you're saying the greatest musical moment you ever had didn't even involve music. How can that be? Because we, as performers, are far greater than what we're trying to do when we play. It's about all the things that emanate from our being.

What emanates from our being has to do with all the things that are important to us. The things we've lived in life, the choices we've made, the things that we aspire to, the things that we devote our life to, the things that we are and would like to be. Those are all things that go way beyond just what fingering I'm going to do here, or do I play that on the D string or should I vibrate that note? Those are all still products and extensions of something that's far greater than that. And that I learned from that moment from Rubinstein. And when he started playing, it was absolutely heavenly. But it didn't tell me anything that I didn't feel and know already just from those five seconds.

A.A.   *That's an amazing memory to share. Have you ever had to deal with a period of doubt about being a musician in your life?*

G.H.   All the time. Every single day. There isn't a day that goes by where I don't question it. Not a day. Not because I don't love music and not because I think I'm doing the wrong thing, but because it's a difficult life. I mean It's a privilege to do something one loves to do. That means so much to actually make a living at it. I count myself amongst the privileged people in this world.

But it's a very hard and stressful life. It's a lonely life. It's demanding. There are many times that I feel like I wish I could do something else because I don't know if I really want to confront the pressure again. And yet at the same time, as I've gotten older, I realize that it's such a privilege that it helps to put in perspective the perception of stress and pressure, and has helped me relieve some of what that is and how it affects me. Because I realized that this is not a finite experience, that there will be a day where I can't do it anymore. And if I don't really relish the moment now, the time will come when I can't do it anymore, and I'll have regrets about what I didn't allow myself to experience.

So I continue mostly because I don't want the feeling of depriving myself of something that I know means a great deal to me. In so doing, in a way, I feel like I'm able to handle the difficult aspects of this life, and with a little bit less concern and worry about it, and let it just happen and let it come to me. So actually, in a lot of ways, I get more pleasure from playing in many ways now than I did, say, 15 years ago. But at the same time, playing is getting harder and harder. It's a curious paradox, because physically, I can't do certain things that I could do when I was 20, 25. On the other hand, I know myself much better, and I know the pieces that I've played a long time so well. Unfortunately, I also know that there's certain things that maybe I'll never achieve. And so there's a level of acceptance, because I have no choice.

For many, many years now, I've asked myself regularly if I'm going to continue with this. Because sometimes I think I wouldn't. Wouldn't I really rather be at a baseball game or lying on the beach? I spent nine days at home at the beginning of July. I don't remember the last time I spent nine days at home. And I have to tell you, I loved it. And I had to go out and play after that, and that was hard for me. I thought, oh God, I have to pack a bag, go on a train, carry the cello, and then talk to the presenter, and all of that. None of which is so horrible. I was enjoying just being home and enjoying Paris. And realizing that it's a different thing than when I was 25 and trying to make my career and gobble it all up and eat it up and spit it out. It just takes more to do it.

So you better know why you're doing it. But that, I never questioned. I never wondered why I'm doing this. I know why I'm doing it. It's my way of expressing and I need to express. So that, I don't question. But do I want to go through all that to do that? That's the question.

A.A.   *Related to that, is there anything you still want to do before it's all done?*

G.H.   Before I hang it up? In music?

A.A.   *Musically or personally.*

G.H.   There are a few places in the world I haven't visited yes, like India or Australia. I should probably go to these places before too long.

In music, I don't know if there's things that I haven't done that I would like to do. Probably if you'd asked me this question 30 years ago, and I was really honest about it, I would have said I still want to solo with certain orchestras. But I came to realize that this doesn't change your life one bit. Because some of those orchestras I did play with, and it didn't change my life. So why would others be any different? They're interchangeable. So I learned that which was good, because that meant stop wanting and longing for things that in the end weren't important.

Personal relationships have not worked out very well. Music is a hard life for that. I've made a lot of relationship choices which were not necessarily the most fruitful ones and have missed having a really fulfilling relationship. I remember a documentary where Rubinstein says the most important thing in life is to get to share our experiences. "Here I played at Carnegie Hall, that's a picture of me at Carnegie Hall" or things like that. And then he said, "The most important thing is to share this." And I've felt this for a long time now, not being able to share these experiences. I've always wanted that. That's been hard to come by. So that's something I would love to have.

A.A.   *And finally, what are you most proud of in your life? Cello or otherwise.*

G.H.   My son. For sure my son. And after that, I would say the impression that I have, maybe only in a small way, made a difference to some people. Maybe not a lot of people, but I do believe that at least to some people, I have made a difference, and that gives me a sense of satisfaction and gratification and a feeling that it's been worth it, beyond just my own personal need to express.

I had an experience a few weeks ago where a student of mine at the Chapelle was preparing for a competition and she played through some pieces on her program. This also happened to be her last lesson as she was graduating. She finished playing and she played unbelievably well. The thing that meant the most to me is, I felt like I made a difference. And now she's doing it and she's her own person. And I got all choked up. I couldn't say anything because I was about to break down. I turned my back and I walked away. I don't know if she knew what was going on, but I thought to myself, this is what it's about. When it happens the way it's supposed to happen. Of course, she plays on the highest level imaginable. It could also happen with somebody who doesn't play on that level. It mostly had to do with the understanding that the time, the discussions we had, and the questions about important matters and unimportant matters, made a difference in her life.

I have a hard time accepting the fact that I'm not one of the young ones anymore. I'm one of the older ones now, and people are looking to me for answers and they're looking to me for guidance and mentoring. And I accept it a little bit more now than I did, let's say 20 years ago. And I figure, well, if they're looking at me and they see it that way, there might be a reason for it. Maybe I should just accept it and then be happy to give.

And sometimes I feel frustrated, I'm thinking, these people don't need a teacher. And then people will say, maybe not in the way some people do, but they need something that maybe I can help them with. Maybe, I don't know. It's true, we all need something. Even people who play already on a very, very high level are still looking for something. Maybe they're looking to turn to certain people who they feel might be able to help them with that. Maybe I'm that person.

A.A.   *Well, from my observation, one of the things I love most about your teaching, is that you have such fantastic taste in the way you make music. And that's something that I think all these people benefit from. Because like I said, they all have great hands, but you're sculpting these final touches that make a performance special. That doesn't necessarily come from just practicing and learning your instrument. That's a wonderful gift to give these young artists.*

G.H.   Well, thank you, first, for saying that. I appreciate that. And of course, that's also important, because we're not teaching these people how to play. We're talking about those things that can make the difference between a good performance or something that maybe can reach a higher artistic level. That's what this is about. It's not, can I play the cello? They all can play the cello. It's not about that, it's about other things. But they're here for a reason and they're looking for something. And I think my role is to help them with that if I can.

A.A.   *You talked about your son, and I know from being a father, there are similarities to being a parent and a teacher. And when you talked about that student who you saw get to a certain place, you are sort of being a parent as well as the teacher. That's wonderful, I think, to get to see these people grow and achieve success. And if you've helped them, which you have, it's even more fulfilling.*

G.H.   Plus, it is very gratifying. You see a guy like Leland, sits down to play the Poulenc Sonata. He can play it, there's no problem. He also plays with a lot of character and everything, it's not like he's just playing the notes. But it's gratifying to see when he responds to some images and things like that. And he says, "No, I love that." It's like, this is what he's looking for. He's looking for those images that he can connect to the piece.

A.A.   *I'd be willing to bet you anything when he's our age, he's going to remember those images that you gave him today, he'll hold on to them. He might not even remember where they came from, who knows?*

G.H.   I don't remember most of those things. It doesn't matter. That's the point, right? You've digested them and they're part of you.

8

Hans Jensen

Hans Jørgen Jensen is professor of cello at the Bienen School of Music at Northwestern University. From 1979 to 1987 he was professor of cello at the Moore's School of Music at the University of Houston. During the summer, he is a faculty member at the Meadowmount School of Music and the Young Artist Program at the National Arts Center in Ottawa Canada under the direction of Pinchas Zukerman. He has been a guest professor at the Thornton School of Music at the University of Southern California, the Oberlin College Conservatory, the Eastman School of Music, the Academy of Music in Sydney, the Royal Academy of Music in Copenhagen, the Tokyo College of Music and the Musashino Academy of Music in Japan, the Festival de Música de Santa Catarina in Brazil, the Jerusalem Music Center, and the PyeongChang International Festival and School in Korea.

Mr. Jensen has performed as a soloist in the United States, Canada, Europe, and Japan including solo appearances with the Danish Radio Orchestra, the Basel Symphony Orchestra, the Copenhagen Symphony, and the Irish Radio Orchestra under the baton of conductors such as: Simon Rattle, Mstislav Rostropovich and Carlo Zecchi. He has given numerous workshops and master classes across the United States, Canada, Europe, Japan, Brazil, Korea, Australia, and Israel.

His former students have been and are members of major orchestras including the New York Philharmonic, the Chicago Symphony, the Saint Louis Symphony Orchestra, the Cincinnati Symphony, the Detroit Symphony, the Kansas City Symphony, the Colorado Symphony, the Gulbenkian Orchestra in Portugal, the Graz Philharmonic in Austria and the Montreal Symphony. Mr. Jensen's former students are currently the principal cellists in the Toronto Symphony, the Detroit Symphony, the Kansas City Symphony, the Copenhagen Philharmonic Orchestra, and the Symphony Nova Scotia. His former students hold teaching positions at Northwestern University, the University of California at Berkeley, the CIM, the San Francisco Conservatory, the Cincinnati College Conservatory, the Royal Academy of Music in Copenhagen, the Desautels Faculty of Music at the University of Manitoba and numerous other music schools.

Hans Jørgen Jensen's students have been first prize winners in competitions such as the 2017 Klein Competition, the 2017 Sphinx Competition, the Casado International Competition in Japan, the Johansen International Competition, the MTNA National Competition, the ASTA National Competition, the Stulberg International Competition, the Chicago Symphony Young Performers Competition, the WAMSO Young Artist Competition, and numerous other competitions. His students have also been prizewinners in the 2017 Queen Elisabeth Inaugural Cello Competition, the Naumburg International Competition, the Lutoslawski Cello Competition, and the Klein Competition.

Mr. Jensen was awarded the prestigious 2010 Artist Teacher Award from the American String Teachers Association (ASTA), as well as the Copenhagen Music Critics Prize, the Jacob Gades Prize, the Danish Ministry of Cultural Affairs Grant for Musicians, the Northwestern Charles Deering McCormick Professor of Teaching Excellence award, and the US Presidential Scholar Teacher Recognition Award by the US Department of Education. He was named the outstanding studio teacher of the year by Illinois ASTA. He was also the winner of the Artist International Competition that resulted in three New York Recitals. E.C. Shirmer, Boston, published his transcription of the Galamian Scale System for Cello Volume I and II and Shar Products Company published his cello method book, Fun in Thumb Position. A new pedagogy book CelloMind was published in November 2017 by OvationPress.

Jensen studied at the Royal Academy of Music in Denmark with Asger Lund Christiansen at the Juilliard School with Leonard Rose and Channing Robbins and pursued private studies with Pierre Fournier, also appearing in his master classes.

The Past

Anthony Arnone	*Where did you grow up and how did cello become a part of your life?*
Hans Jensen	Both my parents were violinists and musicians. My father was concertmaster in an orchestra in Denmark, so I started out playing the violin when I was about five years old. The violin didn't fit me very well, so I ended up quitting after a few years. But, one night, my parents were rehearsing their string quartet in my house, and I ended up just watching their rehearsals for two hours. I was already fifteen at the time, and I told them afterwards that I would just love to be a cellist. A few days later, my parents happily bought me a cello, and I was very excited to play.
A.A.	*You started taking cello lessons right after that?*
H.J.	A week later, I had my first lesson with a solo cellist who played with my father. His name was Peter Popovich, a wonderful German cellist. I played, maybe a year with him. Then, I took lessons from Asger Lund Christiansen. He was the best teacher in Denmark at the time and was the cellist in the Copenhagen String Quartet. After two years with him, I went to the Royal College in Aarhus and studied with Asger Lund Christiansen.
A.A.	*Was there a point when you knew that you were going to be a cellist?*
H.J.	I think that evening, listening to the string quartet. I decided right then that I was going to be a cellist.
A.A.	*Were there other performing cellists that also inspired you around that time? Or was it just the sound of the cello?*
H.J.	At the time, it was just the sound of the cello, but after that, I got inspired by lots of cellists. I was never really interested until that evening, sitting in the corner chair.
A.A.	*Wow, what if that evening had never happened?*
H.J.	It's very strange to think about because I had been to concerts before, but sitting there gave me a different feeling. The cellist was an incredible man who reminded me of a philosopher. He was very warm and I think his personality was what inspired me so much. It's almost as if he was the cello. He's very calm, obviously more than I am but really, it was him and the cello.
A.A.	*Did you enjoy practicing when you were younger?*
H.J.	Yes, but I enjoyed learning to try and conquer the cello fast. After I had played cello for two years, I played the Boccherini Concerto with orchestra, and the year after that I played with a major orchestra as a soloist. I enjoyed the whole process, but I didn't always enjoy every minute of practice. I like seeing a goal and achieving that goal.
A.A.	*Were you pushed hard by your parents or your teachers? Or were you pretty self-motivated?*

H.J.   With the violin, my parents tried to push me since I was younger but with the cello, there was hardly a time where I needed my father's help because he was a wonderful violin teacher. But, once or twice a week, I would practice with him for an hour and a half or longer, and I would do whatever he'd say. So, he taught me a lot. That's why I could learn so fast because he's a very experienced teacher. My cello teacher couldn't understand why I progressed so fast.

A.A.   *Do you think it helped that you already had that experience?*

H.J.   I'm sure it's all hearing the music. Even as a baby, my parents used to take me to all the rehearsals. I know all these pieces, just instinctively. With music, it has as much to do with what we hear as what we do. Many violinists started at a young age, but for cello, it is more possible to have a later start.

A.A.   *I agree, I started late as well. Did your teachers, in high school and college, give you a lot of scales?*

H.J.   We did have to play scales, but extremely slow. It was more for the bow than for the left hand. I would play slow scales for an hour. When I played four octaves really slow, I would sometimes have people come in thinking it was a violin, because of that last octave. Playing that slowly for an hour is really good to teach sound production.

A.A.   *What did Asger Lund Christiansen give you the most? Was he responsible for helping you find a solid technique?*

H.J.   Oh yes, his message was simply that you play, you learn very little, and the little part you learn is really great. For instance, in the Saint-Saëns concerto, he would spend months just on the first page. Learning the first movement really slowly with perfect intonation, vibrato, and sound. You had to dominate and conquer the sound before moving onto the next page. It took me several months to learn the first movement really well.

      That was just his teaching method. He would be very detailed and tell you exactly what to do. He had a very strong sense of sound production and really focused on building the foundation in the low register sound. I mean later, when I worked more with Rose, he taught me to have a really strong sense of a real cello sound, because he was a quartet player, played in an orchestra, and also played solo.

A.A.   *Did he work on physical setup with you?*

H.J.   He would work on how to sit and balance on the chair. One of the things that I've noticed since coming to America is that we focus on the physical detail and setup here. In Europe, people are not as aware of everything that has to do with the physical aspect. I learned more about the biomechanics of the cello much later, when I started to teach.

A.A.   *So, then you went to New York to study with Leonard Rose?*

H.J.   No. Before that, I studied with Pierre Fournier for a short time. I just loved Leonard Rose and Fournier for their sound. It was important for me at that time to study with somebody that had the kind of sound that I liked, the incredible cultivated and refined cello sound. I didn't know Rose as a teacher at all when I was in Denmark.

A.A.   *So, how did you happen to study with Fournier? Did you seek him out and then play for him?*

H.J.   I met him in a master class in Zurich. I asked him at the end if I could come to study with him and he said yes, right away. So, I would fly to Geneva and take lessons and stay there for 3 or 4 days, and then fly back. I did that a number of times.

My plan was to go to Geneva the next year to take a year off and go to another country to study. But then, I met Leonard Rose and I thought New York would be more exciting than Geneva. Because, in Geneva I would not be in the school, I would just be studying privately. In New York, I could be in the Juilliard School. My teacher recommended going to a school where you have chamber music and all the other subjects, instead of studying privately. So, I chose New York because of the school.

A.A. *What was it like to work with Fournier? What did you get the most from working with him?*

H.J. With Fournier, he focused more on the refinement of sound. But I think I learned a lot more from Rose because I was there much longer. Rose worked a lot on the refinement of sound and the bow arm. I used to not be so flexible in my bow because I was gripping the bow a little bit. So, he worked a lot on that, the famous Leonard Rose bow arm.

A.A. *Even though it was a shorter time with him, did you feel like there were things in your playing that you got from Fournier?*

H.J. Yes. I only went there for one year, so that's not how long it takes to really understand a person. With Fournier, I knew all of his features, I had all of his recordings and listened a lot to his sound production.

I didn't think that Fournier was as specific about technique as Rose was. Rose would say, hold the bow, put it like that, and move, and he'd give me all these exercises.

A.A. *And how old were you when you went to New York?*

H.J. I was already 24 when I went to New York. I was there with Leonard Rose for two years. The year after that, I took a lot of lessons with Channing Robbins because, at that time, Rose was always quite busy and wasn't in New York as much. I think Robbins and Rose made a fantastic combination, since Robbins would devote more time to the little details, like the sautillé bow stroke.

I had maybe 12 lessons in the whole year with Rose. But I remember many of those lessons. For example, In the Magic Flute Variation, in the second variation, I'll never forget the sound that he created. I kept asking if he could teach me, and he said, "If you get my bow you can do it." So, I got his bow. It was a Salchow bow, and quite heavy.

A.A. *Could you do it?*

H.J. Not as well as Rose. It actually gave me that depth of sound he had. When I teach it, I always remember that. I also remember starting the slow movement of the Saint-Saëns concerto, on the F hardly vibrating, and then opening the vibrato up. That was ideal for what Rose wanted in that phrase. Though you might not agree with that, it's beautiful and very minimalistic, just letting it flow.

There are so many incidences like that. I was 24 and I had worked hard to get to that level. So, I was much more aware of many little details. Whereas, if you are an undergraduate, you wouldn't notice it or you wouldn't remember it as much. I was like a sponge, just watching him. Even just seeing him in the hallway, I'd get so excited. He was such a legend.

A.A. *I do love the sound of his recordings. Maybe your basic technique was already solid, and you were just refining your technique. You talk about vibrato, and it seems like vibrato is best when you don't notice it in a performance.*

H.J. That's true, it should be that you don't notice it as a listener. But, as a performer, you might think about many things that a listener doesn't notice.

A.A.   *What was your career path after New York? Did you get job opportunities right out of school?*

H.J.   At that time, I had to get a Visa because I needed to stay longer in New York, so I needed some work. When you stop being a student, your Visa runs out a year later. So for two years, I played in the New Jersey Symphony. By having that job, I had some income, but I played a lot of solo concerts in Denmark when I was in school. Sometimes I would sub with a professional orchestra there.

   I remember the first time getting a paycheck thinking, oh my god. I get paid for this. It was really fun. Someone in the orchestra had told me that I didn't practice my parts enough. "You didn't make the orchestra, you never practice." I probably shouldn't advertise that.

A.A.   *What happened after a couple years of doing that?*

H.J.   I started to look for a permanent job that would pay more money. You know, I was trying to be principal chair in an orchestra, I wasn't trying to get a teaching job. I hadn't really discovered my love for teaching.

   But, I already had teaching experience in Denmark. My teacher recognized very early on that I had a special talent for teaching. So, even if I was the youngest student, he used me as his assistant. Once, he went on tour to America for three weeks, I had to teach all the other kids. I was only a second or third year in school. So, I taught people that were much older than me.

   I remember one older student, maybe ten years older than me, asked me how I never missed the high notes. I said, oh I never thought about it and nobody's ever taught me how to do that. Somehow, I just hit the notes. Then, I thought, how do you actually hit a high note? So I said, you know I visualize the note very, very strong in my mind and then I put my finger right in the middle of that note. So, the note sounds really big in my head and I put it right in the middle. That was like, I don't know how to explain that much better. But that was how, I just heard it in my head. I just put it there in the middle of the note. It always worked. Many other things didn't work, but that always worked.

A.A.   *Were the older students okay with having a younger teacher?*

H.J.   I didn't think that I was super helpful, I just asked a lot of questions. But actually, many students wanted me to give them lessons because they wanted extra lessons. They figured that since I was his assistant, when he wasn't there, I could give them extra lessons.

A.A.   *So, you still weren't sure if you wanted to teach or play in an orchestra?*

H.J.   No. I auditioned for the principal chair in Denmark, and I was supposed to go for three months because they wanted to see me on the job. I decided a few weeks before I was supposed to go that I really didn't want to leave America. I love America. So I auditioned for Indianapolis, and I was runner-up for the principal cello position. I started looking for teaching jobs at that time, and I got a job teaching at the University of Houston where I was in a string quartet with Fred Gerlach, a wonderful violinist. So, that's how I got into teaching. And then, very soon I realized, wow this is incredible.

   I got that job because I had taught at a summer program that had an affiliation with the University of Houston. That program was a fantastic recruitment tool because it gave students the opportunity to pay in-state tuition, making it easy to recruit. If they're applying fresh out of high school it's an open game, but you're not supposed to transfer in the middle of the program. I'm very strong about that, not taking a student from another teacher.

A.A.   *How many years were you at the University of Houston?*

H.J.   I was there from 1979 to 1987. Then, I was called up by the Chairman of Northwestern. He called up my colleague and asked about me. He heard that I had a strong class and then I was just invited for the interview. I've been here ever since.

The Present

A.A.   *I think teaching a student how to practice is so important. What are some of your secrets to practicing well and do you consider that an important part of your teaching?*

H.J.   I find that when you get a new student, the most important thing is to teach them how to practice. You get 1 hour with a teacher and around 10–20 hours alone, so it's so important that they learn to spend that time in a very productive way. To teach them this, I simply practice with the students in their lessons and try to talk about all the different ways there are to practice. It's different for different people, but there are a lot of basic ways. For instance, I teach pedagogy and the students are all good at pointing out what's wrong. They all see something, but they don't see that exact little detail that is the reason that there's something wrong. Learning the ability to pinpoint those details is the most important thing in your practice.

Some people get very frustrated very quickly when they don't know how to practice. They waste so much time doing it the same way over and over because they don't have the answer to the problem. I find that's the biggest problem and that's the most important thing to teach. You can't advance to another level of playing until you learn how to practice.

A.A.   *Do you ever have students do things like keep journals? Writing down goals for each practice session?*

H.J.   I think we have to set long term goals, intermediate goals, short term goals. It's really important. And really knowing how to layer all of them. The hardest thing for most people is keeping multiple things going at the same time, and practicing with priorities. Organizing the priorities with the present, the near future, and on building basic technique. Work on what's really weak in your playing. That's all important.

For instance, if a student goes to a competition, I will have them take their whole repertoire, and I will have them go through every piece and mark out everything that's complicated in the piece. It could be a shift, could be a passage, could be a melodic thing. Whatever it is, take all of those and write them down. So, let's say they have between 20–50 different passages. Every day, spend an hour and a half on everything that's hard. Then, play it all over two days. If they have too many passages, just take half of it and start the other half a week later. As things get easier, then they can master it. That's when they have a few titles, especially big competitions where there's a lot of repertoire.

And for that, it's also important really playing through. In a national competition, I think it's important that you really play the first round, let's say, a year before. And then, two months later, the second round. And then, as you get closer, maybe you do it one week apart, and eventually days apart. For example, if you go to a competition and you don't know the concerto really well and you think you're not going to get to the finals, you're not even going to play the first round well because it bothers you that you aren't prepared. So I think, even to play the first round well, you have to know everything so you mentally feel really prepared.

A.A.   *Related to that, do you tell your students to practice performing when it gets close to a performance?*

H.J.   I think it's something they should do every day. Another thing is to play through all the pieces. I mean if you have the people, a really good thing to do, is to just play it in orchestra in front of everybody. That ability to sit down, so you keep the pieces in your fingers is really important.

A.A.   *And also not letting yourself stop to fix things.*

H.J.   Continue, no matter what.

A.A.   *When you have new students, do you have a certain scale routine, or do you hear scales in lessons with some of the students?*

H.J.   I usually teach a scale class. At the college, usually I have an assistant that does that.

A.A.   *So it's something that they have to be accountable for?*

H.J.   They have to be accountable for it, yes. That's really important. I have them learn and play all the major and minor scales in three octaves. Really, really slow and really, really fast. Then, I have them go toe-to-toe where they have to play all keys one after the other really fast. And arpeggios too. But sometimes we don't get to do enough. One summer, I did all 96 arpeggios, 8 for every key. I made it a contest for the students and gave the winner $20 every week, and the same boy won every time. At the end of this summer, he transformed into a completely different player after doing those arpeggios. It's amazing what a difference it makes.

A.A.   *I'm sure he realized it too.*

H.J.   And to think, he did to win the money, but he could play all 96 totally clean. It's hard to do because you get tired and bored going through all of the keys. So we'd split it up over weeks because to do them all at once is too much.

A.A.   *What about nerves? Is that something that has ever been an issue with you?*

H.J.   I like the story that says, 90% get nervous, the other 10% are liars. I think nerves are part of life. It's just how much. I tell my students, if you're nervous, it's totally normal. If you're not nervous before you play, I think something is actually wrong. You should be nervous beforehand, so that when you get to the concert, you're not nervous anymore.

Usually young people don't get nervous. But, I've had some very gifted students that were very nervous, even when they were young. I also have students now that get really nervous when they play because they don't differentiate between practicing and performing. When they are performing, they are still criticizing themselves way too much. But, I can relate to that, I always felt like that. You play, and you're not really happy with the performance.

A.A.   *Yes, a lot of people think you never play 100% when you perform. It's always going to be a little bit under. I sometimes feel like when you perform it accentuates some physical bad habits that you might have. Do you think there's truth in that if you're tense?*

H.J.   Sure, if you're normally tense, you get even tenser.

A.A.   *That's one thing that's helped me as I've become just a more relaxed player. So when I'm nervous, it doesn't lock up my playing as much.*

H.J.   I think the only way to deal with nerves is just to play a lot. A lot of people teach meditation or calm down, but the better you know it, the better you can handle being nervous. If you're nervous and you really play badly, I think that means you're not really prepared. You should be able to be really nervous and still play really well and usually, you end up not being nervous. The better a person is prepared, the less nervous they get.

On the other hand, some people practice for a year for a recital, and the recital becomes too big of a deal. You need to build it up. Before I had important concerts, I would always try to play like eight or nine times at smaller concerts. Finally, I would get most nervous there because I would always think, "Oh if I can't play here, how can I play them in a bigger place?" So, I got even more nervous and maybe didn't play as well there, but you eventually become familiar with the process.

A.A.   *If you had to summarize your teaching philosophy into words, what would it be? How do you feel like your teaching's evolved over all these years?*

H.J.   Yes, I mean you have people that are categorized as really technical teachers and then other people that are really musical teachers. I always thought you have to be able to be both. With the new students, I spend a lot of time on the technical part. And if they don't really master that, then I never really get to the musical part because you can't really be free in the music if you have fundamental problems.

The basics are the ability to practice, play in tune, to have beautiful vibrato and good sound production. They're all really important, and if a person doesn't have that, I will work a lot on it in exercises, away from the pieces. However, people get really bored with just exercises, then you have to try to teach the technique in the pieces.

A.A.   *Do you have specific études or exercises that you've used over the years consistently?*

H.J.   Yes, I mean I like the Duport études. I always use the Starker book for the left hand or the Cossman or the Klengel or some of those books are very good. They're very similar. I think for the left hand the Sevcik are great. I like the 40 variations. To really go through that for the bow arm. And some other shifting exercises are also really great. But I spend a lot of time teaching people to make up exercises within the pieces they are working on. I do think you can teach a lot of technique inside a piece, but sometimes it's hard for people to do everything at the same time.

I try to teach to what the person needs, but for a new student, I try to really work on the technique first. When you get to the higher level, to teach people the different styles, the different composers, different sound production, I mean it's endless. But if you start doing that when there's a basic problem, it's like you're putting a bandage on instead of actually fixing the problem.

A.A.   *When you hear a lot of great students audition for you, do you tend to pick people that are more physically already gifted on the instrument but maybe don't have as much to* say? Or are you more drawn to people that have a lot to say but maybe have more physical limitations?

H.J. Usually, I want to teach students who want to study with me.

A.A. *Well, I mean everybody wants to study with you.*

H.J. I mean, some people really want to study with you. If they're really excited about it and they think I can help them, I think that's really important. I don't want to fight for the student. Somebody that really wants to study with you will be more open to what you're trying to teach them. There's sometimes a human connection with people and if I think that there's a strong one, that's really important. You feel that.

But I'm pretty objective, when you select students just try to select them on how they play without being too personal. Sometimes, it's really hard because you have to turn down people you really love, or someone that really wants to study with you.

A.A. *You have to say no to someone.*

H.J. It's very hard, I really do not enjoy that at all. When you're a young teacher and you don't have a lot of students, it's the opposite. So when you get older, it's not fun to have to reject somebody you like.

A.A. *Do you sometimes see certain problems that you think, "I can really help this one"?*

H.J. I see that sometimes. When you see a person, I always see where they are now and where they are later. I am not sure I always select the right player. It's not always about the ultimate success in the end. When you teach, it's the process of also having fun together with the person. At Northwestern, it's also about attracting students that can really succeed here, because it is an academic school. I look at the whole package. I didn't do that in the beginning. You want people to come to your school where they really fit in.

A.A. *How do you teach a student to keep individuality in their playing, is that something you're very aware of when you're teaching?*

H.J. No, I don't tell them what finger to use or what bowing. I have them do it themselves, and if it's not good, then I spend a lot of time trying to explain why it's not good. So, they learn to do it on their own. After three years, they're all really good at it, even the young kids.

A.A. *That's good to hear. I debate with myself sometimes as a teacher, but especially with Bach when I studied with Colin Carr, he would not give us much, he just taught us philosophies. I used to get very frustrated at the time, but I actually learned so much more.*

H.J. Oh, definitely. You have to think for yourself. When you just follow blindly, you've done it long enough that you remember the system, but you don't learn why you're doing something. For example, in shifting, you have musical slides or transportations slides. If you don't know there is a difference, you can't hear the difference. But if you know the meaning behind the slide, you can bring it out and make it more expressive.

A.A. *But, especially on the musical side of your teaching, do you try to have your students sound different from each other? Or try not to?*

H.J. The more I teach, the more I try to promote individuality in each person. But you can't help favoring a certain sound that you like. I don't always play for the students. I teach them more how to create the sound from their own mind. Because of that, they become more uniquely individual.

A.A.   *Do you think demonstrating is important?*

H.J.   You have to demonstrate. If they can't hear sound, you have to play the sound. We learn by watching people. It's how we learn to walk. We see people walking, we imitate it. The younger the student is, the more you have to teach by showing. Kind of like how a picture is worth a thousand words.

A.A.   *What is the hardest thing that you've found to teach students after all these years?*

H.J.   Patience, tenacity, and consistency. It's hard to change a person's personality. So if a person is very talented but very undisciplined, it's hard to make them become more controlled and calculated. On the other hand, somebody that's extremely disciplined but a little detached or over calculated, it's hard to teach them to be really engaged and emotionally involved. So, you might have to teach the opposite to two people.

There's also the person that is full of passion, but the passion gets to them and locks their arms from their full ability. That's when they need to just step back. The slower you play, the more you can kind of manipulate what you do with things, and the more you can gauge yourself musically. If you play really fast and loud, it's better to just do it the right way so you can last for a long time instead of putting all your emotion in. There's a fine balance and it's different for each person.

A.A.   *Do you tell your students how many hours a day they should be practicing? Do you believe in the 10,000 hour philosophy?*

H.J.   Oh, I think 20,000 or 30,000.

A.A.   *Really? Do you talk about that with your students? Or just tell them practice, practice, practice.*

H.J.   They know. I tell them between 3–5 hours a day. To play two hours is not enough. To play seven hours is probably too much, and you're not concentrating. Because you need consistency. If you do 3–5 hours, twice a week, that won't work as well. So, I think it's the consistency of practicing. If you already have fantastic technique, then it's not hard to retain. They can get away with less. But, if you're building technique at the same time, you probably have to practice more. So, if you're older but haven't really spent a lot of time, you might have to practice a bit more in order to make up for all those hours. I practiced really hard. I did seven or eight hours a day since I started so late. I made up for it within two years.

A.A.   *You mentioned just some of the key things you want to give a student. Intonation was one of them. I find that one, a hard one to teach. How do you work on intonation with a student?*

H.J.   I teach them the theories of intonation. I explain the difference between Just, Pythagorean, and Eco temperament. I find when people have problems to really hear, it's very hard to teach. So, I teach them where all the overtones are on the cello.

A good student of mine was very talented but he never played totally in tune. I taught him about the different harmonics. Then he came to one lesson, and I explained that we had to play really low to get it, compared to equal temperament. The intonation is just lower. When he learned that, his playing changed dramatically, and he could hear far better after doing the harmonic trick an hour every day.

I just finished writing a book about it. I learned this works really well once you understand it and start adjusting everything.

A.A.   *How do you guide a student who is having intonation problems?*

H.J.   I teach them where all the overtones are so they can hear that. Then I teach them the syntonic comma. The difference between Just Intonation and Pythagorean Intonation. I've also developed a system so they can also play the triads with Just intonation, or play triads with Pythagorean.

   I tell them to play triads with low thirds, then do it with high thirds and pick the ones you like, because in the end it's up to what we like. There's no absolute, it's individual.

   I had a student ask how to play with this sort of intonation in a string quartet. I told them that when you know more and you can play better in tune, you can adjust better to what's around you. But you can't lecture other people. They don't want to hear that.

A.A.   *How do you feel about electric tuners?*

H.J.   Oh. I think they're fine. But they don't really work. I mean, you can set them with the Pythagorean and Just intonation, but it's not the same as when you train the ear. We certainly use it today to tune cellos to the same pitch.

A.A.   *Right, but I mean if you're playing a scale and you're using the needle?*

H.J.   I used to use the tuners with drones and drone the dominant while playing scales. So, if you play with a drone, you're going to end up playing just intonation because your thirds will end up matching with the drone. If you're trying to use the Pythagorean, the thirds will be out of tune with the drone.

   I showed it to a friend, and he thought it was amazing. But, he said that when he was teaching, the students start in D major, and as they get higher, they end up in E-flat major. That ended up being the problem. He told me that what I was teaching was nuclear science, but he was dealing with people that modulate in the keys a lot.

   There are many different levels of doing this. What I'm doing is the highest level. So, if you taught it in high school, they probably don't need to be that precise. In that situation, if you have a drone, it is very good. As long as you're close, it's okay. So I think, at different levels there's different ways of teaching these skills.

A.A.   *How do you feel about playing by memory? Is that something you make your students do?*

H.J.   I think it's really important. If you have to compete in competitions, you're freer when you play from memory. People have trouble with it. I spend a lot of time teaching mental practice, sometimes spending hours in lessons without the cello. It's a habit, "You play first, what note? That's an E. Okay, start on the note before … What note? F-sharp. Okay, start on the note before." So, I go through it like that.

   If they can't do it in their head, I have them do it on the cello first. Next, do it on the arms. Then I can see if they move wrong, because they have to sing it in their head. For most people you have the motoristic element and then you have the melodic element. It's important you know what fingers it goes on and what string.

   Other people might have a very strong sense for harmony. So that's also really great. But, if you don't have that, then developing that is not necessary. I think they just need to have a motoristic component, and some people see very clearly the musical page in front of you.

   I learned to do it, but it took a lot of effort. My goal was to be able to play the piece, but see the music in my mind. I could do it, but I don't think it was a success, because I forgot to play expressively.

A.A. *Do you think it also helps a student be more aware of what they're doing physically when they're playing by memory?*

H.J. Oh, I think it's great, but then on the other hand, if it sounds beautiful, it's no problem having music. Especially if you're already in a major orchestra and have a job, it doesn't really matter much. You should do what you want to do.

A.A. *You talked about this a little bit, about the awareness of the use of the body. How important is body movement in playing? Is that something you talk a lot about in teaching?*

H.J. Oh, I think that's really important. The more that you can relate what we do on the cello to natural movement patterns, the better off we are. Most of the things on the cello, we are doing in our daily life. Even the way we move. When you pick something up, think about your muscles when you do it. Between slow and controlled motion and ballistic movement. Ballistic is when you move, you initiate the movement but then inertia carries you through.

When you try to pick something up slowly, you use much more muscle power. You immediately relax your hand whenever you pick it up. You don't naturally grip super hard. It should be the same with the bow. In fact, I think we need to be flexible and have many bow holds so we can be free to move.

But that's only something I developed from teaching. I think it should be very natural, but I think what we learn from Yorca or Alexander Mason. I think all of those things are really important. But that may be because you can't just learn it from the cello, you have to do it from other things.

A.A. *I often use the analogy a lot of throwing a frisbee or tennis, having the torso start the motion of the arm.*

H.J. Oh, absolutely. We can learn a lot from sports. You can relate cello to everything.

A.A. *So, you brought vibrato up earlier. I know you've mentioned before that you have ways you teach vibrato. But, are there some methods that have worked really well for you for a student that has really tight vibrato for example?*

H.J. I have a new method that I use for a lot of the younger students, because their fingers are weak, so they have vibrato problems. So, when they rest their arm way into the string, the finger doesn't have enough strength that it can carry. But a lot of the time, when they have a tight vibrato, I think it originated when they were young. The teacher would tell them to keep the fingers curved, but since their fingers weren't strong enough, they collapsed.

When they keep it curved and are tightening the whole arm, it produces tight vibrato. To fix that, I teach a lot of exercises where they only play it on the harmonics. So, they start out playing just touching inside the string on the harmonics. Everybody can vibrate on the harmonic without problems. And then of course the tennis ball is very effective.

A.A. *I've used the tennis ball often and it is a great teaching tool.*

H.J. Because you learn the basic movement pattern in the bigger part of your body. And, there are different ways of vibrating for different people. Some people have a little bit fatter hands, so they use a lot more rotation. And then there are people who rotate their upper hand. Although, arm vibrato is the most important. But even if it's arm vibrato, it kind of starts in the fingertip. Even if it comes from the arm.

A.A.   *You have to get the whole pad covering the string. So the finger has to rotate.*

H.J.   But, you never thought about it, you have such a natural and beautiful vibrato. I think you didn't think a lot about it.

A.A.   *Well, thank you! But I've definitely had to think about it in my teaching. It's really fascinating to me, all of the different methods there are to learn and teach. I used the matchbox on the hand.*

H.J.   I learned a lot of those things because my father was a very, very, good teacher. So, I already knew everything about vibrato in the violin. Finger vibrato. Wrist vibrato. Arm vibrato.

A.A.   *How do you teach another struggle on the cello, the sautillé stroke? What should the bow hand be doing?*

H.J.   I think it's important that you get the rotation movement, but the most important thing is that you're keeping a little bit of pressure into the stick so that there's tension. Create a loop with the hand, but at the same time keep the tension. After a while, I've found that it becomes very easy to teach that.

A.A.   *I also wanted to talk about the Bach Suites. What is your philosophy on teaching the Bach Suites? What do you think of the historically informed performance practice that's evolved over the last 30 years or so? Where does your teaching fit into that?*

H.J.   When I played with Fournier, it was much more romantic style. But, what influenced me to open up to new ways was really my students when I taught at the University of Houston. That's when Anner Bylsma came out with his recordings. All of my students were listening to it, and after I heard these recordings two or three times, I thought "oh my god this is phenomenal."

   After my students convinced me to change, I started reading a lot of books about Bach because I really didn't know a lot about it. If I teach a younger student, and they're not going to really play the cello well, I don't spend a lot of time on the performer's practice aspect. But certainly, for the college student, it's also up to how much each person likes a certain style, so I have different ways of teaching it for different people.

   You can't live in this day and age without paying a lot of attention to that. I try to implement a lot of the rules from Baroque performance practice into the students.

A.A.   *Yes, it is delicate.*

H.J.   Most of them don't use vibrato when they play now. I remember going to the Rostropovich competition and there was such a variety of different styles in the performances. If it sounds great, either way it's good.

A.A.   *But the education has been very useful too. I think the whole movement that's happened has been great. To insist on one way is sometimes counterproductive.*

H.J.   Yes, the tendency is to play Baroque performance practice in a major orchestra. You can play it if they want to hear the person really playing the cello, and to hear them handle the instrument in a beautiful way. When you play the excerpts, then you have to really show you can play different styles with different excerpts. And this way, you get just in an orchestra. If you play Baroque performance practice, maybe it's not so good for an orchestra. But, I've had students that play it really well in competition, and I remember the judges would say, "Wow, I must say it's not my cup of tea the way he played it, but it was very good."

Sometimes when somebody plays like that, people feel insecure to criticize because they don't really know enough about it. Most of the time, they will tend to give you credit for that.

A.A.   *There are 3 pieces that are not often played in their original version that I wanted to get your thoughts on. The Boccherini/Grützmacher B-flat Concerto, the Fitzenhagen arrangement of the Rococo Variations, and the Feuermann arrangement of the Chopin Polonaise Brillante. How do you feel about those arrangements? Do you discourage students from playing those?*

H.J.   No. I was brought up on the Grützmacher.

A.A.   *Yes, me too.*

H.J.   I love the slow movement, it's the most beautiful slow movement. It's from another concerto. I've had people play many originals, especially if they're older students. I even have them play from the original parts. I think the Grützmacher is great because if you're teaching a younger student, it's about learning to play the cello. All these pieces are great for that.

A.A.   *Do most of your students play the Fitzenhagen version of the Rococo variations?*

H.J.   I've had ⅔ play that and ⅓ play the other. The other version is still very good, but I actually like the original more.

A.A.   *Do you think there will be a bigger shift in the future, since no one played the original until about 20 years ago?*

H.J.   Yes, I think it will shift. The original is just really beautiful, and the flow of the variations come right into the cadenza. The end feels a little funny, but I think the rest is wonderful. I've now taught the original so much that I like it. I think it's much more appropriate since it's much more Rococo style.

A.A.   *What about the Chopin Polonaise?*

H.J.   I think the original is very beautiful, and all the technical things almost destroy the music a tiny bit. But, I have a lot of my students play both. I have the original Feuermann version that is also Rose's version. But it's sort of like putting ketchup on something that's beautiful. I use ketchup sometimes myself. I like ketchup.

A.A.   *Me too.*

H.J.   I definitely teach all three transcriptions, but I also use the originals. Not with the Chopin, nobody wants to play the original.

A.A.   *Yes, when I was in school with Colin Carr, I wanted to play the Feuermann version, and he was against it. But I played it anyway because I wanted to experience the piece in that version once. But I still feel a little guilty.*

H.J.   You feel guilty. I can understand somebody being a purist. I totally understand.

A.A.   *Yes, but like you said, ketchup is good sometimes. I feel like every day I'm reading an article about this shrinking audience in classical music. What sort of changes do you see in the next 50 years in the classical music world? How has technology affected you as a teacher or is affecting your students?*

H.J.   Yes, I think it's fantastic for people from a studying point of view. Being able to go to YouTube and click and see all of these great musicians from the past.

I always tell the kids, make sure you see all, don't just look at the recordings that are done today, you've got to know them all. I think it's like a goldmine and I encourage the students. A lot of the time, I tell them to write down the differences between four recordings.

A.A.   *That's a great idea.*

H.J.   It was so hard in the past to get to see these great artists. You had to go to concerts, although there's nothing like being in the room with a person. It doesn't feel the same way on film. Classical music is too amazing to disappear. People always say it's when people get older or more settled down, they start to favor classical music. Maybe they have more money now, they can kind of live life a little bit slower. When you get to that age, then classical music is much more soothing for your soul than when you were a younger person.

   I think we have an older audience, and it's totally normal. But I think the orchestras in the future will be different. I think they'll require people to break up into small groups, and there will be more teaching, and more involvement in the community. I think that's a good way that music can go. Sometimes seeing an orchestra on stage makes it feel like there is a barrier between the performers and the audience, even if it's a fantastic performance.

   When you're in smaller groups, it's easier to connect with the audience. But, a Rachmaninoff concerto, Tchaikovsky, those great pieces, I don't think they'll ever go away. It's just too exciting and too fun.

   And I think, because of technology, there will be many more ways for people to also learn to promote themselves. It's very integral in that sense but I don't think it'll go away.

A.A.   *How does new music fit into the future of orchestral music especially or chamber music? Orchestras these days tend to program the new piece, and do you think that's working with the orchestras?*

H.J.   That's the difference between Europe and America. In Europe, you have a lot of orchestras that get sponsored by the government, so they don't need to do things that are popular. They have a lot of freedom to program pieces that are not necessarily bringing in the audiences. When the new music was much more Avant Garde, not many people appreciated it. I think the new music has adjusted more toward what people like to hear.

   At universities, you have composers that almost have to compose music that nobody understands, and they don't have to worry if people like it. But, if you have to make a living as a composer, you have to create music that people like. It's a very hard career to go into because even some of the famous composers of the past had critics, but eventually people grew to like it.

A.A.   *To me, it's fascinating that 80% of the pieces orchestra play are by like 15 different composers. I almost wonder if it's becoming so historic an organization and the new music might just have to eventually find a way of fitting in.*

H.J.   Some organizations that are emerging are directing their fascinating music toward younger audiences. They actually have a really strong following and involve a lot of fantastic composers. That world is just exploding with ideas from so many young composers, and there are lots of open minds in the audience.

A.A.   *You've been teaching for a long time and you've seen a lot of great students. Where do you feel like the level of cello playing has gone?*

H.J.   Well, I think every ten years, the level moves up. When I grew up, very few people played the Sinfonia Concertante of Prokofiev, and now you have 12-year-olds playing that piece like it's nothing. The level of technique is rising at an insane rate, and even in other instruments like piano.

I think YouTube has an incredible influence. Even when I went to Australia, some of the students there recognized my students back here, because they had seen them play on YouTube.

When I was in Denmark, people told me they saw my student on YouTube for a competition. Then you have a kid in Denmark that sees that, and they say, I can do that! That's human nature. So, I think the technology is making the level go up much, much faster than before. Everyone has access to watch it.

It used to be all in a pedagogy class, filled with cellists that I'm sure have had an incredible influence on each other. But now, because of YouTube, the whole world is in one class. They all know each other and they have friends there and they watch each other. So, it's a fantastic thing.

A.A.   *On the negative side, do you think there are enough jobs for all these great cellists?*

H.J.   I think it's very hard. I think that people have to learn to use technology to self-promote so they can make an organization. Like, create a string quartet that's really out there. Groundbreaking new ideas. If they successfully create an audience for themselves, they'll attract a manager for their group.

Now it's not just about winning a competition. I try to tell the students that a lot, but it's still hard to find the 4 people that really match together and that really works. Usually, somebody gets a job so the group breaks up.

A.A.   *Sort of related to that, how often do you help a student find success or a job out of school? And do you think that's part of your job?*

H.J.   I stay in touch with people after they leave here. They come back and play for me. People have left for ten years, they come back before auditions. I tell them I'm their teacher for life and their friend for life. If they end up never playing cello for me again, they're still my friend, and I'm still here to help them. I have people that come back here many times.

I spend a lot of time with the students before auditions, so they can really get a job. I tell them, you can't quit if you get discouraged, you have to keep going. I have total belief in people. And I'll go down with them.

Close to the Heart

A.A.   *If you hadn't been a musician, what would you have loved to have done with your life?*

H.J.   Oh, I wanted to be a veterinarian because I love horses. Or, I would have a farm with a lot of horses. Or breeding horses. I love horses.

A.A.   *Do you ever ride sometimes?*

H.J.   No. I still miss that one part of my life. When I started playing music, I gave all of those things up.

A.A.   *What are your most memorable concert moments that you've been involved in?*

H.J.   Before Simon Rattle was famous, he was conducting a concert in Denmark, and I won an award just playing with him. I was playing the Popper Hungarian Rhapsody and the Saint-Saëns concerto. Usually, when you play with an orchestra, it gets very heavy and drags you down. But with him conducting, he always knew what you would do before you would do it. That was the only time I felt that with a conductor, playing as a soloist. He absolutely had a sixth sense. It was incredible.

A.A.   *Did you ever have to deal with a period of doubt about being a musician in your life and how did you get through that?*

H.J.   Before coming to America, I felt stuck in Denmark. I was in a soloist class, and all we did was have one lesson a week, and play a little chamber music. We were supposed to practice all the time. It was just depressing because I had to face myself every day, and I had all day to do it. I was already married, and my wife had a job teaching at the conservatory and accompanying. So when she would go in and work, I'd just stay home and practice.

In the end I had too much time on my hands and was really not enjoying what I was doing. I started losing belief in myself because I was just looking at myself the whole time. I didn't have enough outside perspective.

A.A.   *What got you through that?*

H.J.   It simply was setting goals, that I wanted to go abroad and teach. And thankfully, I got a grant that could support those goals.

A.A.   *What are you most proud of in your life or career that you've done?*

H.J.   I don't really feel proud of anything, but I feel lucky that I ended up in a situation where I can teach and work with so many wonderful talents. When you get older, people really appreciate what you do, seeing that what you do actually has an effect on something. I get the most happy and proud when I see a person get a job. To win a competition is still great, but when people win a job, I find it really exciting because they're set for making their living out of music. It's a feeling that leaves me feeling more lucky than proud.

A.A.   *Is there anything that you have on your bucket list that you still want to do before you're done with all this?*

H.J.   I still would like to have a horse and to have a farm with horses. But, my wife is from Tokyo and is used to a big city and never wants to live in the countryside.

For cello, I just finished one book that I wrote together with Minna Chung, who is a professor in Canada, at the University of Manitoba. But, I have two or three books that I have to finish. I'm trying to cut down on my teaching because the last book was mostly written between 11 at night and five in the morning. I slept very little many times, and I don't want to do that again. So I plan to cut down a little bit on private students so I can write during the daytime, and have more time to spend with my wife.

When I was younger, I always felt that I didn't spend enough time at home with my kids, who are now 38 and 32. We spend a lot of time traveling together trying to make up for the time when they were younger. So I'm trying to cut down a little bit because life is short, you have to enjoy it.

A.A.   *And are you still running?*

H.J.   I've started again. I'm training for two marathons in 2017. Bordeaux actually, because you can drink wine while you run. It's fun, people have costumes on. I'm not going to drink wine during the run, but maybe a little bit afterwards. I've never been to Bordeaux. I started training a couple of weeks ago for it. Because when I have a goal, I like to reach that goal.

9

Paul Katz

Paul Katz is known to concertgoers the world over as cellist of the Cleveland Quartet,
as which, during an international career of 26 years, he made more than 2,500 ap-
pearances on four continents. As a member of this celebrated ensemble from 1969 to
1995, Katz performed at the White House and on many television shows, including
CBS Sunday Morning, NBC's Today Show, the Grammy Awards *(the first classical*
musicians to appear on that show), and in In the Mainstream the Cleveland Quartet, *a one-hour documentary televised across the US and Canada.*

Katz has received many honors, the most recent including the "Chevalier du Vio-
loncelle," awarded by the Eva Janzer Memorial Cello Center at Indiana University for
distinguished achievements and contributions to the world of cello playing and teach-
ing; the Richard M. Bogomolny National Service Award, Chamber Music America's
highest honor, awarded for a lifetime of distinguished service in the field of chamber
music; an Honorary Doctorate of Musical Arts from Albright College; and the Ameri-
can String Teachers Association "Artist-Teacher of the Year 2003." Katz is a passionate
spokesperson for chamber music the world over, and served for six years as President
of Chamber Music America. As an author, he has appeared in numerous publications
and wrote the liner notes for the Cleveland Quartet's three-volume set of the complete
Beethoven Quartets on RCA Red Seal.

In 2011, declaring that "our art is passed from one generation to the next, not by books but by mentoring," Katz launched CelloBello, a website designed to connect cellists of all ages and performance levels. Among the site's resources are "Cello Lessons," consisting of footage filmed in Katz's studio with NEC students; "Legacy" videos from Katz's own mentors; and a blog coauthored by more than a dozen prominent cellists. Through this medium, Katz is digitizing his own life experience as a student, teacher, and artist of his instrument.

Katz has appeared as soloist in New York, Cleveland, Toronto, Detroit, Los Angeles, and other cities throughout North America. He was a student of Gregor Piatigorsky, Janos Starker, Bernard Greenhouse, Gabor Rejto and Leonard Rose. In 1962, he was selected nationally to play in the historic Pablo Casals masterclass in Berkeley, California. He was a prizewinner in the Munich and Geneva Competitions and for three summers, he was a participant at the Marlboro Music Festival.

Katz's recordings include Dohnanyi's Cello Sonata for ProArte Records, and the Cleveland Quartet's recording on Sony Classical of the Schubert two-cello quintet with Yo-Yo Ma. The Cleveland Quartet has nearly 70 recordings to its credit on RCA Victor, Telarc International, Sony, Philips and ProArte. These recordings have earned many distinctions including the all-time best selling chamber music release of Japan, 11 Grammy nominations, Grammy Awards for Best Chamber Music Recording and Best Recorded Contemporary Composition in 1996, and "Best of the Year" awards from Time magazine and Stereo Review.

In September of 2001, Paul Katz joined the New England Conservatory faculty, following five years at Rice University in Houston, and 20 years of teaching at the Eastman School of Music. At NEC, in addition to his studio, seminar teaching and other chamber music coaching, and coaching the NEC Chamber Orchestra, he is founder of the Professional String Quartet Training Program. To date, this program has enrolled six emerging quartets, all of which are now experiencing considerable professional success, including a Grammy award for the Parker Quartet's 2010 Ligeti CD.

Katz has mentored many of the fine young string quartets on the world's stages today including the Ariel, Biava, Cavani, Chester, Harlem, Jupiter, Kuss, Lafayette, Maia, Meliora, Parker, T'ang, and Ying Quartets. One of America's most sought after cello teachers, his cello students, in addition to membership in many of the above quartets, have achieved international careers with solo CDs on Decca, EMI, Channel Classics and Sony Classical, have occupied positions in many of the world's major orchestras including principal chairs as far away as Oslo, Norway and Osaka, Japan, and are members of many American symphony orchestras such as Buffalo, Chicago, Cleveland, National Symphony, Pittsburgh, Rochester, and St. Louis.

Katz has taught at many of the major summer music programs including 20 years at the Aspen Festival, the Yale Summer School of Chamber Music, the Perlman Music Program, the Schleswig-Holstein Music Festival in Germany, ProQuartet in France, Domaine Forget, Orford, and the Banff Center for the Arts in Canada, the Steans Institute of the Ravinia Festival, and is a Director of the Shouse Artist Institute of the Great Lakes Chamber Festival. His hundreds of masterclasses worldwide include many of the major music schools of North and South America, Europe, Israel, Japan and China. Katz frequently sits on the juries of international cello and chamber music competitions, most recently the Leonard Rose International Cello Competition, and the international string quartet competitions of Banff, London, Munich, Graz and Geneva.

Paul Katz plays an Andrea Guarneri cello dated 1669.

The Past

Anthony Arnone   So I want to start from the very beginning. Where did you grow up and how did you first become exposed to the cello?

Paul Katz   Well, I'm from Southern California. I was born in Long Beach. My parents actually were very much working-class parents. I spent my high school years in Compton, California, between Long Beach and Los Angeles. There was only one other person in the entire city that was studying a string instrument privately, a violinist named Elisabeth Matesky. She wound up in the Heifetz class at USC and eventually as a member of the Chicago Symphony! It was just the two of us—not bad!

Both my mother and father were amateur musicians. They met in their high school orchestra when they were teenagers in Chicago. My mother played the cello and my father the oboe. He was in the training orchestra for the Chicago Symphony. When the Depression hit, my grandmother sold his oboe, which ended his dream of becoming a professional musician. Still, my father was musically gifted. Whatever talents I have, I'm sure they came from him. He had perfect pitch and a passion for music that infected me. The house was filled with music day and night, mostly the radio and phonograph, but my dad loved to go to the piano and play and sing his favorites. The radio was always on in the car, and he would sing at the top of his voice and sometimes pump the brakes rhythmically with the music, causing the car to make a stop-and-go stutter down the street! My parents never pushed me to be a musician, but they got a lot of pleasure out of the fact that I decided to go into music, that's for sure.

My parents were also what I would call social activists and very socially conscious people. You know, when I was a very little kid, they always talked to me about doing something for others and making the world a better place. That's how I was raised. They never talked to me about becoming a musician. I discovered I really loved teaching when I got my first cello student when I was 10. My cello student was eight and I got a dime a lesson. When I was in the 10th grade I joined the school's Future Teachers Club and started tutoring math to junior high school kids with learning disabilities. Teaching, not always music, but teaching spelling and math in addition to teaching cello, that's what I did growing up.

A.A.   *How did you first get your hands on a cello?*

P.K.   Well, my parents had three instruments at home—a piano, a flute, and a cello. My parents started me on the piano when I was five and later asked if I wanted to play the flute or the cello. I have no memory of infancy, but my mother told me that she used to play the cello to put me to sleep. So maybe that subconsciously impacted my choice.

I was really fortunate that, despite living in the middle of nowhere, they found me a wonderful piano teacher. This woman was very special. So, at five years old, in addition to teaching me piano, she taught me to transpose the pieces that I played. She taught me all the keys and clefs and encouraged playing by ear. She did all of these things. So by the time I started cello, which was a little before I was eight years old, I already had a pretty good musical background. And even now when I see chords in my head, when studying a score or something like that, I visualize the vertical aspects of music on the piano, rather than on the cello.

A.A.   *Do you have siblings?*

P.K.   Yes. I have a sister Lois who is two years younger than me who played the flute. She was an above average flutist through high school and college. In high school, she played in L.A.'s all-city orchestra and in CA's all-state concert band but didn't continue in music and became a history teacher instead. But our homelife as kids also shaped her. As an adult she has always been a great concertgoer, music is always playing in her home, and one of her daughters, my niece, composes, sings and plays piano.

A.A.   *Talk about your musical path after that?*

P.K.   Looking back, there was one incident that really defined me. I was quite a bit ahead in school and started USC when I was 16. When I was 14, in the 11th grade, I won an award as the outstanding fine arts student in my high school. Not a big deal at Compton High School as there wasn't a hell of a lot of competition. The Bank of America gave this award to every high school in the State of California and then all the winners competed for a statewide prize. There were sculptors, photographers and poets and musicians, all mixed up like that.

So the Bank of America in its wisdom decided that the best way we could compete was to write an essay. And the topic that they gave us was, what is the necessity of art and in particular, your art? Is what you do important for society or for humankind? (In those days, it was called mankind!) Well, I was 14 years old. I had never thought about that for a second before in my life. Though music was my passion and my hobby, as I said before, at that point I was thinking I would go to college and become a social worker or a school teacher or something like that. But I wanted to win that money, which I didn't, but I worked really hard on this essay, and in the process of writing, I came to realize that music is necessary to the world.

Music is what keeps humankind balanced and sane -That was my premise and what I still believe. Can you imagine, it was the 1950s, and I wrote "In this *increasingly technological* world, music is more important than ever." Right? In the process of writing that, I actually convinced myself that it was okay to be a musician. The world needs music and so it's OK to become a musician because playing the cello has a purpose larger than just my personal enjoyment. That realization was basically what turned my head. And so I told my parents that I wanted to become a musician. The next year as a senior, I applied to USC to study cello with Gábor Rejtő. And that was actually the turnaround for me and I never looked back.

A.A.   *And were your parents okay with that?*

P.K.   Well actually to tell you the honest truth, I can't remember, but I also can't imagine any resistance. I doubt that there was resistance because my father had wanted to be a musician and his parents were against it. He wasn't going to make that mistake again with me, right? When my sister and I went away to college, he bought himself an oboe and took lessons, and he set up a table downstairs where he spent many an hour making oboe reeds. He joined various community orchestras in the Los Angeles metro area, attending rehearsals several nights a week.

A.A.   *Were you pretty self-motivated as far as practicing in your teen years?*

P.K.   Off and on. Not always. There were times when I was 10–12 years old, where I know I didn't practice much—I was a misfit in the Compton environment where I was growing up. Several times my mother threatened to stop the lessons and that was the way she would get me to practice. If she threatened to stop, then I would go practice. I remember once when I was about 10 or 11, I wanted to go out and play baseball. And so, when my mother wasn't looking, I took a knife and cut an A string halfway through and then practiced very loud until it broke. "Oh, mom, my A string broke. Can I go play baseball?"

A.A.   *Pretty normal thing for someone that age to do.*

P.K.   I hope so. I'm still living with the guilt.

A.A.   *So you weren't always motivated?*

P.K.   I've often thought about this because I think my motivation had quite a bit to do with my teachers. When my teachers would excite me in a lesson, I would run out of there and grab my instrument and practice. But other than that, I wasn't that consistent. I have to say that as I got older, I was mainly motivated by having concerts to play. Some people are just incredibly self-motivated and I have always envied them. They'll get up and do their two or three hours every morning, whether they have a concert or not. They may not have a concert for six months, but they will still practice. I'm not that type of person because I've got other interests and I never have enough hours in the day to do everything I would want to do. But fortunately, in my professional career, the Cleveland Quartet rehearsed 3 to 6 hours a day for 26 years and played over 80 to 120 concerts a year, plus recordings. So I stayed in shape, even improved.

A.A.   *Your first teacher was Victor Sazer. How did his teaching shape your playing? He was a student of Leonard Rose, right?*

P.K.   Yes, though before Vic, my first teacher in Long Beach was a sweet, amateur player by the name of Louis Miller, a former student of Joseph Schuster. Vic was my second—he was a Rose student, came from a really poor family in Newark, New Jersey, and began cello at 16 years old. And he was one of these wonderful, hungry talents that learned so fast that, despite his late start, still was able to get into Juilliard and was accepted by Rose. He must have also had a lot of scholarship help because his parents had no money. As I remember, he went to the Houston Symphony in the 50s, and this was the time of Senator Joe McCarthy. Vic's politics were on the left, and he was blacklisted and fired along with many other writers and musicians nationwide. To support his family, he left music and actually worked as a machinist and steelworker. And somehow, he just happened to be a neighbor when I was growing up in Compton. I think the way we first met is that my sister was babysitting his children.

A.A.   *What a random way to meet him!*

P.K.   Very random. He eventually came back to the instrument when his daughter Nina came home with a cello in her fourth grade. But I would like to think I can take some small credit for also helping to rekindle his interest. One could say our neighborhood was a culture-free zone and out of nowhere this young kid, me, pops up playing the cello. It was serendipitous! I believe he enjoyed helping me. He started listening to me in the 11th and 12th grades and he made a big difference. He helped me prepare for my college auditions. And over a period of time he himself came back into music. He taught cello and chamber music at Long Beach State College, played in the Pacific Trio, and in his later years was President of the Los Angeles Cello Society. In the nineties, he wrote a really interesting book on cello pedagogy, *Playing Without Pain*, and asked me if I would write the foreword for it. When I read the book drafts. I got really excited about some of the new ideas that he was writing about. He had unique and valuable insights challenging some of the traditional ideas of cello technique. I mean, how many ideas can be truly new to cello technique after centuries of the evolution of playing? There are certainly differing schools and beliefs, but once you are exposed to them when young, you rarely hear anything truly new. What you learn from one teacher usually comes from another in different words. But Vic had some really unique concepts about balance, awareness of the breath, playing from the floor, strength at the tip. There were others I wasn't so fond of, but they still made you think, reexamine. I learned a lot from the book and actually changed my playing back in the early 90s after it came out. And I use many of his ideas in my teaching now. The book brought him a lot of deserved attention and for a number of years he was all over the United States at the major conservatories like Juilliard and Eastman and at several Cello Congresses.

        Vic is wonderfully perceptive, and just as with his politics, has the guts to stick with what he believes, even if it challenges age-old traditional beliefs. He's now 93, lives out in Santa Monica, California, still teaches, and at the urging of his family is writing his memoirs. He's a quiet man, leads a very quiet life, but I think he's made some important contributions, including for me, powerful arguments about why the body should move contrary to the bow.

A.A.   *That's a question I was going to ask you later but yes, I'm very interested in how the torso affects cello playing.*

P.K.　Yes, a lot of that comes from Vic Sazer. It's similar to what I was already doing because Rose taught something very close to that. He taught me to lean on the left side of my butt. But I find contrary motion more dynamic than a static position. The way Vic talks about it is "playing from the floor", using your right foot to move the body left on the down bow, and your left foot to steer the body right, in opposition to the upbow. And it adds such ease and power to the bow.

A.A.　*I've come to believe that the torso usually leads the arms. Sometimes they move in opposite directions and sometimes the same direction, but the torso is always ahead of the arms.*

P.K.　Yes, it definitely should not be just the arms in isolation, but the entire body is interactive. Just like when walking, throwing a ball, or swinging the arms from side to side—the arms go one way and the legs the other. It all happens naturally without thinking—it's the body balancing itself.

A.A.　*I often think of your foot pushing to get the momentum going. It's helped me a lot instead of trying to start the bow motion from the arm.*

P.K.　Exactly. Bravo Tony! Lluís Claret, when I was watching his cello chat on CelloBello recently, was talking about initiating the bow motion from the lower back. We're all saying close to the same stuff in different ways. Except that Vic added something important to that with his "play from the floor." So Vic was an important teacher to me and has made a major contribution to cello pedagogy.

A.A.　*So let's go back to when you started at USC. What did you feel like you got most out of Gábor Rejtő?*

P.K.　He had such refinement and was certainly the first teacher that really got me to honestly listen to myself for detail.

　　　In my first semester studying with him at age 16, every time I came in for a lesson, he told me I wasn't listening carefully. Paul this is out of tune, Paul this is scratchy or Paul, you're playing a sloppy rhythm. I think it's typical when you come in as a freshman to be intimidated by the seniors and graduate students and I started doubting myself and thinking, oh my God, these people are all so good, do I have any talent? Did I pick the wrong profession? That's the way I felt when I first came into USC. And as I told you, I came from a fairly poor family, so my parents didn't have enough money for the USC tuition. So when I was a freshman, I got a job. I was basically the jailer of Clark House where the string and piano faculty taught daytime, and I worked evenings when the building served as the practice room building. Every practice room had a lock and key on it and people would sign up with me. I would let them in, I would let them out. I did that from five o'clock until 10 o'clock every night.

　　　I would do my homework at my desk when I wasn't busy letting people into practice rooms and then at 10 o'clock I would close up the building and practice. I loved playing late at night in the dark. And I would practice until one in the morning, two in the morning. It was dark, I was alone and I felt free and all of that. Yet Mr. Rejtő was never happy with me, he never acknowledged my progress. When second semester came, Clark House, which was a beautiful mansion on Adams Boulevard in Los Angeles, was taken over by a Hollywood studio to make a film. If you ever want to see it, it is *From the Terrace* with Paul Newman and Joanne Woodward.

　　　They paid the school of music a ton of money to rent that building and being poor, the school couldn't say no. And so we were tossed out of there in our second semester and all of a sudden there was no place to practice. So the only way I could find a place to practice was to pull myself out of bed and get to the temporary practice rooms before everyone else at seven o'clock in the morning. So I would get there first, get a room and I would practice from seven to nine o'clock before my first theory class.

As lessons continued in the second semester, Mr. Rejtő said, now you're starting to hear! So what I learned from that, was even though it might be more fun to wail away at midnight, that the mind is sharper, the ears are sharper when you're fresh. Years later I applied that to touring, and found an afternoon nap before the concert does wonders.

A.A. *Did Gábor Rejtő help you a lot with your technique at that point?*

P.K. Yes. Although I have to say that almost all of the technique that (Gabby) taught me, I modified or outright changed. Nevertheless, it's all been valuable. In my teaching, I always have felt that there's more than one right way to do something and the same thing doesn't necessarily work for everybody. He was a wonderful cellist and musician, I remember the things that he taught me and sometimes I will use them today to teach a student, even though I don't do it that way myself anymore. But far more importantly, he was the first sophisticated musician teaching me about phrasing and artistry, how to think and study composers and style and this kind of thing. He was such a high-level artist. He was a very refined player, I'm much more earthy, So I got lifelong artistic values from him more than what I now use technically.

A.A. *How many years did you study with Rejtő?*

P.K. I studied with him for three years. In my fourth year, when I was a senior, he took a sabbatical and wow, talk about the gods smiling on me, that was the year that Heifetz, Piatigorsky and Primrose came to teach at USC. I auditioned for Piatigorsky and got into his very first class at USC. So my senior year is when I started to study with him.

A.A. *And then you went to study with Bernard Greenhouse at Manhattan School for your master's degree?*

P.K. Yes. I had actually heard and met Greenhouse back in the 11th grade, before I'd even met Piatigorsky. Greenhouse came to Los Angeles on tour. He came twice that year. The first time he came he played in the Bach Aria Group and I was thrilled by his playing and his beautiful sound and I was really inspired by him. And then he came back later in the year with the Beaux Arts Trio. I was really excited by his cello playing, it just spoke to me. So I went backstage and told him I was a cello student and I asked him if he taught. He was very welcoming, and I liked his warmth as a person and all of that. I had decided even before I started my undergraduate years that I eventually wanted to get away from home and the idea of going to New York for Greenhouse was always on my mind. So yes, I applied for a master's degree with Greenhouse. Actually, I also applied to study with Leonard Rose at Juilliard, and except for humorous, or I might say maddening circumstances, I probably would have gone there due to the prestige.

I was admitted to both Juilliard with Rose and the Manhattan School with Greenhouse, but a fact forgotten today, is that in those years, which was 1962, Juilliard gave only a bachelor of science degree. Strange, but they didn't offer a bachelor of music degree and they were snotty about it. They insisted I spend an extra semester to get a B.S degree on top of my B.M. from USC where I was second in my graduating class. My parents didn't have the money for an extra semester so I didn't do that.

I remember feeling really pissed, this degree stuff felt so illogical. But besides, I didn't like Juilliard's attitude and so it was an easy decision to study with Greenhouse, whose playing I really loved.

A.A.   *Talk about the experience with Mr. Greenhouse and what was your biggest takeaway from him? What did you get the most?*

P.K.   I got a lot from him. I was really inspired by his sound. I think to that point in my life I had been sort of mesmerized by these big players like Nelsova and Rose who sustained everything. I loved making a big fat sound and I loved getting down near the bridge. As a kid to that point, I was into producing thick chocolate, you know, and Bernie, he just started talking to me about color and nuance in a way that made me want to practice. I got really obsessed with trying to make colors, as I heard him doing. So I found it very inspiring.

Rejtő taught us a squared position in the left hand. I don't think Piatigorsky played that way, but Piatigorsky didn't talk to me very much about my left hand at all. Piatigorsky talked a lot about shifting and fingerings, that sort of thing, but not hand position. But Bernie (Greenhouse), he was the one that switched me from a square left hand to a slanted left hand which really sped up my vibrato. And teaching me to release the non-playing fingers made a huge difference to me in terms of comfort. I really needed that. But you remember I said I sometimes teach things that Rejtő taught me—I will teach the squared position depending on the student and maybe how old they are, and if sound good, I leave them alone

One of the primary ways that I try and help a player decide whether their hand should be slanted or square is to listen to their vibrato. Sometimes students have this machine gun vibrato, a vibrato that needs to be slowed down. Usually turning them around into a squared position will help reduce the speed enough that it might even take care of the problem. And conversely, speaking of me, in my early years I always felt my vibrato was a little wobbly and a little bit slow and I would push, force it, to try and get more intensity in it. So when Bernie slanted me around on the side like that, it really helped me. Bernie was a vibrato maven. He was obsessed with vibrato! I mean he used to talk about his three different vibratos, wrist, arm and whole arm. In addition to all of those things, he took me through a lot of repertoire and was also really on me for my intonation.

A.A.   *Did he help you become more confident?*

P.K.   I think he did. And I needed that after Piatigorsky.

A.A.   *Masterclasses with Piatigorsky must have been stressful.*

P.K.   Many students, certainly me, were intimidated at his masterclasses. I mean he was pretty open about wanting to apply pressure. He compared his masterclasses to basic training in the army. He wanted it to be so tough that when you actually got into battle, which was the concert, it was easier. I'm grateful for that. I suffered but don't regret any of that time with Piatigorsky. It was a complicated relationship because he was also a very warm and perceptive human being. He wasn't entirely old school and just rapping your knuckles all the time, nothing like that. Piatigorsky also was encouraging, but the student up there performing was always the butt of his jokes and I didn't respond well to that in front of my friends.

A.A. *And I would imagine just thinking about it now, he might've been quite different if you had lessons one on one with him. Did that ever happen?*

P.K. Yes, I had quite a few of them during the summertime.

A.A. *And was it a different feeling at those lessons?*

P.K. Yes, as there was no embarrassment. But not dress. I remember it being over a hundred degrees in Los Angeles when I went to Piatigorsky's home for a private lesson. I still had to wear a suit and tie and he wore a suit and tie. It was sweltering, he was in his own home and had a suit and tie on!

A.A. *After Greenhouse, when you went back to study with Piatigorsky, did you feel more confident as a cellist at that point? And did you feel like you had a technique that had served you well?*

P.K. I mean I could say yes, but I don't remember. It's so many years back that some of these memories are very strong, but in terms of my evolution at that point, I don't know.

A.A. *What were the most important things you learned from Piatigorsky?*

P.K. Enormous wisdom about both music and life in general and the psychology of performance, which he was very big on. Losing inhibition. How you sit yourself on stage, present yourself, how to deal with nerves.

A.A. *How would he tell you to deal with nerves?*

P.K. Well I mean, like one of his wisdoms that I continue to pass along is "every talented person knows what they can't do. You sit in the practice room three or four hours a day, your weaknesses scream at you. But when you go on stage, you have to know what you can do and you have to focus on what you can do and you have to bring your audience's attention to your strong points." I'm paraphrasing him, but if I had a Russian accident. It would be pretty close. One day someone asked him, "Mr. Piatigorsky, what are *your* weak points?" He sat for a long time and finally dryly answered, "My fourth finger trill!"

A.A. *Are there other Piatigorsky stories that you often share with your students?*

P.K. Piatigorsky was the first teacher to talk to me about what the instrument *felt* like. Rejtő was always talking about what your hands *looked* like. Rejtő would tell me to put my fingers here or there and hold your hands this way or that. Of course, he helped me and I teach that way today as well, but perhaps I use it differently as I am in search of the final arbiter which is comfort and what does it *feel* like. If it feels clumsy or awkward, it probably is. When you're just 19 years old, you don't think of these things. I don't know why as it is so obvious—How can you play the cello without thinking about what it feels like? But that was revelatory at the time and it made a big difference to me.

  And even though I sort of already knew it, Piatigorsky was the first one to encourage me to tap into, to believe in the power and insight of instinct. Both the physical and the musical could be intuitive. Successful performance depends on trusting and communicating your natural emotional response. As a teacher today I tell students that their right-brain creative response to music can be just as valid and often, more insightful than the logical brain. Today I realize that art is a balance of the rational and the intuitive. Not everything needs to have, or can have a reason, not everything needs to be logical or analyzed. Both logic and imagination are needed—one without the other is insufficient. I love the Albert Einstein quote, "Logic will get you from A to B. Imagination will take you everywhere."

A.A.   *So let's talk about life after Piatigorsky. I'm curious to talk about how you made the switch from being a student to being a professional and if chamber music was always on your mind as a career goal. And did you always enjoy teaching? Did you ever think about being in an orchestra?*

P.K.   Well, I always loved chamber music, but I'm not sure when the idea of doing it professionally became a reality. But when I was just a freshman in college, I was diagnosed with an eye condition called keratoconus. This was a very debilitating condition especially back in 1958 or so. Because of that, I had severe, fairly limited vision when I was in college and it became clear to me by the time I got to be a junior or senior, that an orchestra career wasn't really an option for me. It's "conical cornea" in English, a progressive condition where the cornea gradually pushes outward and becomes pointy and distorts one's vision. I eventually lost my driver's license and was considered legally blind. In the early years of the CQ I pretty much memorized everything—I could see the page and that was a huge help, but I could not really see pitches. I had corneal transplants in 1975 and 1977 and it changed my life.

   Anyway, back when I was studying with Greenhouse, he went to IU during the summers, and taught joint classes with Starker. So for two summers I went to Indiana University summer school with Greenhouse, and while I was there and enrolled in chamber music, I met a fine violinist by the name of Leonard Felberg who was actually 10 years older than me. I guess I was 20, 21 he was 30, 31. He'd just gotten a job teaching at the University of Toledo in Ohio and playing in a faculty string quartet. After a year their cellist left, and he called me and asked me if I'd be interested. I was 22 at that point.

   I actually went and talked to Piatigorsky about it. And this was the side of Piatigorsky that could be very supportive and very fatherly. I hated to leave him, but I was excited about having a job. My parents didn't have money. I remember telling him I was worried about going to Toledo, Ohio, that there wasn't going to be any musical inspiration. "I'm not going to be around great people like you," I told him. I can still hear his exact response, " 'Remember wherever you go, you make your own atmosphere.' He told me to take the job and with his encouragement, I did. There I was at 22 studying with Piatigorsky and this college teaching and faculty quartet jpb fell into my lap. So in my life, I have never gone through the process of a competitive interview or anything like that. It was all set up for me. I played five years in that group until the Cleveland Quartet formed with a full time faculty position at the CIM—again, no interview or auditions!

A.A.   *Did you also teach at a school when you joined the Cleveland Quartet? How did that all start?*

P.K.   The Cleveland Quartet was formed at the CIM. Don Weilerstein, the founding first violinist was already at the institute and already teaching and he convinced the powers that be that a resident faculty string quartet would be a good thing for the school.

A.A.   *So you went right out of school into teaching college at Toledo?*

P.K.   Immediately.

   And the teaching was natural to me. I'd always taught through college. It was part of the way I earned enough money to survive school. You know in Los Angeles you could get a driver's license when you were 16 so when I was 18, 19 years old, I could drive out to Beverly Hills to some wealthy families and make some extra money. And so I did a lot of teaching all the way through school.

The Present

A.A.   *What are some of the secrets to practicing well? Is that something you talk about a lot with your students?*

P.K.   Of course I talk about it with my students and I'm sure as a teacher you do the same thing. There's so much to teach and not enough time to teach it. So I have a studio performance class every week and whenever I can steal some time, I turn that into a discussion class. For example, last week was the first week of school and there wasn't anybody ready to play. So I had a discussion class and the discussion had to do with how to practice. It's a good subject for a class meeting because you have to talk to everybody about it anyway, so it's better to do it with everyone at the same time.

I also love that format because these are smart kids and it's interactive and they come up with valuable things that I sometimes wouldn't have thought of saying. Or they paraphrase me in interesting ways. And depending on their struggles and what is on their mind, they take the discussion in the directions meaningful to them. I have a student from China, an extremely creative, imaginative player, somewhat spacey but sensitive and insightful. The class was talking about practice warm ups, saying all the usual things I talk about when warming up and then she said, "Well when I warm up, I just like to take the cello and play beautiful sounds and move up and down the instrument and I don't play any pieces. I just want to get comfortable at the instrument and make my hands feel good." While I often say words to that effect, it crystallized the conversation and really impacted the class.

I added emphasis by adding that almost every great artist I've heard warming up backstage, and I've been lucky enough to play with a lot of them, is usually not playing pieces. Most everybody's got their own little ritual or whatever it is, but they're basically doing what she said. I love to have those discussions as much as my students.

A.A.   *Do you ever think when people lose themselves musically, while they're playing that they're not always able to really understand what's going on physically in their playing? I often ask students to try playing without being musical for a minute, which often opens their mind more and then they can actually think about what their body is doing.*

P.K.   Yes and no. I think everybody's different. It can cut either way. I mean there are people that are such thinkers, so objective about everything they do that you have to ask them to stop thinking, get lost in the music, tap into their intuitive emotional response. In fact, I believe that too much thinking when you're out on stage can be a negative and many young players make the mistake of thinking their way through a performance. We need thinking on stage as well, but more thinking is needed for the learning process. Focusing listening and expressing, getting in the zone, leads to the performances for most of us. Piatigorsky would say that as you get ready for a performance, you move more to the intuitive side of your playing, though not in a way that clouds the brain.

After so many years and well over 3000 performances, I have found attempting to control everything through conscious direction from the mind is limited—we can only *think* of one thing at a time. We can mentally control a shift, or a phrase shape, or bow distribution, etc., but they cannot control everything, because it all needs to be integrated. The ears are a miracle—they can monitor and merge everything simultaneously. Character, sound, intonation, shaping, rhythm, ensemble, ad infinitum—we *hear* it and unify it. Students trying to control everything by thinking tend to feel overwhelmed attempting to track an infinite number of musical and technical variables.

My own inner game, one of the things conjured up when I go out on stage, is to imagine that my ears are growing very big, that they become huge and that they are like vacuum cleaners that suck up all the sound. No sound gets away from them (at least that's my aim). That's my way of trying to describe this state of hyper-listening awareness.

A.A.   *Do you have a teaching philosophy that you can verbalize? And how has your teaching evolved over the years?*

P.K.   I think I've gotten more articulate over the years, at least I hope I have. One of my conscious goals is to teach students to become independent problem solvers. I want teach them to self-teach, to think, how to solve their own problems. So rather than tell them just do it this way or do it that way, I'll explain to them why. And I ask a lot of questions. That has its pros and its cons because it takes time -often a lot of time. Sometimes I feel my lessons are a little bit slow because I really want them to understand why. But at the end of the day, after they've left school, I believe that will help them the most. I want them to have a knowledge base as they go through life in order to be able to figure out things for themselves.

A.A.   *Most of our lives we don't have teachers.*

P.K.   Exactly. And I mean, I was luckier than many because I not only had five great teachers to teach me how to play the cello, but I was also really lucky that after I was a student, I played quartets with three amazing artists that all love to teach. So for all of those years that I was in the Cleveland Quartet, we were teaching each other. We had endless discussions about bow holds, what it feels like with high elbows, low elbows, what kind of vibratos to use, ad infinitum. I mean, somebody like Don Weilerstein is one of the greatest violin teachers in the world. I played with him for 20 years and learned so much from him through all of those rehearsal discussions. And I hope he learned something from me. In fact, every single person that was ever a member of the Cleveland Quartet has gone on to be an exceptionally well-known teacher. And every single person in the Cleveland quartet loves teaching. That's unique. I mean, over 26 years there were seven of us and I learned from each of them.

A.A.   *Do you demonstrate a lot in your teaching? And has that changed over the years?*

P.K.   Well, I have to say I demonstrate much less.

A.A.   *Many of the other people I have interviewed have said that.*

P.K.   Really?

A.A.   *Yes. It seems to be the trend.*

P.K.   Yes. Well, I mean, part of it is, to be honest, is that I'm 77 years old. I can't play like I used to.

A.A.　*But students can still learn from hearing you play.*

P.K.　Yes. I can still show them a beautiful sound and I can show phrasing and I can share some different vibratos. I can show them a lot, but there's a lot I cannot show. That unfortunately happens to everyone with age. Bernie Greenhouse told me when I was 19 that because I had soft hands, I would play "forever", but he didn't know I would have physical injuries like a rotator cuff tear, which makes it hard for me to get my arm up into some of the upper positions. It's hard to accept that I cannot perform as I once could, but when I feel regretful, I remind myself that I've played many thousands of concerts, had a wonderful performing career, and I get to work with gifted young people that continue to inspire me every day. I say, "Get over it Paul—you still have an incredibly rewarding musical life—enjoy it!"

A.A.　*Do you generally give a student bowing and fingerings? What's that process like in your teaching?*

P.K.　Well, Rejtő gave every student all his bowings and fingerings and you had to do all of them. He would actually be hurt sometimes if you didn't do his bowings or fingerings. He was a little bit defensive about it. His students would go away for the summer and study with somebody else and when we came back, he was really on pins and needles as to whether we had changed his bowings and fingerings. Looking back on it, I don't know if that was a lack of self-confidence on his part. I can imagine that it was, though I didn't feel it at the time. I just felt like he was closed on that particular issue.

　　My next teacher Piatigorsky, on the other hand, would not give a bowing or fingering. He refused to. He made us do everything ourselves. I found that a really valuable process and it fits into my own teaching philosophy of encouraging independence.

A.A.　*Did he suggest something later if it wasn't working?*

P.K.　I remember from time to time he would make fun of a fingering just as he loved to make fun of his students. "Why do you do that?" For example, if we would ask him for a scale fingering he would say, "You should practice many different scale fingerings. The scale fingering you use depends on the passage it is in." I think his road to mastery was just turning the world upside down in every way possible.

　　I will share a story about playing the Dvořák Concerto for him. I walked in one morning, the classes were always at 10 o'clock. "Mr. Katz, you look very tired today." "No Mr. Piatigorsky, I feel fine." "Oh, you look very tired. What are you playing?" I said, "I'm playing the Dvořák Concerto." He said smiling, "Sorry you are so tired— please lay down on the couch." Then he gave me my cello and he said, "You will feel better—now play." He made me play the whole first movement on my back. You know, just trying to balance with my knees, with the cello on my stomach, that's a good example of how he could embarrass you. But while I felt that way many times, on that particular occasion I didn't care about sounding bad because I felt like I had such an understandable excuse.

A.A.　*What was the pedagogical goal behind that?*

P.K.　I think to be flexible, ready for anything. That may be the most extreme example. But we would come into class and he would give us a low chair, or the next time a highchair. One day he would tell us to push our endpins all the way in and another time to pull the endpin all the way out. He would make such requests frequently in the masterclass and then make us play. He couldn't stand rigidity, inflexibility, those kinds of things. For example, it would drive him through the roof if he saw somebody use their hand-span to precisely measure their endpin length

A.A.   *He wanted you to feel free with any sort of circumstance.*

P.K.   Yes! And you know, he was right. I mean, when you go around the world as I got to do for so many years, you will come to a hall that has only a very high or low chair. Once I actually played a concert on a bass stool because there wasn't anything else. And I remember in Toronto, on the last tour of the quartet, just before the concert, my endpin slipped inside the cello, and I could not get it out. There was a stage hand with a pair of pliers who tried everything but there was no way to pull it out. So, I had no choice but to rest the cello on the stage floor without endpin and play the concert that way.

A.A.   *You played baroque style, between your knees?*

P.K.   Yes, sometimes I did. I don't remember but, on that occasion, I decided I was more comfortable with it on the floor. But at scary times like that I would thank Piatigorsky for giving me that sense of possibility and flexibility.

A.A.   *You mentioned scales. How much time do you spend with the students on those? Do you help them have a routine and do you hear scales and related arpeggios, thirds and sixths during lessons?*

P.K.   When I was younger, I taught scales much more than now although I believe in them just as much today. It's a hard call now as the class that I have is quite advanced. I mean when today's kids are auditioning from high school with our most difficult repertoire, like Sinfonia Concertante, it makes you wonder how much you should take of lesson time to work on scales. When I was in college 60 plus years ago, we were auditioning on pieces like the Lalo Concerto and we played scales at our admission auditions. Today, most US conservatories have stopped requiring scales in auditions and juries. How to balance a lesson, what to teach in one hour is always a difficult judgment call that varies from student to student. But there is so much advanced, technically oriented playing today that many of us old folks feel concerned, even compelled to spend our time on nurturing creative, artistic development. I think it's probably been four years now since I've had a scale class. I'm not proud of that. I used to have weekly scale classes and I do believe in that. I really believe in it. But life seems to get busier and busier. Neither my schedule or that of my students makes it easy to schedule both a scale class and a performance class each week.

A.A.   *Do you think it has to do with them being at such a high level? If they were technically struggling a lot more than you might be more insistent on scales?*

P.K.   Definitely. I do regularly assign scales to my freshmen and sophomores. But I don't always hear them in every lesson, and I trust them to do them in their practicing as more independent kitchen work. I admit that in some cases I should be more demanding and wish that I guided them more.

This subject reminds me of another Piatigorsky influence which came up this last week in my studio discussion class on practicing. Piatigorsky admonished us not to warm up the same way every day. He told us that even the greatest artists can get psychologically dependent on a warmup ritual to the point where they simply can't walk out on stage until they've done their half hour of scales, their whole bows, or whatever it is. And his point was that it is nothing more than psychological. Their warmup ritual is not really a physical need. So Piatigorsky recommended that you begin practicing a different way every day. Some days it's good to start directly with the concerto, some days with Bach and sometimes with scales. Or perhaps start with the arpeggios and then do the scales. You can do everything every day but not in the same order. So, you don't get psychologically dependent on a particular order.

I mean, while that kind of freedom is ideal, I have found it doesn't work for everyone. Some of my students require more structure and get better results if I just tell them 30 minutes of scales, 15 minutes of thirds and octaves; then the étude, then your Bach, sonata and concerto. I will help them set up their practicing like that if it's a player that's a gypsy and lacks logic and discipline. I mean there are people that are just so disorganized that you have to spell it out for them. So, in these cases I have them bring paper and pencil and write it all down. Most of the time I don't feel the need to do that with my students. I Just have a discussion on the principles of healthy practice—like we are having now.

Piatigorsky also was the first person in my life who talked about productive practicing being *experimental*. You have to try a variety of approaches, be a creative problem solver. It was his way of saying that doing it by rote, over and over again the same way is inefficient, even a waste of time. I use an image that might be my own or might be his, I can't really remember: You're at the bottom of the mountain and your goal is to get to the top and there are several roads -some will get you there and some will not. So, you might go up one, hit a dead end, and you have to come back down and try another one. But you explore this one and that one and finally you find your way to the top. He described practicing similarly. Practice in rhythms, try different bowings and fingerings, faster and slower, louder and softer. Stand on your head, lay on the couch -anything other than mindless repetition and you will find your way.

A.A.   *It's true. One thing I find myself saying to students which seems obvious when I say it, but if you want to sound different you have to do something different with your body. I think it is so easy to forget that when you're practicing.*

P.K.   Yes! One of my favorite expressions is "There is no progress without change."

A.A.   *Do you practice performing sometimes as well? I mean that's like the flip side of like, I think some of these students always stop to fix something and don't ever know what it's like to play without stopping until they are on stage.*

P.K.   That's really important. That's part of my teaching actually. This was another Piatigorskyism which came from his masterclass. You had to walk in twice a week and perform the piece in concert clothes from beginning to end. It's true that if you know you're going to have to perform it when you walk in, you will practice differently during the week. If you walk into a lesson knowing the teacher is going to stop and start you and you're going to go work bit by bit, then the lesson doesn't give you the motivation to put Humpty Dumpty together.

So, Piatigorsky always made us start with a performance. Even when I had private lessons with him, he would make me perform the whole movement before he would start to teach. Piatigorsky had 10 hours a week of master class with us whereas I have one for 2–3 with my class. So, in my NEC classes I often feel such a pressure of time to let everyone play, that occasionally I don't have them play a whole movement. I'll have them play a big chunk of it. But, even in the worst cases, I never stop them after eight bars. I stress that studio class is for performing.

A.A.   *What's your thought as a performer and as a teacher, of playing things by memory?*

P.K.   As a student I memorized everything but of course because my career was in a quartet, in my career I didn't have to do a lot of that. But my students must play everything except sonatas by memory.

A.A.   *When they come in for lessons.*

P.K.   Well not right away. If they're learning a Bach Suite and they come in for their first performance with the music, that's fine, but they still know they are going to perform it, and t/hat they will need to memorize it. At the beginning of each year I make a point to new students that the weekly studio classes are not workshops, they are performance opportunities. I require them to dress up in whatever they consider their concert clothes and I tell them my Piatigorsky story. But I'm also different than Piatigorsky as this is a different era and there are many different ways to go out on stage, right? They can choose to be more formal or more casual—whatever fits them. I tell them, whatever you would wear in a concert, I want you to wear it here. Psychologically, dressing up feels more like a performance. And also, you learn what's comfortable, if the buttons rattle, if the high heels don't feel good, or whatever. Choosing clothes wisely is part of learning to perform, so I do have them do that.

But back to memory, I do let people play a Bach Suite the first time out if they don't have it memorized. It's a judgment call each time—if I feel they need to be pushed to perform for their peers, but they are nervous that their memory is not yet solid enough for the class, I will respect that. It's important that I am not so rigid with the memory requirement that I set someone up for failure—a truly bad experience can stay with one forever. If it's a concerto, I am tougher. I seldom let them play with the music for the class unless it's a tricky contemporary work like Dutilleux or Carter, If they bring a traditional concerto to their lessons for a couple of times and are still using music, I might say, "Hey Jesse, this is the third week you are playing Haydn D with the music. I'm sure you've got it memorized, so just try it out on me now without music. In this way you'll learn the few little places that you have to work on, and you can then get the memory solid and play it in class next week."

The only way to really learn how to perform is to perform- nothing else can replace it, and the hardest thing about being a student is that you rarely get to perform. When you play only a few times a year, each one of those performances gets magnified in your head and if something goes wrong, you often don't get a chance to try it out again the next night. After playing well over 3,000 concerts in my life it's super-clear that "every concert is a rehearsal for the next concert." So that's why I offer weekly studio classes and make them a performing experience.

A.A.   *Do you think making students play by memory is helpful to get them to know the music better, or do you think it's to free them from the visual so they can focus more on other things or both?*

P.K.   Hopefully both. People differ—sometimes it's liberating and for some people it's a distracting pressure. It's interesting that I've been a chamber player for most of my professional life, yet how much I still believe in memorization. I want, not just for the hands to memorize it, but also for the head to memorize it. I think you can take your listening awareness to another level and hopefully it gives you a chance to open the ears. For me, when I can just close my eyes and play, I hear better. So, I like to teach different mental techniques for memorizing.

A.A.   *I agree.*

P.K.   I have a friend who was talking about how when you play, you use 3 senses: touching, hearing, and seeing. If you can take the seeing out of it, your other senses can be that much more involved. I thought that's a nice way to put it.

A.A.   *Do you make an effort for your students to sound like individuals? Is that something you're consciously aware of?*

P.K.   I'm really super-aware of it. I mean, I'm even proud of the fact that none of my students sound alike and they can sound convincing with interpretive differences. My whole goal is to help a student find their own voice. I don't believe an interpretation can work without authenticity and so I view my role, in addition to teaching style, tradition and musical insights, to help them integrate that with their own musical responses, to find themselves.

       Probably all of my teachers taught me that in their own way. It was one of those values I learned without knowing I was learning it. Ten years ago, I did a video interview with Greenhouse where he says exactly that, and I also remember lessons where he spoke of spontaneity and strength of personality. So I know that Greenhouse felt that way. And Starker would say, "My job is to give you the tools so you can express yourself the way you want to." Piatigorsky definitely felt that way as well—his whole thrust was to free us of inhibitions. Rose might have been less flexible, but I don't really know, as the short time I was with him was all intense technical work. Casals was totally inflexible on any particular day, but after you could play as he heard it, he would tell you to throw it away and become yourself.

       I was influenced by Casals for as long as I can remember. Because of his humanitarian stances and political courage, Casals was one of my parents' heroes, so I was listening to Casals recordings as soon as I began cello as a little boy. I was incredibly fortunate at age 20 to have first studied with Casals in his master classes in Berkeley, California. And of course, Rejtő and Greenhouse were his students and real Casals' disciples. And I then had three summers with him at Marlboro where I played for him in more master classes as well as in the Marlboro Orchestra which he conducted.

       Casals had a power and charisma that you felt as soon as he walked into the room. An unintended result of his power of influence was that many of the cellists that studied long-term with him never quite succeeded in careers because they could not stop imitating him. Bernie Greenhouse told me that too—that this was an unintended negative of Casals' power of persuasion. Bernie's comments further strengthened my belief that to be successful, an artist must find their own voice—performance is all about conviction and authenticity. My job is to help a student unlock themselves.

Greenhouse was proud that he was able to get past the Casals influence and find his own unique voice. Anyway, I don't believe this is any kind of a teaching problem for me—I don't have 10% of the ego or charisma of Pablo Casals—and I shouldn't! I do believe in myself—I'm proud that I've had success as a performer and audiences find me communicative. But I don't feel it's my role to make everybody imitate me—that's never been anywhere in my mind. Yet it's a hard question as a teacher: What aspect of the interpretation of a composition is intrinsic to the work and needs to be insisted upon, and what are merely my more subjective preference or feelings after playing a work for a lifetime—those I can suggest but should be willing to let go of if they don't speak to the player. For example, I really have a hard time accepting a really slow tempo of the C-Major Bach Prelude because I feel that, in addition to a triumphant herald or announcement, there is also a positive joy and a bit of virtuosic mentality intrinsic in Bach's intentions. But what is truly Bach and what is simply a personal conception that I should be willing to let go of—tough question—know what I mean? For me, the answer is, can the player convince me.

Sometimes I'll say, "I really didn't find you convincing. It's not working for me. I don't know whether it's because I've been thinking of the piece differently for the last 50 years and that blocks my appreciation, but why don't we try a few of my ideas?" I'll then help them, but it's really about finding themselves and not trying to make them sound like me. Sometimes I'll say, "Ouch, I think I just made it worse!" Or sometimes I'll say, "For me, that's much better." Perhaps they want to be on my good side, so they usually agree. When they do, it's often because a lightbulb went off and they like the idea and hear something they were missing before. But not always. Most importantly, I got them thinking and listening. And, agree with them or not, I most always respect their decision to do as they believe. That fosters their own journey to increasing conviction and authenticity.

I can illustrate this with a story that goes back probably 30 years, when I was still a pretty young teacher at Eastman. I was teaching a wonderful cellist named Brant Taylor (now in the Chicago Symphony) who studied with me for four years. He came in one day to play the C-Minor Bach Prelude for me. Well as I just said, I grew up imbued with Casals and Casals' approach to the Bach Suites. So I always thought of the Prelude of the Fifth Suite as this big organ prelude. A huge and massive prelude on a grand scale. And then Brant came and shocked me when he started *pianissimo*. It was so wonderful, really full of expression and I went, "Wow! I never thought of that before." The story illustrates two of my beliefs—you can and should learn from your students and the lesson was proof that there's more than one way to play a piece.

A.A.   *Well, that leads me to another question specifically about the Bach Suites. There has been such a shift in performance practice over the last 20 years or so. How do you feel about H.I.P. when you teach Bach? It sounds like you might be a little conflicted from some of the things you said earlier.*

P.K.   No, I wouldn't say I am conflicted. I have my own really deeply held beliefs about Bach, but the wonder of the Suites is that there is more than one truth, and it's important to acknowledge that. I mean, if you put on 30 recorded performances of Bach, you're going to get 30 different interpretations, so nobody plays them the same way. In general, I recoil from rigidity—there is more than one valid way to play *anything*, and especially Bach!

Casals used to make a point of this. He played Bach every day of his life and each day played it differently. And there's this video interview I did with Bernie Greenhouse which is on my CelloBello.org website, where he relates how he studied the D-Minor Suite with Casals. For days, Casals made him play every note in unison with him, made him copy the bowings, copy the fingerings, copy the rubati until Bernie could play just as Casals, and after he could do it, Casals said, "Now, change it. Play it differently. I'll show you what I mean." And he picked up the cello and played it in a totally different way. I hope you will watch the interview.

There's been so much important scholarship in the last 100 years. Over my lifetime, through study of Baroque performance practice, conversations with colleagues (and as I said—students), I have evolved from the Casals' influence. I have a baroque bow in my studio which has helped both me and my students tremendously as one of the most difficult decisions about Bach is finding the right bow stroke. I have found that when I take the baroque bow, even on a modern cello with four steel strings, so many of the passages sound instantly better. So I like to lend that bow to my students and when they have the sound in their ear, then give them their own bow back and have them imitate the sound. I have found that very useful.

A.A.   *What is the hardest thing to teach a student?*

P.K.   Whatever they can't do.

A.A.   *That's also what Joel Krosnick said.*

P.K.   Well, I think that that's a good answer, as people are so different. But that being said, I will add a little something to that.

I think when people are emotionally closed, that's tough. To get them to tap into, to believe in their talent, to trust and express whatever their inner response to music is, that is my job. Sometimes with gifted people you just know it's in there but then, how do you give them the necessary confidence or the permission or whatever it is to enable them to let go and get it out? You will hear one of my students tomorrow- really gifted and potentially an emotional player, but he doesn't believe in himself. I mean this guy has great chops. Won a national competition this year with the last movement of the Kodaly unaccompanied and Arpeggione Sonata. Somehow I got him over that hump for the competition, got him to open up and express himself. He's talented instrumentally and musically, but one senses some kind of emotional reserve. I can't expect an instant change. I need to be patient and give him time—let him, help him evolve—he's still young.

A.A.   *Do you think people play like their personalities for the most part?*

P.K.   Yes, I do. I really believe that. Maybe you're going to ask this question later, but while it's on my mind, one of my pet peeves is the person that comes to me for advice on achieving a career and then asks, "How can I be different?" And that always bothers me because I know that the key is not to be different, but to be yourself, to be sincere. You've got to find yourself and if you're putting something on because you think that's what you're supposed to do, it never works.

A.A.   *When you pick students to come study with you, what do you look for the most? Someone who has a lot to say, but maybe physically has more challenges or someone like the student you were just describing who is physically really gifted but isn't as comfortable expressing themselves?*

P.K.   I mean that's a really good question and a difficult one. And that's changed a little bit for me over the years.

I remember during my Eastman days, when I was still young, I took a few students I somewhat regretted. I remember one boy in particular. He came in and he impressed me as being so musical and rhapsodic and a free spirit and everything. And I really liked all of that. But he was sloppy as hell and played out of tune. And I thought, "Oh, all he really needs is my wonderful teaching. I just have to instill a sense of integrity and get him to listen better." And I never could do it, or perhaps I should say, he could never do it.

I now believe that by the time somebody is 17, 18 years old and they come in, there's a core that's already formed. I mean, of course, everybody's going to have their strengths and their weaknesses, but I'm looking for integrity and honesty. I want somebody that's musically really responsive, but not into showbiz just for the sake of showbiz. I turn away from shallow playing. And additionally, these days it's got to be somebody with real physical talent for the instrument. The instrumental level is so high, that a physical gift is a necessity.

But in the end, when it's all said and done, if I feel there's artistry in somebody, I'll go for that every time over the technique.

A.A.   *I imagine it must be hard to decide sometimes with so many talented kids.*

P.K.   Yes. It's a hard call. I mean, I love to have people that have chops. What teacher wouldn't—it makes our lives easier. But if I'm considering somebody that I'm going to be working with for four years and they can play the notes but don't have much musical response, I know that after a while it will start to drive me crazy. It's more about me than them—that kind of talent may be very deserving and go far, but they frustrate me and I feel they need a different type of teacher. On the other hand, if there's somebody that really has something to say and has to work a little harder to master the instrument, I'm willing to help with that. To me, that's more rewarding. And I guess really selfishly, as I get older, I'm looking for students that I feel will be rewarding. When I was younger, I used to think more about taking on a challenge as a way that I could develop myself as a teacher. I don't think that way at my age anymore.

I also have to like the person. So in addition to the audition, I always try and give them a lesson, talk to them a little bit, even if it's on Skype or something such as that. And I know these kids are growing up and a year or two more of maturity can help a lot, but if somebody is really screwed up emotionally, I get a little bit scared by that because I've had a few bad experiences. I have a bleeding heart, I think I'm very supportive and can help people get through a lot of emotional stuff and I actually like doing that. But I also know that I cannot solve everybody's psychological problems. For me, it is important to have a personal relationship with my students. I want them to know, to feel that they can come to me not only with their cello or performance issues, but personal problems if it is something I may be able to help with. But there have been some really gifted people that I was not able to stand on their feet because they had too much emotional baggage. And I've tried. It saddens me. I have tried.

A.A. *Do you ever talk to students about how much they should be practicing? And how do you deal with motivation?*

P.K. Yes, especially if they're not developing as I want them to—if I suspect a problem. I'll begin by asking them, "How much did you practice this week," which all by itself already sends a message. Depending on the response, the conversation can go in many directions. But at NEC now, we're pretty lucky with a wonderful level and motivation is seldom a concern here. I mean we've got terrific cellists and these kids are all motivated. Early in my teaching life I taught at lesser schools. I know what that's like and I know I'm a better teacher because I didn't always get to teach the most wonderful talents. Working with the less gifted is how you cut your teeth as a teacher and that's how you learn. I still feel tremendous reward if I can help somebody that's not so gifted, but in terms of the few people that I take for my class at this time of my life, everyone has a future. They are pretty self-directed and pretty hungry. The only motivational problem I sometimes see comes from fear of failure which can lead to procrastination and a temporary blockage which stops practicing. It's natural, particularly as they approach graduation and fear the cold, cruel professional life ahead. But I believe in everyone I teach and so I need to help them get through that.

A.A. *What are some of the technical exercises or études that you use to teach and has that changed over the years? Do you do a lot of Popper études or other things?*

P.K. Yes, I mean at this point, it's almost all Popper and Piatti, and Grützmacher Book 3 sometimes because there's some tough ones there. And every once in a while my students remind me of Duport or Franchomme. The Queen Elizabeth Competition last year accepted Duport. When I was younger and also when I was teaching kids that weren't quite as advanced, I used Franchomme and the easier Duport studies a lot more than I do now. But nowadays it's getting fairly common that entering freshmen have already played all the Poppers.

A.A. *Wow! So it is truly a High School Book of Études.*

P.K. Yes. Absolutely. Finally, but once through at a young age does not mean you have mastered them. And they are often played with bad physical habits. If I spot a technical weakness or a bad hand position or something like that I want to correct, I'll reassign an étude to correct the problem. Or just redo them to achieve a higher level. Especially Popper for the left hand. If I want to work on their bow technique, I'll often use Piatti which is so great for virtuoso bow strokes, besides being more fun and musically more rewarding than the Popper.

A.A. *We talked earlier about bowings and fingerings. You said you see it as freedom, but do you maybe guide them at some point with just philosophies, especially fingering?*

P.K. I want my students to go through the process of finding their own solutions, and then correct them as needed. I have fingering principles that I explain when correcting a bad fingering. I correct a lot of fingerings. I'm a big believer in half steps when possible as opposed to whole step shifts or longer. I don't like successive shifts on consecutive notes. I don't believe in leaving the hand open in extensions as it blocks vibrato and causes fatigue. One cannot stop and discuss every student misjudgment, but if I see a bad fingering that is causing a musical or technical problem, I'll usually ask them to find another one … and lead them there but usually not give it to them. And it's amazing how, when they are challenged, they will figure it out. Finding good fingerings really does take experience so I want them to start that search early, but with my oversight providing guidance.

When I was younger with serious eye trouble, I got in the habit of writing the finger number large and clear over the note. I couldn't see pitches accurately, so it was a really useful cue as to what note to play. I guess it was habit forming and perhaps the reason I still like to see fingerings, even though I had corneal transplants and see better today.

I have always spent a lot of time finding good fingerings. They matter a lot to me and I pride myself on finding helpful solutions. But I must say I admire musicians like the violinist, Arnold Steinhardt—there are no markings in his part. I mean, how can anybody play that beautifully with nothing in their part? That's not me. I put fingerings in. But even then, I'll go back five or ten years later and I'll say, "Why did I do that?" And then I'll find a better one. In one of my video interviews with Janos Starker when he was well into his seventies, he talks about how he still is always looking for better fingerings. So if a young player uses a bad fingering, I insist they find a better one, but I don't beat up on them too much, as I view it as a lifetime pursuit.

A.A.   *Do you have certain techniques you use to teach vibrato and do shy away from fourth finger vibrato especially?*

P.K.   It used to bother me when I was growing up that some of my teachers would say vibrato can't be taught. So I'm really proud of the way I teach vibrato. I spent so many years working on it and, of course, I learned a lot from my teachers. Both Greenhouse and Starker were wonderful at teaching vibrato. If you go to my website, CelloBello. org where I have dozens of lessons, the topic I probably cover the most completely is vibrato. You know, all the educational experts say your videos shouldn't be longer than three or four minutes. But that is only time for a small conversation, it isn't very holistic. So I have had to make four or five different videos on vibrato to really talk about all the aspects of vibrato and to cover the subject in some depth. And I need to make a couple more. I think of vibrato as an important expressive tool in terms of creating mood and character. And it is an essential part of each person's individuality. So I talk about vibrato a lot in my teaching.

A.A.   *I'm guessing most of your students have a pretty nice functioning vibrato and you are able to help them use it more as a color.*

P.K.   Well, everybody's got a vibrato, but some people have vibrato problems, and there is always more to teach as it's an expressive tool with endless possibilities. When you teach cellists from all over the world, you hear different vibratos that often reflect a cultural difference. A lot of the Asian kids come with a very fast, narrow vibrato. Nothing to do with talent, it's what they grow up hearing. France is a bit the same way. French pop singers, like Edith Piaf have rapid-fire vibrato that goes into the ear of anyone growing up in France. Those quick vibratos certainly can be an asset in exciting, dramatic moments, but to my ear they sound too hot in tender, more relaxed moments.

A.A.   *How do you teach a clean spiccato? How do you view the wrist and finger's role with that?*

P.K.   When I was an undergrad, for my senior recital I played the Francoeur Sonata and I had a hell of a time, as I recall, because I had this spiccato that only worked fast. I had a good spiccato except it only worked at high speed, and my left hand wasn't quite good enough to stay with it, right? The way I remember it, the Francoeur Sonata in my senior recital wasn't too good and so I was eternally grateful when I got to Rose a year later and he taught me that I could slow it by initiating the motion from the forearm instead of doing it solely from the wrist. He taught me how to bounce at any speed.

Rose had a way of teaching off-the-string strokes that spoke to me and I believe I adopted the method for myself. But when you've studied something 60 years ago and you use and teach it throughout your lifetime, you don't know exactly how you might have changed the original. But I know that Rose is where the original thoughts came from. Rose talked about all bow strokes in the lower part of the bow as whole arm strokes, finessed by the wrist and fingers. He would have us practice bouncing a bow in a slow tempo off the strings in the lower part of the bow: Bum-bum-bum swinging from the shoulder, getting faster, faster and faster until you reach a point where you can't go any faster because the whole arm motion is too big and clumsy to go past a certain speed. He would then have us continue to accelerate by slowly working out to the middle of the bow where the forearm would take over from the whole arm and you could move at very fast tempi. It's difficult to describe in words but you can understand it better through one of my lesson videos on CelloBello, "Spiccato: Slow to Fast", which comes originally from Leonard Rose.

A.A.   *So, your spiccato as a kid was fast.*

P.K.   It was very fast—it was wrist spiccato. But what Rose said was that a wrist spiccato has a kind of limited range of speed, whereas if you use your forearm along with the wrist, you have greater range of speed, the ability to slow it. And I found that to be true. When I put my forearm into the spiccato I was able to control it. Of course, as in most things physical, not everything works exactly the same for everybody, so when I'm teaching spiccato anything is ok as long as they have control at different speeds.

Concerning spiccato, I also tell this other illustrative story about a time in California when I was on the jury for a high school solo festival. Kids go and play a solo piece to get a rating. I got there early with some time to kill and was walking through the hallway looking for the cello room when, by mistake I happened to open up the percussion room. A kid with a snare drum was about to take his jury and I suddenly felt curious. "What do you do for a snare drum jury?" I thought.

So I decided to watch. This kid started on his snare drum playing slow sixteenth notes, accelerating faster and faster until he evolved into a rapid snare roll. Then he started backing out of it, decelerating, gradually slowing down. And the way he got his A or A- or B grade depended on how evenly he could do his accelerando and ritardando. Additionally, the longer it took him, in other words, the more gradual the accelerando and ritardando, the more control it showed and the higher his score. I saw this and I thought, "Wow, what a great way to practice spiccato."

Some people are forced to play every perpetual motion piece at the same tempo as that's the only speed their spiccato works. I didn't want to be one of those people so I practiced accelerate-decelerate exercises myself and eventually found it quite easy to master different speeds. It took me a while, but that's how I now teach spiccato to my kids. I have them start at the frog and tell them "Pretend you're bouncing eighth notes in a Mozart symphony or a Haydn string quartet, bump, bump, bump, bump." Then

I'll have them accelerate and when the whole arm won't move faster, transition to the middle of the bow switching to the forearm. The ritardando is a little bit harder, but you do gain spiccato control at all tempi. One actually learns to make a smooth evolution of tempo and transition from whole arm to forearm quite inaudibly.

A.A. *There are three pieces that are really commonly played that aren't original versions, the Fitzenhagen version of the Tchaikovsky Rococo variation that everyone plays. The Chopin Polonaise, and the Boccherini/Grützmacher Concerto. I'm just wondering what your thoughts are on each of those three.*

P.K. It's funny. It might be a shortcoming of mine but I'm happy with either version of Rococo Variations. We don't know exactly what Tchaikovsky felt about the modifications or I would respect that. It's not my favorite piece of music and so I think the *spirit* of Tchaikovsky is what counts … I don't know. The piece is a wonderful learning vehicle for virtuosity and color and beauty of sound. Beyond that, maybe it's a rationalization, but I don't think Tchaikovsky would care so much.

There is certain repertoire which I feel is so sacred and so special that I consider that every marking of the composer needs to be carefully adjudicated and paid attention to. So a Beethoven Sonata, a Brahms Sonata, what we know about the Bach Suites, although that's a big rabbit hole, is sacrosanct in my mind. I have spent a good part of my life worried about interpretive approaches and solutions to those immortal works. I don't feel that way about Tchaikovsky Rococo Variations.

A.A. *Do you teach, then, mostly the Fitzenhagen? The one that you and I learned on the cello?*

P.K. Yes I teach the Fitzenhagen. Of course, it's easy to teach the original if somebody wants to learn it. That is fine with me. For me, the finale of the Fitzenhagen is more effective but the variations of the original are more logical. The last variation in the original makes total sense whereas at the end of the Fitzenhagen, after the fermata to the end, you wonder, "Where did that rhythmic motive come from?" Of course it comes from a whole variation using the two 32nd notes followed by a 16th in Tchaikovsky's original version and is compositionally more logical. What I advise my students is to learn Fitzenhagen, because for orchestra auditions, for example, that's what people expect. Of course for their recital, if they want to do the original and that's interesting to them, that's fine. In other words, I don't have very strong feelings about that piece.

A.A. *Yes.*

P.K. I guess, I feel a bit the same about the Chopin Polonaise, although, that's a more special piece and I love it. Chopin's Sonata I played often. I care a lot about it and have researched it as there are so many different editions of that piece. But when I went back to the original Chopin' Sonata—Franchomme Edition (Franchomme was the first cellist to play it), I unfortunately found it often more confusing than helpful because so much of the sonata has since been changed. And as we know, Chopin was constantly rewriting, so I've never settled right and wrong in my own mind. I'm talking about Chopin's Sonata now, I'm just not sure what's a good edition. I haven't read anything definitive that is able to separate the changes that Chopin made from the changes that editors or cellists have made. I have studied the Franchomme, but frankly, I think what's commonly played today and the newer editions makes sense to me, too.

The Polonaise is interesting. Several years ago I met Feuermann's granddaughter, a wonderful woman, a cellist that lives in New York. I got to know her and she gave me an amazing 6 hour video interview (again published in segments on CelloBello), an oral history based on what her grandmother, Feuermann's wife, and her mother, Feuermann's daughter told her about Feuermann. She feels a responsibility to his memory and is very dedicated to his legacy. All of his surviving belongings and some of his manuscripts and that sort of thing have been passed down to her. She's the only surviving relative now of Feuermann, a direct descendant. The point is, she has the manuscript of the Feuermann version of the Chopin Polonaise in Feuermann's hand, which she showed me. That was very special to me. I was delighted to see it's basically what I've taught and played, and it's a little more brilliant than the original.

As you know, Feuermann died when he was 39. She told me that at the time, he was editing much of the repertoire for International Music. He had prepared his Chopin edition for International, and I guess they had a copy of it. It was published a few years after his death with Leonard Rose's name on it. If you look at the manuscript in Feuermann's hand and then you look at the Rose edition, they're the same. She told me that her family greatly resented this and that Leonard Rose was a name not to be spoken in her home. That saddens me for as you know, I feel I owe him a lot.

A.A.   *But philosophically, you don't have a problem with not playing the original Chopin version of the piece?*

P.K.   Right. I don't have a problem with it. I would make a point of fidelity to all markings if there was any reason to believe they were truly Chopin's wishes, but too much is unknown about changes Chopin undoubtedly made. Again, when we get into the Romantic Period where freedom of self-expression is the highest of values, I view markings from that period with a little bit of a different attitude. For the Classic and the early Romantic, I am much more of a stickler for editions and historical accuracy and that sort of thing. A less literal approach, more interpretive freedom fits the mentality of the Romantic age. I think the spirit of the era allows more freedom. So yes, it's fine with me. It's great in its current form. I do hope Chopin doesn't mind.

And as to the Boccherini, I learned the Boccherini-Grützmacher Concerto when I was a kid. I played it. But as a hybrid, I guess it fell out of favor, and I have not taught that piece probably in 20 years.

A.A.   *That's surprising to me. Have you taught the original Boccherini B-flat?*

P.K.   I don't know it, never played it, and I don't really remember if I may have taught it. I don't think so. I remember hearing Yo-Yo play it at Ravinia with the Chicago Symphony maybe 20 years ago. It was a bad day as he got mixed up and lost. He told me afterwards that he learned the Boccherini-Grützmacher when he was a kid, and it was so ingrained in his head that he just got confused. He said that he should have used the music but didn't, so he took a couple of wrong turns. He still played really beautifully and it was no fault of his that I didn't enjoy the piece that much. I missed that wonderful second movement.

A.A.   *Do you think many of your students have played the Grützmacher when they were younger before they came to you?*

P.K.   Yes, but I can't remember any cellist from any of our four cello studios at NEC playing a Boccherini Concerto. Sonatas, yes. But neither the Grützmacher nor the original have been played in a jury here, and I've been here for 18 years. Interesting isn't it.

A.A.   *Yes, surprising for sure!*

P.K.   But what's getting to be more and more common now is that many of the lesser known sonatas by Boccherini are being played, and there are some beautiful ones. It used to be that one heard only the A-Major Sonata. But in fact, at the Queen Elizabeth Competition last year, contestants were required to play a Boccherini Sonata other than the A Major, and not with keyboard, but as a cello duet. They had staff cellists that accompanied all of the competitors, and there were several Boccherini Sonatas from which to choose. They were all hard as hell, transparent, up in thumb position, requiring lightness and elegance. And these kids were nailing it.

A.A.   *We talked a little bit last night about the movement of your body when you're playing. We talked about that in playing. But we didn't talk about your thoughts as a teacher. Is that something you talk to your students about? To have them physically try to move more and move in a certain way?*

P.K.   Yes. Especially when I first get a student. There's a routine I go through to explain the advantages of contrary body motion. I have a new student who you will hear today. She is a wonderfully gifted girl, really, really tiny, so I have been working with her to help her get maximum strength at the tip. I just assigned her the Elgar Concerto in order to work on the opening for sustaining power and strength. So it will be interesting for you to see whether she's been able to incorporate that today. I mean, if she's got it, she's got it and I will move on in the lesson. But if I need to work with her, I'll work with her on it while you're there so you can see what I do.

In general, I'm really conscious about how the body integrates its various parts. And chair height. After all the Piatigorsky stories I told you about, playing on a couch and on high and low chairs and all that, I still do believe there's an optimum chair height. The trick is to know what's optimum and healthy so you can use it in your home on a daily basis, but yet to be flexible enough to adjust to adverse situations. I have a little bit of residual low back trouble. I fell off a hill and ruptured a disc at the Marlboro Festival when I was 28 years old, so I've always had lower back problems, and as a result, I've studied healthy sitting a lot. The way the body works has always been fascinating to me and I've spent a lot of time with non-cellists as well as cellists. Yoga, Pilates, tai chi people, I have engaged them all in countless conversations about how the body works and, specifically about a healthy way to sit. In certain areas of physical motion there are conflicting ideas between them, but amazingly, they all are in agreement as to how one should sit in order to protect the lower back. These principles have helped me, virtually eliminated my lower back pain, so I teach them.

I make a big point to teach my students these fundamental principles, and then, depending on the height and the build of the student, I help them individualize. Endpins are another variable to take into account. Big, tall people I encourage to try a bent-endpin. People with long arms, a long torso, or knees that stick out past the cello usually benefit from the bent pin. Shorter cellists do better with a straight endpin. There's a whole thing that I go through when I get a new student.

A.A.   *I loved getting to watch you teach yesterday and it made me think more about the Bach Suites. Because sometimes I talk with my students about acquiring a "Bach" accent, like a French or German accent.*

P.K.   What a nice way to express the search for a Bach style.

A.A.   *I wonder, because I felt like you were wanting the same sort of thing from them, for them to find that "Bach" accent. Do you think they need to hear a lot of good baroque playing or is there a way they can find that accent just by the process? How do you help them find that accent in their playing?*

P.K.   Well, let's see. You heard me teach Bach twice yesterday, right?

A.A.   *Yes, the D-Minor Prelude and the C-Major Prelude in the second lesson.*

P.K.   Right. Both of those lessons were the second time that I was hearing those pieces from that particular student, so you missed my introductory spiel in their previous lesson about how to approach Bach. We had a lengthy discussion about the aesthetics of Bach in both of those lessons- sorry you didn't hear it. Bach interpretation is one of those topics that I also often use in my studio class discussions because the topic is so endless. I mean, I expose them not only to my beliefs, but to different approaches, different beliefs, and tell them my job is to help lead them eventually to their own philosophy. In general, I talk about being true to all composers, but in the case of Bach, what does that mean?

One often hears, "To be true to the composer, you must play exactly what's on the page," but in the case of Bach, there's not that much there. Even if one wants to be literal with their interpretations, play only what's on the page, it's problematic. First of all, there are no dynamics from Bach at all, right? That doesn't mean Bach didn't want us to use any, but that he expected the player to be creative in his own way and is allowing, *expecting* the performer to use his own imagination. Importantly, there's no autograph in the composer's hand. The bowings are a huge issue as they don't agree between the Anna Magdalena manuscript and the other copyists, they often do not follow sequences or patterns in a logical way, and in many instances are even difficult to decipher. This music has survived through countries and cultures and hundreds of years, not out of fidelity to Anna Magdalena's bowings, but because Bach gave us a miracle in communication, a universal message. My belief is that joy, grief, pride, and the infinite number of characters expressed in the Bach Suites are what's most important, why this music survives. Our job as performers is to communicate those feelings to today's listener. That most likely will be different in today's world than it was 300 years ago in a small German town, but in my mind, bringing the "message" alive, is how we stay true to the composer.

A.A.   *The Bach Suites seems to be becoming more popular, don't you think?*

P.K.   Yes! How amazing is that?! I did talk to the first student I taught yesterday about the sadness, melancholy, the private, almost prayerful suffering I feel in the D-Minor Prelude. That kind of discussion, to me, is what makes the music universal. Music is a miracle of communication. Within any piece of music, there are moods and characters inherent to those notes. The notes sit silently on the page and it's up to the performer to realize, communicate the human emotion they contain. And I think generally, the greater the music, the more complex the emotional content can be. It's a little bit like what we were talking about with the C-Minor Suite. It's so sad and grieving and personal and private, and yet at the same time, it's heroic, and epic. You can view it both ways. In life, we experience complex mixes of emotions, and I believe works of great depth do the same. Bitter and sweet, strength and vulnerability, etc. I heard somebody else say this once, and I borrowed it: It's like a jewel that you turn, and as you turn it, you see different colors and shapes, all wonderful. A musical diamond can also be enjoyed from many different viewpoints. It's what makes differing interpretations valid.

But not every interpretation is valid. To use the D-Minor Suite as an example, if you play it fast and brilliant and flashy, I mean, it's just not going to work, because you're violating something which is inherent to the character, right? It's not believable because fast and flashy is not compatible with those notes, or one might say, with Bach's message. Some may play it a little faster, some a little slower, we all can use differing dynamic shapes, articulations and on and on, as long as we stay true to the inherent character. That Prelude is beautiful with not very much vibrato and it is helpful to know that during the time of Bach there wasn't so much vibrato used. But in my view, vibrato is also possible, as long as it doesn't cross a line that we can all intuitively hear is inappropriate. To repeat, I think the way to be true to the composer is to communicate to today's audience what that message was in the time of Bach.

Here's something about Bach I find really interesting. When I was a kid, I was very influenced by Casals who always talked about following the "natural shape" of a line, meaning that when the line goes up, you crescendo, when the line goes down, you diminuendo. That's what he did in the Bach Suites too. That's how I learned to play the Bach Suites. It's an expressive approach, and as Casals said, it does feel "natural." But as I got older and studied and learned of Baroque performance practice, I came to understand the value of a *harmonically* based way to look at the suites, that shaping can, should acknowledge the motion of the bass, illuminate the harmonic progression. Casals was not privy to historical performance practice, but yet he brought the suites to the attention of the world, which sort of proves my point.

It's really a lifetime pursuit. Here I am starting to push 80 and there are still so many questions. I remember the video interview I did with Greenhouse where he talked about Casals, who was probably more in his sixties or seventies at the time that Greenhouse studied with him. As I told you earlier, Casals played for Bernie to show him how he could change the interpretation at will and play beautifully in a different way.

This illustrates one of my favorite little sayings, "out of discipline comes freedom." Remember that Casals first made Greenhouse copy him. They played that D-Minor Prelude in unison for days until he could do everything that Casals was doing, and only then did Casals turn him loose and say, "Now make it your own." I think there's amazing value in that story.

So in my practicing, rehearsing and teaching, I love the detailed process of being really picky. I work hard getting kids to listen to everything, expanding and elevating their listening and then forcing them to make their own decisions. That's why I tell them to take their own pencil and write in their bowings and fingerings. The process of writing something down forces decisions, makes them think. I believe that out of that decision-making process, they learn trial and error and find their own way.

A.A.   *How important do you think listening to recordings or YouTube is in that process?*

P.K.   Every once in a while a student will say to me, "Oh, I'm afraid to listen to somebody else. I don't want to be influenced." I don't believe that. I say, "No, listen." What I really tell them to do is go to as many live concerts as possible. Don't let YouTube be a substitute for the live concert. Every time there's a cellist in Boston, every time there's a recital you can go to, even your own peers, go and you'll hear some things you like and some things you don't. But then run to your cello afterwards and try and recreate the sounds that you loved.

   I tell them, in terms of YouTube, that the only danger is, for example, that you decide you love Jacqueline du Pré playing the Chopin Sonata and you never listen to anybody else. If you listen to Jacqueline du Pré play it 100 times, you will probably develop a bias that wouldn't be healthy. So of course, listen to her every once in a while, if you love that recording, but listen to others at the same time. Yes, I think of listening to many different performances as research, a different kind of research than going to the library and reading books on baroque practice. But, I mean, it's all valuable.

A.A.   *You mentioned that Piatigorsky would often try to have you endure the hardest circumstances so that when it came time to be on the stage, you're ready for anything. I think the flip side of the coin is maybe to instill confidence in a young student so they feel they can get on stage and feel good about what they're doing. How do you feel about that with your students? Do you try to see where they are at and work both directions?*

P.K.   I'm very much into the psychology of teaching. It's on my mind all the time. I mean, it's quite instinctive with me. Almost everything I say, there is a little bit of radar going out there, kind of watching for the reaction. For example, yesterday I knew Joe was not reacting well to my picking. I think he was feeling a lot of pressure from me. I just made the conscious decision while I was teaching him that, "That's okay, I think he needs me to be hard on him today." It might be a hard day today, but it's going to be useful later because I've spent a lot of time propping this guy up. I think that he's one of these people who is always looking for sympathy. I need to give him some of that without caving into it. I mean a year ago he cried in a lesson because he felt that everybody in the class was so much better than he was. That was real, so realizing his insecurities affects my approach.

A.A.   *He's a very talented guy.*

P.K.   He's a super talented guy, yes. But he's the guy that an earlier teacher virtually destroyed. What a pity—why would a teacher do that? So now I spend a lot of time trying to get him to believe in himself. But not just for Joe but for everybody, how do a teacher give a person the confidence and the security to go out on stage and play and, at the same time, be critical enough as a teacher to raise their level—to get them to listen at a higher level and critique themselves. It's very tricky to do both.

The Future

A.A. *Okay, let me shift gears a little bit. A lot has been made about shrinking audiences in classical music. Where do you see the future of classical music going in the next generation? And related to that, how has technology changed the music world? Has it been good or bad for music?*

P.K. I am an optimist in the extreme. The *economics* of the large forms, the opera and the symphony orchestra are problematic, but not the interest and love of the public. There is a devoted segment of the population that will continue to support culture, the fine arts, and what we do. I feel quite good about the future of classical music. I have always felt that. I think my ideas were formed during all the touring that I did for 26 years with the Cleveland Quartet. We played in huge halls to thousands, and of course, sometimes to practically no people at all. And I spent a lot of time thinking about that during the six years that I was President of Chamber Music America, because I was obsessive about what's the best way to help the field and help the future of chamber music. I've seen it all and I don't believe it's only about superstar names. It is clear to me that when classical music is professionally presented, audiences are there.

In terms of players, the level of performance is better than it's ever been. But not only the level, but most importantly the passion, the commitment, the interest. I mean, with young people, it's wonderful to see that they have as much passion and dedication as generations before them. Also, what's different from when I was a kid is that now it's a completely global world. Think of all the students coming from Korea and China. There's an amalgamation of cultures and playing styles going on and large segments of those huge Asian populations have been exposed to Western classical music and care about it. That also helps insure the future.

A.A. *That was another question I was going to ask about. The level of play over the years, has it changed?*

P.K. It's a little hard on my generation's egos, but the truth is that when I was 17 years old, I didn't play the way these kids play today! I'm sure I didn't. Most of us didn't. I wasn't a prodigy or a generational talent, but I think I can say I was one of the better players around. But it's actually rewarding to see your students surpass you, at least instrumentally. I view this in the context of the evolution of the human race. I mean, when I was a kid, who thought the four-minute mile would ever be broken, right, and now, dozens of runners have now done it. Look at all the track and field records being broken- all human physical endeavors have progressed upward. There's an evolution of the species in this way.

Built into the human spirit is the instinct to pass knowledge on to those younger than us, each generation standing on the shoulders of the previous. This is how we progress as a species. My generation benefited from a Leonard Rose, a Gregor Piatigorsky, a Janos Starker, and now cellists of my generation have gone out into communities large and small, teaching at conservatories and universities everywhere. You, Tony Arnone, are the generation behind me and now you are part of this transmission of insight and tradition. The passing down of values and knowledge results in a rise in excellence. So quality performance is clearly in very, very good hands.

As I started to say, audience turnout depends much on the abilities, even the intentions of the presenter. During the years that I toured with the Cleveland Quartet the majority of chamber music societies were run by well-meaning mom and pop operations. They were volunteers, often European immigrants that loved string quartets and put together five or six concerts each year for themselves and a like-minded circle of friends in their community. We owe these people a lot for bringing classical music and chamber music to this country-that's how so many Friends of Chamber Music all over the US began. But in those days, there wasn't much interest in outreach or even the idea of building audiences. On the other hand, even in small places like Lawrence, Kansas, or Sedona, Arizona, where audience-building was a goal and where the presenter had a sense of social responsibility, audiences could be large and enthusiastic.

A.A.   *And related to that, with the globalization of so many different kinds of music and with so much new music being written, is the audience getting pulled too many directions? Can an audience handle Beethoven and a new piece?*

P.K.   There are too many presenters that feel the best way to attract an audience is to dumb down. I have never found it necessary, or in most cases, even successful. I have never responded well to "Oh, please, don't play a modern piece." The Cleveland Quartet took the position, which we were quite hard and fast about, that if they wanted us, they had to accept a new work. We were enough in demand that we could force the issue.

A.A.   *At least one.*

P.K.   One, yes. Right. We were not a new music quartet. But we commissioned works regularly, and we tried to tour with a contemporary work on each program we offered. Very rarely would we back down on that. We believed that if it was a good piece, then it was up to us -that if we played it well, the audience would get it. And as part of our obsession to be understood, we often spoke in the concert about the work, even gave short demos. I mean, my own father was a fine amateur musician and passionate concertgoer, and he still hated Bartók! But yes, I think performers have a responsibility to music of their time. I also have seen that very young audiences respond to new works. The globalization of music and exposure to different cultures makes concerts more interesting and it seems to me new audiences are responding to the variety. In my own experience of playing concerts, I have not found that the size of the audience depends upon whether or not a new piece is on the program.

A.A.   *Do you think these days, where everything is so accessible on your phone or on your computer, there needs to be something different to draw people to actually come to concerts?*

P.K.   I mean, outside of playing naked, what can you do that's different? Because everything is on the web—anything and everything is there. The Internet offers a wonderful world of musical diversity. Even so, the blessed fact is that a live concert is just a better experience than anything you can get off of the internet. You just don't get the emotional involvement and fulfillment through headphones.

A.A.   *I agree with that. But what I've encountered is that a lot of people think there should be more of a visual component to the music, or something that makes it more visually engaging. I don't know how you feel, but people's attention spans are getting smaller and smaller.*

P.K.   It's true that attention spans seem to be getting shorter and it's a problem. When I began my website, CelloBello.org, I had wonderful educational media experts from PBS helping me, and they kept emphasizing not to make my video cello lessons longer than two minutes because they didn't think most students would watch a video of three or four minutes.

They were the experts and so I listened to them and started my website that way. But I've departed from that now. I've decided that if there are certain topics that need a four minute or even an eight-minute lesson, then I'm going to make it an eight-minute lesson. The attention span thing is difficult, but I still have no doubt that engaged kids are capable of absorbing more than a sound bite.

But you asked about the visual. It is true that the way music is presented and the way musicians market themselves has changed. Women play in low-cut blouses and short skirts, and groups like the 2CELLOS, terrific male cellists, are successful in large part as they put on a visual show. But they still play the hell out of the cello. I don't know if I have an answer or much of an opinion about that. I hope there's room for everything. But remember, the visual has always been important. Piatigorsky gave me explicit lessons on how much cuff of my white shirt should show, how to tailor my suit, and how to hold my head to impress audiences. As long as musical artistry and instrumental excellence stays primary, let each generation be themselves. And don't forget, it's also true that there are still plenty of beautiful concerts, traditionally presented.

I'm open to changes of attire and presentation because in the 1970s, when the Cleveland Quartet started, we were the revolutionaries of that era. We were the young people of that time, all under 30, and we decided not to wear white tie and tails. We quite consciously decided that we wanted to get classical musicians out of the ivory tower and more humanly relatable. We began wearing suits, and over time, dressed down from there. Sometimes we didn't even wear a tie. We dared to wear colored shirts. It upset a lot of people. My mother-in-law sarcastically remarked once that I looked like I just came off of the golf course.

So now the next generation is taking it a little bit further. Some people can do it tastefully, and some people can't. T me, if the playing is excellent, if the music is really wonderful, the other stuff doesn't really bother me.

A.A.   *We have a quartet residency program at the University of Iowa. We've got five or six quartets that come through. Really top-notch quartets that usually will play a very new piece. I sometimes ask how they feel about the longevity of these new pieces, and the answer I usually get is they don't care. They're just trying to get them out there, and make sure people hear them. I wonder if there's a difference in your mind between having people enjoying the live experience of this music? Or if these pieces are as dear and valued as some of the others that are played, or if that even matters at this point*

P.K.   I do believe that as performers, we have a responsibility to champion composers and the works that we believe in. But, speaking for myself, when listening to a new piece of music on YouTube, for example, it very often doesn't get through to me whereas, if I'm in the hall, the same work will speak to me.

A.A.   *But do you want to hear it again?*

P.K.   Yes, of course, often I do want to hear it again. When I hear a new work for cello or string quartet that I like, I'll write down the name in order to tell my students about it, usually one of the young quartets I'm mentoring. Sure. It's interesting that your groups say they don't care about longevity, and in an important way, that's admirable. I mean, every quartet that we commissioned I hoped would become an immortal masterpiece, but we learned it and played it our best whatever it turned out to be. There's no way to know what will endure, that's out of our hands. All we can do, and what we should do, is present everything we play the best we can, and hope audiences love it. If it doesn't survive the test of time, well, that's okay, not every piece can be a masterpiece. Out of all the quartets that we commissioned, it's too soon to know if any of them are going to survive the test of time. I don't know.

Close to the Heart

A.A.   *If you hadn't been a musician, what would you have loved to have done with your life?*

P.K.   Probably social work or psychology. That's what I was considering before I had the epiphany writing my essay at 15. I told you about that at the beginning of this interview. I mean, I think both a strength and a weakness of mine is my empathy for people with problems. I've only had two students leave me in 55 years, but both of them left me because they didn't think I was hard enough on them. Sometimes I say to myself, "I should be pushing my kids harder. I'm too nice to them." But going back to your question, I have a natural interest in what makes people tick, and I cannot help but be sensitive to their moods and their feelings.

    I also have a huge political interest. I mean most of my time now, when I'm not professionally engaged, I'm listening to the news or reading about the political situation. I took time off before the 2016 election to go up to New Hampshire on behalf of Hillary Clinton. About a month ago, I offered myself to go to Texas because of the Senate race against Ted Cruz, who I consider a dangerous politician lacking in morality and with no feeling for the less fortunate. I could easily see myself in politics because I'm concerned about humanity and society and how my own personal beliefs fit in with what the world needs. In fact, it's one of my personal conflicts. Remember I told you that I decided to become a musician only when I realized that the arts are important to the quality of life, that the world needs music, that it's not a frill but an essential form of human expression. Yet, very often in times of a political crisis or something awful going on, I can feel really guilty that I am practicing my cello instead of taking part in social action.

A.A.   *Did you ever have a period of doubt about becoming a musician? If you did, how did you deal with that?*

P.K.   Not really. I mean, in terms of giving myself permission to become a musician for the reasons we are talking about, yes. But as I told you, that was at the fairly young age of 14–15. The only other time was a couple of years later when I was a freshman and Mr. Rejtő was pretty hard on me. I had a bit of the same self-questioning feeling that my student Joe had, a lack of confidence, and wondering whether I should be doing something else with my life. I was a 16-year-old freshman, and there were many other cellists that I thought were much more advanced than me and that intimidated me.

The other life lesson that I tell my students is—it's easy for me to say now because I have had real celebrity- but I don't feel ambition for career or fame was primary in what drove me. I just loved music. I never dreamt of fame when I graduated and took my first job on the faculty of a small, unimportant music program like the University of Toledo in 1964. Certainly as a member of the Toledo Quartet, I never thought of an international career.

That doesn't mean that I wasn't success conscious. I was, but I wasn't primarily driven by that. I just, I loved playing. I've always loved the rehearsal process, probably more than being on stage because especially after the stress of the Piatigorsky master class experience, I got nervous on stage. That was serious pressure, but the rehearsal process, which is the socialization of making music with others, the collective thinking about music, probing, discussing interpretive ideas—I love that. If I hadn't made money and if I hadn't had a career, I truly believe I would still have had a very fulfilling life teaching and playing on a more local level. That's what I try and pass on to my students. They are all gifted and deserving but not many will be lucky enough to enjoy my career success. Yet hopefully they can have just as rich a life making music as I have had. I tell them, "don't go into the profession to become rich and famous. And don't choose the profession solely out of your competitive nature because you want to be better than somebody else—remember that Piatigorsky was unhappy because Casals was more highly revered. It's a big, talented world and no matter how amazing a musician and cellist you become, there will always be those that surpass you in some way and, or, are more successful. Be the best that you possibly can—the striving to reach your own potential is in itself fulfilling. Be driven to express yourself with the instrument. You can have a very meaningful, fulfilling life that way, whereas, if your primary motivation is to be Yo-Yo Ma or to make a lot of money, you're setting yourself up for failure."

A.A.   *You have had so many concerts in your life. I would love to hear some of your most memorable experiences. They can be memorable for whatever reason, musically or otherwise.*

P.K.   Well, let's see. Sort of on the positive side, I guess, our first Beethoven cycle in Alice Tully Hall in New York. I mean, those 5 concerts were a very heady experience and it was greeted with terrific success. There was tremendous stress getting ready for that and its successful completion was very confirming. I kind of pinched myself and said, "Wow, maybe we are good," because starting out, you don't really know about yourself until you get that kind of critical public affirmation.

This was probably 1974 or 1975. We were in Cleveland from 1969 to 1971 and then we went to replace the immortal Budapest Quartet at State University of New York in Buffalo. That move shaped our career as we inherited their residency which included playing the complete Beethoven quartet cycle every year. We won the position by playing the one Beethoven quartet that we knew, Op. 59"1. I'm sure the search committee didn't know we only knew one Beethoven quartet! We won the position and moved to Buffalo in our third year. We were supposed to play the complete Beethoven cycle, but that of course was impossible. What we did in the first year was to learn and play half the Beethoven cycle, and, the Guarneri Quartet played the other half, Talk about pressure, right? They were already world famous and had recorded the cycle for RCA. Then the next year, in 1974, we reversed the process and learned and played the half of the cycle that the Guarneri played the year before. The Juilliard Quartet, at the height of their career, was engaged to play the quartets we had done the year before. Once again, pressure. And finally, in our third year of the residency, we played the complete cycle for the first time at State University of New York in Buffalo. The Beethoven cycle then became central to our career. We recorded the complete cycle twice, once in analog and later in digital. And we played it in cities around the world—New York, Washington DC, Tokyo, London, Florence, Paris, etc. Memory of the exact number fails me at the moment, but we played at least 30 complete cycles and hundreds of all-Beethoven concerts.

P.K.   To go back to your question, what will always stick with me was our final tour, particularly the final 3 concerts, in New York at Tully Hall, the last concert at the Eastman School of Music where we were in residence for 20 years and, which as I recall, actually turned out to be on Beethoven's birthday, December 16. And the very last concert of all, which was December, 17, 1995, in Severance Hall in Cleveland. Those concerts, of course, were very emotional.

    Martha's last concert with the Cleveland Quartet in 1980 was also very emotional for all of us as we were the original CQ formation and never had had a change in personnel. Her final concerts were a Beethoven cycle in San Francisco. We don't usually finish Beethoven cycles with Opus 131, but for some reason that I don't remember, that was the order for that particular cycle—the last piece on the last concert was Opus 131. I mean this was our 11th year, we hadn't ever had a change, and I think the whole quartet was pretty close to tears. And then, at the worst possible moment, the variation movement of the C-sharp minor Beethoven Quartet—get this—my C string popped.

A.A.   *Oh no!*

P.K.   Who knows why, but it's the only time in 60 years of concerts a C string broke. We stopped, I went backstage and put on a C string but couldn't take time to stretch it out. By the time we got to the last movement, the open C string, which is the leading tone in the finale's key of C# minor was so flat, it was more like a whole step. So wherever I could, every time I saw an open C, I put my first finger down next to the nut and tried to raise the pitch.

A.A.   *What are you most proud of in your life?*

P.K.   That's a hard question. I hope my music making has meant something to other people, both as a teacher or to somebody in the audience that was moved, that came away enriched by the concert. I mean, that's why I play. That's what drives me.

    I tell my students, when you go to a concert, there could be a wonderful player up there, but if it's all about themselves, you feel their ego in a negative way. We all have heard that, know it and recoil, right? The musicians I admire and the musician I've tried to be, is somebody not involved with promoting themselves, but who is in the music and striving to communicate it—it's all about the music and not all about us. Such intention is so important for a performer. It's also a very good way to deal with nerves. When I'm on stage preoccupied with something like intonation, that's stressful.

Better to be preoccupied, even at a subconscious level with "What an amazing phrase this is. I want to make it beautiful for somebody out there," something like that. Yes, it's a coping mechanism that helps nerves, but it's also something that drives me in a completely basic way—for me it is a reason to be.

From a non-performance standpoint, I'm very proud of the Cellobello.org website. When I'm not teaching or playing right now, much to my wife Pei-Shan's chagrin, I'm preoccupied with that. But I feel like I'm really doing something important for the world and for the world of music and for cellists. I think it came at the perfect time in my life because I had just entered my 70s and wasn't playing 100 concerts a year anymore.

My obsession is to get the website to the point that when something happens to me and when I'm no longer here, that I know it's not going to fold. I need to know, to be certain that it will go on. I'm thrilled that I've been able to get funding to hire a professional administrator. This is a real crossroads and I am hoping the site will go through the roof with professional expertise. Somebody spending eight hours a day on the website that knows what they're doing. I dream of just sitting back in my old age with a smile. Of course, I also know I'll never really stop. I want to keep making cello lessons for the website, but it's time for me to pass the running of the website on to somebody else. That's really my goal.

A.A.   *Do you have anything on your bucket list that you still want to do before it's all said and done?*

P.K.   Not only continue teaching, but to perform for a few more years and hope I don't get booed off the stage! I had a glorious career as a member of the Cleveland Quartet but other things are now more important. I have always said, and it's true, that if I had wanted a career, I wouldn't have ended the Cleveland Quartet. I played in a couple of serious but short-lived trios after the Cleveland Quartet. Today I love performing chamber music with some incredible artist friends that I admire, particularly sonatas with my pianist wife, Pei-Shan Lee.

Quartets have to practice much more than trios do. If you're playing 90 to 110 or 115 concerts a year, teaching a full cello class, and trying to record and raise a family, there's a lot of stuff that you never get to do. Looking back, I have no idea how I handled all of that, and additionally, I was 12 years on the Chamber Music America Board, 6 years as V.P and 6 as President. Anyway, after the Cleveland Quartet, I looked forward to trios and sonatas and I did quite a bit of that for a few years, and I still do. That's what I'm doing now, but less and less. I just cannot say to myself, "Okay, you don't need to play cello anymore." I can't let go of it, but at 78, I sort of practice minimally and I'm much more into the CelloBello website. That's really where my passion is right now. I'm proud of the way I teach and I think I have things of value to pass on. To be able to put lessons online continues to be really exciting to me and I hope that they will be useful to somebody. And I am also focused on building a global cello community through the website, involving as many of my wonderful cello colleagues worldwide as possible. So CelloBello continues to be a hugely important and rewarding part of my life and I worry that it will end with me. I need to make the website sustainable, find a successor or successors, and step back. We are currently moving forward with a totally Chinese language version of CelloBello, and I look forward to the development of a new CelloKids, with special age-appropriate graphics and featuring teachers who specialize in teaching young children.

A.A.   *If you had a desert island playlist. What are some pieces that would be on it? Pieces that are most meaningful to you?*

P.K.   One of them would be the Bach Gamba Sonatas with Pablo Casals, because I grew up on those when I was a kid, and because, for all the reasons I don't have to regurgitate, I was influenced by Casals, admire and love him.

Two CQ recordings. The first Cleveland Quartet recording of the Brahms Quartets—that really put us on the map and continues to be a lot of people's favorite. During the 26 years of the quartet I almost never listened to our recordings as I was too self-critical and found it stressful, sometimes even upsetting. With some distance, I can now actually enjoy them, and am really surprised, thrilled at how good they actually are. The second recording would be the slow movement of the B-Flat Brahms Sextet. I added narration and turned it into a birth announcement of my second child. It was played around the country on radio and I got dozens of letters and compliments. It's because of the memories associated with these works that I would choose these recordings.

Then, for sure, the Beethoven Emperor Concerto with Rudolf Serkin and Bruno Walter, which was a very early LP. I mean, when I was a very small boy, we were still listening to 78 rpm. My parents got an LP player somewhere around when I was 8 years old. I listened to that Serkin recording day after day. There were some places where he played these little obbligato passages in the right hand and would linger on a note, hold a special note. I would run out of the room, sometimes crying, because it was so beautiful that I couldn't stand it. Looking back on it, it was just incredible how I was so emotionally overcome—that may be where I first fell in love with Beethoven. Wow, talk about being brainwashed by a recording. I mean, even today I almost can't listen to another performance of the Emperor Concerto without missing those Serkin rubati, and I've heard some really great performances, for sure.

One more recording that I think of right now is the Piatigorsky recording of the Schubert *Theme and Variations* that I believe he himself arranged. It's on video also, and to see him play brings back so many wonderful, powerful memories. And in the last movement, he does a series of down bow staccatos that are totally super-human. I don't think there's ever been anybody that can down bow staccato as he could!

10

Ronald Leonard

Ronald Leonard has been known and admired as one of America's leading cellists for many years. He was principal cellist of the Los Angeles Philharmonic, where he performed many times as soloist in works by Schumann, Barber, Brahms, Beethoven, Lalo, Tchaikovsky, Berio, Barber, Tchaikovsky, Elgar, Strauss and others. Some of the conductors for these performances were Zubin Mehta, Carlo Maria Giulini, Simon Rattle, Michael Tilson Thomas, Mariss Jansons, André Previn and Esa-Pekka Salonen.

Mr. Leonard has always been active as a teacher, having been Professor of Cello at the Eastman School of Music, Piatigorsky Professor of Cello at the University of Southern California Thornton School of Music, and most recently a cello and chamber music faculty member at the Colburn School Conservatory of Music where he retired in 2018. He has also taught and performed at many music festivals, including Aspen, Marlboro, Musicorda, Sarasota and the Perlman Music Program.

Chamber music has always been an important interest in Mr. Leonard's life, and he has performed with many of the world's top artists, including Rudolf Serkin, Felix Galimir, Itzhak Perlman, Pinchas Zukerman, and Richard Goode. He has been a guest artist with many of the finest string quartets—the Guarneri, Borromeo, Juilliard and American, to name a few. Mr. Leonard performs on a Peter (of Mantua) Guarnerius cello, which is the only known instrument from the hand of this fine maker.

The Past

Anthony Arnone	*Where were you born and raised? How did you get your start on cello?*
Ron Leonard	I was born in Providence, Rhode Island, and I got started on the cello because of my parents. There were seven children in my family, and my parents wanted each of us to have music in our lives. They insisted that we all start on the piano, and after we had done that for a little while, they had each of us pick out an instrument that we wanted to play. For me it was very easy. They took me to a cello recital one night and I thought, "That's pretty cool." It was that simple.
A.A.	*Do you remember who played?*
R.L.	I don't. I know he was an older man and that he was a big name at the time, but I don't remember who he was.

I studied piano for about ten years. After a couple of years of piano, I started on the cello. I was very fortunate to have had a fantastic first teacher, Alice Totten, who was very demanding. At the same time, she thought I was something special. She gave me a lot of her time, and she really believed in me. She lived for a long time; I think she was 90 something when she died. She gave me a love for cello. Between that and the support of my parents, you can't have a better start.

A.A.	*How old were you when you were studying with her?*
R.L.	From about ages eight to fourteen. One thing I really respect about her was that by the time I was fourteen she thought it was time for me to move on to somebody really famous. She sent me to Boston to study with the first chair of the Boston Symphony Samuel Mays. I was 16, and I was getting out of high school. Sammy Mays thought it was a good idea if I went to the Curtis Institute of Music to study with Leonard Rose. I auditioned and was accepted, and this was when Leonard Rose first went to teach at Curtis.

He had just left the New York Philharmonic, and he was starting his solo career at that time. I studied with him for four years, and again, I think I lucked out. He practically treated me like a son, and he was tremendously supportive of me. He thought I was really going to go places. For instance, when I graduated from Curtis, I had the opportunity to go to play principal cello in the New Orleans Symphony. The New Orleans Symphony at that time was a very good and young orchestra, and the conductor had been the assistant concertmaster of the Philadelphia Orchestra. He invited me to go there to play principle cello. I told this to Leonard Rose and Leonard Rose said, "Well you know, that's wonderful but you know what I'd really like you to do is audition for George Szell for the Cleveland Orchestra, because in that orchestra, you will get the best education you could possibly ever have."

He called it the most professional orchestra in the United States. The people in the orchestra were very proud of the orchestra, and Szell I knew would be very hard to work for, but it was worth it. I've always appreciated the fact that he told me that and that I started out right there. He thought I would learn a lot in Cleveland, which I did. I learned how to be a real professional player in an orchestra, including how to prepare for the orchestra.

He called me one time and he said, "There's a young cellist in Cincinnati who I think should study with you." This is when I was in Cleveland. I was 21 years old. At that time I was the youngest guy in the Cleveland orchestra, and so I said, "Okay, fine." I had never done any teaching, and this cellist came every other week from Cincinnati down to Cleveland to have lessons. I learned quite a lot by all of a sudden having to teach and explain all of these things that I just did naturally. At the same time, I had a good background of Leonard Rose's teaching. Two years after being in Cleveland, I was offered the principal cello job in Rochester, New York and to teach at the Eastman School of Music. I began by teaching beginners and amateurs, so I had a very busy teaching schedule and a very busy orchestra schedule.

A.A.   *I'm curious, did you have to audition? Was this similar to how things are now?*

R.L.   Yes, I did have to audition. I played for the conductor, Howard Hanson, who was also the director of the Eastman School of Music at that time.

A.A.   *Was there a screen back then?*

R.L.   No, this was one on one. By the way, the audition for Szell was also a one-on-one situation, something that could not happen today. It'd be totally illegal. I guess Szell liked what he heard, and at that time the conductor had entire say. Now with orchestra committees, everything is a whole different ball game.

When I started teaching, I had to work with people who were older and didn't have much technique, so I had to wing it and figure out what I was going to tell these people. Based on my studies with Leonard Rose, I developed a process of approaching both young students and amateurs. Shortly after I was there, I started teaching in the collegiate department. After about five or six years, I don't remember just how long, the man who had been the principal cello teacher there retired.

Then I was made head of the Cello Department of the Eastman School of Music, all so around the age of 26 or something like that. I was all of a sudden teaching these very talented college students. Some of my students were doctoral students who were older than 45 years old, and here I was 26 years old teaching these old people. That was an interesting experience.

A.A.   *You mentioned drawing on your experiences studying with Leonard Rose. Could you talk about a few things that were most important that you got from working with him?*

R.L.   There were two things: a wonderful bow technique and sound. Those were the things that he was interested in, and those are the two things I have been totally interested in my whole life with my teaching.

A.A.   *Did you learn mostly by him telling you what to do, or by him demonstrating?*

R.L.   He demonstrated quite a lot. He was a perfectionist like you wouldn't believe. In lessons, he would demonstrate something and if he happened to miss something, he would be very upset with himself and then sit there and practice five times, seven times, eight times, or ten times. That also helped me to figure out how to practice some things. He was famous for his bow technique and for his sound. I'd like to think that that's what I really got the most from him.

A.A.   *Was there a point when you knew that playing cello is what you wanted to do with your career?*

R.L.   By the time I was 12 or 13, it just didn't occur to me that I would do anything else. There was nothing else that I wanted to do, and here I am.

A.A.   *Did you enjoy practicing in your teen years?*

R.L.   Well, like every kid, it was a strain to get me to practice. It wasn't that I was all that anxious to practice all the time, but all of my brothers were practicing. Imagine in the house there were seven kids who were practicing various instruments at the same time. My parents gave us duties, but I could get out of them if I practiced. That was an easy call.

A.A.   *What inspired you to choose music as a lifelong pursuit?*

R.L.   Ever since I was nine year or ten years old, we traveled around all of New England as a family unit giving concerts. There was saxophone, clarinet, harp, cello, violin, piano, tap-dancing, and we all sang together.

A.A.   *Were your parents musicians?*

R.L.   My mother was a musician and oddly enough my father was totally tone-deaf. He adored my mother. She played piano, violin, and trumpet, and he would go with her when she played for weddings and in bars. She taught piano, and she taught in the public schools. They wanted all of us to be involved in something. Whether or not we went into it as a profession, that wasn't the idea.

A.A.   *Did your siblings continue to have music as part of their life? Do any of them do it professionally?*

R.L.   Actually it always ended up being a part of their lives, but there are two of us who ended up with music as our main profession. I had an older brother who was a wonderful pianist, and he was mostly a jazz pianist. He traveled around the world, did all kinds of jazz and Broadway. He traveled on the Queen Mary, going back and forth to Europe playing concerts.

A.A.   *How long were you teaching at Eastman?*

R.L.   I was there for 17 years. I stayed in the orchestra for eleven or twelve years. Then I dropped the orchestra because I was doing a little bit of concertizing and a lot of chamber music. I was going to places like the Marlboro Festival in Vermont in the summers. I wanted to just have as full a musical life as possible. I always loved chamber music.

A.A.   *I worked at Marlboro one summer while studying with my teacher Colin Carr. I loved being in that environment, and I even sang in the choir when Rudolf Serkin played the Beethoven Choral Fantasy. That's one of my favorite musical memories.*

R.L.   That's one of my favorite memories too. I visited Marlboro once before I went there, and he played that piece. The very opening was so astounding; I don't think I've ever been that amazed by the sheer intensity of one person. It was mind-blowing.

A.A.   *And then was it from there that you came to Los Angeles?*

R.L. Yes. I had a funny period of time where I joined the Vermeer quartet for one year. I always thought that chamber music was the way I wanted to go. As a matter of fact, I actually turned down the principal chair of the Philadelphia orchestra at that time to play in that quartet.

I figured at the time that the only way I was ever really going to know what the quartet life was like was if I did it then. I knew it wouldn't happen later, so I felt I had to get it out of my system, and it was a wonderful quartet with beautiful players. The life and the whole chemistry of it didn't work for me, so I just stayed for one year and then went back to Eastman.

I had also auditioned for the Los Angeles Philharmonic principal chair. They asked me to come in, but I said, "No, I'm in a quartet." I decided I didn't want to go to Los Angeles, so I went back to Eastman, but it was somehow different when I returned. All of a sudden I felt like I wanted to get out of there. The job in Los Angeles was still open at that time, so I called them and then ended up in Los Angeles. It was a pretty weird way of taking a principal cello job.

A.A. *Yes, do you think it was being away from Rochester for a year with the quartet that made you realize you didn't want to stay there?*

R.L. Yes, somehow when I went back, it didn't feel quite the same to me. I had a wonderful time while I was there. The orchestra was very good, and I had wonderful students. I just thought it was time to move on. I stayed in the LA Phil for 24 years, and during all that time I was also teaching at USC. Eventually I was the Piatigorsky chair at USC. Then along came Richard Colburn. When he started this school (The Colburn School), he wanted me to teach there. I had been teaching in the prep department here ever since I came to Los Angeles, which is around 1957. I have been working with young kids, teaching at USC, and at the same time I was also playing. I was very active in the studios. I look back at it and I think I was absolutely crazy, because I was just going 24 hours a day, running from one thing to another.

Richard Colburn got the idea of starting this conservatory, and so I decided it was the thing to do. Turns out that that's one of the best things that ever happened. There was a committee of five or six people who had weekly meetings with Richard Colburn over a period of two years. In those meetings we brought in visiting conductors, visiting teachers, and visiting educators to discuss what we wanted to do at this school.

We tried to look at every angle possible, including what kind of a building we wanted to have. It was a wonderful committee, and it turned out to be a tremendously successful adventure. The school is spectacular.

A.A. *It's tuition free, right?*

R.L. Yes. When this school was started, Curtis had always been tuition free, but everybody had to pay for their own housing. When they started this school, it was a free ride for everything including housing and lessons.

A.A. *Is it still like that?*

R.L. Total free ride. We think that it had a very strong effect on music education in the United States, because since then there are quite a few schools who are just about the same way.

Curtis is now totally free too. They have dormitories there as we do, and there are quite a few schools that are pretty much free ride. These young kids today have the wonderful opportunity to choose between several schools where there is a wonderful faculty: Rice, New England, Curtis, Northwestern, and others.

These students, the better they are, have more possibilities, so we get a good share of those really talented students. I think it has made quite a change in the music schools in this country.

The Present

A.A.   *If you had to summarize your teaching philosophy, what would it be?*

R.L.   Well I would say that you can never forget the basics, no matter how well you play. You have to know what you're doing with both hands. You have to realize that scales and arpeggios and all those wonderful things are terribly important, that you've really learned the fingerboard from doing them.

Bowing exercises are very important. I can't tell you how often I've gone through the same spiel with incoming students. I want them to move the bow a certain way, and they need to know where the middle of the bow is, how to divide it, and what direction it's going in all the time. The left hand is the same thing.

There's a basic hand position that's terribly important. I keep coming back to the basics. I've made it one of my important things in my daily routine of practicing. I still practice scales. I still can't play arpeggios in tune, but I keep trying. Every day I do fairly basic double stop exercises with the left hand for intonation and hand position.

There's a certain way I work on a bow hold. I always realize that there are many ways that people can play really very wonderfully, but there's an overall technique that seems to work for most people. It's not that I or anybody has the correct way of holding the bow or moving the bow, but there are certainly things that get in the way when they're not disciplined in what they're doing.

A.A.   *I do think that's one thing I love about cello, is that you just can never master it.*

R.L   Perfection is an ideal that we all strive for, but it's impossible.

A.A.   *When you pick students, what's more important in a potential student: what they have to say or their physical approach?*

R.L.   I'm pushing for someone who has something to say. That's much more important than being perfect.

You can work with those physical problems and get around them. A lot of times it's not easy. Some people come in and play perfectly, but it sounds empty. It's very difficult to come to decisions, because there are so many young people who play so wonderfully today, it's just astounding. I don't think there is any teacher who hasn't kicked himself that he didn't accept this student or that student. We've all wished that we had taken certain people who wanted to have great careers, but it's very, very difficult to try to figure out who is the best one for you to accept.

A.A.   *One thing I spend a lot of time on is trying to help my students learn how to practice, and I'm wondering if that's something you also do.*

R.L. I spent today with one of my young students, a 16-year-old girl. This is a girl who can play Ligeti Sonata faster than anybody you could ever imagine, and she's starting on Rococo Variations right now. The whole lesson, I picked three or four variations, and I showed her how to practice those variations. For instance, in the second variation with all those scales, instead of the written rhythm, I had her practicing them in triplets. What it does is it forces you to stay slow. Usually you look at the page and you play just the way it's written on the page. I find in my own practicing all of a sudden, I'm playing too fast. I showed her how to practice that variation, and I worked with her on the first variation playing with a lot of double stops. Then I would have her playing the first three notes, and you have to lift the bow after the slur to get back to the frog. You practice it very slowly, get a little bit faster, and then realize that you can play it that way.

You have to relax the hand and drop the bow on the up-bows. You forget about shifting; you forget about all the other things. You'll learn the bowing pattern, and then you're all set for the variation. That's what I did with the whole piece. I just tried to get her to think about how she was going to practice everything in that piece.

I have a thing about having people count out loud when they're practicing, because I find that a lot of very talented people don't realize whether there are actually four beats in a bar, or three beats in a bar. If they do, they don't realize what the third beat does or what the second beat does, especially in a piece like Rococo Variations which everybody's heard a million times. They play it and they don't think.

It's not early computer language. It's not ones and zeros. It's one, two, three. It's one, two, three, four. When you practice a scale, it's not a matter of just playing four notes on a bow, but you should have in your mind that you're playing in three-four time, four-four time, six-eight time. There's always a meter. If they're playing a variation that's in 4/4 time, a fourth beat has a different feeling from the downbeat.

A.A. *Do you give a scale routine that you teach to your students?*

R.L. Yes I use the Galamian book, except he has one set of fingerings that fits all the scales. From my vantage point, that's too mindless. I think when there's a scale with open strings, you should use the open strings. For example, I want you to play a C-Major Prelude with no open string. Let me see how you do that. That's going to be the weirdest thing imaginable. Why should I play a D-major concerto scale with a D-flat major fingering? It doesn't compute.

I do use the Galamian though. Rhythmically, it makes sense with so many bowings. In that book there are three octave scales, and he adds a couple of extra notes at the beginning, and adds a couple of extra notes at the end. These turnarounds are so you can play bowings, anything that divides into 24: 2, 3, 4, 6, 8, 12.

Practicing with a metronome is critical. I tell my students they have to practice with a metronome all the time, including slow movements, so that there's a sense of what the pause is. But, if you sound like a metronome, then you're doing something wrong.

A.A. *Do you make an effort to keep students sounding like individuals? I know old school teaching would be, "These are my bowings, these are my fingerings, and this is how it's done."*

R.L. Well I must admit that I tend to have them follow my markings a lot. Every once in a while, one of them comes in with a bowing or fingering that I'd never thought of and I'm always thankful for that. It's surprising to me how many poor fingerings and bowings that students can come up with, so I don't want to waste the time.

A.A.   *Right. If you feel that they're saying something that maybe you wouldn't quite say the same way musically, I would imagine you're more lenient on that.*

R.L.   Of course, absolutely you're looking for individuality. I'm very happy when their vibratos are different, then the approach is different. I think this is even better when the basics are worked out carefully. If a student plays with an unmusical fingering I ask them to find another fingering, and then I ask them what's better about that fingering. Most of the time it'll end up being a fingering that I would choose.

A.A.   *What is the hardest thing to teach your students?*

Vibrato is a very difficult thing to teach. It may be the hardest. I find each student moves in a different way. For me the most important thing is what you're doing with the thumb. All of us are taught that we put the thumb under the second finger. I always studied what I was doing, and I looked down at my left hand one day and I said, "Well, I've been telling all these people that the thumb belongs here, but I don't do that."

I noticed that we talk about the fingers being curved but straight up and down, and I don't do that either. It's always tilted. My left hand is more like a violin. The thumb for me has to be behind the first finger, because the amount of pressure you use on the thumb is usually too much. When you bring it back you're more inclined. I have people making a fist and practicing with thinking of the vibrato being on the low side always and never going to the upper side of the note. These are always pulling the finger backwards to vibrate. People's hands are so different, and they move in such different ways. Every case is different.

It's also very difficult to teach a student to take time. They're in such a hurry, but that's a double-edged sword too. You tell them they have to practice slowly, but at the same time just practicing slowly isn't going to teach you to play fast.

With practicing, I read every once in a while about some wonderful musician who says you always have to practice musically. I question that. People go into practice with absolutely no vibrato, and they played this horribly loud, pressed sound, which just drives me crazy. I can't understand why anybody would want to listen to that sound. Yes, you have to practice slowly with and without vibrato, listening to the intonation very carefully. I find over and over again that someone will come in and they already have a preconceived musical idea about what they're going to do just from having heard. They don't know the basic rhythms that are there, and the intonation can be all over the place. The goal is to sound musical, but you have to get there through a series of rather painful exercises and careful attention to physical problems.

That happens all the time with students. They try to play Baroque Bach, but they don't know anything about Baroque music. I'm not a Baroque specialist, but I know enough to know when I hear bad Baroque.

A.A.   *Since you brought that up, if the students coming in are fairly new to Bach, do you try to approach them learning it with an ear toward the Baroque period?*

R.L.   Well I would say much more so now than I used to, because when I was in school my hero was Pablo Casals. Now Pablo Casals, if he were on the scene today, nobody would think it was all that great. It has changed so much, and the Baroque influence on how to play Bach is very strong now. I use a lot less vibrato than I used to do in Bach, but I will never be thought of being a Baroque specialist.

A.A. *How do you work on intonation with your students?*

R.L. Drone notes are very good, and double stops I think are extremely helpful when slow. I practice perfect fourths a lot, which are very hard to play in tune. I practice whole tone scales and sixths. I practice one octave scales and sixths but without any extensions. I feel that extensions are very dangerous, because people get their hand in an extension position where they can't ever vibrate. Anytime there's an extension, for me it's a delayed move. You only move to it when you're going for the note. In the major sixths, the fingers have to be spaced by half steps all the time, never a whole step between any two fingers. That helps you get across the string, and it's great for the hand position. One octave, any key, and anywhere on the fingerboard, you can do it.

A.A. *Are there certain technique books that you use?*

R.L. Well I don't do a lot of exercises. I used to teach a lot more Popper études and Piatti Caprices. I do some, but I think it's enough with scales, arpeggios, and double stops.

A.A. *Do you force students to play by memory?*

R.L. I see students practicing a passage eight or ten times and they're always reading the notes. I tell them, "Now look, you're playing two octaves or whatever it is, why are you imprisoned by reading the notes every time you're doing that?"

When you're practicing, it's important at any stage to get your eye away from the page. Why should I look? I can think about how it feels, but it's not on the page. Practicing by memory has to start young.

Some people have real, real hang-ups with it, and I understand that Rostropovich didn't allow anybody to come into a lesson with the music. That's fine, except Rostropovich had a photographic memory. We all wish we could do that.

You can't expect anybody to look at a piece and have it memorized the next day. I try to have them do as much from memory as possible, and they have to get out and perform it from memory. If they screw up, such is life. Go out the next time, and you do it again.

There are people who just have hang-ups with memory. If they play well that doesn't concern me, I'm not going to put somebody down because they do or don't play from memory. As a matter of fact, I was a judge in a competition one time, and this violinist came in and he played either the Brahms Sonata or Mozart Sonata from memory. A piano member of the faculty said, "I would never vote for somebody who plays a Mozart Sonata from memory with a pianist. It's insulting to the pianist." I said, "Please, how's the performance? Tell me how that is."

One of the important things in performing is always you want to be free. If you're sitting there and you're always reading the music, you can't be free. I've realized as I've gotten older how important it is to free yourself from watching. Although when I practice, I'm watching where I am, I try and look around the room. It's not to be theatrical, but it makes such a difference for some people.

A.A. *Do you give students detailed hours of practice or a goal to work on?*

R.L. I tell them to use the first hour for scales and arpeggios. Some of them do it and some of them I know don't. Some people waste so much time by practicing the same thing too many times without actually thinking about what they're doing. They just do it over and over again. I heard a pianist practicing about six bars of a piece as I went by his practice room at about 10:00. I went by at 11:00 and he was still practicing those six bars. At 12:00 he was still practicing those six bars. Now to me, that's the height of stupidity. You cannot possibly gain anything from practicing that way. There aren't enough hours in the day.

A.A.   *How important is body movement and playing?*

R.L.   Obviously you don't want people to be rigid. I have them do a lot of shifting from side to side and moving forward. I don't insist on any particular position for their feet. I have them practice moving their body against the bow and moving the body with the bow. I've suggested some of them take dancing lessons or motion lessons. With the bow, I use simple terminology of push and pull. The resistance is always at the tip.

As a matter of fact, when people play loudly thinking of down and up bows, they think of pressing down. I think of pulling the string to the side instead. The fallacy is that you always have to be at the bridge to play loud, but it depends. It depends on how fast the bow is moving.

A.A.   *You talked about Leonard Rose demonstrating sometimes, but do you also demonstrate a lot in your teaching and has that changed over the years?*

R.L.   I demonstrate small passages. I rarely will sit and play a movement of a piece for a student. They're not there to hear me play. I don't worry, and never have, whether I sound particularly great in a lesson. It doesn't bother me. I'm much more interested in getting from this point to that point by moving a certain way.

A.A.   *They get the concept of what you're trying.*

R.L.   Yes.

A.A.   *There are three pieces commonly performed that are not all quite originals, including the Boccherini Concerto that Grützmacher arranged, the Fitzenhagen Rococo, and the Chopin Polonaise. What do you feel about all of those?*

R.L.   I think Fitzenhagen did us a big service. I know a wonderful artist who would take umbrage at that statement. I've looked at the original of course, and it's too long and anticlimactic.

With the Chopin Polonaise, when I hear the original version, I think it's the most boring piece in the world. Even Rostropovich's recording of the original is not very interesting. When Rostropovich doesn't sound interesting, there's something wrong.

A.A.   *Good point. What about the Boccherini/Grützmacher? The B-flat?*

R.L.   There are two or three versions of the Boccherini, and I learned the Grützmacher. Nobody plays it these days.

A.A.   *Everyone plays the original Boccherini?*

R.L.   Yes, which I think is a better piece. I think it sounds better, but I've only played the Grützmacher. It reminds me of the Haydn in D major. I learned the Gevaërt edition, and I don't play that anymore. I more often use the original, but I actually liked the Gevaërt edition better, but I don't play it because I know the snobby critic is going to say, "What's this that I think he's doing? This is the 20th century." Well, that's all well and good, but for my taste, Grützmacher did a good thing.

The Future

A.A.   *A lot has been made of the shrinking audience in classical music, so where do you see the future of classical music going in the next generation and how is technology positively or negatively affecting classical music?*

R.L.   The whole music world has changed a lot. People use the computer for the music instead of buying music. It's very freeing and a big help. I think you have to be up on technology, and you have to sell yourself. You have to know how to deal with audiences, you have to be able to talk about the music, and you have to project ideas to the audience. For me, I've just spent my life playing the cello. But now, technology is a big thing. Look what you see these days. The more you learn about technology the better, and you have to be a real entrepreneur now in order to be a soloist.

A.A.   *How do you think new music fits into the future of orchestral music?*

R.L.   Well, with minimalists for instance, I find it the most boring thing in the world, and I find it painful to play because you repeat and repeat and repeat. It's bad for you physically. I don't find it appealing at all. But I enjoy the challenge of playing new music because you have to know your instrument very well. You have to be quick; you need to have great rhythm. But, I cannot imagine a life playing in the Kronos Quartet. I need to hear a major chord once in a while.

  I go to performances of these pieces, and people think they're fantastic. They go crazy. The same thing with minimalist music; they love it. I know that I have not taught enough contemporary music to my students, but these days they bring things in themselves so we can work things out together.

A.A.   *Do you think orchestras will continue to try to bridge the gap?*

R.L.   I think so. It's always been historically important to play new music. When I was growing up, the Bartok quartets were the craziest thing that one could think of. Now I really love those pieces. There are a lot of pieces like that; over the years they get into your system. But, when I hear a piece where there's nothing to hang onto, it's cacophony and my life is better without that.

A.A.   *Have you seen the level of cello playing change over the years?*

R.L.   Yes. I'm very glad that I'm looking at it from this vantage point. I wish I had some recordings of what I sounded like when I was 16 or 17, but when I hear these 15- ,16- , 17-year-olds, I know that I didn't play that well at that age. The level is really outstanding.

A.A.   *Are there enough jobs for cellists in today's market?*

R.L.   No. There aren't, and yet every time there's an opening in a major orchestra, they hear many, many wonderful cellists and violinists, and they don't pick anybody. Sorry, that doesn't compute. I don't understand that.

A.A.   *Would you say it because two factions of the committee are not agreeing and so they just can't take anyone?*

R.L.   Well, I think it's gotten to the point where unless you play absolutely perfectly, they don't want you. I've got a pretty good track record of my students getting orchestra jobs, and I try to instill in them the idea that you cannot play at an audition the way you think somebody wants to hear it. You just can't do it. I can't play Brahms third symphony slow movement the way I think this committee wants to hear it. It has to be what I think is right within the confines of general tempo and taste. When people come in and play perfect auditions, I don't mind mistakes. For instance, when I auditioned for the LA Philharmonic, I played for Zubin Mehta. He wanted to hear *Don Quixote*, and I played a run in that piece that was so ridiculously out of tune and he just laughed. He thought it was hilarious and it meant nothing to him. He was interested in personality.

A.A.   *How much do you help a student find success when they're done with school? Do you consider that part of your job?*

R.L.   Well, I wish I had more contact with my students when they leave, but for the most part you kind of lose track. It's very hard to keep in contact. It's a little bit easier now with the internet.

A.A.   *I would imagine if a student wrote or asked you for a recommendation, you probably would still do that.*

R.L.   Yes, absolutely.

Close to the Heart

A.A.   *If you hadn't been a musician, what would you have loved to have done with your life?*

R.L.   I've thought about that and I just can't imagine. It has only been cello and music. It's great because I was not a brilliant student academically. I was always smart, but I was always lazy academically. I think I could have taken any kind of a job, but it just happened that I hit on music.

A.A.   *What are maybe two or three of the most memorable concerts you've been involved in?*

R.L.   Well, you mentioned Serkin playing the Choral Fantasy at Marlboro. That would be one of them. Another one would be a concert that I heard of Andres Segovia. That was many, many years ago. A few years ago we had Menahem Pressler at the Colburn School. He was a guest artist here, and he played here when he might have been 93, or 94. He played a Chopin Nocturne as an encore, and it was one of the most breathtaking performances I have ever heard in my life. I was not the only one who felt that. It reached everybody.

I have one experience when I was principal cellist of the L.A. Philharmonic when Bronfman played a Prokofiev concerto. It was a stunning performance, and at the end of it, everybody cheered. It was a standing ovation. I left the hall and went down to my car. I got about four miles away, and it suddenly dawned on me that it was only intermission. I raced back to the hall, and I could hear over the intercom, "Ron Leonard, where are you? Where are you?"

A.A.   *Did they wait until you got back?*

R.L.   Yes. It was just about 10 minutes away. That was maybe 20 years ago, so I can't even say that it was a senior moment.

A.A.   *Have you ever had to deal with a period of doubt about being a musician in your life, and how did you get through that?*

R.L.   Never. It's never entered my mind. Maybe I'm arrogant, I don't know. I feel like I've been unbelievably fortunate in my whole career.

A.A.   *Well what are you most proud of in your life and career?*

R.L.   Well, a lot of it was so great. I've always had wonderful jobs and worked in wonderful places with a lot of great people, but The Colburn School is the thing I'm most proud of. There's a wonderful faculty and a wonderful work environment. Colburn's main idea was that the school should be run by the ideas of the faculty and not the administration. We're trying to keep it that way and still have the same committee that started it. Not everybody is still here but it's been approached in a way where we try as best we can to make all our decisions based on what we think is best for the students, not what some music organization or administration thinks we should do. We've certainly made mistakes, but it's a phenomenal thing.

A.A.   *Is there anything you still want to do, any projects or bucket list things?*

R.L.   I want to enjoy walking, that's all. That's where I do my best thinking and where I enjoy nature, and it's a great climate here in L.A. When I have time, I walk three or four miles a day. I live in an area where there are a lot of steep hills, so it's tough on my body.

A.A.   *Do you ever think you will retire?*

R.L.   I have recently retired although I never thought I would. However, I practice daily, including scales and arpeggios. I also still teach a little and perform.

A.A.   *If you had to pick three desert island pieces, only three pieces to listen to ever again, what would those be?*

R.L.   The Schubert cello quintet, even though I've played it a thousand times.

A.A.   *Never gets old, does it?*

R.L.   No. Other than that there are just too many wonderful pieces. It might not necessarily be classical music. It could be Frank Sinatra, and there are a lot of jazz players that I really enjoy.

A.A.   *Who were some of your favorites?*

R.L.   Erroll Garner, Dizzy Gillespie, and Stan Kenton. That all shows my age, but they were fantastic and imaginative musicians. Sinatra was one of the greatest.

11

Laurence Lesser

A native of Los Angeles, Laurence Lesser was a top prizewinner in the 1966 Tchaikovsky Competition in Moscow and a participant in the historic Heifetz-Piatigorsky concerts and recordings. Mr. Lesser has appeared as a soloist with the Boston Symphony Orchestra, the London Philharmonic, the Los Angeles Philharmonic, the New Japan Philharmonic, the Tokyo Philharmonic and other major orchestras. His New York debut recital in 1969 was greeted as "triumphant" and "magical." His Tchaikovsky Rococo Variations in Hamburg, Die Welt stated, "could not have been more thoroughly realized than is this staggering performance."

As a chamber musician he has participated at the Casals, Marlboro, Spoleto, Ravinia, Music@Menlo and Santa Fe festivals. He has also been a member of juries for numerous international competitions, including chairing the Tchaikovsky Competition in Moscow in 1994.

A 1961 graduate of Harvard College, where he studied mathematics, Lesser went to Köln, Germany the following year to work with Gaspar Cassadó. Just before, he played at the Zermatt master classes for Pablo Casals, who declared, "Thank God who has given you such a great talent!" He won first prize at the Cassadó Competition in Siena, Italy, in 1962. When he returned to Los Angeles, he studied with Gregor Piatigorsky and soon became his teaching assistant and regular faculty member at the University of Southern California.

During the remainder of the 1960s he was a frequent contributor to the artistic life of Los Angeles. Notably, his 1965 performance of the Schoenberg Cello Concerto to inaugurate the Bing Auditorium at the Los Angeles County Museum of Art was its first hearing with orchestra after Emanuel Feuermann introduced the work in the late 1930s. He recorded it the following year for Columbia Masterworks. He left Los Angeles in 1970 to become Professor of Cello at Baltimore's Peabody Institute.

Lesser was invited in 1974 by Gunther Schuller, the then President of New England Conservatory, to head NEC's Cello Department. In 1983 he was named the school's President, a position from which he retired in 1996 to return to performing and teaching. A high point of his tenure as President was the complete restoration of the 1000-seat Jordan Hall, one of the world's greatest acoustical spaces.

Teaching has always been an important part of Lesser's artistic activity. His former students, numbering in the hundreds, are soloists, orchestra section leaders and members, chamber musicians and teachers, active throughout the USA and in many other countries around the world.

In September, 2005 Lesser was named "Chevalier du Violoncelle" by the Eva Janzer Memorial Cello Center at Indiana University.

Lesser's previous recordings include the complete Beethoven with pianist HaeSun Paik on Bridge Records. His recordings of the complete Bach Suites feature his transcription for cello of the composer's version for lute (its manuscript is the only extant original source in Bach's hand.) Other labels include RCA, Columbia, Melodiya and CRI.

The Past

Anthony Arnone: *Where did you grow up, and how did you first get exposed to the cello?*

Laurence Lesser: I was born in Los Angeles in 1938. My mother had conservatory education as a pianist in the Chicago Musical College. My father was not connected to music, but when asked if he was a musician said, "I pay for the lessons."

I'm the youngest of three boys. All of us had some beginning piano. I was about four or five when I started. In those years, my parents used to take me to the Los Angeles Philharmonic Youth Concerts, and they'd ask, "Is there any instrument you're interested in?" And I said, "I want to play the double bass." They thought it was too long for a little boy, and on my sixth birthday they gave me a cello. I don't seem to have ever been able to get rid of it.

A.A. *I know you've had some amazing teachers.* Looking back, what do you feel you got *from each of them?*

L.L. The first teacher of any length that I had was Gregory Aller here in Los Angeles. He was a musician from St. Petersburg, and his progeny are very famous. I studied with him from about the age of eight or nine until 12 or 13. He was an old-fashioned teacher but with a great love and passion for what he was doing. He was in his 70s and had a lot of young students in this area. He was a very warm person. He took me through the Dotzauer Études, the Kummer, and a little Goltermann. That was how I began.

After that, I went through a period when I just didn't want to work anymore, but it was recommended that I study with Gábor Rejtő, who was teaching in Santa Barbara at the Music Academy of the West, but he was not coming to USC for one more year. It was arranged that I would have lessons for a year—I was then approaching 15 years old—with Kurt Reher, who was the principal cellist of the Los Angeles Philharmonic. Kurt Reher had studied with Emanuel Feuermann in Berlin before the Nazis came. He had a brother Sven there. Their heritage was Norwegian and they got Hindemith to write the duo for viola and cello, which is dedicated to them.

I studied with Kurt Reher for one year, and I remember that he talked to me a lot about Feuermann. Feuermann was always saying that you have to be so well equipped in what you're doing on the instrument that when you walk on stage, even if you're not in the mood to play, you can do a proper performance. That's what I remember Reher told me.

The following summer, I went to Santa Barbara for individual lessons. From that fall of 1954, Rejtő was teaching at USC, and I was his student for a couple of years.

A.A. *While you were still in high school?*

L.L. Yes

A.A. *At this point, did you know you wanted to be a cellist? Or did that come later?*

L.L. Well, that's a different part of the story, but what I will say is that it was clear that I was gifted on the cello, that I was encouraged very much to do it, and that I loved doing it. I was very shy and very awkward. When my parents had people over, they said, "Oh, Larry, play something for them," and I was shy about it until I started. Then they couldn't get me to stop, because I loved playing.

Those Rejtő years were very formative, because he took me through a lot of the repertoire. In that period, I played a certain number of recitals for the Young Musicians Foundation and various places around here. He also taught me a lot of fundamental technique. He had also studied with Casals.

In high school, I was academically gifted and very interested in mathematics. When it came time to enter college, I was interested in pursuing mathematics. My mother was always on the side of music, but my father was always dubious that music was a possible profession. He was very pleased that I ended up going to Harvard College in the fall of 1956.

While I was there during my first year, I had lessons once a month at the Longy School of Music with Maurice Eisenberg, who had been a student of Casals. Although I didn't see him enough to really have a strong impression, I was not very comfortable with his approach, but it was only for that year.

During that year, I was in classes with freshmen who were intending to go into mathematics who I thought were vastly more gifted than me in mathematics, and I was lonely with the musical part of my life. I took a leave of absence from college after my first year and came back to Los Angeles. I enrolled at USC School of Music for the fall semester, and life took its twists and turns. That was a wonderful experience for me. It was my first encounter with people like Ingolf Dahl, great piano teachers like John Crown and Lillian Steuber, and the mainstream USC faculty. It was all held in Clark House, a wonderful Victorian mansion on Adams Boulevard. Sadly, it's gone. It was a really wonderful place to come together and feel like you were part of a community.

So I was here with Rejtő again, and two things happened. I felt, with no disrespect to USC, that I was missing something by not being at Harvard. The family had a bad period of time financially, and I couldn't really afford to stay in school. In the second semester, I did whatever freelance work I could, and I went on a very strange tour for what I call a pops chamber orchestra for the Columbia concert circuit out of New York City. We played 53 concerts in 63 days and traveled by bus all the way from New York City to the south and then all the way west to Roswell, New Mexico, Carlsbad, New Mexico, and then back again.

By that point, I said, "I think I better go back to Harvard." I did, and I met a cellist who was in that group who said, "Well, you should be playing for Leonard Rose. He's my teacher." It was arranged that I do that when I came back, and Rose said he would teach me privately. I came back to Harvard in the fall of 1958, and for three years I went about once a month to New York to have lessons with Leonard Rose. It was not an ideal situation. I was trying to straddle two careers, and Harvard is not an easy school. What I learned from Rose was tone production with the bow. He was very influenced by Galamian. Hold your bow and use it like you're using a heavy paintbrush to go back and forth against the side of the strings.

I remember the one thing that was good for me but irritated me at the time was when I was learning Rococo Variations for the first time. As I was learning it, he said to me, something that I later on understood but at that time really galled me, "You know, this is really a very easy piece. Once you know it, you just play it." I was sweating bullets trying to learn it. He was also hard on me about intonation.

Anyway, I was very interested to go to Europe to study cello. By the time I came back, I stayed a math major, but I had made up my mind that I was going to be in music. Sometimes it was very, very clear to me that that's what I wanted, that's what I would do, that's where I belonged, and no matter how it turned out, that was going to be it. My father was dubious about that. He was the son of poor, Eastern European Jewish immigrants in Fall River, Massachusetts. He went into law, which is not what he wanted to do, but it was something a Jewish kid could do. He was always talking to me and my brothers that it is very important in your life to do the thing you love and just go for that. Even though he was questioning my choice to go into music, he knew that it was what I wanted.

I applied for Fulbright, and I got it. I wanted to go to Germany because it was the source of so much of our great music, and also the source of such atrocities. As a Jewish kid, I really wanted to see why. During that period of time, I had my first musical contact with Piatigorsky. He was not teaching, but he was the president of the Young Musicians Foundation.

I would come home in the summertime and spend part of the summer working on a recital program, which I did with a wonderful pianist named Ellen Mack, who's still teaching at Peabody. We would prepare a recital program and play it somewhere, usually it was in Schoenberg Hall at UCLA, and Piatigorsky always came. He would invite me to come to his house a few days later and give me his impressions of the whole recital. That was my first pedagogic contact with him, and he was just such a great wonderful warm person.

When I said I was going to Europe, he thought that was a good thing. He had been the principal cellist with the Berlin Philharmonic when he came out of Russia. That was his first real job after studying with Hugo Becker and Julius Klengel. When I got the Fulbright, they said they were sending me to Cologne, Germany. I said I wanted to go to Berlin, Hamburg, or Munich. They said, "Well, you can do that, but if you want the Fulbright, you have to go to Cologne." I asked, "Why?" They said, "Well, because the most important cellist teaching in Germany right now is in Cologne, and that's Gaspar Cassadó."

I only knew about Cassadó because of a Frescobaldi Cassadó Toccata, which I learned much later was not written by Frescobaldi at all. I had studied that with Rejtő. When I spoke to Piatigorsky about Cologne, he thought I should do that. He told me he would never go back to Germany, but he thought that was a good thing for me to do and that he knew Cassadó from the 1920s in Berlin. He remembered Cassadó as being a great cellist.

I went to Cologne for the year, and I studied at the Hochschule there. Cassadó was the most famous student of Pablo Casals. He was enormously important for me because he was the first teacher I had who was really talking about left-hand technique, articulation, and structure. He was not a textbook teacher, but it was clear that those things were important. He had come from being, as a young person, the Kreisler of the cello to somebody who was trying very hard to be young. Piatigorsky always said it's important to be your age when you're there. It was not quite natural because Cassadó wanted to be young. He was the first cellist who played with steel strings, he had all kinds of contraptions on his instrument to make it louder, and the bow itself had a huge cork apparatus held over the frog so that when you held the bow, it was like holding a small pipe instead. If your hand was bigger, you had more leverage. Cassadó was very nice to me, and I think he respected me as a talented kid. He was generous to me.

Then I came back. I had gone on a draft deferment at the time. I went into Piatigorsky's class starting in January of 1963. I would say that Piatigorsky for me was just the right person at the right time, and I was around him from 1963 to 1970 here at USC. I consider him my primary teacher. Piatigorsky had a philosophical point of view about how you play and a sense of what the music was about. He was not particularly explicit in technical information, and he didn't play a lot in class, but if he picked up a cello, I was sure to position myself in class so I could stare at what was going on. I learned so much.

A.A.   *When you started with Piatigorsky, did you have a sense of what you still needed in your own playing?*

L.L.   I didn't. By that time, I'd been playing a fair number of concerts, and he was a teacher who taught by example and by indirect suggestions. Although, sometimes his suggestions were very specific. He would say, "Well, why don't you use third finger there?" He was more concerned with what you were trying to make the music sound like, not so much about how to hold and do things, although he did have a few basic exercises. He taught us, for instance, that you should be able to play any note with any finger at any time and that you should be able to change from one finger to another without anybody knowing.

He recalled that he had gone once to play a bunch of concerts in Copenhagen with Itzhak Perlman, Daniel Barenboim, and Pinchas Zukerman. They were doing a Beethoven string trio with Pinky playing viola. Pinky wanted something up-bow, and Itzhak wanted it down-bow, and Piatigorsky said, "I don't care. Just tell me which one. It doesn't matter to me." I learned everything from him by hearing what he believed in, by hearing how music was put together, and by listening for quality of sound. He said, always in French, "C'est le son qui fait la musique." It's sound that makes music.

A.A.   *Would you say that helped you become more of an artist at that point in your life?*

L.L.   Oh, absolutely. He was an astonishingly natural player. He just picked up the cello and played. We all aspired to that. He recalled when he was a pupil of Klengel in Leipzig that Klengel would kind of pair up students and say, "Why don't you go listen to Mischa Schneider's vibrato?" and then everybody would huddle around him. Klengel could barely play at all at his advanced age. He just sat at the piano and played accompaniments for the pieces the student was doing in front of the class. That was a model for Piatigorsky, a real sense of community among the students. We had that in Piatigorsky's class.

I came in 1963 in January. In the fall of 1963 he asked me to be his assistant, and he said that would be very good for me. I was used to teaching little kids, but suddenly I'm teaching Nathaniel Rosen. Nick was ten years younger than me, so that was kind of easier on a personal basis. For three years I gave Nick a lesson every week. Later on, and more recently, he said something very generous to me. I don't know whether you know Narek Hakhnazaryan, but he studied with me for two years just before he won the Tchaikovsky Competition.

A.A.   *I certainly have heard him play. He's amazing.*

L.L.   Nick very generously said to me after Narek won the Tchaikovsky, "Well, you're the only American teacher who has had two cellists win the Gold Medal of the Tchaikovsky Competition." It was very generous because he was studying with Piatigorsky.

A.A.   *That's nice.*

L.L.   Nick, Jeffrey Solow, Paul Tobias, Steven Kates, and Myung-Wha Chung came. I could go on and on. There was a family feel to it because Piatigorsky promoted that sense that we should learn from one another. He also saw all of us individually at his house from time to time.

We always met at the class two days a week. Sometimes it was Thursdays and Sundays. He liked Sundays because there was no traffic, and he had learned to drive when he was in his 50s. He was a terrible driver.

Around that time, actually, my first place to live on my own was a three-minute drive from where he lived in very modest housing, and he had a very lavish, wonderful home. Very often I would drive him to the conservatory.

I learned so much from him about life. He taught me about the attitude of a musician and through watching him and hearing how he would make suggestions to other people. It couldn't be better. He said, "I don't care about diplomas, and I don't care about degrees. But, if you could have a diploma that said you are a free artist, that's what you should aspire to."

The Present

A.A. *What are some of your secrets to practicing well, and most importantly, do you consider that an important part of your teaching? Do you spend time in lessons helping a student use all the hours they have during the week efficiently?*

L.L. It's true that when you're teaching very young people that you're dealing with fundamental issues of how to do this and how to do that. I start working with people on tone production with their bow and learning how to make the instrument ring. We play an instrument that's not terribly loud, and only manage to project if we learn how to get the resonance of the instrument for what we want it to be. I work on that at the very beginning. There is somebody who wrote a book about cello technique having to do with left hand technique, such as where the fingers are pointing and that they're perpendicular to the floor. I try to teach some of those fundamental things.

In terms of time, it seems to me that this is not just technique. You have to have an idea of what it is you're trying to say or play. If you don't have an idea, you can fool around, you can doodle around, and maybe once in a while you'll find something good. I think the important thing in that case is if something good happens, stop for a second, and try and figure out what it is you did, why was it good, and capture that.

I think Piatigorsky said, "It's wonderful if you can have a place to practice where your cello can be open and sitting there waiting for you, and that if you can practice off and on many times during the day without trying to cram it all into one two-hour period, you're better off. Because every time you sit down to it you should be fresh and eager and have some idea of what you're looking for."

Young people have trouble in dealing with time, and not everybody has a practicing situation where they can do what Piatigorsky suggested. But, I do encourage them to sit down and practice as long as they're concentrating on what they're doing. Never sit down and practice mechanically because you're wasting your time. Always stop when you feel your mind is wandering. Go off and do something else. If you have other classes you have to study for, go study for them for a while, go take a walk, go have a meal, or talk to friends. When you're working, you have to be absolutely focused in on it like a laser beam.

Maybe the single most important thing that I talk to people about is you have to understand what it is you are trying to get the music to say. Since you're in the game this far, you obviously have music in you. How do you get it out? Open your mouth and sing because we don't, for the most part, think about what we are singing when we sing something. It just comes out. It's inborn, and for me, it's the most significant source of information. Some of them are very shy to sing. I say to them, "You're preparing for a life in front of people. If you can't sing for me or for yourself, you're in the wrong business. It doesn't mean anybody's expecting you to walk on stage and sing an aria." You just have to learn. Then the next thing, really hardest thing is when I tell them, "I want you to open your mouth and sing this phrase." It's amazing to me that even if it isn't exactly the way I think about it, it always comes out sounding musical because it's natural to them. I say, "Let's begin to try and figure out what it is you did." If it's a short phrase, I'll say, "What was the most intense note in that?" Then, something very dangerous happens. They sing it, but it's not natural anymore. They sing it what they think intellectually is supposed to be the most important note. And I aid them by saying, "You've got to get past that. You've got to learn how to separate your analytical tools from your emotional tools so that you can say that's the note that I'm aiming for. Now you can figure out a way to move the bow or to find a shift or whatever it is that brings that note out. Now you begin to have something you want."

Piatigorsky used to say, "People are less limited by what they want for themselves than what they're able to do." If you don't want anything, you don't get anything. For me, I always think about the fact that there isn't enough time. I will go through a piece and talk later about all the details. I never start somebody working on a piece with bowings and fingerings.

A.A.   *I was going to ask about that.*

L.L.   I just won't do it. When they come in, I like to joke with them. I say, "You know, I'm hoping you'll find some better ones than I know. I'm going to steal them from you." But sometimes they come in, and it's not very good. Then I have something specific to talk with them about that becomes generally useful later on. Then I become more and more analytical about shifting. There are two things I do at the very beginning when working with people these days. I'm well known during first lessons to make the statement, "I want you to understand my ambition is to get rid of you." They're usually a little bit uneasy about that.

A.A.   *I remember you saying that at NEC, actually.*

L.L.   My ambition is to get rid of you. Then I explain by saying, "I am hoping in the period of time we're working together to give you guiding principles so that you can be your own teacher. Right now there are two teachers of you in this room. One of them is much more important than the other, and it's you. I'm trying to teach you how to teach yourself."

The next thing I'll say is, "So, tell me, in your life up until now, can you remember a day when you had the cello in your hands, whether orchestra rehearsal or practicing or a lesson or chamber music or whatever it was, and how many hours on a really long day," and most people will say, "Oh, maybe eight," or somebody will say, "Maybe nine or ten." I ask, "So, how many hours are there in a day? And they go, "Twenty four." So

I say, "Even on the day when you were playing the cello more than any other day you can remember, there were more hours in that day you were not playing the cello." Why do so many people pick up the cello and behave like they're from a foreign planet as if it is not related to how they use their body the rest of the time? Maybe this is some of the attitude of Piatigorsky. I'm trying to use common sense as a way of finding solutions, and it doesn't all happen in one lesson. It's an attitude that's very important for me.

A.A.   *How do you feel about students getting to know recordings or YouTube these days?*

L.L.   It doesn't bother me at all. When I studied with Rejtő, he forbade us to listen to recordings because he said we'd never have our own ideas. I would say that if you listen to a recording and you're inspired by it, you internalize what that's about, and then it's yours. You're not copying anymore. You just can't sound like somebody else. You can be influenced by somebody, and that could be from many different areas. It could be from different kinds of music. You could hear a sound that really resonates with you emotionally.

A.A.   *What do you think is one of the hardest things to teach students after teaching for so many years?*

L.L.   I don't know it's the hardest thing, but I try very hard to encourage and empower people to be themselves and to figure out who they are. As I just said, I encourage them to take influence wherever they get it and not be afraid to say what they feel. I have a funny way of encouraging people. I say, "Suppose you came in for your lesson and you're ready to play. Now wait a minute. I have to ask you to do something before you play." They'll ask, "Oh, well what is it?" I say, "Please take off all your clothes. Well, of course, I don't want you to do that. But, what I want you to know is that what we're working on is harder to do than that, is riskier than that, because the world is not asking to see your skin, they're asking to know what's underneath your skin. If you're afraid to do that, let's find a way to give you the courage to do that, to be able to communicate."

I love amateurs, but in my work I don't work with amateurs, except for encouragement. I say, "We're aiming to be professional, and being professional means not just that you're paid and living on what you do but that you're doing it for other people. You have to know that people come to a concert not to "get" you, to figure out what you did bad, but they come because you have something to give them that they don't have. By and large they don't play music, but they love to hear it and they need you. You have a responsibility to give something to them."

A.A.   *Do you demonstrate during lessons? How important do you think that is in teaching?*

L.L.   I demonstrate when there is something physical more easily explained visually. I am always trying to help students find their own answers, but some things need to be shown.

A.A.   *When you get to hear a lot of potential students at auditions, what do you look for and what's more important to you? Is feeling they have something to say on their instrument or their physical ease on the instrument more important?*

L.L.   I listen to a lot of people every year, and I'm pretty quick in understanding what I'm after, but I always am very careful to review it. I am discouraged and not inclined to invite somebody who it seems doesn't use the ear well for intonation. If I feel that there is no discrimination in that area, that's something I know I can't fix, so I won't teach that person. If I find somebody whose music making is mechanical or uncommunicative,

I don't work with them. I'm looking for somebody who has some musical spark in them. They don't have to be physically perfect. I'm in my 80th year. I just can't work with beginners anymore although I've done a lot of it in my life.

A.A.   *How do you feel like your teaching has changed from maybe your early first five or ten years as a teacher?*

L.L.   I felt that as I began to figure out how the machine works that it was my responsibility to make everybody work the machine perfectly, and I was extremely analytical and specific. I've moved far away from that because, while I have all of that as a pool of information that I can share as needed, I'm trying to get people to learn how to find those answers themselves. I'm trying very hard not to be invasive.

In the technical approach, I ask them how they use their body when they're doing other things. If you're picking up something of a different shape, what do your fingers do? I'm trying to get people to learn which part of their body does what.

There's a muscle called the trapezius muscle. It connects the shoulder blade to the spine, and it's a place where when I was growing up I always felt a lot of tension. I've learned a lot since then and I usually don't get physically tired from playing. After I played the Bach last night I was kind of drained emotionally and mentally, but I could've played it five more times. When I'm moving, I try to move in a way that is like how I use my body when I'm not playing.

A.A.   *Right. How do you feel about body movement, such as in the torso? Is that something you try to work on with a student?*

L.L.   Well, I try and work on the upper body. I think that people have to be well seated. They have to have good posture. They have to feel, like the Alexander method talks about, like they are playing with a long spine. You don't have to be on the front of the chair. You have to be somewhere where your feet will really be supported. Your feet should be on the ground and your spine should be going straight up all the way to the top of your head, and you don't want your neck sticking out like a pigeon. Tuck your chin in and try and do that way and leave it alone. Don't shake it around a lot. Then, hang your shoulders from the spine and hang your arms from the shoulders, and apply all of that from the back side of you into the instrument.

A.A.   *When you do longer bows, do you believe in starting a motion from the torso or your arm?*

L.L.   I would say you've got to figure out where the motion is coming from. It depends which string you're playing on. You see, if you play on the D string, let's say, the motion of your bow arm is going pretty much from side to side. If you play a down bow on the C string down bow, the motion of your arm is like you're pushing the elbow behind you.

We're dealing with arcs. The bridge is shaped like an arc, and the strings are in an arc disposition. Your arm is attached to the shoulder. You put it out, it makes a circular motion. Different parts of the motion come from different places, but if you do it just from the forearm it's going to be very tight. The big motions come from the arm and ultimately back to the shoulder and the upper back.

A.A.   *Do you use the torso to start the bow's motion? Sometimes I feel it's like throwing a Frisbee. That same kind of motion to get the momentum started. Sometimes it helps me to get my torso ahead of my arm.*

L.L.   I don't care about those things. I find that sometimes if you hold the bow on a string and move the cello back and forth, the moment of truth is where the hair touches the string. I did it with a very fine player this year, and it made a big difference because she was kind of floating with the sound. I said, "Okay. What I want you to do is while your bow is going this way, I want the cello to go that way," and she began to feel the relationship with the string.

A.A.   *Do you make students play or perform by memory and how important is that?*

L.L.   I have a mixed answer about that. My late wife, a great violinist from Japan, Masuko Ushioda, seemed to me like she could play any piece by memory once she looked at it. She just absorbed those details very, very quickly, and I've never been very good at that. In my life now, it's very rare for me to play without music. When I grew up, I did it a lot, and I would say there are a lot of nerves on stage. I'm kind of forgiving about that.

What I've learned to do when I play from a page of music is to remind myself that it's just a visual reminder of what I'm supposed to be doing. My mind and ear are focused on what it is supposed to sound like. If, when you play music, you're staring at it like you're following a road map, then I think it's very limiting. I will make people memorize pieces, and a lot of them have much more ease at it than I do, but I don't enforce it. It's not a very high priority.

A.A.   *Do you tell your students approximately how many hours they should be practicing?*

L.L.   Never. I'm very much motivated by the work I'm trying to get accomplished when I'm practicing than how many hours I'm doing it. If I find my students haven't been working, which is evidenced to me by the product that they bring to the lesson, I say, "Let's figure out what's the best way for you to get this work done." I never say, "You have to do four hours or six hours a day." I will often say to them, "What time of the day do you practice? When are you fresh?"

A long time ago Andrés Díaz was my student. He used to come to the conservatory at 6:00 in the morning and practice every morning for two or three hours. Everybody knew he was a really good cellist, and so the whole Cello Department was beginning to come in early. A lot of people say, "Well, I've got all my other work done," and they start to practice at 9:30 or 10:00 at night. It's just nothing; they don't have the emotional or physical energy left to do it.

A.A.   *Do you have any principles in selecting fingerings or bowings for that matter?*

L.L.   Well Piatigorsky was not a big scale person.

A.A.   *I've read that.*

L.L.   He said that you should find the scales in the music you play. Your fingerings and your bowings should match to what the music needs. If you do enough music, you will have covered all of those different options. I think the single fingering I dislike the most is going from, on the A string, first finger E in the fourth position to fourth finger D in the first position. You're going such a great distance for the result. Sometimes you're better off staying in a position. Anner Bylsma is a very good friend of mine. He says you should stay in one position.

In Beethoven, for instance, I will offer fingerings that resemble how a piano would sound, but without the glissandos. Sometimes I go across a string on a different finger.

For example, going from C-sharp to F-sharp, I would change fingers instead of just going down and across.

For bowings, I'm very big on trying to get people to look at original source material. That doesn't always mean so-called urtext editions, which I think are sometimes very faulty. When I grew up, everybody was playing international editions done by Leonard Rose, and I was his student for a while during college years. It was the least expensive thing to buy. International editions were also based upon how to get around the copyright laws. They would always put a few wrong notes in and say, "Well, it was a different piece, a different rendition."

If you take the Schumann Concerto and you look at an orchestra score, it has what the composer wrote because it doesn't have fingerings and bowings. In one place near the beginning, there is no slur the first time, but the second time there are five notes and a slur. Why did he do that? The bowings are your job. It's just like the cook in the kitchen has to determine how much salt to put in the food. You eat it, you don't want to measure it. It just has to taste good.

In the Fourth Suite Prelude, in the little cadenza after the low C-sharp, there is this wavy line in the Anna Magdalena manuscript. Does that mean it's all in one bow? I can't put it all in one bow, but can you make it sound like that? There is the same marking in the lute version of the fifth suite (the only extant source in Bach's handwriting). There's no bow, so clearly it is an expressive marking. It means it's cadenza-like.

A.A.   How have people changed their approach to Bach over the last 30 or so years, and how has that affected your playing or teaching of it?

L.L.   I love Anner Bylsma, and I'm very interested in that Baroque approach. I find that I did not grow up with that approach, and so what I do is kind of a hybrid of it. You'll hear it in my playing. I don't belong to the Baroque police, and I don't believe in the people who say, "Don't look at Anna Magdalena because it's such a mess. You won't learn anything there." I've studied it very carefully.

Anner Bylsma hasn't played the cello for at least 12 years because he has a muscular ailment, so he has no strength in his hands. He's become almost doctrinaire on the subject and says that Anna Magdalena's bowings are exactly what you should play with all their variety. You could look at his book called *Bach the Fencing Master*. Anner is a very dear friend of mine. It was very painful for me when I made my recording and sent it to him saying, "I can't do all of that." He wrote back and said, "I never was trying to tell other people exactly how they should play." What I do is really a hybrid, as it always will be. I'm informed, but I also think the people who are Baroque specialists have learned a lot. But there's an awful lot they have not been able to learn. I think that the human voice and your personal feelings have to be central to what it is you're saying.

A.A.   What is your philosophy on teaching pieces or playing pieces like the Grützmacher Boccherini in B-flat, the Fitzenhagen Rococo, or the Chopin Polonaise?

L.L.   Well, of course, part of my very early career was playing the Grützmacher Boccherini. I'm a little bit more forgiving about it now, as long as you think about it as an expression of a certain moment in music when that was the thing to do. A wonderful example is Fritz Kreisler's transcription of the Paganini Concerto in one movement. He makes it sound like Paganini was a Viennese composer. Kreisler was such a great artist that it's really interesting to know about that. Should everybody do it? No, of course not. Should people play the Boccherini these days? Only if they talk about it as that.

A.A.   *The Fitzenhagen Rococo, what about that?*

L.L.   That's all I've ever played. I think either is fine. I recently played the Schubert E-flat Trio, and it's the one piece that he actually heard in his last year of life. A lot of people said in one of those house concerts, "Oh, Franz. It's too long. You have to cut the last movement." He made some cuts and he sent a letter to the editor saying, "Please, when you publish it, remove these sections." But, the original manuscript still exists. That was the first time in my life I played it. It's so fantastic. Why would one throw it away? If somebody wants to make the cuts, they should make the cuts. We wouldn't have any other writings of Franz Kafka if his friend Max Brod hadn't disavowed what Kafka said when he said, "Destroy all my manuscripts." He didn't and there we go.

A.A.   *Good thing.*

L.L.   I don't know any composer who doesn't change something after the manuscript after they hear it. If you just go to the manuscript, which is very valuable, you don't have the whole story. Like Piatigorsky said, "You shouldn't try to be more Catholic than the Pope."

The Future

A.A.   *I'm wondering about your thoughts on the next generation of cellists and the number of jobs, especially with orchestras. All the technology and the internet, do you think that's a bad thing for classical music?*

L.L.   Orchestras will modify their activities gradually to incorporate current realities. But I imagine that the pool will not grow much, so seats will stay very competitive. This means that cellists entering the workforce will need to be nimble and creative in finding places for themselves.

A.A.   *Have you seen the level of cello playing change over the years? And are there enough jobs for young cellists leaving school?*

L.L.   The general level of proficiency of cello playing has risen continuously over the last many decades. Probably the same on many other instruments as well. One report I heard is that Richard Strauss was surprised at how accurately cellists could play his orchestra parts, he didn't expect it. I also heard Gingold say something like that. But, along with that, composers keep upping the ante with new demands. When Schuppanzigh complained to Beethoven about the difficulty in the late quartets, Beethoven supposedly answered, "What do I care about your miserable fiddle?"

A.A.   *How much do you help a student find success out of school, and do you think that is part of your job?*

L.L.   If I am asked to recommend someone for a job I am always eager to do it. The most important way I can help current students is to make their playing as good as possible and to teach them to be open to what comes their way. I am a big enemy of their waiting for the "ideal" job to come in their direction. If they are good "searchers" they are usually good "finders."

A.A.   *I'm curious what your thoughts are on new music in the orchestra setting. Do you think it's working?*

L.L.   Depends who the composer is. There are less than 1% of the composers whom we still revere. It has to be given a chance to be heard.

A.A.   *There's a certain population that enjoys the new music but is there enough of an audience?*

L.L.   I don't think you'll find a general audience going to hear an evening of contemporary music. I run a series at the conservatory called First Monday, which probably existed when you were there.

A.A.   *I think so. Yes.*

L.L.   It started in 1985. It's in its 32nd year. I very often will, in the middle part of the program, introduce something that I think people are not expecting, newer music or different kinds of music, and people like that as long as they have something safe surrounding it to hang on to. People are curious, but they're afraid. A lot of people say, "Oh, I don't understand anything about music so I can't enjoy it." I think that's more often than not the fault of the performers or the organizations for not approaching the audience. I don't think you need to pander to an audience, but I think you have to lead them.

Close to the Heart

A.A.   *If you hadn't been a musician, what would you love to have done with your life?*

L.L.   I can't imagine not having been a musician. I started out trying to be a mathematician. I wouldn't have continued down that road. I think I came to an end of that road. This is something I would never do, but I love cooking. I would never want to run or work in a restaurant, because I think that's a really terrible job. But, anything dealing with that I would love. I think it's no different from music. Food and music, it's all the same stuff.

A.A.   *Those are two of the best things in life, I think. What are a couple of the most memorable concert experiences you've ever had that come to mind?*

L.L.   Well, when Piatigorsky was about 70 years old, the Israel Philharmonic came and he played *Schelomo* in Carnegie Hall. It was just astonishing. It was like a young great artist was playing. It was just so enrapturing. I was at his last concert, which was the *Don Quixote* in Philadelphia. He was a month and a half away from dying, and he couldn't breathe right. It was so painful to hear that same person play. He shouldn't have been on stage. Those are two concert experiences that are memorable for me. I'll leave it at that.

A.A.   *What are you most proud of that you've done in your career with music?*

L.L.   I was president of the New England Conservatory for 15 years. The thing I'm most proud of during that period of time is the restoration of Jordan Hall. It was built in 1903 and we did the restoration in 1995. People don't associate me specifically with having done that, but I supervised rescuing one of the greatest acoustical spaces in the world. I'm very proud of that.

I'm proud of how many of my students have found their ways in all parts of the world. It isn't just the exalted ones like Narek, Sharon Robinson, or Andrés Díaz. Carter Brey was my student at Peabody. I can go on and on. There are a lot of people who are teaching and playing in orchestras or string quartets. I'm very proud of that, and that's my professional career. In my life, I'm very happy about my family.

A.A.   *Is there anything you still want to do on your bucket list before—?*

L.L.   Before I pop off?

A.A.   *Before you pop off.*

L.L.   Yeah, I'd like to learn how to play in tune. I've been playing the cello for a long, long time, and I still can't play in tune. I am still trying. That's sincere. I really work at that every day when I practice. I've done an awful lot of things in my life that I'm very happy about, and I'm grateful for that.

12

Raphael Wallfisch

Raphael Wallfisch is one of the most celebrated cellists performing on the international stage. He was born in London into a family of distinguished musicians, his mother the cellist Anita Lasker-Wallfisch and his father the pianist Peter Wallfisch.

At an early age, Raphael was greatly inspired by hearing Zara Nelsova play, and, guided by a succession of fine teachers including Amaryllis Fleming, Amadeo Baldovino and Derek Simpson, it became apparent that the cello was to be his life's work. While studying with the great Russian cellist Gregor Piatigorsky in California, he was chosen to perform chamber music with Jascha Heifetz in the informal recitals that Piatigorsky held at his home.

At the age of twenty-four he won the Gaspar Cassadó International Cello Competition in Florence. Since then he has enjoyed a world-wide career playing with such orchestras as the London Symphony, London Philharmonic, Philharmonia, BBC Symphony, English Chamber Orchestra, Hallé, City of Birmingham Symphony, Leipzig Gewandhaus, Berlin Symphony, Westdeutscher Rundfunk, Los Angeles Philharmonic, Indianapolis Symphony, Warsaw Philharmonic, Czech Philharmonic and many others.

He is regularly invited to play at major festivals such as the BBC Proms, Edinburgh, Aldeburgh, Spoleto, Prades, Oslo and Schleswig Holstein. He is also frequently invited to be a jury member of international competitions such as the Rostropovich

International Competition in Paris, the Schoenfeld in China and the Enescu in Romania.

Teaching is one of Raphael's passions. He is in demand as a teacher all over the world and holds the position of professor of cello in Switzerland at the Zürich Hochschule der Kunst.

Raphael has recorded nearly every major work for his instrument. His extensive discography on EMI, Chandos, Black Box, ASV, Naxos and Nimbus explores both the mainstream concerto repertoire and countless lesser-known works by Dohnanyi, Respighi, Barber, Hindemith and Martinu, as well as Richard Strauss, Dvořák, Kabalevsky and Khachaturian. He has recorded a wide range of British cello concertos, including works by MacMillan, Finzi, Delius, Bax, Bliss, Britten, Moeran and Kenneth Leighton. For the Chandos Walton Edition he was privileged to record the composer's Cello Concerto, originally written for his master, Piatigorsky.

Britain's leading composers have worked closely with Raphael, many having written works especially for him. These include Sir Peter Maxwell Davies, Kenneth Leighton, James MacMillan, John Metcalf, Paul Patterson, Robert Simpson, Robert Saxton, Roger Smalley, Giles Swayne, John Tavener and Adrian Williams.

Alongside his solo career, Raphael has a long-standing and distinguished duo with pianist John York. With a rich history of many international recital tours and numerous recordings, the duo celebrated its 35th anniversary in 2017 and look forward to future collaboration in 2018. Raphael also greatly enjoys touring with his very successful piano trio—Trio Shaham Erez Wallfisch—which he and his colleagues Hagai Shaham (violin) and Arnon Erez (piano) founded in 2009. Four recordings have been released so far, each receiving the highest critical acclaim.

The Past

A.A.   Where did you grow up, and when was your first experience with the cello?

R.W.   I was born and raised in the UK. My first experience with the cello was actually prenatal because my mother was working until the day before she went into labor. I had my ear against the back of the cello growing in the womb.

A.A.   So you had a head start on all these pieces.

R.W.   Although, when choosing an instrument, my parents actually suggested that I start with the violin. I certainly didn't show any interest in the violin, so that didn't stay. Then I tried the piano and that also didn't stay. Since my parents were both very busy professional musicians, they didn't really have any time to push me in any particular direction. Then, the cello was just there, so I decided to try the cello. I started when I was 8 but didn't become really interested in it until around the age of 12 or 13.

A.A.   *Was there a pivotal moment that got you hooked on cello?*

R.W.   I always had very good teachers. Even if I wasn't particularly interested as a child, whatever I was learning was correct and gave me a good start, so I think that was very important. I was really just captivated by the cello, but I wasn't really sure if I really wanted to do cello because I was even more captivated in theater at the time. I used to spend my vacation time doing youth theater things instead of doing youth orchestra things.

My mother used to work at the Maida Vale Studios in London, which is the home of the BBC Symphony Orchestra. One day, she just happened to see that they were rehearsing that morning for a concert later that evening, the Brahms Double Concerto with Ida Haendel and Zara Nelsova with Sir Adrian Boult conducting.

She just had this flash of inspiration that I needed to be there to hear it and she took me along that evening. The amazing impact of the Brahms Double at close hand and those two ladies playing, especially Zara Nelsova's sound, stayed with me and changed my life. So the next day, I decided that all I wanted to do was to spend my days playing the cello and try to make that sound. And that's exactly what I did.

A.A   *Did you ever get to tell Zara Nelsova?*

R.W.   Yes, I did. She thought it was very funny.

A.A.   *And when you play that piece do you still think of her? Because I know earlier you said you got to be close.*

R.W.   Yes, I always think of her for many reasons, but I've always found her performances really top notch.

A.A.   *So, we talked about when you knew you wanted to do this for the rest of your life, but let's talk about your early path in music. Who were the biggest influences for you as a young cellist?*

R.W.   I had several teachers right at the beginning, probably because of my mediocre interest. They were colleagues of my mother, and they probably thought that they couldn't help much. But I became really interested around 13 or 14, and my teacher was Olga Hegedus. It's funny because in Hungarian, Hegedus means violin. Cello is "gordonka" in Hungarian.

Anyway, she was co-principal of the English Chamber Orchestra cello and was a lovely, lovely lady. As a teacher, she was very gentle and very encouraging. I enjoyed her lessons very much. I was beginning to have a little success on the cello back then, winning a few scholarships already, and I began to see that maybe I wasn't so bad at cello.

My parents caught on that I was really becoming totally obsessed with it. My father was a pianist, and was playing some concerts with Amaryllis Fleming at that time. Amaryllis was one of the main British soloists at the time. This was just at the beginning of the Jacqueline du Pré era when most other cellists were then finally pushed aside. I mean, to be a cellist of 45 years old when Jacqueline du Pré turned up was bad news, you know, because there was no hope. She was, that was it.

A.A.   *I can imagine.*

R.W.   Amaryllis was a very busy soloist and didn't teach very much, but my father was doing some recitals with her and she agreed to take me on. That was very lucky because she was extremely strict with me. It was Sevcik, Feuillard, scales, and arpeggios you know, which coincided with my new passion really for it. So it all worked out. I was happy to learn a Popper study a week from memory even while I was a full-time student in high school.

So even for a short time, she was a great teacher. Those intense couple of years brought me to the age of 16, where I had the opportunity to leave high school. Most of my friends went on to do "A Levels" which is the next step before University, from age 16 to 18. But, the headmaster at my school was not going to allow any concession for practice time, meaning I would have to do a full curriculum, all sports and everything.

Fleming suggested that I should use the gap of time between June and September of break that I had to study with her friend Amedeo Baldovino in Italy. Baldovino was the cellist of the Trio de Trieste, which is one of the greatest ensembles ever.

So, I learned Italian and went off on my own to Italy at 16 years of age. It was great, and it was all to the imagination of my teacher, Amaryllis to see that this would be a really important thing for me. Baldovino was actually the first male teacher I ever had; they'd all been ladies up to that point.

My goodness, he knocked me into shape. Just for a few months, I was an apprentice to him, I lived in his house and worked with him nearly every day. He and Piatigorsky were probably the two most important teachers. The others were all great, but those two really stood out. I continued my relationship with him the following summer, and although it was a relatively short time, it was very intense, very important. Then I went to The Royal Academy of Music for three years.

A.A.   *Who did you study with at the Royal Academy of Music?*

R.W.   With Derek Simpson, who was in a quartet and also a wonderful and practical teacher. His teacher, who was also his father-in-law for a short time, was Douglas Cameron. Douglas Cameron had taught generations of really fine cellists in England. His cello is in that box. It's just this adventure, because that cello is a Montagnana and belonged to Douglas Cameron. When he acquired it, probably before the war, he had it all that time and then he sold it to another of his students, Keith Harvey, who had it for many years.

When Keith sold that cello, it went to an amateur cellist in Germany. By that time, the value and cost both increased so much, professionals could no longer afford to buy it. It was up to rich amateurs. That amateur died not too long ago, and the family sold it to another collector in Britain who lent it to me. I know that cello well.

A.A.   *Then you went to Piatigorsky?*

R.W.   After the academy, I went to Piatigorsky.

A.A.   *How did you feel about your playing then and what did you feel like you still needed to learn right before you went to Piatigorsky?*

R.W.   Well, I knew I needed lots of things since I had a very good education and was 20 by then. Technically, I was in a good position to go and have help with in the sort of highest artistic way. I already knew that Piatigorsky was not going to be like Navarra who would say, "Well, you must put the little finger exactly in this and that and that."

Navarra had a very specific style of teaching, very much in the French tradition and was very dogmatic. Piatigorsky's style was the complete opposite of that style. It was an artistic experience.

A.A. *Is that what you felt like you needed?*

R.W. I'm not sure. I didn't know what I really needed, I just knew that this was a good thing to do, and I trusted the advice I'd been given. People told me that if I wanted an amazing experience, go there. It seemed like a very exotic thing to do, because going to Europe to study from England was not too expensive, but going to Los Angeles was going to be. My family normally wouldn't have been able to afford that, but there were many bursaries and scholarships available, which I applied for and I competed for. They ended up covering enough money for the airfare and the fee for one year at USC.

I was lucky enough to stay free of charge with people, friends of friends, as a guest in the house. I think I drove them mad with the noise, but they were great. After the year, Piatigorsky told me that I had to stay another year, and said not to worry about anything. I didn't have to worry. I don't know what he did, but there was no fee to be paid.

A.A. *After those two years, what were some of the things you learned?*

R.W. Well everything. I was so full and inundated with experiences and influences from Piatigorsky specifically. He just opened up possibilities of my expressive playing. He taught in very broad brush strokes and taught me how to approach music. The fine business of how you do it, actually, that's up to you. You've got to see where the goal is and listen, open your eyes, and open your ears.

I think that's what makes that kind of teaching long lasting. Because if you tell them the recipe, then that's the end of it. Instead, you tell them they have to find their own way and not give them any fingers or bowings. It was style really; a style of approach, which is difficult if you are not technically sound.

I think that's why the people who played the most in the class were the people he knew could take what he was doing. Everybody else could observe and take in what they can, but he liked to work in that way with people. I mean there are just so many examples of ways he would show you, because he wouldn't always demonstrate it exactly. Sometimes he would demonstrate, and he would also tell a lot of stories and parables.

A.A. *Were lessons generally in front of other students?*

R.W. Always, unless it was at his house when he invited you over for special sessions. Otherwise, it was always a performance—which is good so you were always nervous, always a state of adrenaline.

A.A. *You could always watch him teach other people as well?*

R.W. Absolutely. You wouldn't wander around, you'd stay in the room.

A.A. *What a great way of learning other repertoire.*

R.W. That's right, because there were many things that I didn't play to him, which of course I regret, but then I realized other students had played it already. Certain pieces, he would ask for again and again so you'd think that you were done with that piece, but you were not at all done with it. He wanted to see how it's going, developing or if you hadn't touched it for two months.

A.A. *You had to be ready for anything?*

R. W. Yes. You realized that you can't just sit, it was never safe. We often had visitors in the class from outside, and they would come in and listen. A lot of people would turn up and he would always ask either of us to play something, especially for them.

A.A. *Would you say he was nurturing as a teacher?*

R. W. He was very nurturing yes, because he took us all individually for what we were. I was known as the "Eager Beaver" because I was and still am very eager, that's my nature. I was almost always quantity over quality, because I just wanted to learn stuff. It was a joke at the time, which I didn't quite understand. I remember someone told me, "You'd be better off if you keep bringing the standard stuff, don't bother with all that obscure stuff."

But Piatigorsky liked the obscure stuff. I remember I learned the Dallapiccola *Ciacccona, Intermezzo e Adagio* for cello which he didn't know, but he loved it, and he used to ask me often to play it to people. I remember distinctly that he called me one day one afternoon I was practicing at my place. He said, "I've got some ideas, come over," and he'd been thinking about the piece without playing it. He said, "Try this," and it was amazing.

A.A. *Did you enjoy practicing?*

R. W. Yes, I loved practicing. I mean I just enjoy it. It is such a gift to enjoy practicing because for me it's never been a chore. It's a chore of course occasionally if you have to practice a piece you don't like, that is a chore. It's something I miss if I'm not doing very much.

A.A. *Even when you were a teenager, you didn't need to be pushed to practice?*

R. W. No, because my father, if he wasn't concertizing, was in his studio practice. If my mother wasn't working, she'd occasionally practice at home. So strangely enough, it was normal for me to hear somebody practicing in the household.

My mom has told me that when I was working away at home, my father would come out of his studio, he'd hear me and go back in, and vice versa. His, "Are you okay?" was like a pacemaker.

A.A. *Did your mom ever come in while you were practicing?*

R. W. There were times where she would yell through the door.

A.A. *Your F is sharp.*

R. W. Exactly, which never goes down very well with kids. With our own, I was terrible. It took a long time for Simon, who's the cellist in the family, to actually come and say, "Dad, can you help me with this?" I wasn't his teacher, and if I did try to help him and give suggestions, he never thought it helped much.

The Present

A.A. *As a performer, what are some of your secrets to practicing well, and do you consider that an important part of your teaching?*

R. W. Well, I think if you practice well, it's an amazing thing, because it means you are constantly searching for a key through to whatever you are playing; a way to do it. There are so many levels of this because as a professional musician and doing the kind of playing that I do, there are so many pieces on the go. I consider it a bit like having a back burner and a front burner. There are things that I need to keep going slowly, knowing the date at which I have to play them, and other things that are right there in the front that I have to be ready for soon. Then the part at the back moves to the one at the front, and so on.

Teaching helps me with my practice as I'm teaching so many of the main pieces and repertoire all the time. I'm demonstrating all the time, so even if I'm not having to play them that month, they are in my fingers.

That's a good thing and the students are always a reflection of what you are thinking. You can change your idea time after time, and they are quite used to that.

A.A.   *What about teaching your students to practice, is that something you do?*

R.W.   Yes, I've tried to teach them how to use time well. Not to bash away at things endlessly, and to realize that sometimes a small amount regularly is more effective than the set goal of making yourself practice for X number of hours. In my own experience, I tried to explain the value of time in practicing. I love to practice in the morning when everything is going, and that's when I get all my ideas.

I usually learn things very quickly first thing in the morning, and change all the ideas that I've had late in the afternoon from the day before. I enjoy that process very much, and I'm always quite amused at the fact that whatever I thought was a brilliant idea in the evening was totally useless the next morning.

I like to try to be organized with practicing because I find that I have great plans which are rarely achieved. I often ask myself the question, "What do I want to achieve?" I ask my students that question too, asking what they want to get out of their lesson before we even start. I think that it's great if there's one thing that they can ask for and that I can answer. Whatever it is, if the goal is to play a passage without rushing, or playing it controlled, I try to be specific and ask, "What's next?"

A.A.   *I might try that; I love that idea of asking them before a lesson even starts.*

R.W.   Like when you go to the doctor, they ask, "Well, what can I do for you?" I think for teachers, it should be exactly the same thing because it might not be at all what you think.

The other day, a student came in, who's a difficult student. He's a challenge and he has big problems physically and the intonation is tricky. Anyway, he came in and said, "Well, I have something to tell you; I've decided to give up." He's a 26-year-old, so I said, "Okay, tell me about it?" We were going straight into another kind of lesson, and I ended up finding out that he doesn't want to give up playing the cello, but he no longer wants to pursue it as a profession. We had such an interesting lesson and the question was just, "Okay, what's new today?"

A.A.   *How do you deal with nerves or has it been an issue for you?*

R.W.   Well, it's never been a shattering issue for me, because I think my early enjoyment of being an actor helps, and Piatigorsky talked to me about that actually. He told me that it was a good thing that I wanted to be an actor, because I have experience of projecting. One of his big parable lessons was to the student who came in and played with zero expression.

Whenever he tried to get the student to play warmly or softly, nothing worked. Eventually he told him to put the cello down, and told him to just say "I love you" and then "I hate you." The guy asked, "That's all?" Piatigorsky said, "Yes, go away and practice." So the next week the student comes back claiming he'd been practicing and said, "I love you, I hate you."

The whole idea of this was if you can't say something with expression, how are you going to be able to play it? I could see what Piatigorsky connected between my passion for acting and my passion for cello and told me that I bypassed that problem because I'm a natural communicator. Realizing that connection helped me too. For instance, I've heard other musicians tell me that when I play, it's not about me, but rather I am merely the messenger of the composer. So what is there to be nervous about? It's not you, you've got this big thing to tell people, so that helps with nerves too.

Nerves are fears about yourself; that you are going to fail, you're going to mess it up, you are going to forget, all of those things. All are technically possible, but they can all be dealt with in the right way by balancing them out.

I think as far as the practical thing of actually, "Are you shaking?" Because some people have a bad tremor, and it's worse when the adrenaline hits. But there are ways around that too, and I learned from a violin teacher that in playing long notes, just play them with movements like slow waves.

Then, instead of thinking that you're shaking, you actually go with the flow. If you practice, you relax everything and you let go into the string. You are constantly listening to other people, watching other people, how they deal with it, and what it looks like, and how it sounds.

It's a sort of continual learning process, but I think the other main thing about nerves is preparation, because if you are very well prepared you are less nervous. If things aren't very well prepared, you are going to be nervous because there's a lot to be nervous about.

A.A.   *If you had to summarize it, what is your teaching philosophy?*

R.W.   I tend to think on the hoof, probably because my best teachers have always been very practical teachers, and deal with the problems. If I see a specific problem that I know I can help right away, I would rather deal with that problem right then so that the chain of events won't have a kink in it.

If somebody comes with a problem that is rather obvious, I'd talk about the problem first. So often in teaching, we have to backtrack a lot, otherwise you won't get anywhere until it gets sorted out. I tend to take things a bit like a plumber coming to an emergency.

A.A.   *How do you keep each student sounding like an individual? Do you insist on bowings and fingerings?*

R.W.   I don't insist, but if they ask, "Could you finger and bow this?" I tell them "Here are some ideas, here's some shortcuts, try this" or I say, "Here are two or three."

A.A.   *You don't say, "Here's mine, do this."*

R.W.   Sometimes, If I'm specifically asked for the fingerings, I'm not going to hold back and respond like Piatigorsky would. He hated giving students the fingerings, so he finally gave me a whole lot of fingerings. But the next lesson, I came back and played and he said, "This is terrible. Who gave you these fingerings?" I told him he did, and he responded with, "Did I tell you to use them"?

So, that's another lesson. Don't just take everything. If you buy someone's edition of something and you follow the fingerings and it doesn't sound very good, you don't have to use them. Use your brain.

A.A. *Do you make a point to try and let each student find their own voice, technique aside?*

R.W. I definitely think so. One of the best students I had was an extraordinarily gifted Canadian-Korean guy, Dong Kyu Am. He actually had been a pupil of my late sister-in-law, who was a wonderful teacher in Edmonton, Alberta. She said, "Well, DK would like to come and study with you," and I thought, "Oh, this is going to be tough," because he's a really prodigious talent, but a very huge personality. It will be interesting.

Some of his ideas were wackier and mad, but it was amazing. He went through phases of playing everything with all five fingers like Shafran. He devised fingerings in things that you'd never think of. So I figured that since he was really thinking and trying really hard, I didn't want to stop him from doing this.

About four years ago, he went in for the Prague Spring Cello Competition. He was a post grad in Switzerland and he went into it very well prepared and was terrific. DK was sailing through, round after round. They knew this guy was something special.

He got to the final four, playing with the orchestra. I was really concerned because he was playing Dvořák, and it was his own Dvořák, it was a very special version. I warned him and said, "Don't do that, because they are not going to appreciate it," but he did his thing anyway and came in second.

A.A. *Wow that's fantastic.*

R.W. He could have won that competition. He really should have won it because the girl who won it bored me a bit, a little too neat and tidy. But DK, he is an interesting guy. Eventually, he made a recording which is absolutely fabulous, one of the best performances I've ever heard of Rondo Capriccioso on any instrument. It is the most beautiful playing, and all I did was just let him do it. He was very respectful and always wanted to try everything that I was doing. I just told him, "Look DK, you do it better than me. Just do it like that."

A.A. *Sort of related to what you were just talking about, when you are selecting students, what is more important in a potential student-- their musicality or the way they might physically handle the instrument?*

R.W. Well, I think they both go together. I think personality is very hard work with the extremely introverted people. I mean there are obvious personalities that you take to. There's somebody open, bright and questioning; that's always a great thing. That's the ideal, but I've learned to have patience with people, to see how things develop. Very often, they change quite radically.

A.A. *How many hours a day do you think a student should be practicing?*

R.W. Well, I would say minimum four. Certainly, if you are doing twice the amount, the likelihood that it's excellent practice is less. If you can do four hours and really concentrate, and not necessarily consecutive hours, that would be a good thing. Just like any athlete, you have to do that much at least.

A.A. *How do you work on the intonation with students? What is your opinion on tuners?*

R.W. Oh no, I'm not a great believer in tuners. In fact, I feel that one shouldn't use those like wind players do, and I've seen a lot of string players doing that. I suppose there's a certain physics interest in that, but I think that tuning is much more to do with the relative open string, relative to the key, relative to other players, and relative to the piano. They are all different kinds of intonation, and it all has to do with the awareness of it all.

A.A.   *But if a student's playing flat all the time or something like that?*

R.W.   Oh my! Actually, working at intonation, I'm sure you agree is like building roads, it's terribly hard. A lot of kids don't tune the instrument well, not tuning to other notes, to fourths and fifths and thirds and don't hear the difference in minor third and major third. I'm a great believer in playing a lot of double stop scales, and a lot of scales generally. I'm always practicing scales, enjoying them and the benefit afterwards, feeling very focused.

A.A.   *What are some of the études or studies that you've generally used over the years, and have they changed over your teaching?*

R.W.   Well, like most people, I use the Popper Études and I always dabble in some Duport I love the Feuillard Daily Exercises because they are a copy of Sevcik, the bowing ones, so you don't need to plow through the entire book, which is like a death sentence. I think if anyone's going to buy a study book, the Feuillard is still one of the best because it's got fantastic left hand shifting exercises, all the scales are written out. It gives you all the bowings you could ever need.

A.A.   *Two, three and four string crossing exercises.*

R.W.   All different rhythms and then Piatigorsky gave us two exercises to do with crescendoing and détaché. Using your forearm like a violinist, starting very small to large, opening your arm. Once you know all of that, it's basically just like the Saint-Saëns pattern on either of the three strings. It can be slow or fast, but not accelerating. The point is to control the dynamic. That is really important that when you play crescendo, you aren't just pressing into the string, you are using more bow sometimes. Using a lot of bow per note was very important, and the other one is about replacing fingers. It is a very simple exercise, but you take a note and play the same note legato hardly noticing the change. You might do one, three, two, four, thumb, and you can choose any note.

The idea is the closeness of the fingers, and it is a practical exercise and you can learn it in a minute. I'm always looking around for stuff and I develop a lot of my own exercises from shifts or moments in repertoire, and then I play it in all keys.

When I warm up, one of my favorite things to do is play a melody right away with cold fingers, but I take it very slowly in high positions and come down chromatically. After my four minute routine, I feel ready to go.

A.A.   *Do you make students play by memory?*

R.W.   Well, I try to encourage it because I find it harder to learn from memory when you get older. When you are 18, 19, 20 it should be very good.

A.A.   *Do you have principles in selecting bowings and fingerings?*

R.W.   I use what I learnt from Baldovino. He had a small hand, and his style of playing was avoiding shifts, so he had a phenomenal thumb technique. He would find ways across the strings and play with the thumb. I learned Schumann and Haydn D major with him with those kind of fingerings. That gave me enough to be a basis to process different fingerings to other pieces if I need them. Using the thumb like a finger all the time is just gold. I hand a lot of fingerings that I got from him to my students, showing them how much easier it is with them. Something that I always look for is to shift with semitones so that the left hand positions are very solid. If I can find ways to use the best finger on the best note, then I work around that.

A.A.   *Do you ever use your fourth finger up in thumb position? That was a Tortelier thing.*

R. W.   Sometimes, but not as much as him. I have quite a short fourth finger, so it doesn't particularly lend itself. It's very interesting, I mean Rostropovich had an enormous fourth finger. He told me once that he was apparently in his mother's womb for 10 months and it grew longer.

A.A.   *How do you teach a clean staccato and how do you view the role of wrist and fingers?*

R. W.   Very, very important and what I'm fascinated in. Only a few days ago, I was teaching a very gifted young girl from Moscow who came to play for me, and she played with a typical Russian bow hold. It is fantastic for certain massive bow strokes, but if you try and play staccato like that, it won't work at all because you'll totally lock the wrist.

I suppose my influences from the beginning were very good and old fashioned. Basically, I get my students to sense the stick in the most sensitive part of their fingertips, where all the nerve endings are.

It's this kind of thing that you can do with a pencil, and never have to feel it unless you are doing some massively heavy stroke. I'd always tell them to pick up a pencil and you'll see how easy it is, and where your fingers should be. Then, when it comes to staccato, I said the bow is like a horse and you are the jockey. When you watch the jockeys, they are way up in the horse saddle, and all the front all the weight is off, allowing the horse to jump to do its thing and they are just guiding it. That's exactly what you do with your fingers you are guiding this amazing piece of wood, which loves to jump if it's allowed to go.

So when they hear that, it immediately helps because they suddenly feel the life inside the bow. They lighten their fingers and just guide the energy. Piatigorsky used to make us just dribble the bow along from high, just to see how long we could go and. I find that helpful for staccato and then coming along with those kinds of exercises. Then seeing if they are going to start the staccato from the string, or if they are going to drop the bow onto the string or do both. You can do one that starts from the string or off the string, different speeds different rhythms I mean different triplets of course, whatever they may be. I think the main thing is to realize how much the bow is going to do things on its own, and guide it.

A.A.   *Do you play with a bent thumb on your bow hand?*

R. W.   Well I have a short thumb, but there are times when it straightens out, but it's generally flexible. I know a lot of people with double joint or hyperextension, it's a very tricky thing isn't it? I find a lot of Asian students have that.

A.A.   *Double jointed.*

R. W.   Super double jointed. I'm kind of double jointed, but when you can't maintain that, it's almost impossible to help actually. It's terrible to try and play 5ths with a thumb that goes backwards.

A.A.   *What is your philosophy on teaching the Bach Suites, especially with the performance practices that have evolved over the last 30 years?*

R. W.   I've practiced Bach when my wife happened to be nearby and I heard her say "You must be kidding, you can't do that!" The result of all of that is that now when I play Bach, I play with a baroque bow that I carry around everywhere. I have a couple of them and it has taught me so much about everything really. Have you used one?

A.A.   Yes.

R. W.   So you know exactly what I'm talking about. I always give one to my students just to let them try, and they often go out and buy one or borrow one after. It makes such a difference in playing chords. It's all about the bass and the harmony. It adds up and illustrates the music, it really does.

   I think that's been extremely helpful in my practice, in the lightness and the speed of articulation as well. The baroque bow is more lively and is just more interesting. Of course, I look at the manuscripts and all but I get a little frustrated with the Anna Magdalena because it's very odd. Not just with the bowing problems, but also the sense that it was done in a hurry. There are one or two weird notes there, but if you really are going to be super religious and are going to do everything, you are going to play all the weird notes in it too. Some of them are not so weird, I mean there's some places in the Sixth Suite Prelude where there are notes that most people haven't played but are rather good, but you never know because it's not his handwriting.

A.A.   *There's been such a great awareness of the baroque style in the last 30 years or so. Is that a good thing in your eyes?*

R. W.   Absolutely, it is a great awareness, but I have to say it's not as great as one would hope. I was just listening to a competition where there were well taught violinists playing too. Well taught in the sense that Russians were usually teaching them, and they could play the violin. But, whenever they played Bach there was just no idea. Even the way that they played chords was aggressive, which kind of works in modern world music, but just doesn't sound good. I found that weird because it'd be easy for them to go listen to someone else play it, and then make up their own mind, because the old style of playing was okay but we know more about it now.

   Honestly, I don't think enough teachers are open minded enough to take that on and encourage it. I know that in some international competitions if somebody came along and played the baroque bow, they might get disqualified. Which is weird isn't it? I mean it brought the music we are going to see.

A.A.   *I'm curious how you feel about pieces like the Grützmacher/Boccherini B-flat Concerto, or the Fitzenhagen version of the Rococo Variations, or the Feuermann version of the Chopin Polonaise—how do you feel about these? Do you prefer the original versions?*

R. W.   I feel strongly about them and especially the Rococo because I made a modern edition of the original version.

A.A.   *I read that recently in an interview that you did.*

R. W.   Well, it took a long time to actually do it. It was one day in the Piatigorsky class and he came in and told us that we all had to play the original version. I didn't know what he was talking about. He had just gotten hold of this Russian edition from Moscow and he re-printed the original. We were interested and some of us learnt it; I took it as far as I could, because I saw there was actually a lot of interest. Not many people know the original Rococo because everyone plays the Fitzenhagen version. One of my first professional engagements I played the original, I had handwritten parts that I copied out myself, and lugged them around in a suitcase.

It took around 20 odd years of persuading, trying to get it printed. I recorded it for Chandos back in 1983, but no one could really find the music for it. Chandos had bought our score, but there was no cello and piano reduction, so students couldn't just go to the shop and buy the Rococo in the original version. Finally Peters did it, and they've done it pretty well, although I put in some fingerings that I regret.

A.A. *Well, people change them anyway.*

R.W. Yes they'll do that, and they also printed the orchestra parts, so I felt job done.

A.A. *Do you feel that it's wrong that people are learning this?*

R.W. Not wrong, no Rococo is not wrong. We know historically because of the letters, that he did not like what Fitzenhagen did to his piece. With Grützmacher, I think it was just that Boccherini was this obscure composer at that time and he'd written something nice. Do whatever you like with it, and now we know these pieces are very beautiful in their original state. But, I grew up with Casals' recording of Boccherini B-flat, and it's fantastic. I used to listen to that endlessly, I remember even going to the recording sessions of Jacqueline du Pré in Barenboim, where my mom was playing in the orchestra. I went and heard all of that Boccherini B-flat. She did it in such style, it was just crazy, I wouldn't play the piece.

A.A. *If students come in and they want to learn Rococo, do you insist that they learn the original version?*

R.W. If you are going to learn it with me, we are going to do the original. If they come along and play the other one, I'll show them the original. I'll say, "Look, you've got a whole other variation you can play."

With the Chopin Polonaise, I've always had trouble with that piece because I like it and I love the sound when people play it well in the crazy version. It's obviously a piano passage, it's so much a piano, it's just daft. I've learnt it in the sort of Leonard Rose version, the only one I've ever performed is original. I decided that I didn't need to play that piece at all. Even though I could play the original piece, I ended up avoiding it, really.

The Future

A.A. *In today's day and age, the audiences for classical music seems to be shrinking. Where do you see the future of classical music going in the next generation?*

R.W. The weird thing is that maybe these audiences are shrinking, but the number of people learning instruments is growing like a tidal tsunami. Of course you ask, "Well who is going to listen?" My answer to that is that not all of these people are going to be professional musicians. Presumably, they will be interested in music and they'll go and listen to some. I honestly think that pessimism is the thing that is hurting the industry. For instance, some musicians are demanding far too much money which is crippling the market. You mentioned certain people coming to Iowa earlier. There is a star system, but if those stars come to small places for nothing or don't charge a crazy amount, then the money could be spread out more. We wouldn't feel as much pressure in the industry and there wouldn't be this bizarre fascination with youth and inexperience. That is happening much more than it used to. Back when I was 14, the cellists and artists that came were all in their 40s or 50s. Today, nobody is interested in 40s and 50s because they are interested in the conductors and musicians in their 20s. It's gone mad, and is now just a panic to sell seats because people find it so exciting that person is just out of wearing diapers.

It's unfortunate we have to live through this period, because it's very hard for people like me, or those close to my age, to compete with totally inexperienced people. And how are we supposed to attract the people that aren't coming to the concerts? What can we do?

There are many people who feel that Yo-Yo Ma is cool, not only because he was very good when he was very young, but also because of the way that he's being portrayed. Other fabulous cellists are on the same track. It's a certain thing that creates the star when people will come and pay. There's something not quite right there and it ought to be fixed in the near future.

A.A.   *How do you think technology has affected what we do?*

R.W.   I think it's affected a lot. I love the process of recording, and I'm very grateful that it is possible to improve something beyond all imagination with editing and so on. I'm probably the first to admit that it's not exactly how I played it. The majority of it is just how I played it, but there are definitely parts where I could never play it as accurately as it sounds. If you accepted it for that, then you also are in awe of the incredible standard of playing in the earlier days when people just played without any hope of edits.

A.A.   *What about things like the internet?*

R.W.   If it's used well, I think YouTube is an incredible archive and encyclopedia of knowledge. I think it's bad when it's used by far too many people of inferior mediocrity on posting themselves up on the same YouTube as the great people. I think a lot of young people compare themselves to other young people far too much. What they should do is only listen to dead people, the great dead people. Because then they realize that they are not in competition with these people, but these people are a thing to aspire to.

A.A.   *Have you seen the level of cello playing change over the years?*

R.W.   Most definitely getting better and better, absolutely.

A.A.   *Are there enough jobs for cellos in today's market for these great cellists coming out of school?*

R.W.   No certainly not. There's more and more competition, and it's very interesting how so many of the solo cellist positions are not being filled because they are being constantly on trial because the choices are enormous.

A.A.   *Pick one of them.*

R.W.   Just pick one of them. It happens everywhere, so they don't want to give a contract or anything. The general standard of execution of being able to play the instrument is pretty remarkable across the board. It is also remarkable because obviously you can see and hear a lot of these people also on YouTube. There are people that I've heard, Brinton Smith—He is one of the most amazing cellists I've heard in recent years. But, nobody's heard of him, what's going on there? Maybe you know of him, but I'm very curious.

A.A. *I definitely know of him, he's in Texas.*

R.W. Maybe it's just his choice, because he has chops to beat most people. I mean that is extraordinary cello playing. Why does he never play? Why has he not recorded more stuff? Why is he not known? I'm sure he's exceptional, but I think he's not alone.

A.A. *How much do you help a student find success out of school, and do you consider that part of your job as a teacher?*

R.W. Yes, that's the hard part. I think a real teacher should help and is the person who is the real sort of a guru, the one you go to all the time. Having said that, Piatigorsky didn't really do any of that. He wouldn't introduce you to managers or tell you to go and audition here or there, that wasn't in his remit. But I do help my students. A lot of them are doing auditions for orchestra, or going in for competitions, or I'm writing them letters of recommendation, or doing whatever I possibly can. But there's certainly also that strange thing that once they are out there, you are suddenly in competition with them. It's in a weird way because it's not direct competition, but there is enough time in between that there is just enough space for it.

Close to the Heart

A.A. *If you hadn't been a musician, what would you have loved to have done with your life?*

R.W. One of the glib answers I've given is a Delicatessen owner, but not really. It's hard to answer, because I've always been interested in theater, but I think that I could've been a good counselor. I'm interested in people.

A.A. *It's half the job of being a cello teacher.*

R.W. Yes! My sister is a psychoanalyst, but I'm not quite sure if I could deal with crazy people all day. It's a difficult job. I often look at people who do normal jobs and finish it at a normal hour, and then go enjoy something else. In a way, anything like that might be quite enjoyable.

A.A. *Could you name a couple of your most memorable concert experiences that you've been involved with? Not necessarily because there was a big success with the audience.*

R.W. Well it's usually certain pieces, because I'm a great champion of the underdog piece. I told you earlier, one of my favorite pieces is the Finzi. I made a short film about that which is on YouTube. When I played that at the Proms in London, that was a very big audience that was a live broadcast all over the world. I wasn't nervous about that at all, but I was very uncomfortable because it was unbelievably hot in there. It was a very hot night, nobody wore jackets, it was wet, and people had fans. This piece is colossally difficult, it's really one of the most technically demanding pieces in the literature.

I just wished it hadn't been quite so wet playing it, but I was just so excited doing it, because I loved this piece, and here I was playing it to all of these people then. What more could you wish for if you believe in something like that. I was sitting there and that's it and I played the shit out of it and it was great. I was very proud of that. That was something, and there have been several situations like that where I'm playing something I totally believe in, but have to persuade other people to believe in it. For me, other things like playing the Schubert Quintet with the Amadeus twice was one of those amazing, music making at its best. It was exciting, spontaneous, and fantastic; edge of your seat.

They were a really big quartet really big and Norbert Brainin, the leader was one of the most inspired musicians. You never knew what the power phrase was going to be, so it's as free as possible and I just love that kind of thing. That would be high on the list. As far as just playing, certainly sitting down with one of the students and playing in a house concert with Heifetz and Piatigorsky playing Dvořák Sextet. I don't remember much about the music, but it was just a feeling of wow. Nearly every time I sit down and play on stage, I feel that this is where I'm happy.

A.A. *Did you ever have to deal with a period of doubt about becoming a musician and how did you get through that?*

R.W. Subsequently I've had many periods of doubt, and that's not because of the music at all. It's because of the absolute hell of the profession frankly. Sometimes you feel you are just up against an impossible situation. What's got me out of that is not only my family and my fantastic friends, but actually music itself. The fact that I love to get up in the morning and play. Even if nobody wants to hear it, I'm happy.

A.A. *I still feel like just tuning the cello brings me a lot of happiness.*

R.W. That is an amazing thing! We are so blessed with that.

A.A. *What are you most proud of in your career?*

R.W. In my career, I think my recordings. I mean recordings are something that will last a long time, and it is also a moment of time of certain things that I've done many, many years ago. I hear myself and I try to stay as good as that moment in time, but I am very proud of what I've done with British music particularly. I keep on doing it, and when I occasionally look back, I think about how far I've come and that I've got to keep going.

That box I gave you, is actually only about a third much less than even a quarter of just concertos I've recorded of British composers. I've done all of the regular ones and many of the irregular ones and new ones and things that have just been composed, and it just keeps going on and on.

In the end, I think about what I have done and what has been useful. And that is really useful to think about because I've helped the composers, I've opened repertoire up for other people in the future, and given people pleasure at the same time, that's good.

A.A. *Is there anything you still want to do before you are all done? Like a bucket list of cello, or anything else for that matter.*

R.W. What I'd really love to do is play all the Beethoven string quartets, and not for money or anything. I'm actually starting this summer on it, and the trick is to get people who are like minded. Not just on an amateur level, but you don't want to be a string quartet. Just to work on a couple of pieces for a short time, and just play them to have that experience. I know I'm not going to play in a symphony orchestra, because there's a whole lot of repertoire that I've never played. But, I've played a lot of chamber music, piano trios, quintets and sextets, and I think that the string quartet repertoire is still the best music ever written for our instrument.

When I hear a great quartet, a young quartet, I just think they are so lucky but I know how hard it is, it's hard as hell. But if I can do it for fun like a good amateur, that would certainly be a wish list I'm starting this summer. We'll be doing a Schubert quartet, Beethoven, and the Brahms Clarinet Quintet. Just rehearsing for four or five days, that will be great and it will be fun to play it in a tiny place if I can do that regularly.

A.A. *Get through all the Beethoven Quartets.*

R.W. And then the Schubert Quartets and so on, but Beethoven would be a good start. Have you done it?

A.A. *I haven't played all of them. I've played the majority of them and I think I've gotten to read all of them but I've never gotten to perform all of them.*

R.W. That's already more than I have.

A.A. *I doubt I'll get to perform all of them either.*

R.W. Actually the performing side is not at all what I'm interested in. I just want to sit and rehearse them. I want to just learn them and get some feeling with this amazing stuff. As much music as possible in that sense.

A.A. *There are still some great pieces left that you haven't gotten to experience.*

R.W. Many. I would also like to play Dvořák much more, because it doesn't come up very often. I play a lot of all these things because I'm always playing new ones. I brought along the Castelnuovo-Tedesco, which I just recorded last week, and you can see that this is how it works, this is my dirty laundry, my typical working part. Every single note has been thought, rethought, and then some, there is no note which hasn't had any thought put into it. Not just for reading purposes, it's just because I don't allow anything not to be tried. That's why if a student asks to see my part, I warn them that they might not understand any of it. That is hours and hours of work, and even some of it right at the very last second.

A.A. *You might even make a few more changes.*

R.W. Well I just left a lot as I went along, because of course then you record it and you hear it straight away, and change right away, because there is no way that's going to work.

A.A. *Well wonderful, thank you for all your thoughts.*

R.W. It's been a great pleasure.

13

Helga Winold

Helga Winold worked at Indiana University Jacobs School of Music from 1969, where she taught private cello, cello literature, cello pedagogy and chamber music until becoming Professor Emeritus in 2008. That same year, she was honored at Indiana University with the President's Award for Distinguished Teaching. Now living in Tampa, Florida, she still maintains a busy schedule of private teaching, master classes, solo and chamber music recitals, and is currently affiliated with both the University of South Florida and the University of Tampa. Many of her students have gone on to important performing positions in professional orchestras such as the Los Angeles Philharmonic and the Philadelphia Orchestra. Other former students have gone on to significant teaching positions such as the University of Pennsylvania and the Freiburg Hochschule für Musik.

As a performer, Helga Winold has played solo and chamber music recitals in many of the leading music centers of the United States, Europe, and Asia, including appearances as soloist with the Munich Philharmonic, presentations of the complete Beethoven cycle of works for cello and piano in Vienna and other cities, and performances of contemporary works for cello. As a researcher and writer, Helga Winold has made important contributions in several areas, including research on movement in string playing with Professor Esther Thelen under a grant from the National Institute for Health. She has published numerous articles in the American String Teacher, Strad

Magazine *and other publications, and given master classes, guest lectures, and seminars at universities in the United States and abroad. She is the author of* Cellocity, *a highly successful method book for beginning cellists, which is available for free on her website winoldsmusic.com.*

The Past

Anthony Arnone	*Let's start from the beginning. Where did you grow up and how did you first become exposed to the cello?*
Helga Winold	I grew up in Munich, Germany, and I was lucky that my father, an engineer, helped to develop the Munich public transit system right after the war. With that position came free tickets to the opera. I didn't see a movie until years later, but my sister and I were at the opera practically every week as kids. We knew every opera singer, and we could sing many of the arias, so, it was clear to me that I wanted to be an opera singer. Here was no question in my mind. The only problem was that I didn't have a good singing voice.

In school, I was always rather tall, and in third or fourth grade I had a music teacher who said, "You're tall. You should play the cello." So, I went home and said, "I'm going to play the cello." My parents said, "You're not even practicing piano enough. This is ridiculous, why would you want to play the cello too?" So even though I was taking piano lessons, I secretly practiced the cello at school on borrowed instruments, and finally at Christmas, I had the courage to play some wonderful pieces on the cello for my parents. I suppose I played well, because my parents said, "All right, you can play the cello." That's how it all started.

A.A.	*Wow, just because you were tall and someone suggested it?*
H.W.	Yes, and I guess it seemed like the cello's sound was the closest to the voices I heard and admired so much at the opera. My parents let me take group lessons at school, and eventually private lessons. A year or two later, I was playing in the church chamber orchestra. I was very lucky because there was a small, beautiful, Baroque chapel very close to where we lived. The *Generalintendant* (or Director) of the Munich Opera would come to the chapel to conduct our chamber orchestra there. He knew all the star singers of the Munich Opera, and so they came along to sing. We played all of the beautiful Mozart and Haydn masses. I especially remember playing the *Seven Last Words* of Haydn. I had never seen four flats before and was desperately trying to figure out where they might be on the cello. There was just one other cellist, who was a good cello student who knew what he was doing, and I sat next to him, watching where he was playing the notes.

A.A.   *Did you like to practice when you were younger? Was that something you enjoyed, or did you have to be pushed to go practice?*

H.W.   No, I wasn't pushed at all and I truly enjoyed it. In Germany it's not common for there to be practice rooms at school, or even at the Conservatories, so I didn't have a place other than my house to go and practice, so I would often go to the basement and practice there.

Practicing was often an escape of sorts. At home there were constant disruptions and also constant demands on what you ought to be doing. My mother didn't drive, so I was her chauffeur. My father loved to take very long walks when he was home, which was rare, usually only on weekends. So practicing the cello gave me a good excuse. "I'm sorry, but I really have to practice." I not only enjoyed it, but it was my way to go off and be by myself. I really do enjoy practicing, you know? It's very weird, but I do. I like it. Even today, I feel like I haven't brushed my teeth if I haven't practiced.

A.A.   *Did you continue to play the piano as well?*

H.W.   Yes, although most of my piano playing has consisted of sight-reading songs (German Lieder) I still play simple piano parts to accompany my students when the opportunity arises, but I am by no means a pianist. My mother had a beautiful alto voice, and so from a very young age I played along when she was singing Brahms, Schubert, and Wolff songs. I wasn't really serious about cello until I was about 11 or 12. At that point, we had just moved from Munich to Cologne because my father got another job. I went to the Musik Hochschule Köln and tried to find a new teacher.

I remember one thing clearly from that time, I think I was around 12 years old then. One of the students was playing a recital at the Hochschule, and I went just out of curiosity. She played the Brahms E-Minor Sonata, and I sat there absolutely mesmerized. I thought, "I'd do anything to play this piece." I know that was my first glimpse into what I really wanted to do, and I kind of stayed with that. I even remember the name of the woman, Betty Hindrichs. I don't know if she ever became a professional cellist, but she was just so wonderful.

A.A.   *Did you ever get to tell her that story?*

H.W.   No, by the time I was old enough to think about telling her, she was long gone from the Hochschule. As a young girl, I took lessons from a number of students from the Hochschule, some better than others, and when I turned 15, the lone professor of cello at the Hochschule accepted me as his student. His name was Adolf Steiner, and he was a student of Hugo Becker, who was a student of Grützmacher and that whole line of cello pedagogues. Steiner was a very conscientious teacher. He was also very hard on his students. There wasn't a lesson where we didn't have to play our four-octave scales, arpeggios, thirds, octaves and sixths. There was no way around that. I remember the first couple of lessons, on the street car home I tried to recall everything he'd said so he wouldn't have to repeat it at the next lesson. At first, I had to work on Franchomme and Piatti, then Grützmacher Études, etc. and you never could show up with music. He said, "If you show up with music, you might as well go home." Everything had to be memorized.

A.A.   *Even the études?*

H.W.   Yes! We were all horrified, especially with the Grützmacher Études, Volume 2. But it was actually good training. It was kind of frustrating to memorize études, but on the other hand, it taught me a lot. I remember the first couple months it would take me maybe a week to learn half a page securely by memory. Then it would be a page per week, then it would be two pages. Because you develop a routine in anything you do a lot, learning to memorize is something that has helped me throughout my whole career.

Steiner was a good teacher. He went very methodically through the repertoire, as we all do. The only thing was that his teaching method was from the Becker school, so what he did with the left hand was very rigid. Open position was a bit square and closed position was slanted, and each finger had to be over the note exactly. A shift could never be heard, so you had to go as fast as you could, which made for a very jerky and kind of stiff left hand. You weren't allowed to leave the position until you arrived at the next one, so it was a sudden motion. As for the right hand, he taught the bow Becker style as well. You stretched the fingers for the lower strings and bent them when you changed to a higher string. So it was very finger-oriented. I continued to study with Steiner when I became a full-time university student at the Hochschule.

When I was around 20 years old, I went to study with André Navarra for two summers in Sienna, which was absolutely fabulous. Sienna is a beautiful city and Navarra was incredible. He could play like an angel and could do anything. Lying down, standing up, sitting with one leg out, really in any position. His bow arm was probably the best I've ever seen in the whole world. It was just unbelievable. Not that his left hand was bad either. We all just worked and sweated and came back and listened to what he said and got really inspired by him.

A.A.   *Were the lessons in a masterclass setting?*

H.W.   Yes, masterclass, the whole time.

A.A.   *Was everything usually memorized as well?*

H.W.   Yes, most of us had everything memorized. At that point we were playing mostly concertos and Bach, mostly standard repertoire.

After university, I performed quite a bit, but the problem was that given my prior training, I didn't play horribly, but I had to basically warm up for at least an hour before I was loose enough to really be able to perform. I was so drilled in the regimented German style—Adolf Steiner style—that I just had to practice a lot until my fingers were tired enough to let loose and I could finally really perform.

When I was about 24 or so, I heard Janos Starker play. Naturally, I knew many of his recordings and thought, "How can he play so easily and I work so hard? I really need to go and find out what I can do to make life a little easier." I mean, you can't just practice five, six hours a day and never trust that it is going to be alright. Starker was in Düsseldorf and gave a masterclass, so my quartet went and played for him. He had just started teaching at Indiana University, so he didn't have that many students yet. When I said I'd really like to come and study with him, he said, "Sure, come on over," and offered me an assistantship.

A.A.   *Before that, were you going to school in Germany?*

H.W.   No. I can't remember exactly when I completed the *Reifeprüfung cum Laude* (graduating with honors), and then the *Privatmusiklehrer Prüfung* (teaching degree) but I was already performing quite a bit. I was playing and making money at the Cologne radio station, which was wonderful. First of all, it was in my hometown. Secondly, Stockhausen was there, as well as many other contemporary composers, right in Cologne. They were writing, not just the big pieces that became famous, but also radio plays, or *Hörspiel Musik*. This was basically before TV became popular, when radio was what people listened to. That was how you got your culture, listening to the radio. There were marvelous radio plays written by first rate authors to make money, and also to become well known. Locals would go to their theater in town, but the whole country would listen live to the radio. The radio was the major way of conveying art.

A.A.   *This must have been a great time for new music in Germany.*

H.W.   Exactly. In the late 50s and early 60s, new music was very much appreciated and promoted by the radio station in Cologne. The symphony orchestra was excellent, and I went to observe many of their rehearsals and concerts. It was a wonderful time for me to be living and working in Cologne. I was part of a group of musicians who would be called to go to the radio station to record music for the radio plays. We would be in the radio recording studio with the composers to record their compositions, but sometimes, the play's author would be there as well, and might say something like "I need two more minutes here." The composer would write something, we would record it, and it was fantastic. It was really an exciting time to be there. This is why, when I went over to study with Starker at Indiana in 1963, I was convinced it would only be for one year, and then I would go back to my life in Germany.

A.A.   *Boy, were you wrong.*

H.W.   Yes, was I wrong. Yes, Here I am—still in America. And ironically, the first man I met at Indiana University became my husband. Did you know that?

A.A.   *No. Tell me the whole story.*

H.W.   Well, Dr. Charles Allen Winold was my academic counselor. He was the official counselor for foreign students. Then they were called "special students." Not that every student isn't special, but that was the thing back then. He wore many hats at that time. He taught theory; usually three courses with enormous amounts of students in them. He also was Director of Undergraduate Studies and Associate Dean to Dean Bain. In addition, he managed the orchestra program and had four orchestras to keep in order.

   Allen had studied German in the United States and was a Germanophile. When I sat in his office he spoke only German, and very strange German at that, which I found odd. He had memorized Egmont to impress me with Goethe Deutsch, which he did. On the other hand, I was furious, because I was only going to be in the States for one year, and I was not going to speak a word of German because I wanted to practice my English.

   So that's how we started. After a year, we got married and then I brought him with me to meet my family in Germany over the Christmas holiday, and that was that. Back in Bloomington that January, Starker said, "Great. You just go on and get a degree," and so as I had two German degrees, I thought, "Well what else is there?" There was the doctorate. So, for better or worse, I completed the first doctorate to be granted in cello at Indiana University. It was a very strange and funny thing, because everybody thought I should know more than the faculty, since most of them didn't have a doctorate, and I actually didn't know more. I didn't know half of what they knew, that was perfectly clear.

A.A.   *Was the DMA program fairly new at IU?*

H.W.   Yes it was. I think there were a few violinists at the time. Then it started growing.

     For me, the program naturally involved a lot of studying while still trying to get my cello practice in, but Allen and I decided we wanted to have children. My daughter was born three weeks before my orals, and my son was born a couple weeks before my finals. It made for exciting times with little sleep. After finishing the DMA, I jobbed around. I played with the Louisville Orchestra, under Jorge Mester at the time, which was fun. He was great to play with, because he was a string player himself.

A.A.   *Was that a full-time job?*

H.W.   No, I didn't do it full time. I just played the regular season concerts.

A.A.   *At that point, when you were done with your degree, were you thinking about a career in orchestra or teaching?*

H.W.   I was teaching all along. I actually taught my first student when I was 14. I remember her very well. She was the daughter of a wonderful publisher in Germany. The girl I taught was named Bettina, and my daughter is called Bettina, I think because of her. She was a great student. Then I had a whole bunch of students in Cologne and Düren, which is not too far away. I always loved teaching. It was obvious; I really, really enjoyed teaching.

A.A.   *So after you finished your degree at Indiana University, you were in Bloomington playing in an orchestra but still teaching as well?*

H.W.   Yes, but that was natural as Starker's assistant. I was both Starker's student and did a lot of his teaching as his assistant while I was getting my doctorate, because he was gone so much. This was at the high point of his career, so basically, he would be gone for three weeks, appear, be there for two or three days, and be gone again. He could be rather hard on students, especially back then. He would tell you everything you were doing wrong, rightfully so, but he wouldn't remember what he said at the last lesson, because three weeks would pass in between.

     In the meantime, you would work your tail off fixing what he had told you to do, and then he would never mention it again. He wanted his students to be good, but was less interested in how they became good. He showed students how he played, and then expected them to play better after he'd shown them what he did. It seemed he was asking "I showed you, so why aren't you that good?"

     He was very nice to me in that he really trusted me with his students. He would always say, "Oh, wow, so-and-so has really made progress. You must have given him the right message." Something of that sort, sometimes tongue in cheek, but he meant it. I had taught so much more and longer than he had. He had never taught much before he came to IU. He had taught a few students, but not really consistently.

A.A.   *As a cellist, what did you feel like you got most from him?*

H.W.   Musically, I think his way of looking at rhythm and timing. Timing, I think, was one of his real strengths. It would be very logical. He would tell you simply if you are going to make an accelerando, you would start from one note to a beat. Then you would go to a couple of notes per beat, and finally to a whole unit per beat. By just feeling the larger beats, you would make a very organic accelerando, and the opposite, naturally, by feeling smaller units.

I remember lessons where he would sit and say, "Now watch that this finger is vibrating and that the bow is straight, and that you prepare the string change, and look at the phrase." Then he would come and move my head and say, "Now your head is supposed to go up and then down as you breathe." While I was trying to follow all of these instructions, I would ask myself "why should I also move my head?", especially since anyone who has seen him play anything knows he's famous for not moving a lot, right? But if you watch his gesture, there is always this tiny preparatory movement of his head that puts the timing of the note exactly where it should be. Anticipation was one of his big concepts. Part of that was this head motion, and part of it was getting your arms ready to do whatever was needed.

Starker also talked a lot about timing in musical phrases and shifts. He talked so much about preparing shifts that I think we all spent more time preparing than shifting. Students tend to exaggerate what they are told. He would say, "Feel the preparation of the shift," and he would go and throw our elbow in a circle who knows how far back and then land wherever. It was the same over-preparation with the right arm. Naturally we saw him doing very small motions; but since he told us to do it, clearly, we all exaggerated.

Starker didn't have much patience. You were supposed to bring in new pieces all the time. He was not happy hearing something he had heard before. It was not very easy to do, and I think we would have learned more if he could have followed up on some of the things we played only once. He played until he fell in his grave. Even when he was in his late 80s, just before he died, he was still playing. He couldn't really sit anymore, so he was propped up with pillows on a horrible chair, and the cello was kind of just hanging there slanted. There was not much sound but he played in tune. I always swore there were magnets on his fingerboard and in his fingertips, because he just never played out of tune. I don't know anyone else that can do that, it's just absolutely miraculous.

He tried to tell us about the incredible flexibility of his left hand, and would demonstrate it by playing any number of difficult passages with ease, and we were all green with envy about it. I wrote about that in one of my first published articles, entitled "Musical Aspects of Motion Analysis," which explains that with one impulse you can play many notes, which we all do, right? How else could we play quickly? Otherwise, it would be like pronouncing one letter at a time to say a word. I think finding the right movement impulse for the left hand, in fact for both hands, is the key, and that is very hard to explain unless you have felt it.

A.A.   *It sounds like what you are saying is to have the hand feel the rhythm that's there, too.*

H.W. Sometimes the movement impulse coincides with the rhythm, other times it does not. When it doesn't coincide, then we say that the passage does not play easily. Starker's teaching of the bow arm helped me to gain a more flexible forearm. Maybe I played smoother because of lots of Popper, which I hadn't done before. Steiner didn't do

Popper, he was a Grützmacher man. With Starker it was Popper, which naturally helped me a lot.

In the summers, while I was a doctoral student, Bernard Greenhouse came to IU as the cellist of the Beaux Arts Trio at that time. We were privileged to get lessons from Starker and Greenhouse, and could go into either of their studios, which was incredible. Paul Katz came for the summers at IU at that time, and Paul and I would sit at this restaurant we called "The Chatterbox" where we would discuss our lessons. Paul would ask, "What do you think about Starker insisting 'pronate, pronate, pronate'?" and I would reply "What does Greenhouse mean? He keeps saying, 'pull back, pull back, pull back.' What does that mean, Paul?" and he'd respond, "You know, I'm really uncomfortable with this pronating business," etc., and we would debate for hours. It didn't look to us like either of them used pronation or pulling back that much, but they kept telling us these things.

Starker was into pronation. You pronated. And if you didn't do it, you were damned. So naturally, we as students had all our elbows up high and then pressed down from there, which makes a wonderful squeezed sound. Just lovely. And so I still didn't know what Greenhouse meant with the pull back. I had no idea. So I kept trying to figure out what to do.

You know, Greenhouse wasn't very tall. He certainly wasn't a strong guy. I mean not a muscle man, but he no doubt produced the most beautiful sound in this world and I tried to figure out how he did it. I couldn't understand what he meant by "pull back" until one day he played Schubert's E-flat Trio with the Beaux Arts Trio. He was sitting up there playing the opening solo of the slow movement exquisitely, yet he looked like he was doing nothing. Suddenly I thought, "I think I've got it. I think I've got it! He's just using the gravity of his arm toward his body. Ah!" Just like I was inspired to play the cello seriously the moment I heard the Brahms' E-minor as a child, I had that same physical feeling of suddenly knowing something: how to produce much better sound much more easily. Navarra used gravity and momentum, but he didn't explain it, or maybe I just didn't 'get it'. I got that from Greenhouse. Finally I understood what "pull back" meant and I have always, ever since, felt so much better. I'm forever grateful to Greenhouse for that.

Between gravity and momentum, I was able to find my sound. Now I can't even avoid it. By "pull back" I'm not talking about pulling my shoulder back, I'm just dropping my arm against my body at the various angles that we create with the bow. It's such a simple concept, but you see most cellists "pronate and then squeeze" and then there's not enough sound at the tip.

A.A.   *And were there a lot of the students during the year who stayed there in the summer?*

H.W.   Bloomington was very nice in the summer because it became a smaller university. There were only two orchestras, instead of the normal six that we had during the year. It shrank, because many people either didn't want to spend the money or didn't want to be burned out by too much teaching and too many courses. We had the festival orchestra, where faculty and students played together, and we always did one opera in the summer. It was a much more intimate group which was very nice.

A.A.   *What was the class of cellists like at that time? Were there many international students? Women?*

H.W.   A lot of both. The class was often more than half female and there were always international students. When I came there, Tsuyoshi Tsutsumi was a student. We have been good friends ever since, I just love Tsuyoshi. He was just wonderful as a student, and then much later he came back to join the faculty after he taught in London and the University of Illinois. What an artist and a great human being! When he came to Bloomington, those were the glorious years when he and Starker were there, and I was lucky enough to be there too. That was really incredible, because we all worked together. We were constantly sending students back and forth between the three of us***. I might have had a student working on a piece and, when I felt they were ready, I would recommend that they play the piece for either Tsuyoshi or Starker, depending on what I thought they needed. Likewise, if a student had a problem with a piece, we could send that student to the other studios so they could get help with their problem. That was an incredible time.

A.A.   *So how did that work? Your transition from being there as a student, and obviously being Starker's assistant and knowing people there, to then being on the faculty at IU. Was that your first academic job as well?*

H.W.   Let me think. I think there were only one or two years in between when I just taught privately and jobbed, mostly in Louisville, until I joined the faculty.

A.A.   *Were you playing with orchestras?*

H.W.   Yes, but then Starker asked me to teach at IU. I was adjunct at first. They needed somebody right after I was finished with the degree, while my kids were very little. Gary Hoffman taught at IU at the time. Gary was 23, and was building a successful career. He would call me from wherever he was and ask me to teach his class. When Gary left, I was appointed to one of those famous "part-time jobs." I was "part time" for 17 years, although I was really doing full time work, including a class of at least 14–16 cellists, as well as teaching cello pedagogy, cello literature, and chamber music, not to mention recitals, hearings, committee assignments, etc.

A.A.   *Why didn't they give you a full-time job?*

H.W.   Well, I think Dean Bain thought it was so much easier to keep paying me as "part time" faculty. He could save a lot of money and didn't have to pay benefits. It didn't hurt that they knew that I was pretty much tied to Bloomington because of my husband Allen's position at IU. I actually got promoted while I was in this "part-time job" to Assistant and then Associate Professor, but never full-time. It wasn't until 1986 when two administrators, Professor Anya Royce and Dr. Vernon Kliewer said, "This is just not right. You have a class like everybody else." They mentored me through the process of getting the full-time and tenured appointment.

A.A.   *Did you ever look into teaching at another school? And did you ever get offers?*

H.W.   No, that was my mistake. I didn't dream of leaving Bloomington. I loved Bloomington. I loved my husband, so I just didn't consider ever leaving. Also, Allen was diagnosed with cancer in the late 80s, right around the time that I became a full-time faculty member. We had a strong support network of friends and an excellent medical team, neither of which we wanted to leave behind.

A.A. *And he was working there as well, so I would've made it a little bit harder, I suppose.*

H.W. Yes. There were times when Allen had other offers, and maybe we should have tested the waters, but we really did like Bloomington and IU and it all worked out. I did get the full-time job, and had it until I retired in 2008.

A.A. *Although you didn't really retire, because you're still working all the time. But, 2008, from Indiana.*

H.W. Yes, in 2012 Scott Kluksdahl called me and asked me to teach while he was on sabbatical.

A.A. *Did you know him already?*

H.W. Yes. Did you want to know how we met?

A.A. *Sure, yes.*

H.W. It's a great story. About 20 years ago or so, a freshmen, one of many, many freshman I have taught over my career, showed up for his lesson. Usually at this first lesson you ask about what they've played, how they warm up, and what they do for technique. This student said, "Well, I usually play scales, first slowly and then faster." So I asked him to demonstrate this, and yes, he could play them well. Then I asked if he'd done some octave work and he said, "Sure." And after he played the octaves well, I asked "Have you also played thirds?" to which he responded "Oh yes, thumb position and lower positions." Wow! I mean, there was nothing he hadn't done and also he played his concerto beautifully.

    Finally I asked "Who's your teacher?" I didn't always ask that, because sometimes it's impolite. He said it was Scott Kluksdahl. I had heard of Scott's name, but didn't know him personally. So, out of the blue, something I've only done once in my life, I asked "Do you have his phone number? I really would like to call him." The student gave me Scott's number and I called him that same night and said, "You won't believe that I have never done this, but I really want to tell you that you have taught this kid so beautifully. I have to tell you, I'm thrilled to have him as a student and you must be just a fantastic teacher." Scott was very nice on the other end, what else could he do anyway? That was the beginning of what is now a very dear friendship with Scott, who is an excellent cellist and teacher.

    Many years later, in 2012, when Scott asked if I would teach his class for his sabbatical, I said to Allen "Wow! Can you imagine a winter semester in Florida? Not a bad idea." We rented a little house up the river in Seminole Heights, which is really nice, and fell in love with Tampa. So much so, that we bought a condo and moved there. The Dean at the University of South Florida (USF) then offered me the adjunct teaching position that I still have now. I also teach at the University of Tampa, which is a private university in a very picturesque setting here in Tampa. Somewhat ironically, I'm back to "part time" positions again.

A.A. *So you thought you were just going to come for a sabbatical replacement, but ended up never leaving?*

H.W. Yes! We actually moved out of Bloomington after 50-some years, which wasn't easy.

The Present

A.A. *I'm excited to learn more about how you think body movement affects cello playing. Not so much fingers and hands, but maybe more torso movement. How important is this in your teaching?*

H.W. I find this very important, because I don't think there's any movement in our arms that doesn't have repercussions in every other part of our body. Every part, even in the toes. If I swing my arm, my body takes up the slack, unless I stiffen it. Nobody in the world would swing a rope and not move their body, right?

A.A. *Right. Counter motion?*

H.W. Yes, the body always needs to react to stay in equilibrium. That means you have to change the balance of the torso as your arms move. If I need power here in the upper half of the bow, for instance, if I wanted to make a crescendo or speed up to the tip, my body will go to the left and my weight will go from the right side to the left as my arm moves to the right.

A.A. *I agree. And of course, we have to play sitting down. I've often asked students what's the first muscle used when you're about to play the first note of Dvořák Concerto and they're thinking arms or shoulders. But I think of my foot.*

H.W. Exactly!

A.A. *Is this something that you spend a lot of time on with students?*

H.W. I try, and it's not easy. The head movement frees the breathing and you should lift the head before starting a sound in the tempo of the music. This is also important before up beats, which often occur after dots or held-over notes, so that the head's downward motion coincides with the down beat. You know how many people gurgle when they're playing? Good cellists, including Casals, breathe like that because everything is tight around the shoulder and neck. I think methods like the Alexander Technique are helpful, but it's about understanding the complete picture.

A.A. *I agree. I sometimes see people trying to sit up so high when they play, to the point where it doesn't help.*

H.W. It feels like they have a screw from the top of their head all the way through the chair.

A.A. *Yes. And I've caught myself. If I feel a little nervous, sometimes I feel like I sit up way too straight. I need to let myself be in the cello a little bit more. And I really sound much better all of a sudden!*

H.W. Exactly. This reminds me of a very interesting study I was part of some years ago with violinists, in Freiburg, at the Institute for Music and Medicine. The institute owned force plates that were normally used to measure weight shifts from one foot to the other when someone was standing on them. I wondered whether you could use them to measure the weight shift when sitting on them, so I just sat on one and moved from side to side and it worked! It worked the same with bottoms as it did with feet. It would be red when you sat on your left side, and then it would go orange to yellow, and then red on the right side as you shifted, it showed very clearly where your weight was centered.

I then experimented by having two violinists, each sitting on a force plate, playing side by side, looking at one music stand like they would in an orchestra. I measured their movement on the force plate, and also observed their bow arms at the same time.

What we found was that the violinist who was sitting quasi-concertmaster on the right, or outside, had a wonderful bow arm and used her bow beautifully the whole way. She could fluidly switch her weight from one side to the other, with no problem. However, the other violinist, sitting on the left, or inside, sat with her weight mostly on the right buttock and was totally restricted; she was squished. She never ever put her weight on her left side. She couldn't, because by shifting she wouldn't be able to see the music.

This made me realize that our students are forced to sit like that for hours in orchestra. For cellists, it's the same thing. We are either staring to the right or to the left for hours at a time. No wonder our neck and back are twisted and painful. That's why I always tell my students to switch seats every time they can.

A.A.   *That's really interesting, sometimes with students. I'll put the stand up high, just to get them to use their body differently.*

H.W.   Yes, exactly! Students should try all sorts of stand placements when they practice.

A.A.   *When you were picking students at auditions, what did you look for most in students? Was it more if they were physically gifted? Or was it more if they had something to say, but maybe they weren't as physically gifted?*

H.W.   It was a mixture of both. If a student really couldn't play, we probably didn't take them. Josef Gingold was such a wonderful, wonderful violin teacher, just a miracle. He taught 40 hours a week, from morning to night, when he was at IU. He was passionate about teaching and had a wonderful philosophy: he believed everybody deserves a good teacher. He always took at least three or four Music Education majors that weren't perhaps the greatest violinists, but they were fine musicians. He said, "These guys will have the capacity to do more good than many of my students, and I really want to spend my time working with them." That made for a very nice atmosphere. Also, my husband made sure that the Music Education students would have the same course numbers for lessons, so that no teacher could see from the class roster if students were Education or Performance majors.

Not all of the other teachers took Ed. students. In spite of Gingold, there were still violinists that said they wouldn't even look at one. I don't think Starker ever took an Ed. student. He would listen to them from time to time, but wouldn't take them in his class. I was always happy to do so because those are the students that will inspire young players and help educate future audiences for all of us.

A.A.   *Do you use specific études in your teaching? Has that changed over the years?*

H.W.   I am not an étude lover. Honest to goodness, the truth is I think études are something for lazy teachers. You don't learn to play octaves from Popper or Grützmacher or others and you don't learn to play sixths or thirds from études, but études really do test if you can master the techniques. They are also great as reading exercises, especially Popper, because they go into far-away keys, so you have to catch on fast.

A.A.   *So do you spend a lot of time working on pure technique?*

H.W.   Definitely, I practice simple motions, trill motions, shifting motions, octaves, thirds and sixths. I remind my students that we need all of these for our concerti, and we should also be able to play these passages in other keys. So I'm not an étude fan, but I use études when I have lazy students. I might say, "Bring me that étude next week" just so I know they have practiced.

A.A.   *Through all the years of your teaching, were you an active performer as well?*

H.W.   Yes, I've always played but I perform less these days as I have gotten older. Though I still play regularly. I love playing so much, especially performing chamber music.

A.A.   *Do you teach your students how to practice? And what are some of your secrets to practicing well? I guess those are two different questions, but is that something you spend a lot of time with your students?*

H.W.   Yes, for sure. That's one of the reasons why I don't think they should spend hours and hours on études. Part of how to practice would be to separate the hands to see where the problem is. Don't just play without thinking, but rather figuring out "How do I get there? How do I make it faster and easier? Do I have a clear musical goal and how can I translate that, both physically and mentally, into the appropriate movements?" This helps students with the exercise of deciding how to "chunk" musical letters together into words, phrases and find the bow movement to pull it all together.

A.A.   *Do you make students bring in things by memory, or perform by memory? Is that an important part of a student's development?*

H.W.   Yes. I mean, people don't memorize so easily anymore.

A.A.   *I know.*

H.W.   Do you find the same thing?

A.A.   *Yes. And I just don't know how hard to push sometimes. I think back to when I was in school, where we pretty much had to memorize everything; maybe not the first week or the second, but by the third or fourth week, you should have whatever it is memorized.*

H.W.   Yes. I usually say, don't memorize, just practice by memory. It's not memorizing.

We play a piece from beginning to end when it's a new piece and we need to learn it. Then we practice it in parts. The only issue is to not always start practicing from the first four or eight bars. I start, maybe the second week, practicing from the last eight bars, or from the development section. If you really work and concentrate on two or three lines at a time, by the time you're even halfway in tune, you know the piece by memory.

By the time something's in tune, and I really know what to do with each note, the printed page is not telling me anything new. After I've played a part of a piece roughly 30 or 40 times, what the heck does the page tell me? So I always say, just put your music away. Of course, you have to know what you want. I don't say put the music away before you know what you want to express, but once you have made your decision about fingerings, bowings, and rough phrasings it's not going to tell you that much, because you'll have gone through, part by part, when you practiced. However, it is very important to look carefully at the music and the score *after* you've memorized it, so you can check everything and look for different ideas for interpreting the piece at that point.

A.A.   *Do you find that some people play better by memory? I always feel like I play better when I play by memory.*

H.W.   I do too. I don't like to have the stand between me and the audience, although, I feel when I play sonatas that I should have a stand there because a sonata is a duo rather than a "solo cello" performance accompanied by a piano.

A.A.   *You don't have to look at it then?*

H.W.   No, I only have one line, which is easy to memorize, so I don't have to look at it. The pianists, on the other hand, have so many notes and such a vast repertoire of their own, that I feel it's impolite to ask them to memorize cello sonatas. So for politeness's sake, I will put a music stand there. I concentrate better and am also more aware of my own movement when I play from memory.

A.A.   *Do you have a teaching philosophy? And how has it evolved over the years?*
They're two separate questions in a way, but we can take them on one at a time if you like.

H.W.   As far as a teaching philosophy, my main goal of teaching is to figure out what a cellist would like to express, what would they like to say. It's not that I impose what I think they should do, but I try to find out what they really want. What sound is in the back of their mind, or maybe in the front of their mind, and try to help them to do what they really would like to do. Then I take into account their physical abilities: is there something in the bow arm that hinders them to get to where they want to be or is it because the left hand is giving them trouble as well? Then from there I try to help them to be successful, but hopefully coming at it from what is in their mind.

I was always interested in how the body works in relation to playing the cello. My whole life I have been studying the components that make string players translate music from their mind into appropriate movements, studying the interaction of mind and body.

At first I tried to get together with people in the Kinesiology department, who study the science of movement. Naturally they study sports, but I thought "Well, in a way, playing the cello is a sport." For my first experiment, I worked with a cello with a fingerboard made of metal, in order to measure finger pressure. That turned out to be a disaster because when we turned on the camera lights to film the experiment, the warmth of the lights completely messed up the calibrations of the metal fingerboard! They went absolutely wild! The kinesiologist I was working with also thought it was ridiculous to measure finger pressure because the measurements were so small compared to the things they were measuring. They were used to using force plates to measure impetus from an athlete prior to attempting a high jump or throwing a hammer. With these types of forces you can really see much larger differences than those caused by finger pressure on a cello fingerboard.

However, we did learn a few interesting things. For instance, at one point the calibration was working, and all we did was play one finger after the other on one string ... 1st-2nd-3rd-4th and again 1st-2nd-3rd-4th. I thought that it would be clear that 1st and 2nd fingers would use more pressure, and that there would be less and less pressure as the weaker 3rd and 4th fingers played. To test this, I and my students played 1st-2nd-3rd-4th fingers slowly at first, and then faster. When we saw the results, I thought "Oh, the calibration is way off," but it was consistent. The faster we played, the stronger the 3rd and 4th finger pressure measured. The impact of the 3rd and 4th fingers increased, because we started rolling the hand. So by doing this, there was more speed from further away as the weaker 3rd or 4th fingers hit the string, while the 1st and 2nd fingers stayed closer to the string, so in fact, the impact when playing faster was almost equal between all fingers.

It was through the kinesiologist, who wasn't exactly thrilled to be working on cello fingerings, that I met Esther Thelen, a developmental psychologist at Indiana University. Esther studied how babies learn to move and control their movement. She was fantastic to work with, she wrote books and articles, and she was internationally renowned, and the nicest person you can imagine. I went to her and said, "You know, I'm really interested in cello movement." And she said, "Oh, this is fantastic. See, I study the beginnings of control of movement—you study the highest control of movement. That's what we do, right?" and then she opened her lab to me and the cello studio.

She had a wonderful state of the art lab with all this fabulous equipment, and she had NIH grants. We could put little wires on every joint we wanted to study, each with tiny LEDs attached, and then measure milliseconds of movement. It was incredible, so we did all kinds of experiments. Many cellists took part in the experiments, even including Starker.

We tried to learn about both hands, but the left hand was very difficult, because you couldn't always see all of the fingers. Despite the fact that we had three cameras, fingers would get in the way and obscure the view. Because of this, we really didn't do a whole lot with the left hand, but we did a lot of studying the right arm. It was so much fun to be in the lab with other cellists, and we would do all kinds of experiments. My favorite article we wrote about these experiments was the one in *Strad Magazine*. The whole article was about spiccato, studying movement of all of the joints of the bow arm as people played faster and faster spiccato. Sadly, Esther died of cancer and I will miss her forever.

A.A. *It sounds like she was an amazing woman. I have found with some students that they haven't found their voice yet. Do you ever find students that you feel may have a sound that is fine but just haven't quite found their own voice yet?*

H.W. Absolutely. That's one of the hardest things. The more distinctly they want to make a sound, the easier it is to help them. If they don't have a clear idea, it's the hardest thing and you may just want them to imitate someone they like. But how much should they imitate and how much should they come up with their own sound? It depends on the student.

A.A. *Well, I'm going to ask you about recordings in a minute, but this is related to the question of how do you keep each student sounding like an individual. Do you give them bowings and fingerings from the start? Do you let them discover? What's that process like for you?*

H.W. That's a combination too. Obviously, you first have to give them fingerings and then hopefully they come up with some of their own later. Then we can discuss what's good about their fingering and then I might have suggestions that would make things easier.

A.A. *You mentioned imitation a few minutes ago. What is your feeling on the value of recordings, and do you think it's a good thing for a student to first start imitating or listening to recordings—good recordings hopefully?*

H.W. Yes. I don't like students to listen to recordings before they learn a piece because to me, that's like seeing the movie before you read the book. It's someone else's interpretation of the work, and that interpretation may not truly be one that speaks to their own 'reading' of it. I hope that they don't listen to recordings before they look at the piece, but I recognize that it's almost impossible nowadays, since it's so easy with YouTube.

Sometimes I do listen to recordings, though. If I have to learn a piece really quickly, especially a piece of chamber music or something that I haven't played, it makes it a lot easier to get started if there's a recording. But ideally, we should just come at something like a new landscape or a new language; first have your own discovery of it, even if it may be totally wrong. It's more valuable than just saying, "Oh, we're just going to do what everybody does in the recordings." It was great when we had to go to the record store.

A.A. Or even the library.

H.W. Yes, the library! I remember that as a kid, if a piece was on the radio, you sometimes got inspired. "Wow, that is something I'd like to see and hear." Being at the record store and having a nice person that would let you try every recording, because you couldn't afford to buy it, was great too. I do think you should look at the music and see what you come up with, and then after that, get your cello out.

A.A. *Sometimes I think there are certain performance traditions that get started with piece, possibly because people don't know exactly what is in the score. Are these "traditions" justified?*

H.W. I'll never forget Piatigorsky asking, "What's the hardest cello concerto we ever play?" Everybody said, "Haydn D" or "Prokofiev Symphony Concertante." He said "No—it's the Saint-Saëns Concerto." We all went "What?" and he said "I played it when I was nine. It was no problem. Then I played it when I was 12 with an orchestra and it was still no problem. Then I played it when I was 16 with Bruno Walter conducting. When we got to the opening, Bruno Walter said, 'What does it say in the opening, what dynamic?' I looked at the score and realized I had been playing *fortissimo* when it actually said *mezzo forte*." Then Piatigorsky continued to take us through more of the movement, he said "At the end of the first section, where I was used to taking all kinds of time, Walter said 'it is only *poco ritardando*, just in the last measure.'" In the end, that's why Piatigorsky said it's the hardest concerto, because he finally had to look at the music and not just imitate what everyone else was doing.

A.A. *That's so true. Zuill Bailey just came to Iowa recently and did a class on Saint-Saëns Concerto and was saying almost exactly what you were just saying. He said that he used to feel like the piece was all about him, and then he woke up and now it's actually about the music. It sounds like what Piatigorsky was saying as well.*

H.W. Exactly.

A.A. *What have you found is the hardest thing to teach your students?*

H.W. I really don't know. It depends what they have a problem with. Every student is so different.

A.A. *Do you talk with students about how much time to practice? Do you agree with the 10,000 hours philosophy that probably you and I have both gone through when we were younger? Do you talk about the hours needed? Obviously it's quality as well.*

H.W. Yes, I guess it takes a lot of hours to learn how to practice well. I try to get them started doing essential things and not wasting time, but then I think we all have to waste some time. It's impossible not to. I still waste time practicing. It's really hard to get to the essentials. You have to do some unessential things, to figure out what the essential thing is in that particular practice.

A.A.   *How has your teaching has evolved over the years, are there things now that you're glad you have learned?*

H.W.   I feel like I should apologize to students from 20 years ago, from 30 years ago.

A.A.   *Many others I have talked to have said the same thing about their own teaching.*

H.W.   Yes, hopefully I will never stop learning and finding new things.

A.A.   *Okay, we talked about this a little earlier, but do you have principles of selecting fingerings and bowings?*

H.W.   Right. Yes, I always quote Julius Klengel who said, "I take a new piece and then I noodle around and finally I find something that feels comfortable. That is what I take as my principal of fingerings." Cellists often say that you ought to shift on the half-step if possible. I don't know how that evolved, but I've heard it many times and it doesn't make any sense. The only thing that makes sense to me is something I learned from Tadeusz Wronsky. He was a wonderful violin teacher from Poland who taught at Indiana University for about ten years. He said basically to shift on the beat or on the sub beats, so they won't be as audible, and any shift on the last of four notes will sound sloppy. Shifts are less audible on accented notes.

A.A.   *Okay, what about vibrato? Do you have a favorite way of teaching vibrato?*

H.W.   That's a really difficult question. It's always lucky when you have a student who starts vibrating and it works. Then everybody says, "Oh, what a teacher!" She can teach me vibrato, but you did nothing. If it doesn't work, I think it's one of the hardest things to teach. I have tried everything possible. One of the ways I was taught, strictly in the Becker method, was to keep the hand quiet and just move the finger as fast as possible.

I was forbidden to do a vibrato trill. The vibrato trill was sloppy and horrible. It has taken me many years to allow myself to do it. I still feel sinful about it, but I think it's very helpful in loosening the fingers and warming up. For instance, when I vibrate, I feel movement in the shoulder joint and loose muscles in the upper arm. I have the feeling that my whole arm is really free and wiggly. All the muscles are loose, nothing is tense. I quite often use that as a way of teaching vibrato; start with the vibrato trill and then keep one finger vibrating as the other finger joints move.

I know a more common way to teach vibrato is by quickly moving the hand up and down the fingerboard, shifting from larger to smaller motions, and finally letting the hand just vibrate. The only way of teaching I am totally against is turning the wrist back and forth to get a really wobbly vibrato. When students come with that approach, the only way to get them on track is to keep them from touching the neck of the cello with the thumb.

My newest idea is to have both hands on the fingerboard and vibrate with both arms. That's my newest invention, and it quite often works. Since the right arm has never been asked to do vibrato, it's free. At least for some people, this has freed them up, and they no longer have tension in the shoulder or elbow joint. By trying it with both arms, they can feel how the left arm is so much more tense and can compare it to their right arm, and thereby discover a more relaxed motion for their left arm.

A.A.   *I need to try that out.*

H.W.   Yes, it's one of those elusive things to get right. It's very difficult, Gingold used to say, "I won't touch vibrato with a 10-foot pole."

A.A.   *Since we have a bow sitting right here, maybe we can talk about spiccato or sautillé. I've read a lot of different things about those bow strokes. Some people believe it's a stroke generally from the string and you're pushing maybe downward, some people believe in a circle or an oval—different directions. You're approaching the strings at different angles. What are your thoughts?*

H.W.   I don't do any of those. I have also read tons of method articles and most of them say, "If you play on the string and you go faster and faster, the bow will come off." Now, I have never seen it come off from being on the string. You can practice for 200 years, trying to make the bow come off, and have no luck. I believe that the bow actually likes to jump more than it likes to be on the string. We are actually doing a difficult job just keeping the bow on the string. If you drop a bow on the string, it will bounce by itself. It's much harder to play *legato* then it is to bounce the bow. For *spiccato*, we need to create a half-circle, where the bow touches the string at the bottom of the stroke.

A.A.   *The swinging.*

H.W.   Exactly! If we swing our arm, it creates a half-circle and a pendulum. We have three pendulums built into our arm; the whole arm swings from the shoulder, creating two bounces in an up and down-bow. During the down bow, the arm is actively raising the elbow, and with the up bow, the arm drops passively. The bow changes are in the air, and the bow approaches the string on a tangent: like an airplane landing, not vertically like a helicopter. We can use this whole-arm pendulum at a slow speed, near the frog, or at medium speeds, more toward the middle of the bow. For triplets, the up-bow on the second triplet will be more active.

   For faster speeds, we use the forearm pendulum. If you pronate your arm in playing position for the middle of the bow and push the forearm out, your arm will use force to swing out, but then return back passively, creating two fast bounces with one impulse. You can also make four bounces with two impulses, etc. Watch that the upper arm is moving slightly as it is generating the spiccato. For very fast spiccato, you shake your whole arm from the shoulder and it will move the wrist passively, which is the smallest and fastest pendulum. Let the bow bounce closer to the string for sautillé.

   Lastly, we need to be able to change from on to off the string. We pronate and feel more weight on the index finger when we're on the string, and we play spiccato by dropping the bow on more hair and using rounded fingers. For spiccato across the strings, the pendulums will turn into appropriate circles, around the shoulder, elbow, and wrist.

A.A.   *Let's talk about the Bach Suites a little bit. Because so many of the people I've talked to said that when they were students, there was no real historically informed practice. There was more or less one way to play Bach. Obviously that's changed over the years. Have your feelings on the Bach Suites changed over the years? Is that something you talk about with your students?*

H.W.   Yes, I do. I certainly went through a huge development, but there are different ways of looking at it. I grew up in the 50s, so as a young cellist, Historically Informed Practice was just beginning. We were still told to play metronomically at that time and not to do anything to distort the rhythm and evenness.

For Starker, the most important thing was smoothness. It was flawless, very even playing, and his bowings were romantic, kind of Popper-ish. We had to do these bowings, there was no way around it, and it wasn't easy for me. I was in my mid 20s and came from Germany, where there was already quite a movement toward looking at manuscripts and Baroque playing. Starker certainly played the Suites wonderfully, flawless in his own interpretations. It's still the most in tune Bach there is. It's just that at that point, I thought I knew better because I had looked at the Anna Magdalena manuscript. It was still impossible to get the Kellner manuscript, because it was in East Germany and you couldn't get to it.

Actually Wronski, the wonderful Polish violin teacher from Warsaw Conservatory, snuck out a microfiche copy of the Kellner manuscript for me. I sat in the library to read it. It was terrible to read on the film, because you could only see small parts of it at a time, you couldn't see a whole page. You could see a few bars and then had to scroll. I thought my issues with bowings would be solved between the Anna Magdalena and Kellner, but sadly no. Both of them are probably copies of copies of the actual manuscript and so we still have to guess at Bach's original intentions for articulation.

Another thing I think is interesting is that Bach was so into rhetoric. The only book in his library besides the Bible was a book on rhetoric. In the middle ages, rhetoric was a subject of study, just like philosophy or Latin. Rhetoric is not just talking, it's elevated speaking and articulation. This helps to explain why in the Cantatas and the Passions, Bach composed not only the music but the words. His music is punctuated with syllables (*notes inégale*) that allow emphasis to be placed where one feels the emphasis is needed, as if reciting a poem. This gives us much more musical freedom, allowing us to place the emphasis where we feel the emphasis is needed, using timing of notes to communicate. This is in stark contrast to a metronomic, even approach.

A.A.   *Do you talk about some of the Baroque techniques with your students, such as audible shifts or amount of vibrato?*

H.W.   Absolutely. Too much vibrato can get in the way. They should have the feeling that they could still vibrate on a note. When you don't use vibrato, the bow will become a lot more important as your voice. You cannot hide behind gorgeous vibrato. You really have to speak with articulation and then every single sound becomes more of a creative thing with the bow.

A.A.   *Have you gravitated to the Anna Magdalena bowings? I certainly had to unlearn many bowings from my youth.*

H.W.   Absolutely, same here. It's a real problem for the young cellists if they play competitions, because you don't know what the committee wants to hear. Many of them do want to hear eight notes slurred in the G-Major Prelude, and some judges might be horrified if you do the original bowing.

A.A.   *You mentioned intonation a few times too, and that's obviously a big thing with students. Sometimes it becomes too big, I think. That's all they are thinking about. Do you have ways to work on that with them? Do you believe in drone notes or using a tuner or have other ideas?*

H.W.   Yes, all of them. Playing double stops with open strings is the first important step to being in tune. You also need to listen to the ring of the instrument, if it's out of tune, the overtones won't ring freely. I find it very hard to hear quarter tones because they interfere with the ringing of the whole instrument.

A.A.   *How important do you think demonstrating is for a student? Has that changed over the years for you?*

H.W.   I think it's important. Piatigorsky had a student who couldn't play a passage, so he demonstrated it so that the student could see how wonderful the passage sounded and how easy it was to play. At one point, Piatigorsky slipped and played really badly, and then suddenly the student played it really well. Something happened when the student saw that Piatigorsky was having difficulties too, it gave the student confidence that he could play. I think you should be able to demonstrate. I really think so. Starker would demonstrate all the time. We all sat there and said, "Lord, we can never do it like that."

A.A.   *There are three pieces that I've been asking people about, which are all very famous transcriptions, and wondering about your experience and your opinion on them. I'll just list all three and then we can talk about them. The first one will be the Boccherini/Grützmacher B-flat Concerto. The second one is the Rococo Variations, which I think everyone in our generation has grown up playing the Fitzenhagen arrangement. Then the Chopin Polonaise, which few people seem to play the original. I learned the Feuermann version, which I love, but there are differing opinions. What are your thoughts on those three pieces?*

H.W.   Yes, I still reluctantly teach the Grützmacher version of the Boccherini. The main reason being that the other one, the original, is so much harder. Students can easily play the Grützmacher before they can play the original. I think the cadenza of the first movement is still one of the best cadenzas we have. So why not? They should know it's the Grützmacher version, and that the second movement comes from a different concerto.

A.A.   *You said reluctantly. Do you feel we should be learning the original Boccherini?*

H.W.   Not necessarily. Although it's not my favorite piece, I think the Grützmacher is a perfectly good piece and it can be played as Grützmacher wrote it. It's a good teaching piece. Students should know of the original B-flat Concerto, so they know what Grützmacher did. It's really a beautiful example of how people in the 19th century loved to transcribe.

Grützmacher dug up a lot of Boccherini and other music that was not known and at least made it known. We also don't know what happened with Valentini and Locatelli. They are certainly not all originals, no question, but still good pieces.

As for the Tchaikovsky I really must say I do like the original, simply for the reason that it's musically so much more logical in its structure. He has fun with the pickup notes of the theme in the first variations including the D-Minor Andante and the trill variation. In the later variations Tchaikovsky uses the pickup as a down beat. However, I don't particularly like the ending of the original. The ending variation leaves you disappointed. I think that Fitzenhagen's version has a really good ending.

For the Chopin, I like the original better. It's easier for the cello, but Franchomme and later Feuermann made these arrangements to show off the cello. I think Chopin wrote it for a daughter who could play the piano well. Her father couldn't play the cello very well, so he wrote a very easy cello part and gave all the virtuoso lines to the piano. I still think these sound much better on piano. Maybe we should perform both versions and let the audience judge.

A.A.   *That's what many people have said, but if a student comes in and wants to learn the Feuermann?*

H.W.   Well, it's a great piece. If you can play it, it's wonderful.

A.A.   *A lot has been made of the shrinking audiences in classical music. Certainly more orchestras are struggling, and there is a big push to include new music and music of lesser known composers. Do you think the audiences are connecting with this? Are we going in the right direction? Is it working? Do you see orchestras changing their model in the future? And to further muddy the waters, how has all of our new technology affected our audience's ability to absorb music that is challenging?*

H.W.   Yes, it's really difficult, the constant input of new things. I fear it is inbred in human nature that our eyes seem to enjoy anything new, more so than our ears. It's really weird, but almost everyone is willing to look at a brand-new picture or a brand new building with crazy architecture and is willing to take it in, but they won't even try to listen to anything new. I'm not even talking complicated compositions, just simply new sounds.

I think that hearing performers speak about a piece before they play it is very helpful for the audience, especially for understanding new pieces. I heard the Juilliard quartet do this when they played Elliott Carter Quartets. Their introduction and explanations were excellent and received very positive attention from the audience. It was clear the audience was fascinated and more connected to the performers and the piece because of this.

A.A.   *Do you think the technological age has helped or hurt music?*

H.W.   I think it's a bit of both. Starting out with recordings on wires, okay, it helped and we've come a long way since then! It's great that we can hear some old recordings and learn from them, but it eliminated so many possibilities of getting jobs and making money.

A.A.   *I remind young students that 150 years ago, if you wanted to hear a certain piece, that you had to go here it live. That was the only way to hear music.*

H.W.   Yes! How can we make a concert an event that you don't want to miss?

A.A.   *It wasn't that long ago, but now anyone can hear everything from their couch. Why do you need to go out and go to a concert? I'm curious to see how that's going to be remedied. Many orchestras are trying now to incorporate visual elements, as you said, as a way of drawing people.*

Back to the new music for a moment. We have a quartet residency program at the University of Iowa, which is great. Many of the major American quartets have come through, as well as a few European ones. They quite often will play a piece that was commissioned for them and play it at a very high level. But it's not something that I would want to just sit and listen to.

I'm very impressed by the performance and there's certainly more interest in hearing it live. I've asked the performers if they think there's longevity with these pieces? Many of them said, "We don't care." We just want them to be heard.

H.W.   It's always been that way. I think it will always take time to let the cream rise to the top. It's too hard to know what pieces will become part of the repertoire. I think we can't judge our own age.

A.A.   *We have to wait.*

H.W.   We have to wait; we know now that Stravinsky and Bartók and Schoenberg and all these guys were the cream of maybe a thousand composers that did similar things.

A.A.   *Have you seen the level of cello playing change over the years?*

H.W.   I think there have been wonderful cellists for a long time. I think that Jean-Louis and Jean-Pierre Duport were as good as cellists as anybody today, as were Boccherini, Kraft, Servais, and Grützmacher. I honestly think that saying nobody could create a tone before Casals was detrimental to cello history. If you hear Beatrice Harrison play the Elgar, it's fabulous. I mean she could really play! More people were playing well then, but we probably will never know. On the other hand, I think there are probably more people playing cello now at a higher level than there were 100 years ago.

A.A.   *Related to that, do you think there are enough jobs for cellists in today's world?*

H.W.   No, there are clearly too many cellists and too few jobs. Every time I see a little kid carry a cello case, I think, "Do you know what you're in for?" Not only just the work that goes into it, but also the lessons and transport. I say to everybody, "You have to love it beyond everything else, because the risks are enormous that you won't make a living."

A.A.   *It seems to me the types of ways to make money with your cello are growing with the crossover of music genres and how connected we all are through the internet.*

H.W.   Yes, you're absolutely right. It's amazing what cellists can do when they're creative. They find all these venues that we couldn't think of, because it was so limited when we were younger. Now there are more possibilities if they can find them, and whatever they do on Facebook, YouTube or other platforms to communicate and do interesting things is amazing. I really admire that. There is a lot of creativity with today's younger generation.

I like what they do at Juilliard, they have students not only play a chamber music recital, but also organize concerts and outreach. It really helps get them ready for the real world.

A.A.   *Do you feel that it's part of your job as a teacher to help a student find success outside of school? After they've graduated or even while they're studying with you?*

H.W.   Yes, if you can you help them. I write a lot of recommendation letters and offer suggestions while they're studying. I talk to them as much as possible after they leave. Quite often, I don't hear from students, but then run into them years later, and they say, "I am still teaching and every time I do certain things, I think of you."

Close to the Heart

A.A.   *If you hadn't been a musician, what would you have loved to have done with your life?*

H.W.   I would have loved to have been a handyman or a woodworker, because I love getting things to work. It doesn't really matter what it is. I'm so happy if I put a new electric device in, or if I fix something that's broken and make it work again. That makes me feel like I've accomplished something. You can really see and feel that it works again. It's such a contrast to practicing, where sometimes you can practice and practice and practice and then you may sound worse afterwards. It's such a satisfying thing to do something concrete; when it's done, it's done and it works.

A.A. *Did you ever have a period of doubt, even as an adult, about what you were doing and thinking maybe it's time to go another direction in life?*

H.W. I really never thought of changing directions. I had my doubts about if I did something well. Maybe it's just that I thought I could never do anything better. I guess that's why I still haven't retired at 82.

   I remember once asking a retired pianist friend to play some chamber music. He said, "I'm retired." I said, "You mean you don't play piano?" and he said, "I am liberated." I thought that sounded more like imprisoned. Maybe I'm in prison, but I wouldn't feel liberated if I didn't get to practice. I still feel so lucky to play my cello.

A.A. *Is there anything on your bucket list that you still feel you would love to do before everything is all done?*

H.W. What interests me is the interplay of culture and nature. I would love to go see Machu Picchu. I was fascinated by the museum in Mexico City. I would love to go to Petra in Syria. Old cultures and their expressions of art or architecture within nature are more interesting to me than sheer nature.

A.A. *Are there any musical moments in your life that are most memorable? They could be with your cello or just a musical moment you have experienced.*

H.W. Well, Fritz Wunderlich singing has always been memorable for me. I played in an orchestra in Cologne when I was a student, and I got to hear him sing several times while it was being recorded. If I want something special, I still listen to Wunderlich singing songs or arias.

   There are also two pieces by Alban Berg that are important to me, the Berg Violin Concerto, and his opera *Wozzeck* is one of my favorites. In fact, in Bloomington, my son got to play the part of the little boy going "hop-hop, hop-hop" at the very end of the piece. It was really something. But it was a haunting experience for my son, who would wake up at night and cry, "Mom, are you dead?" He understood what was going on in *Wozzeck*, and I sometimes thought, "What did that do to my poor kid?"

A.A. *What are you most proud of in your life or career?*

H.W. I cannot be proud. I actually hate that expression "to be proud of something." I think it's always a coincidence. You can be proud of your part in preparing something, but success is a coincidence of luck and ability, and so why should I be proud of that?

A.A. *Maybe I should ask what has brought you the most joy?*

H.W. Probably various chamber music performances. The coincidence of excellent musicians and beautiful music and nice people is something that to me is the most precious thing in the world.

A.A. *Do you have any desert island pieces? If you had to go to a desert island, and you could only bring one CD to listen to. It doesn't have to be classical.*

H.W. I think I would enjoy the quietness. I quite often enjoy silence, because we hear so much and there's so much input to deal with every day. There's nothing like silence.

This reminds me of another Piatigorsky story. It's so funny, because I really only met him once. He was telling a story about how he was in a certain restaurant every day, and they would play this awful music. The waiter came and brought in a celery and carrot dish, and Piatigorsky took a handful and stuck them in the waiter's mouth. The waiter went, "Why are you doing this?" and Piatigorsky said, "That's what you do to my ears."

A.A. *When you were in school, were there many female role models?*

H.W. Not many. There was Zara Nelsova. She was the most prominent, and I really admired her. I heard her in-person in Cologne. She was supposed to play the Lalo Concerto under a conductor named Scherchen. Scherchen was very famous for doing a lot of new music. He was a very good conductor, and I went to most of the rehearsals because I could sneak in at the time. I was at the first rehearsal of the Lalo, and Nelsova came in and started playing the first movement. At one point, Scherchen stopped and said, "Let's leave this 'shit' piece and get to the better music." Nelsova got up and said, "If you think that about this piece, I'm not going to play it."

She wasn't that famous yet at that time in the 50s, but she actually did this! The concert was the next day and the orchestra played a Gluck Overture. Then she came on and played the Sixth Bach Suite and then was an intermission. She played the Kodaly Solo Sonata afterward, and then the orchestra finished with a Symphony. She did not play the Lalo, because she wouldn't put up with the attitude of the conductor. I thought that was so fantastic.

I saw her when she was older at the Cello Congress in Arizona, back in the 1980s. She always had a seemingly tight bow arm but still produced such a beautiful sound.

I think the funniest memory was at that Cello Congress when she and Starker played this Boccherini C Major duet. There she was, probably in her eighties, in her typical dress with a skirt 20 yards full, with a shawl and everything, like she used to wear. They were both looking at one music stand and neither could see so well anymore. Here she was in her skirt and Starker on the side, trying to see. Naturally they both hadn't looked at the music and neither could see well, so they both started getting closer and closer to the stand to see the notes. He was surrounded by her skirt, and they were doing a hilarious job playing this duet.

A.A. *Did you see it as more of a challenge for women to be successful in classical music during those early years in your career?*

H.W. It was clear as I grew up that women had a very hard time finding an orchestra job. The Vienna Philharmonic wouldn't take any, and Berlin didn't take any until 10 or 20 years ago. You knew you couldn't land a position in a good orchestra.

You know when I was younger, at first women weren't even invited to audition for orchestra jobs. Then, over time women were invited but rarely, if ever found work. The auditions were mostly token efforts to include women, or minorities for that matter. Finally, in the 60s, they introduced the idea of screened auditions so that players were evaluated on their playing and not their appearance.

A.A. *Was that on your mind when you were in school?*

H.W. Yes, but then I knew what I really wanted to do. I wanted to teach and play chamber music and I wanted to have a balance in my life of different musical things. I was incredibly lucky to have found this balance.

Index

Lightning Source UK Ltd.
Milton Keynes UK
UKHW031432090222
398433UK00003B/49